ARAMCO AND ITS WORLD

ARAMCO AND ITS WORLD

Arabia And The Middle East

Edited by

Ismail I. Nawwab   Peter C. Speers   Paul F. Hoye

Main Research and Writing:
Paul Lunde and John A. Sabini

Caption Research and Writing:
Lyn Maby

Aramco Dhahran Saudi Arabia

Second Printing
1981

ISBN 0-9601164-2-7
Library of Congress number 80-67897

Arabian American Oil Company
Washington, D.C.
1980

Printed in the Netherlands
by Van Boekhoven-Bosch B.V. and Boom-Ruygrok B.V.
of the Elsevier-NDU Graphic Division B.V.

Preface

Aramco and Its World had its origins in the late 1940s when Aramco (the Arabian American Oil Company) was moving through a period of tremendous growth and expansion in all aspects of its operations. This involved the rapid enlargement of Aramco's work force of many different nationalities and especially the growth of its American manpower, which increased threefold between 1945 and 1950. To provide these many hundreds of newcomers with basic information about the company and its place in the world oil industry, and to help them adjust to work and life in a strange land among a people whose language they did not understand and whose culture sometimes seemed almost incomprehensible, Aramco in January 1950 issued a series of five spiral-bound booklets with the general title *Handbooks for American Employees.*

These booklets, though intended for the information and instruction of Aramco's own employees, attracted widespread interest outside the company and the demand for copies was so great that two years later, in January 1952, a revised hardbound edition was published that consisted of two volumes entitled *Aramco and World Oil* and *The Arabia of Ibn Saud.* A single-volume edition containing the same material, further revised, appeared in 1960 with the title *Aramco Handbook.* When a fourth edition was published in 1968, it was apparent that the book had become much more than a "handbook for employees," and accordingly it carried the additional subtitle *Oil and the Middle East.*

This book may thus be considered the fifth edition of a work first published some thirty years ago, and it continues the trend away from the specific (a "handbook" designed for a particular group of Aramco employees) and toward the general. At the start of the 1950s, when the first *Handbook* appeared, most Westerners considered Saudi Arabia and the rest of the Middle East exotic and mysterious lands, and comprehensive, accurate, up-to-date books about the area were almost nonexistent. Today, although the Arab world has again assumed a pivotal role in world affairs, with a powerful day-to-day influence on the lives and fortunes of many millions of people in the West, it still remains in many ways a relatively unknown and insufficiently understood part of the world. *Aramco and Its World* is therefore no longer simply a handbook for employees of Aramco but, in this edition, can contribute to increased understanding of Saudi Arabia and the Middle East by a readership which now includes many with no direct connection with the Middle East, Arabia, or Aramco and some with little or no knowledge of Islam, the Arab world, or the oil industry – but with an interest in these things and a desire to learn something about some or all of them.

An Introduction

Some of the most crucial events in the history of mankind took place in the area and during the time span that this volume attempts to survey. Agriculture began in Mesopotamia and later, in this "land between the rivers," the first cities grew up, with the attendant development of laws, crafts, trade, and writing. From the broader area we call the Middle East came the basic elements of mathematics, the wheel, the architectural arch, sciences such as astronomy and medicine, and the framework of organized trade and commerce. From this region, too, came the three great monotheistic religions: Judaism, Christianity, and Islam. Indeed, civilization itself — the triumph of human experience over time — began in the land that lies between the valleys of the Nile and the Indus.

Over the past six thousand years great cultures have sprung from this source and ebbed and flowed across the map of the Middle East. Some of them rivaled and even surpassed the levels of culture later reached by the Greeks and Romans of classical times, who rightly acknowledged their debt to the civilizations of Mesopotamia and the Nile. And when the lambent Greek and Roman civilizations dimmed and sank into the shadows of the Dark Ages, their afterglow lingered in the Byzantine lands — which included Syria and Egypt — and much of their scientific and practical knowledge and philosophy was preserved in the new classical language, Arabic, by the new torchbearers of civilization, the Muslims. The great flowering of Arab culture between the ninth and thirteenth centuries owed much to this heritage. When the Golden Age of classical Islam ended it was passed on again, vastly enriched, to the renascent West which in turn came once more to play an important role in the political, economic, and cultural history of the region.

No one volume can do full justice to such an immense sweep of history. Nor can it completely satisfy the often conflicting demands of scholars, technical experts, and ordinary readers. To provide fully for the needs of the specialist is possibly to confuse and probably to bore the layman; and to design this work entirely for a popular audience might have invited the scorn of the more informed. To compress the developments of several thousand years of history into a readable and reasonably brief narrative has inevitably sometimes required painful omissions, extensive generalizations, and occasionally a narrow focus on particular details to the exclusion of other significant material. Moreover, to achieve a point of view that is not entirely Western, yet still clear to Westerners, has sometimes required a considerable degree of simplification.

Like the *Aramco Handbook* that preceded it, therefore, *Aramco and Its World* is a compromise that it is hoped will appeal to the general reader and at the same time succeed in presenting accurate information that is based on sound scholarship and, wherever possible, on firsthand knowledge of the events and places discussed.

In conclusion, something should be said about the spelling of Arabic words. The use of a single, logical scheme for spelling these words is desirable both for the sake of consistency and because it helps the reader with some knowledge of Arabic to recognize what the original was and assists the reader with no such acquaintance to know approximately how the original is pronounced. Every European language has developed its own system for transliterating Arabic and in English a number of systems, each with points in its favor and each differing slightly from the others, have become established. The system used in this book is a compromise among two or three of the most widely accepted of these, with some modifications aimed at simplification. The Arabic letter *hamzah,* sometimes represented in English by an apostrophe ('), is not transliterated; and an inverted apostrophe (') is used to depict the letter *'ayn,* as in Ju'aymah and the Ka'bah. *Aramco and Its World* departs from this compromise system in two particulars: for words which have commonly accepted forms in English, these forms are used (for example, "caliph" for *khalifah* and "Mecca" for *Makkah*); and where certain Saudi Arabian place-names have acquired particular spellings through long years of usage and acceptance in Aramco, these spellings are followed (for instance, "Abqaiq" instead of the more correct *Buqayq,* "Dhahran" instead of *al-Zahran,* and "Al Alat" instead of *al-'Alah*). The spelling of Persian and Turkish names (many of which are Arabic in origin) follows the style of the Merriam-Webster dictionaries.

Finally, it may be helpful to explain four common Arabic words that the reader will come across repeatedly in this book. The word *al-* (joined to the following word and with a small *a* unless it comes at the beginning of a sentence) is the definite article and corresponds to the English "the." The similar *Al* (always with a capital *A* and never joined to the following word) means "House (or family) of," as in Al Sa'ud, the name of the ruling family of Saudi Arabia. *'Abd* means "servant of," and in conjunction with the name or one of the attributes of God it is very commonly used to form Arabic personal names such as 'Abd Allah ("Servant of God") or 'Abd al-Rahman ("Servant of the Merciful"). The word *ibn,* sometimes pronounced *bin,* means "son of" or "descendant of the House (or family) of," as in Ibn Sa'ud or Ibn Rashid. Its plural is *banu* or *bani* ("sons of"), as in Banu Musa or Bani Hilal.

Acknowledgements

Aramco and Its World has been the work of many hands, and the editors wish it were possible to acknowledge in some detail the contribution made by each of those who have participated. Space does not allow this, however, and no more than a brief mention can be made of all those who have taken part in its preparation. Each of them can take credit for the success of the book, but none of them should be held responsible for any errors that may be found in it.

The editors wish first of all to thank John J. Kelberer, Faysal M. al-Bassam, and Majed Elass – members of Aramco's senior management – for their personal as well as corporate support.

The many others who have contributed to the completion of the book as scholars, writers, researchers, and reviewers and in other ways include past and present employees of Aramco and others with little or no direct connection with the company. Among them have been Bakr Abbas, Osmar Abib, Donna Aldrich, Barbara Andon, Robert Arndt, Lawrence E. Bagnoli, Thomas C. Barger, Ann Barlow, Brainerd S. Bates, Frank W. Blue, S. D. Bowers, H. M. Brown, John M. Curry, Fred H. Drucker, John H. D'Souza, D. R. Fate, Harold W. Glidden, Marny Golding, T. F. Harrington, George F. Hourani, Cathy Hoye, Yusuf Ibish, Karen Irwin, Libby Jackowski, Albert Jamme, F. Johansson, Martin Judd, Abdallah S. Jum'ah, Frank Jungers, W. J. Kelley, Dickran Kouymjian, Leslie G. Lewis, A. A. Lughod, Robert L. Maby, Laila Madonian, James P. Mandaville, R. E. Martin, H. L. McAlister, Elizabeth Monroe, Mark Morgan, William E. Mulligan, John M. Munro, Libby Murrell, Nawal Naoum, Mary Norton, Peter P. Pease, Peter K. Pestoni, George S. Rentz, Bonita Slusser, Thorn K. Snyder, Ellen Speers, E. Myrl Squyres, Sharon Kay Swearingen, Caroline Stone, William F. Todd, William Tracy, Petronella van Gorkom, F. S. Vidal, and William A. Ward.

Credit for the design of the book belongs to Don Thompson of Aramco's production staff.

The majority of the photographs connected with Islam, Saudi Arabia, and Aramco are by S. M. Amin, A. G. Daghish, David Denning, Sa'id Ghamdi, Geoffrey Hunter, Michael Isaac, A. A. al-Khalifa, A. M. al-Khalifa, A. A. al-Mentakh, Burnett H. Moody, Khalil Abou el-Nasr, E. E. Seal, Thomas F. Walters, and A. L. Yousif – all of them now or in the past Aramco staff photographers. Most of the drawings and all the maps and charts are by Don Thompson.

Additional photographs and drawings are by Robert Azzi, Rick Bloom, John E. Burchard, Tor Eigeland, Harris Foster, Steve and Claudine Furman, Marny Golding, Christine Kokesh Hill, Peter Keen, Sydney King, Dickran Kouymjian, Chris Kutschera, James P. Mandaville, Roland and Sabrina Michaud, Joe Mountain, Ed Mullis, Robert Yarnall Richie, Don Rokke, Brian Smith, Max Steineke, Katrina Thomas, William Tracy, Nik Wheeler, Penny Williams, and Adam Woolfitt. Other illustrations have been taken from *Facts about Oil*, Humble Oil Company, International Publication Services (Beirut), Iraq Petroleum Company, the Metropolitan Museum of Art (New York), the National Museum (Damascus), National Photo Company (al-Khobar), Petroleum Information Bureau (London), and SIPA Press (Paris).

Contents

Contents

OIL AND ARAMCO

Charts And Diagrams

Contents

Maps

ARAMCO AND ITS WORLD

BEFORE ISLAM

In the Middle East, as elsewhere, geography and ecology have been among the important architects of history.

During the last Ice Age — which ended about fifteen thousand years ago — parts of Europe lay under a sheet of ice. The mass of cold air this generated blocked off the Atlantic rainstorms and sent them across North Africa and the Middle East, creating a climate that supported park and grassland and fed lakes, streams, and great river systems — some still visible today as dry wadis in the Arabian Peninsula and the Sahara. The climate also nourished a wide variety of animal life, now vanished from the area, which Paleolithic man hunted and memorialized in rock carvings in the midst of now nearly lifeless desert.

Later, as the European ice cap melted and the Atlantic rain path moved northward again, progressive desiccation set in, turning the grasslands and forests of the Middle East into steppe and desert. The process was gradual, however, and for long periods the climate of early historical times remained more temperate than it is today. Up to the second millennium B.C., Libya was rich in olives, wine, and livestock. Egypt was a land of marshes teeming with wildlife, and lower Mesopotamia a marshland covered with extensive reed forests — as it is today.

In the marshy river valleys of the Middle East man first attempted to live in settled communities.

As desiccation progressed, however, areas with favorable conditions were reduced considerably. By the dawn of history the habitable area of Egypt was already confined to the cliff valley of the Nile in the south, spreading across the Delta in the north. To the north and east of Egypt, the area of favorable conditions narrowed down to a great arc pressed between the Anatolian plateau and the Arabian Desert. Stretching from the head of the Arabian Gulf northward to include the land watered by the Tigris and Euphrates, west across present-day Syria, then south to include the whole eastern shore of the Mediterranean and the lands behind it as far south as the Gulf of Aqaba, this region has been aptly called the Fertile Crescent.

The earliest agricultural sites in the world have been found in the foothills of Kurdistan in the Tigris Valley.

As the highlands turned into steppe and desert, man was forced to descend into the river valleys in search of game and edible vegetation. By Neolithic times mass migrations were common and agriculture, perhaps the most revolutionary development in man's history, had made its first appearance. Agriculture is believed to have originated in the Tigris-Euphrates Valley, where very old agricultural sites have been found in the foothills of what is now Kurdistan. Excavations at Jericho in the Jordan River Valley have also revealed evidence of settled farming going back to 8000 B.C. Irrigation, a separate and later development, probably originated in Mesopotamia too and did more than simple agriculture — which in earliest times, before the discovery of crop rotation, probably involved a constant search for new and fertile soil — to tie human groups to specific localities and so foster the growth of permanent communities. Both agriculture and irrigation developed in the Nile Valley as well, probably independently but a little later than in Mesopotamia.

Another development closely connected to agriculture was the introduction of pottery — possibly an outgrowth of the need to store food surpluses and seed for planting. Peoples of what is known as the 'Ubayd culture (from a site in southern Iraq) were, despite the lack of the potter's wheel, among the world's first master potters. They left a trail of distinctive sherds running up the Tigris and Euphrates Valley and as far south as Tarut Island in what is now Saudi Arabia, which probably indicates the spread of the new science of agriculture as it radiated slowly outwards.

Prehistoric peoples developed distinctive cultures and, chiefly through trade, cultural contacts with one another. Peoples speaking Semitic languages, whose origins are unknown but who first appear in the lands of the Fertile Crescent and the Arabian Peninsula, undoubtedly had cultural and commercial contacts with the peoples of the Nile, for Semitic elements are found in the earliest written records of the Egyptians. Strictly speaking, the terms "Semitic" and "Semite" refer respectively to a group of related languages which includes Akkadian, Aramaic, Syriac, Hebrew, Arabic, and others and to a group of peoples speaking these languages.

The culture of prehistoric peoples eventually flowered into what we call civilization — at which point they possessed writing, monumental architecture, religious art, legal codes, and complex political systems. This efflorescence first occurred in the fourth millennium B.C. in the southern reaches of the Tigris-Euphrates Valley and, a little later, on the banks of the Nile.

Today Westerners regard the birth of Jesus as occurring in very ancient times. But Jesus was born into a civilization whose past was twice as long as the period since his birth. Abraham was born about nineteen hundred years before Jesus, in the Mesopotamian city of Ur, which was already about a thousand years old. When Moses lived in Egypt, the Pyramids were already monuments of antiquity, the earliest of them some sixteen centuries old. And when Joshua fought the battle of Jericho in about 1210 B.C., Canaanite settlements were already some eighteen hundred years old.

During those centuries, the history of the Middle East was as dynamic as it was prolonged. Empires rose and fell, civilizations appeared, rose to their zenith, and sank into eclipse or were absorbed by rivals or engulfed in new waves of conquest. As recently as 1975, for example, Italian archaeologists, after digging for more than ten years in northern Syria, unearthed the state archives of an ancient city called Ebla, previously known only as a name mentioned in Sumerian and Akkadian records. Discovery of the archives — some 16,500 clay tablets so far — disclosed that Ebla was one of the major urban centers of northern Syria about 2300 B.C. It dominated its neighbors and traded with the kingdoms of Mesopotamia. But by the time the Patriarch Abraham was born Ebla had vanished, leaving no more to history than occasional references in the annals of its neighbors.

Yet there was continuity as well. The conquerors learned the arts of civilization from the conquered, each civilization borrowing technology, law, and sometimes elements of language and religion from its predecessor. Even today, social patterns, customs and beliefs may go back thousands of years. The past is always present in the Middle East.

In this long and complex history, geography remains a constant, and it is geography that can supply a thread to guide us through the historical maze, or rather two threads — the two river valleys where the seeds of civilization first germinated.

The first thread is the Tigris-Euphrates Valley, whose rivers rise in the Anatolian plateau, now in Turkey, and flow southeastward through Syria and what is now Iraq, creating the land of Mesopotamia ("between the rivers" in Greek) before meeting near the head of the Arabian Gulf. The second thread is the Nile, rising in two sources in East Africa and flowing in two streams northward to Khartoum in the Sudan, where the streams meet and roll in a mighty flood between cliffs and deserts northward through Egypt to spread into the Delta before emptying into the Mediterranean.

Like the Nile itself, the history of Egypt, despite interruptions and upheavals, appears to flow with an impressive unity, whereas in Mesopotamia the historical chronology, as well as the hydrography, is more irregular, with nation succeeding nation, empire swallowing empire, and people with new names and of diverse origins taking turns at the center of the stage.

These two cultural areas, Egypt and Mesopotamia, were at times brought together by conquest, first by one, then by the other, again by outsiders. Cultural contacts and borrowings multiplied and deepened; yet each area retained a distinctive character, just as each of the rivers maintained a recognizable physical thread throughout the centuries.

EARLY MESOPOTAMIA: The first civilization on earth, as far as we know, was that of Sumer — a name, incidentally, unknown to archaeologists as recently as 150 years ago. A people speaking a non-Semitic language, the Sumerians first appear in the southern part of the Tigris-Euphrates Valley in the fourth millennium B.C. There are several theories as to their origin: that they came from the north, or from the Indus Valley, or that they were the descendants of the indigenous 'Ubayd culture. Most probably they came from Central Asia, in small groups, across the Iranian Plateau. Although they all spoke the same language and had a common culture, the Sumerians did not form a unified state but lived in a cluster of independent city-states often at war with one another. The Sumerian cities best known to us are Ur, Erech (Uruk), Lagash, and Nippur, all originally on the river banks but now left, literally, high and dry by the gradual diversion of the rivers. Eridu, for example, a Sumerian seaport for the Arabian Gulf, is now 130 miles inland.

The Sumerians seem to have been the first people to use the potter's wheel, a technological innovation of great importance. They also built elaborate irrigation systems, traded with their neighbors and other peoples,

Gray stone statue represents a respected Sumerian scribe of the period of Ur-Nina, king of Lagash in the twenty-fifth century B.C.

MEDITERRANEAN   SEA

BLACK SEA

CASPIAN SEA

Byblos

Euphrates River

Tigris River

Sippar
AKKAD

Heliopolis
Memphis

SINAI

EGYPT

White Nile River

Abydos

Thebes

FIRST CATARACT   Aswan

Nile River

RED

SEA

THE MIDDLE EAST IN THE TWENTY-FIFTH CENTURY B.C.

Cities — Ur, Eridu, Lagash, and others — and a system of writing have been developed by a non-Semitic people in southern Mesopotamia. Akkad to the north is inhabited by a Semitic people. Elam to the east largely controls the far-flung maritime trade of the time, which includes Dilmun as a flourishing entrepôt. Northern and southern Egypt as far as the First Cataract have been unified in the Old Kingdom, with its capital at Memphis in the north. The Great Pyramids of Giza are already in existence and the basic forms of Egyptian religion, art, and writing have been established. Byblos and other cities in the Levant maintain trade and cultural links with both Mesopotamia and Egypt.

drew up codes of law, introduced a monetary system of weighted metal rings, and used wheeled vehicles and the architectural arch. Through their interest in astrology, they discovered many of the laws of astronomy. They could solve simple equations and calculate the square and cube roots of numbers and the areas of squares and rectangles. To this day their sexagesimal system of numbers is reflected in the division of the hour into sixty minutes and the circle into 360 degrees.

Despite the lack of building stone in the river valley, the Sumerians constructed impressive buildings of sun-dried brick, notably the imposing tower temples known as ziggurats — artificial heights on the floodplain reflecting, perhaps, ancient memories of the mountains in their original homeland. Ziggurats, whose construction continued long after the Sumerians, are thought to have inspired the biblical story of the Tower of Babel. A large part of one ziggurat survives at Ur today.

Brick set in bitumen lines the stairway of the ziggurat of Nanna, the moon god, built at Ur at the end of the third millennium B.C.

But the Sumerians' most important innovation was the development of the art of writing. From their original pictorial writing they evolved a cuneiform script — arrangements of wedge-shaped strokes impressed on clay tablets which were then dried in the sun or baked. Many of these hard clay tablets have survived, most of them commercial documents (contracts, receipts, deeds, and wills) but others containing medical prescriptions, proverbs, poetry, and chronicles.

The splendor of Sumerian culture burst upon the modern world when Sir Leonard Woolley opened the royal tombs at Ur in the 1920s and exhumed the possessions of the rulers along with those of courtiers, wives, and guards who apparently were killed to accompany the rulers into the afterlife. The graves have yielded superb examples of sculpture, furniture, clothing, jewels, musical instruments, and eating and drinking vessels, all of skillful workmanship and a high level of art. Among the objects found have been a harp inlaid with gold, silver, and lapis lazuli; a gameboard of shell, bone, and stone squares set in bitumen; and a ceremonial helmet of beaten gold in the form of a wig. Despite their many cultural achievements, however, the Sumerians were unable to unite politically and were eventually overshadowed and then absorbed by such peoples as the Akkadians and

A gold ceremonial helmet found at the royal cemetery of Ur reflects the splendor of Sumerian art.

the Amorites, both part of the larger group known collectively as the Semites.

The first of these peoples to attain political dominance in Mesopotamia were the Akkadians. About 2360 B.C., Sargon I of Akkad (which lay somewhere north of Sumer) extended his power beyond a single city-state and created the first Semitic kingdom, a development that was to lead to the later Semitic empires. The Sumerian cities along with their culture were absorbed into a blend of Sumerian and Semitic culture which was to enlighten most of the civilized world for centuries to come and which continued to flourish even after the Akkadian kingdom was overrun by barbarians from the Taurus Mountains and the Elamites of western Iran captured the city of Ur.

In the third millennium B.C. a wave of immigrants from the west, the Amorites, had entered Mesopotamia and settled on the site of the already ancient city of Babylon. They subsequently absorbed the culture of the Sumerians and Akkadians, gradually pushed back the Elamites, and founded the Old Babylonian Empire. Their greatest king, Hammurabi or Hammurapi, inaugurated a reform and unification of the Sumerian-Semitic culture, which henceforth may be called simply Babylonian.

Hammurabi's reforms were religious, social, and political, but he is best known today for his legal code, which sought to harmonize the laws that had evolved through the centuries in Mesopotamia. This code has been found carved in 3,600 lines of cuneiform writing on a diorite column at Susa — modern Dizful in Iran. Punishment under the code was harsh, but in many ways the code was also humanitarian. It provided, for example, state compensation to the victims of crimes. During Hammurabi's rule, and under the rule of his successors, Babylon enjoyed a state of security that permitted two centuries of intellectual development, particularly in mathematics and astronomy, up to the sixteenth century B.C. New forces now enter the history of the Fertile Crescent with other peoples, bringing the hitherto self-sufficient and relatively isolated river valleys of Mesopotamia into the larger stage of the outside world. At the dawn of the second millennium B.C. an Indo-European people entered Anatolia and founded what was to become the Hittite kingdom. At about the same time, the Hurrians, a people speaking neither a Semitic nor an Indo-European tongue, moved from the area of Armenia into northern Mesopotamia; and the Kassites, Indo-Europeans long settled in Iran, moved west into Babylonia. The Hittites, one of the first people to successfully smelt iron, raided Mesopotamia and added northern Syria and the Cilician plain to their empire, whose center remained in Anatolia. They borrowed the cuneiform script and adopted much of Babylonian culture, especially its literature and religion. The Hurrians, under an Indo-European warrior class, learned the arts of horsemanship and carved out the Kingdom of Mitanni in northern Mesopotamia, with their principal city at Nuzu near modern Kirkuk. So strong was the attraction of the ancient civilization of Mesopotamia that the newcomers adopted its language and culture. The Kassites, meanwhile, occupied Babylonia, so that about 1400 B.C. the Fertile Crescent was divided among the Kassites in the southeast, the Mitanni in the north-central region, and the Hittites in the northwest. A fourth contender for power was Egypt, which had pushed up the Mediterranean coast into Palestine, Lebanon, and southern Syria, and whose parallel, but very different, civilization had been developing since the fourth millennium.

EGYPT: In contrast to Mesopotamia, Egyptian civilization has a perennial quality, an aura of unity and permanence that resembles the flow of the Nile itself. As Herodotus observed twenty-five hundred years ago, the land of Egypt is literally the gift of the river. Life itself depended on its waters and on the silt brought by the annual flood to fertilize the Delta and the narrow strip of river valley lying between two vast deserts. Civilization flowered here a little later than in the Tigris-Euphrates Valley and, in the soil of the Nile, grew a distinctive form and character of its own.

The Nile flows some nineteen hundred miles through Egypt without tributaries and with no great natural physical barriers from the Sudan to the Delta — a geographical unity that also encouraged political unity and resulted in a strong central government that could guarantee the efficient use of the life-giving waters for the entire country. From this need emerged the office of the pharaoh, who, with a retinue of priests, attempted to guarantee the annual rising of the Nile by religious

observances. As strict adherence to the prescribed observances was thought essential, a rigid conservatism in religion and politics evolved. Art was similarly formalized, with its conventions remaining essentially unchanged for three thousand years, most of it devoted to religious ends, particularly the glorification of the pharaoh.

During the centuries, as pharaoh-worship became more intense, a great part of the wealth and labor of the kingdom was diverted to his glorification. Massive stone buildings were erected in his honor, and his exploits were depicted in painting and sculpture, or written in hieroglyphs on the walls. As his powers were believed to continue after death, his body was carefully preserved and his possessions — or, later, artistic representations of them — were buried with him. Above all, his tombs were built to last forever and, in the early form of the pyramids, they practically have done so. Eventually, as this mortuary cult penetrated other levels of Egyptian society, anyone who could afford it arranged to be buried in an elaborate tomb with evidence of his wealth around him, even including the bodies of sacred animals embalmed as mummies. These burial customs have preserved for us an extraordinarily vivid picture of life in ancient Egypt.

This preservation of the past was in itself a cause of traditionalism. As building stone was readily available, Egyptian structures (unlike those of Mesopotamia) endured, and each successive generation lived, literally, in the shadow of its own past. Even the climate fostered conservatism: the absence of rain and the dry desert air preserved the more perishable materials of art such as wood, paint, and cloth, and the written records on papyrus.

Historians traditionally divide the history of Egypt into four periods, interrupted by episodes of internal turbulence, foreign rule, or both. The four periods are called the Old Kingdom (from about 3000 to 2270 B.C.), the Middle Kingdom (about 2100 to 1700 B.C.), the New Kingdom, or Empire (1550 to 1090 (B.C.), and the Late Period (712 to 525 B.C.). After the fourth century B.C. Egypt, while still important in world affairs, was rarely independent and usually subservient to other empires.

The Old Kingdom was created by the unification of the Kingdom of the North and

Late Hittite statue of a king reveals the strong influence of Assyrian art.

At Giza near modern Cairo, the enigmatic Sphinx (a royal head on a lion's body) stands at the beginning of Egyptian art and history.

Egyptian artists excelled in free-standing statuary such as this figure of Tutankhamen harpooning, made of wood overlaid with gold.

MEDITERRANEAN SEA

BLACK SEA

CASPIAN SEA

HITTITES

Nineveh
Assur
Haran
Byblos
Mari
ASSYRIA
BA

Tigris River
Euphrates River

Heliopolis
Memphis

SINAI

EGYPT

Asyut

Abydos

Thebes

White Nile River

FIRST CATARACT Aswan

Nile River

RED

SECOND CATARACT

SEA

THE MIDDLE EAST IN THE EIGHTEENTH CENTURY B.C.

Northern Mesopotamia is controlled by a new element, the Assyrians, with cities at Assur and Tell al-Rimah (near Nineveh). In southern Mesopotamia, Babylonia flourishes during the distinguished reign of Hammurabi. This is a period of great prosperity for Canaan, the commercial center through which pass much of the trade and cultural influences of the civilized world. In Egypt the Theban dynasties of the Middle Kingdom push the boundary southward to the Second Cataract.

the Kingdom of the South by the Pharaoh Menes of the First Dynasty. The capital was in the north at Memphis, near modern Cairo. During this period the most important pyramids were built, and the basic forms of Egyptian religion, art, and writing took shape. As Egypt had to import wood and certain metals, its merchants carried on trade with neighbors, exporting gold, ivory, ebony, and manufactured objects, and importing such things as cedar wood from Lebanon. After about eight centuries of relative peace and prosperity, the Old Kingdom collapsed from internal strains, and the dynasties of various cities competed in civil war.

When Moses lived in Egypt, the Pyramids of Giza were already ancient monuments, some of them sixteen hundred years old.

About 2100 B.C. a dynasty of Thebes in the south seized power and founded the Middle Kingdom, the second period of Egypt's greatness. The Theban rulers pushed the boundaries southward as far as the Second Cataract of the Nile, now in northern Sudan, conducted trade with Syria and Palestine and drained and cultivated the Fayyum, a large fertile depression in the desert west of the Nile. In 1700 B.C., the Semitic Hyksos from Asia — the so-called Shepherd Kings — conquered the Delta and ruled there for 150 years.

Another Theban dynasty ended Hyksos rule in 1555 B.C. and created the New Kingdom or Empire, the zenith of ancient Egypt's power and splendor. In this period the northern borders of the empire reached into Syria, gifts were exchanged with the kingdoms of Mesopotamia, the great temples of Karnak and Luxor were built, and pharaohs were buried with pomp and luxury in the cliff-tombs of the Valley of the Kings. In this period too, the Pharaoh Ikhnaton tried to reform the art, literature, and religion of his times. He moved his capital to Tell Amarna, where he encouraged a lighthearted naturalistic style in art, one of the glories of which was the famous bust of his wife, Nefertiti. He introduced colloquial language into literature and even tried to remove dogma from religion, substituting the worship of the sun-god for that of the old god Amon — a change in which some have seen the beginnings of monotheism. On his death, however, Egyptian religion, literature, and art reverted to the old fixed forms.

Ikhnaton's son-in-law Tutankhamen, though a weak king who died young, is well known today because of the magnificent art

The building of the pyramid tomb of an Egyptian pharaoh was a tremendous engineering feat involving 100,000 to 200,000 workers — laborers, overseers, masons, architects, scribes, paymasters, interpreters — many tons of sand and stone, and up to twenty years of work. The core of the pyramid was built in horizontal courses rising like steps, each level a bit smaller than the step below. As the courses rose higher, inclines of sand and rubble were constructed along each side and fitted crosswise with logs to facilitate the movement of wooden sledges on which building stones were dragged up the ever-rising surface. Once the core of the pyramid was completed, the outer casing of stones was laid, beginning at the peak. As the casing proceeded downwards, the inclines were gradually removed until the lowest course was finished and the monument stood as a true pyramid — its smooth sides sloping down in an unbroken surface from peak to base. The tomb of the pharaoh, often with false doors and misleading tunnels, was secreted in the base.

BRIAN SMITH

The splendor of Egyptian art supported religion and the state for three millennia. Opposite page: The pharaoh was considered to be a reincarnation of the falcon-headed god Horus, shown here on the Temple of Isis at Philae. This page, top left: A giant head of Ramses II bears symbols of the goddesses of Upper and Lower Egypt. Top right: The funerary mask of Tutankhamen was intended to preserve some of the godlike power of the departed pharaoh. Above: Two of the four colossal statues of Ramses II in front of the temple of Abu Simbel. At right: The temple of the Roman emperor Trajan at Philae.

BLACK SEA

MEDITERRANEAN SEA

CASPIAN SEA

HITTITES
Khatti
Amida
Assur
Nineveh
Arvad
Hamath
Byblos
Kadesh
MITANNI
Sidon
Tyre
Damascus
Tigris River
Euphrates River
Megiddo
KAS-
Gaza
Heliopolis
Memphis
Nile River
al-Qusayr
Abydos
Thebes
EGYPT
FIRST CATARACT
Aswan
RED
Nile River
SEA
SECOND CATARACT
FOURTH CATARACT

THE MIDDLE EAST IN THE FIFTEENTH CENTURY B.C.

Egypt reaches its zenith in the New Kingdom, and the capital at Thebes is embellished with the monumental temples of Karnak and Luxor. The empire extends from the Fourth Cataract in the south to the upper Euphrates in Syria. The expanding Hittite Empire is encroaching upon both the Egyptian Empire and the Kingdom of Mitanni which, with Assyria in a period of decline, is dominant in northern Mesopotamia. A Hittite raid brings down the First Dynasty of Babylon, but it is the Kassites who inherit political power in southern Mesopotamia.

objects found in his tomb in 1922. The strongest of the pharaohs of the period were Ramses II, called the Great, who fought and concluded a treaty of peace with the Hittites, and Ramses III, who had to contend with raiders from the sea, possibly the Philistines who eventually settled in Palestine. During the third period of eclipse, starting about 1090 B.C., Egypt was ruled by foreigners, including Libyans and Ethiopians, and in 712 B.C. was invaded by a people called the Assyrians, the new ruling power in Mesopotamia.

During the Late Period, beginning in the eighth century, native rule was reestablished within Egypt, but efforts to restore its previous power and cultural predominance were challenged by younger rivals in the eastern Mediterranean, and attempts to reconquer the former empire were blocked by Nebuchadnezzar of Babylon. In this period too, Greek merchants flourished in the Delta and the Pharaoh Necho reportedly commissioned a Phoenician admiral to sail around the continent of Africa. In its final centuries ancient Egypt was more often than not ruled by others: the Persians, who in 525 B.C. annexed the country for two hundred years; the all-conquering Alexander the Great in the fourth century; and his successors, the Ptolemies, a Greek-Macedonian family. During the two and a half centuries that the Ptolemies ruled, the city of Alexandria developed into the center of Greek culture. In 31 B.C. Cleopatra, the last of the Ptolemies, in alliance with Mark Antony, lost the Battle of Actium to the forces of Caesar Augustus and Egypt became a Roman colony.

The culture of ancient Egypt may seem alien to Westerners today, but it fertilized Western civilization, first through interchanges with the cultures of Mesopotamia, and then through the Mycenaeans of Greece, who borrowed greatly from Egypt and passed on much to the later Greeks. Classical Greece and ancient Rome looked on Egypt as a treasure house of wisdom. Imhotep, a genius of the Old Kingdom, proficient in architecture and astronomy, was revered in the ancient world as the father of medicine, and Egyptian medicine reached a level not achieved in Europe till the end of the Middle Ages. The Egyptians were the first people to build monumental stone buildings and their architecture, sculpture, and painting still rank among the

After accepting the surrender of the Egyptian kingdom, Alexander founded the capital that bears his name.

When Cleopatra ruled in the first century B.C., Alexandria was a city of culture and grandeur, second only to Rome.

Quest For The Past

Until two hundred years ago, sources for the history and culture of the ancient Middle East were few and limited: the Bible, Greek and Roman authors (particularly Herodotus), accounts by such Muslim travelers as 'Abd al-Latif al-Baghdadi and Ibn Jubayr, and vague accounts passed on by nomads who had glimpsed traces of abandoned civilizations beneath shifting sands.

It was not until 1748, when the ruins of Pompeii were dug from the ancient ash of Mount Vesuvius, that man began to search systematically beneath the ground for knowledge of his vanished past and, through the science called archaeology, assess and add to those sources. And it was not until 1871 — when Heinrich Schliemann, stripping away the earth in layers, century by century, discovered classical Troy — that archaeology started to become a true science. In the Middle East, however, the quest for the past had been under way since 1798, when Napoleon invaded Egypt and, beneath the Pyramids, said to his troops, "Soldiers, forty centuries are looking down on you."

This was more than rhetoric: the future emperor had brought with him nearly two hundred scientists and scholars to study the Egyptian past. The result was the famous *Description de l'Egypte* — a meticulous account of the antiquities, geography, and monuments of ancient and modern Egypt. Painstakingly researched and lavishly illustrated, this work opened the eyes of the Western world to the splendors of ancient Egypt and established Egyptology as an important discipline.

The most important challenge facing the early Egyptologists was how to decipher the baffling hieroglyphic system of writing. It was not until 1821 that the brilliant French linguist Jean-François Champollion unlocked its mysteries. The key, one of the treasures brought back by Napoleon's expedition, was a slab of fine-grained basalt found near the town of Rosetta on the banks of the Nile — and hence known as the Rosetta Stone. As it was engraved with three blocks of scripts — hieroglyphic, hieratic (a cursive version of hieroglyphic), and Greek — the Rosetta Stone offered the possibility of deciphering the language of ancient Egypt by comparing it to a known language: Greek.

Examining the Rosetta Stone, Champollion realized that the hieroglyphic system of writing consisted of a combination of alphabetic, syllabic, and ideographic signs. His first success in determining the value of some of the alphabetic signs in this complex system came when he succeeded in reading names of Ptolemy and Cleopatra on a bilingual Greek-hieroglyphic inscription on an obelisk found at Philae. Then, assuming that the signs enclosed in "cartouches" — oval rings — were personal names, he compared the relative positions of the cartouches in the hieroglyphic text with the personal names in the Greek and thus determined the values of P, T, O, C, L, E, M, R, and A in the alphabetic system of hieroglyphic writing. As the names of Ptolemy and Cleopatra also occurred on the Rosetta Stone, Champollion was able to vindicate his method and, moreover, provide scholars with a fundamental technique for deciphering other unknown languages.

In Egypt, meanwhile, the soaring interest in Egyptology had resulted in a serious problem: Egypt was being looted of its treasures by an antique-hungry Europe. The seriousness of the problem was first noted by a French archaeologist named Auguste Mariette who, in the 1850s, excavated the great Avenue of Sphinxes at Luxor and the tomb of Tiy, a noble of the Egyptian Fifth Dynasty.

Excavations such as this were a valuable contribution, but in noting the looting of Egypt — and acting to prevent further looting — Mariette contributed much more. He helped establish, in 1858, the Egyptian Museum. He drafted strict restrictions on the export of antiquities. Perhaps more importantly, he also trained the first generation of Egyptian archaeologists.

Unfortunately, Mariette was too late by centuries. Looters had been plundering Egypt since the pharaohs were first buried. In 1875, for example, investigations disclosed that one family of professional tomb robbers had found and hidden the mummies and treasures of no less than forty ancient Egyptian kings. It is easy, therefore, to understand the excitement of Howard Carter — and the world — when, on November 26, 1922, Carter opened the undisturbed tomb of Tutankhamen and gazed upon the treasures of the young pharaoh who had died some 3,270 years before.

The King Tut treasures were the most famous archaeological discovery ever made — as well as the most dramatic. In 1906, Carter, a young and gifted archaeologist, persuaded George Herbert, Earl of Carnarvon, to finance years of work in the Valley of Kings near Luxor. The site he chose had been thoroughly picked over by several generations of archaeologists, but in 1922, just as he was about to abandon hope, Carter discovered a single stairway leading down into the earth, cabled Carnarvon, and, in an agony of impatience, waited three weeks for his patron to arrive. Finally, the door of the tomb was slowly opened and they beheld the untouched gold and other goods of the long-dead pharaoh.

Elsewhere in the Middle East the search for the past was less dramatic, but was certainly more difficult. This was particularly true in the Tigris and Euphrates Valley, where the great civilizations of Sumer, Akkad, Nineveh, and Babylon had arisen, flourished, and vanished.

Some of these civilizations had been known to historians from biblical references, but it was not until 1840 that archaeology began to confirm such references. In that year Paul-Émile Botta, the new French consul at Mosul, noticed the strange mounds that dotted the flat, muddy landscape between the Tigris and Euphrates rivers and decided to explore them. Botta started digging at a site called Kuyunjik — where he very nearly found Nineveh — but then learned that in the nearby village of Khorsabad there were a large number of ancient bricks marked with traces "like a bird's footprints." Excited by this news, Botta dispatched two workmen who, almost with the first shovelful of earth, came on massive walls carved with the reliefs of mythical animals. Summoned by the workmen, Botta galloped to the site and found himself gazing on the walls of the summer palace of Sargon II, King of Assyria.

(Continued on page 20)

Quest For The Past

Botta's discovery of the palace was, of course, important. But his subsequent discovery of a hundred tablets bearing the "bird's footprints" was immeasurably more valuable. For those "footprints" were cuneiform inscriptions and the tablets would provide the clues needed to break this ancient code, one of archaeology's greatest achievements.

Unlike Champollion, the men who deciphered cuneiform had no convenient Greek inscriptions to help them and, furthermore, could only guess at what language, or languages, lay concealed by the enigmatic script. Nevertheless, as early as 1802, a young German schoolmaster named George Grotefend had, in response to a beer-hall bet, made an astounding breakthrough. Working from no more than some poor copies of ancient Persian inscriptions, he deduced that the inscriptions were trilingual. As he did not know what three languages were represented, he decided, like Champollion, to begin with names. Since the names of the Kings of Achaemenian Persia were known from Herodotus and other sources, Grotefend reasoned that he might be able to match some of the recurring arrangements of signs in the inscriptions with the names of known rulers. Grotefend eventually was able to read the names of three rulers — Darius, Hystaspes, and Xerxes — and to identify correctly nine signs of the Old Persian cuneiform syllabary.

The next step was not taken until 1837, the year that Grotefend finally published his observations. In that year an Englishman, Major Henry Creswicke Rawlinson, dangling at the end of a rope on the face of a cliff near Bisitun in Persia, copied fourteen columns of cuneiform writing inscribed on the rock. Later that year he also published translations of the first two paragraphs.

Finally, a few years later, Botta found his hundred tablets and supplied the final clues; by a fortunate chance the tablets turned out to be Sumerian-Assyrian lexicographical texts. With these, and with the values discovered for the Old Persian texts at Bisitun and Persepolis, Rawlinson and others were soon able to read Assyrian cuneiform tablets and, within a decade, understand the principles of the cuneiform writing system.

In 1845 another discovery shook the scholarly world: Austen Henry Layard, perhaps the most famous Assyriologist of all, had, with the help of a Bedouin shaykh, uncovered the royal palace of King Assurnasirpal II, who reigned in the city of Nimrud from 883 to 859 B.C.

Layard was even luckier with his subsequent excavations. Returning to Kuyunjik, which Botta had abandoned, he found the great palace of Sennacherib, with its walls of glazed bricks. Later he found the library of Assurbanipal, the grandson of Sennacherib, which contained the oldest major work of literature in the world, the Epic of Gilgamesh, cut into hundreds of tablets buried in the palace rubble.

The Epic of Gilgamesh was translated by a man originally trained as a bank-note engraver whose secret passion was Assyriology. His name, too often unremembered, was George Smith. Gripped by the story related in the epic he was translating, George Smith was dismayed to discover that the end was missing — so dismayed that when *The Daily Telegraph* offered 1,000 guineas to anyone who could find the missing tablets, George Smith decided to undertake the search himself. By a stroke of the extraordinary luck that blessed those early Assyriologists, in just five days of searching in the vast heap of rubble at Kuyunjik he found the missing tablets — 384 of them. Back in England, he claimed his prize, deciphered the tablets, and — in another spectacular discovery — found that the story of Gilgamesh also told the story of the Flood.

To some, the golden age of archaeology may seem to have occurred in the nineteenth century. In fact, exciting discoveries have been made regularly since then. At the turn of the twentieth century Robert Koldeway began to excavate Babylon and struck the great wall of the city in just fourteen days. Not long after, he discovered the ruins

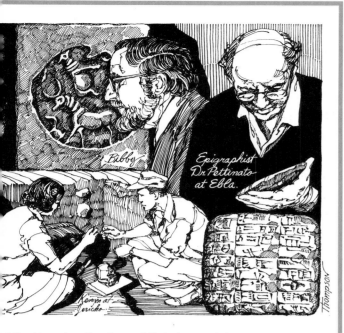

f the Hanging Gardens of Babylon and then a ziggurat he identified as the Tower of Babel. In 1928 Leonard Woolley xcavated Ur and went on to find, below Ur, an eight-foot eposit of clay that tended to corroborate both the biblical ccount of the Flood and the story of the Deluge in the ilgamesh Epic.

More recently, Kathleen Kenyon's important excava-ons at Jericho and Jerusalem have thrown much light on he prehistory of man outside the great river valleys of gypt and Mesopotamia; Mortimer Wheeler's discoveries n what is now Pakistan have revealed a flourishing urban ivilization contemporary with Ur; and Geoffrey Bibby's xcavations in Bahrain have shown that this small island ad an advanced culture contemporary with the oldest vidence of civilization from Mesopotamia and India. inally, in 1975, in what is potentially one of the greatest iscoveries of all, a team of Italian archaeologists in Syria rought to light Ebla, thought to mean "City of the White tones."

Unlike the lucky Layard, the Italians had to dig nearly ourteen years at Tell Mardikh, forty miles south of Aleppo, efore they unearthed, in 1968, a basalt votive statue with n Akkadian inscription mentioning the name "Ebla." oncluding that Ebla and Tell Mardikh were probably dentical, they continued their search and in 1975 found housands of cuneiform tablets from what, apparently, vere the state archives of Ebla.

Although it had been virtually unknown — except for are references in Akkadian and Sumerian tablets — it now ppears that Ebla was powerful enough to withstand the etter-known states of Mesopotamia, and that it possessed far-flung commercial empire. Although the translation nd interpretation of the tablets will take years, it seems hat these texts were written in a northwestern Semitic anguage and that they are considerably older than any ther known Semitic texts.

The discoveries at Ebla have been described by one of he archaeologists as "a kind of earthquake which puts nany theories in doubt," and which, he implies, may chart ew routes in the continuing quest for the past.

world's supreme works of art. Above all, the Egyptians developed and preserved a civiliza-tion of the highest order while most of the world was still submerged in barbarism.

LATER MESOPOTAMIA: In Mesopotamia, meanwhile, a people called the Assyrians had ended the period of anarchy following the breakup of the Hittite Empire. One of those Semitic peoples who had been settled in Mesopotamia since the third millennium, the Assyrians took their name from Assur, the name of their national god and of their first capital on the upper Tigris. Later they moved their capital to Nineveh, and in the ninth century B.C. they welded a new empire out of the neighboring states of Mesopotamia. The Assyrians later extended their boundaries to embrace all of Mesopotamia and parts of Egypt, Armenia, and Arabia.

The Assyrians were famous for their military proficiency. They fought with iron weapons, perfected the technique of the siege, and developed a deadly combination of ar-chers, heavy infantry, and cavalry. Even their art glorified war; their famous manheaded winged bulls conveyed vivid images of power and terror.

Assyrian achievements were not exclu-sively militaristic: they also built roads and introduced a government postal system and the use of silver currency. The Assyrians also compiled in royal libraries a wide range of written documents. Indeed, the 22,000 clay tablets found at Nineveh were one of the most important archaeological discoveries of all time and included the Epic of Gilgamesh, a poem of three thousand lines which relates the Sumerian legend of a hero-king.

Nevertheless, it was militarism that even-tually brought about the downfall of the empire. It drained the treasury, decimated the empire's agricultural labor force, and alien-ated its subjects. In 612 B.C. the ruler of Babylon and the king of the Medes joined forces to destroy Nineveh. The Assyrian Em-pire collapsed and Nineveh became a byword for vanished glory. With the Assyrians routed, the city of Babylon experienced a brilliant cultural revival as the capital of the Neo-Babylonian or Chaldean-Babylonian Empire, Chaldea being the name given to the southern-most part of the valley of the Tigris and Euphrates. Under Nebuchadnezzar in the

The winged manheaded bull, a benevolent being often seen in pairs as gateway guardians, had a long life in the successive civilizations of the ancient Mid-dle East.

The central figure of a literary epic written more than a thousand years before the *Iliad* or the *Odyssey*, Gilgamesh was the hero par excellence of the ancient world, symbolizing man's vain drive for glory and immortality.

Objects from Iran to the western edge of the Fertile Crescent reflect three millennia of art. From Ugarit, a cosmopolitan Canaanite center on the Syrian coast, comes the ivory head seen at top left. Directly above is a tablet from the fifteenth century B.C. bearing the Ugaritic cuneiform alphabet. Massive winged bulls with human heads (left) guard the gateway built in the time of Xerxes I, fifth century B.C., at the Persian capital of Persepolis. At nearby Pasargadae, the winged guardian of the bas-relief above wears a tiara of Egyptian inspiration. Facing page, top: Parade helmet of iron and silver is an example of Palmyrene art of the first century A.D. Gypsum statuette of Urananshe, leader of the temple choir at Mari on the upper Euphrates, dates from about 2500 B.C. Directly opposite is a ceramic-brick bull from the Ishtar Gate in Nebuchadnezzar's Babylon.

THE MIDDLE EAST IN THE SEVENTH CENTURY B.C.

Assyria, at the height of its power, controls all of Mesopotamia including Elamite Susa, the Levant, and much of Egypt and Armenia. Detente with Assyria allows Urartu to recover from Assyrian assaults of the previous century. The Phoenician cities of Tyre and Sidon pay tribute to Assyria but preserve their commercial freedom, while their colonies as far away as Carthage flourish. Caravan routes and the spice trade provide continuing prosperity for the kingdoms of southern Arabia. Overextended, the Assyrian Empire soon comes under pressure, and Egypt regains its independence in midcentury. The Chaldeans of Babylon combine with the Medes and the Persians to destroy Nineveh in 612 B.C.

The ruins at Babylon bear mute testimony to the greatness of one of the mightiest cities of antiquity.

Monumental basalt lion stands over a fallen enemy at Babylon.

sixth century B.C., Babylon became synonymous with splendor and luxury. The Hanging Gardens, a late form of the ziggurat, were one of the Seven Wonders of the World and the royal palaces, the city walls, and the gorgeously decorated Ishtar Gate were equally magnificent. Herodotus, visiting Babylon, said that no one could believe the fertility of the surrounding plain if he had not been there. Because of the great advances in astronomy and astrology made during this period, astrologers for many centuries thereafter were simply called Chaldeans.

Although humane compared to the Assyrians, the Babylonians continued the practice of deporting subject peoples. The best known of these deportations was the Babylonian Captivity of the Hebrews during which, the Bible says, Daniel went into the lions' den and Belshazzar, at a feast, stared in terror at the writing on the wall.

But the glory of the Neo-Babylonian Empire was short-lived. In 539 B.C. it surrendered to the Persian conqueror Cyrus the Great, thus ending Mesopotamian independence for more than a thousand years.

OTHER ANCIENT PEOPLES: There were also, during these periods, many ancient peoples who did not rule over extensive empires, but who nevertheless played major roles in the history of what is now called the Middle East — and also made important contributions to Western culture. Among the best known were the Canaanites, the Hebrews, the Philistines, the Phoenicians, and the Aramaeans.

Canaan is a geographic term designating the region of southern Syria, Lebanon, and Palestine, and including such towns as Jericho, Lachish, Byblos, and Ugarit. Famous later as "a land flowing with milk and honey," Canaan attracted diverse peoples from Paleolithic times onwards — Semites, Hurrians, Hittites, and others. By the third millennium B.C. this amalgam of peoples had reached a high stage of development. From one of the Semitic peoples in Sinai, for example, the world probably received the alphabet.

Through trade, the Canaanites absorbed Egyptian and Minoan influences from the west and Assyrian-Sumerian influences from the east. They worshipped a fertility goddess, Ashtoreth, and a god, Baal, the "giver of life,"

whose name appears in place-names where his temples once stood — such as Baalbek in northern Lebanon. The Canaanite civilization reached its peak from the fifteenth to the thirteenth centuries B.C. and its history then merges with that of the northern branch, the Phoenicians, and other immigrant peoples such as the Hebrews and Philistines.

Because they left an indelible record of their history and ideas in the Old Testament, the Hebrews are better known to posterity than many other peoples of the Middle East. In fact, however, they were politically of secondary importance compared to their more powerful neighbors; their fame rests primarily on their outstanding contribution to literature and religion.

The Hebrews seem to have developed from a group of related semi-nomadic tribes with a common patriarch, Abraham — a situation still paralleled among Bedouin tribes today. As told in the Book of Genesis, their early history is closely intertwined with that of Mesopotamia, where civilization was thousands of years old when the Hebrews emerged as a people, settled in Canaan, and eventually, under King David in the tenth century B.C., conquered it. Earlier some Hebrew tribes had settled in the Delta of the Nile until, oppressed by the pharaohs, they were led out of Egypt by Moses.

Living at the crossroads of the powerful empires of Egypt, Assyria, Persia, Greece, and Rome, the Hebrews were able to rule this territory only at intervals between the thirteenth century B.C. and the Roman destruction of the Temple in Jerusalem in A.D. 70. Despite this, the Hebrews left a rich legacy of poetry, history, and religious thought.

The Philistines, a people from somewhere in the west — possibly Crete or Mycenae — disputed control over western Canaan with the Hebrews for centuries, a contest that was never finally settled in favor of one or the other. With control of iron as one source of their strength, the Philistines welded the cities of Philistia — Gaza, Ashkelon, Ashdod, Ekron, and Gath — into a confederacy that dominated the major commercial route between Egypt and Syria. They worshipped gods similar to those of the earlier Canaanites and at some period in their history abandoned their original tongue in favor of a Semitic one.

The Phoenicians never formed a unified

The Art Of Writing

Aleph, the first letter of the Canaanite alphabet, was gradually transformed into the letter "A" of the European languages.

To the best of present knowledge, it appears that the world's first system of writing was evolved by the Sumerians toward the end of the fourth millennium B.C. in the southern reaches of the Tigris-Euphrates Valley. Not long after that, the Egyptians developed a system of their own.

The Sumerian script is called cuneiform — an arrangement of wedge-shaped marks impressed with a stylus on wet clay tablets, which were then dried or baked until they were nearly indestructible. Cuneiform was adapted by later Mesopotamian peoples to their own quite different languages and was in use by the Persians as late as the first century A.D., over thirty centuries after its earliest development. The Egyptian script — hieroglyphic (meaning "sacred carving" in Greek) and a later cursive form called hieratic — lasted as long but was confined to Egypt.

The Sumerian-Assyrian and Egyptian scripts were not true alphabets — that is, systems of writing in which one symbol stands for a single sound. They were transitional systems representing a stage beyond simple picture-writing or ideographic writing (a somewhat more advanced system in which pictures can be used to represent not only objects but also some abstract concepts) but not yet a true alphabet. Cuneiform writing was pictographic in its origins, and Egyptian hieroglyphics remained strongly pictorial throughout their very long history, but both systems of writing developed a number of additional signs which had no meaning in themselves but were a guide to the pronunciation of the symbols.

The next stage in the development of writing was the use of syllabaries (sets of signs representing syllables rather than whole words or concepts). Both the Egyptians and the Assyrians developed syllabaries which they used as a further help in reading their hieroglyphic and cuneiform writings.

The final step was the creation of a true alphabet, and this probably took place in Sinai. The Egyptians had penetrated the Sinai Peninsula in search of the turquoise mined there by the Semitic inhabitants. Hieroglyphic inscriptions have been found in Sinai and it can be assumed that the local people were familiar with Egyptian writing. From it they took the Egyptian syllabary and reduced it to some thirty letters, which they applied to their own Semitic language. It was at about this stage that they or, according to some scholars, Semitic peoples further to the north in Palestine took the crucially important step of converting these from a syllabary to a system in which each sign or letter represented a single sound.

The Semitic invention of the alphabet had great advantages over the mixed and complex writing systems of other peoples. It required the memorization of only a score or so of characters and even people without a long and arduous education in sacred and historical matters could easily master it. This took writing out of the exclusive hands of priests and scribes and put it at the disposal of all who took the trouble to memorize the alphabet.

Soon the Phoenicians — the Greek name given to the seafaring Canaanites of the Syrian-Lebanese coast — were spreading the alphabet throughout the Mediterranean by leaving examples of this priceless tool in the form of orders, invoices, bills of lading, and receipts wherever they went in search of trade.

The Aramaeans, a closely related Semitic people who were also traders, contributed to the spread of the alphabet too. They adapted it to their needs and, as their language became the lingua franca of the Middle East from Egypt to Persia for more than a thousand years, introduced the alphabet wherever Aramaic was spoken. As a result, the Semitic alphabet became the remote basis of virtually every alphabet used in Asia: Arabic, Hebrew, the many Indian scripts, Burmese, Thai, Malayan, Tibetan, Manchu, Korean, and scores of others.

In Greece, a regular port of call for the Phoenicians, the alphabet was modified. Because the Indo-European languages of the West put more emphasis on vowels than the Semitic tongues, the Greeks assigned certain of the borrowed letters to vowel sounds and invented and adapted others to accommodate the sounds of Greek. But even then the Semitic alphabet remained the basis; as written in the sixth century B.C., Greek retained nineteen of the original Semitic symbols.

From Greece the alphabet spread to the Etruscans, who introduced still more modifications, and then, as altered, to the Romans. Thus the alphabet entered Europe and the New World where, today, it still bears a name directly derived from the first two letters of the Semitic alphabet, for "alpha," the name of the first letter in the Greek alphabet, comes from "aleph" and "beta" is from the Semitic "beit" or "beth" — thus "alphabet," the key element in the art of writing.

Bronze figures covered with gold leaf were among the Bronze Age finds at Byblos, considered by the Phoenicians the most ancient city on their coast.

The political, administrative, and religious center of the Persian Empire was at Persepolis, a city of palaces and ceremonial staircases built primarily by Darius I and his son, Xerxes I.

state and the boundaries of Phoenicia were vague. But they were the greatest seafarers of the ancient world; from the independent ports of Tyre, Sidon, Byblos, and Tripoli on what is now the coast of Lebanon, and Aradus in Syria, the Phoenicians, beginning about the twelfth century B.C., ranged throughout the Mediterranean and into the Atlantic, founding colonies — essentially trading posts — in Cyprus, North Africa, France, and Spain. They also sailed along the west coast of Africa and may have reached Britain, where they are thought to have traded for tin in Cornwall.

The Phoenicians carried many items of trade, especially cloth in rich shades of Tyrian purple, a dye made from the murex, a shellfish found on their coast. They also disseminated the Canaanite alphabet, especially to the Greeks, who passed it on to Europe.

Of all Phoenician colonies, Carthage, in what is now Tunisia, played the most spectacular role. Founded, according to tradition, by Elissa, or Dido, a fugitive princess of Tyre, Carthage outstripped her mother-city and became strong enough to challenge the Roman Empire. In the three Punic (Phoenician) Wars of the third and second centuries B.C., Carthage almost defeated Rome in a long contest for control of the Mediterranean world. In 217 B.C., under Hannibal, a Carthaginian army accompanied by elephants crossed the Alps into Italy and threatened Rome itself. But the Romans won the final battle. In 146 B.C. they took Carthage by siege, destroyed the city and — according to legend — sowed salt on its site. The Phoenician cities of the eastern Mediterranean, meanwhile, had fallen to the army of Alexander the Great and were eventually absorbed into the Roman Empire.

The Aramaeans are chiefly remembered for the extraordinary diffusion and longevity of their language. They appeared in Syria sometime before 1200 B.C. and made the already ancient city of Damascus their capital. A commercial people like the Phoenicians, they penetrated other lands in pursuit of trade, spreading their language — which was closely related to other Semitic tongues in the region — until it became the lingua franca of the Middle East for more than a thousand years. The Egyptians and Persians used it in their diplomatic correspondence and the people of Palestine spoke it during the lifetime

of Jesus. Parts of the Old Testament were written in it and it is likely that Aramaic oral materials, if not written documents, predate the Greek in some books of the New Testament. Aramaic is still spoken in a few Syrian villages and many Oriental Christians — in the Middle East, on the Malabar Coast of India, and even in the United States — have their gospels and part of their liturgies in a form of Aramaic called Syriac.

THE OUTSIDERS: From the sixth century B.C. to the seventh century A.D., a period of more than a thousand years, outsiders ruled in the Fertile Crescent and the Nile Valley. Non-Semitic peoples from the east and the west — Persians, Macedonian Greeks, Romans, Byzantines, Parthians, and Sassanians — governed part or all of the Middle East and each made a contribution to the intricate mosaic of Middle Eastern culture.

The conquest of Babylon by Cyrus the Great of Persia in 539 B.C. was an early step in the formation of the greatest empire the world had yet seen. Persian rule eventually extended from areas now in Pakistan and Afghanistan through the Fertile Crescent into Egypt, and northward through Asia Minor to the banks of the Danube. Only the mainland Greeks, at the battles of Marathon and Salamis, were able to withstand the Persian advance. Despite its size, the empire was highly centralized, with a remarkably efficient administration and excellent communications based on the use of fast horses. The Persians showed unusual tolerance toward their subject peoples, allowing them to retain local customs and religions as long as these did not conflict with Persian hegemony, and they permitted peoples deported by the Assyrians and Babylonians to return to their homelands. The Persian religion, Zoroastrianism, had a high ethical content and Persian art was eclectic: the great complex of palaces at Persepolis shows elements borrowed from Mesopotamia, Egypt, and Greece, but assimilated into a distinctive Persian style.

After a little more than two centuries, the old Persian or Achaemenid Empire was overwhelmed by the conquests of Alexander the Great in 334-323 B.C. It was in Babylon that Alexander died in 323 B.C., after wresting the ancient city from Persian rule and after completing his conquest of the whole civilized world from Macedonia to India. Greek culture, which already had been spreading over the Middle East, continued there in Hellenistic form through the succeeding era of the Seleucids in Syria and the Ptolemies in Egypt, as well as the later Roman and Byzantine empires, down to the age of Islam.

In the first century B.C. the tide of Roman conquests swept away such personal dynasties and absorbed their fiefs into the Roman Empire. Rome itself gradually became orientalized by the older and richer cultures of the Middle East — a change reflected in the Roman poet Juvenal's complaint that Syria's Orontes River was flowing into the Tiber. But as the tendency of the Roman Empire was toward uniformity, Roman art and architecture eventually blanketed the civilized world — as witnessed by the remains of Roman cities at such places as Baalbek in Lebanon, Palmyra and Bosra in Syria, and Jerash in Jordan.

The vitality of Persia was shown in its revival in the Parthian Empire (250 B.C. — A.D. 226) and in the Sassanian Empire (A.D. 225-650). The Parthians kept the power of Rome from going east of the Euphrates. The frequent occurrence on Bahrain Island, as well as on the western shore of the Arabian Gulf, of certain types of Parthian pottery indicates a close relationship between Mesopotamia and the Arabian Gulf, at least during the second half of the Parthian Empire. The Sassanians were often more than a match for Byzantium in war and made significant achievements in architecture, art, and textiles. The historic and fertile region of Mesopotamia attracted both the later Persian empires. Ctesiphon, on the Tigris southeast of Baghdad, was the Persian capital when the Sassanians were conquered by the Muslim Arab armies in 637-650.

Another of the great outside powers that ruled and influenced the Middle East was Byzantium, heir to the Roman provinces in Syria, Asia Minor, and Egypt. In A.D. 330 the Roman Emperor Constantine I moved his capital from Rome to Constantinople — on the site of an old Greek town called Byzantium. At the end of the fourth century, when the Roman Empire broke in two, Constantinople became the capital of the eastern, and more brilliant, half. Byzantium was Greek in language, Orthodox Christian in religion, and Roman in political institutions. In 636 the

Byzantine armies were defeated by the Arabs at the Battle of Yarmuk and Byzantine power withdrew into Asia Minor and the Balkans, where it continued to flourish although in a steadily diminishing area until the Ottoman Turks took Constantinople in 1453. The Battle of Yarmuk was not the first appearance of the Arabs in history, but until then they were peripheral to it. Now they step into its full light.

THE ARABS: The Arabs themselves call their homeland the "Island of the Arabs," a phrase that is effectively, if not literally, true. Cut off from Africa and Asia by water on three sides — the Red Sea, the Gulf of Aden, the Arabian Sea, the Gulf of Oman, and the Arabian Gulf — Arabia was for centuries also sealed off from the Fertile Crescent to the north by a sea of sand and stone as forbidding as the coral reefs and shoals of the coast. Invaders could and did breach this barrier but it was a formidable challenge; as a result the peninsular Arabs enjoyed long uninterrupted periods of separate development.

But as the Island of the Arabs was also located athwart the ancient trade routes that linked the Mediterranean world with the Far East by sea and land, the Arabs almost inevitably became the middlemen of East-West commerce. Although the West could rarely reach them, they could reach the West; as a consequence they found themselves in contact not only with material products of both worlds, but also with their inventions and discoveries. They were, in effect, middlemen for the passage of ideas as well as things between the Orient and the Occident.

Other geographical influences were climate and terrain. The Arabian Peninsula — a veritable subcontinent one-third the size of the continental United States or Western Europe — is sharply divided into two different regions by the amount of rainfall each receives. The southern mountainous fringe of the peninsula receives abundant rains from the monsoons blowing off the Indian Ocean, and these regions — in ancient times part of Arabia Felix (Happy or Fortunate Arabia) and today comprising Yemen, Hadhramaut, Oman, and the 'Asir province of Saudi Arabia — are relatively green and fertile. The northern and central parts of the peninsula — that is, the coastal area north from about Jiddah and the vast

The Seleucids, Greek successors to Alexander the Great, ruled Syria and Mesopotamia, introducing Hellenistic styles of art, as in this bust found at Hatra on the Tigris.

A great elliptical, barrel-shaped vault — 120 feet high at the crown — spans what was once a palace hall at Ctesiphon, the Sassanian capital on the Tigris.

interior — receive little rain and are mostly desert except for occasional green oases where groundwater is near the surface.

Corresponding to these differences in climate and terrain is the clear distinction in Arab tradition between the Arabs of the north and the Arabs of the south. The Arabs of the north had a heterogenous social fabric; the southern Arabs formed a homogenous society. The northerners were divided into camel-herding nomads and sedentary oasis-dwellers. The nomads, organized on a tribal basis, depended for their livelihood on their herds and hence moved constantly in search of pasture over a vast and forbidding area, while most of the sedentary people dwelt in far-flung oases, hospitable dots of greenery surrounded by the harsh desert. The southern Arabs, on the other hand, lived in a densely populated, rain-fed area rich in vegetation, and resided in towns and villages. These population centers developed an urban culture that had a vigorous material and political growth, flourishing for almost a millennium and interrelating and interacting not only with the rest of the Arabian Peninsula but also with the whole of the ancient world.

The Arabs of the north, furthermore, spoke Thamudic, Lihyanite, Safaitic, and Arabic; those of the south spoke several related Semitic tongues but, in ancient times, not Arabic. There were even differences in physical appearance (perhaps the result of differences in living conditions), as there still are today. These differences were not, of course, absolute; in early times there were Arabic-speaking nomads in the south and colonies of southern merchants in the north (at al-'Ula, for example).

One thing stands out clearly: despite the diversity of the Arabs there was an essential unity. Regardless of the political, cultural, social, and economic differences arising from the complex interaction of man and nature, all the inhabitants of the peninsula were recognizably one people: the Arabs.

THE SOUTH ARABIANS: It was in the south, during the millennium preceding the birth of Christ, that the first advanced civilizations in the Arabian Peninsula developed. The earliest of these was the Sabaean, named for the Kingdom of Saba or Sheba, whose queen (according to the Bible — and the Quran)

For centuries, the number of a man's camels was a measure of his wealth among the nomadic tribes of Arabia.

An ancient village in southern Arabia is sheltered by walls of a canyon cut deeply into the Hadhramaut plateau.

Early Times

For many years historians regarded the ancient Arabian Gulf as no more than an artery of seafaring and trade between Mesopotamia and the lands to the south and east. In the 1950s, however, an archaeological expedition reported that the islands and coast on the western side of the Gulf had not only played a vital role in the economy of the ancient Middle East, but had developed an autonomous civilization going back to the third millennium B.C.

In the 1970s, moreover, the Department of Antiquities of Saudi Arabia excavated evidence confirming that soon after 5000 B.C. peoples on the western coast and islands of the Gulf had contact with the 'Ubayd culture of Mesopotamia. An Aramco geologist reported, furthermore, that during an early rainy period — some twenty to thirty thousand years ago — the Arabian Peninsula was inhabited by Stone Age man.

The Rub' al-Khali, now the largest sand desert in the world, was a quite different place then. Because the climate as a whole was milder, there were numerous lakes and streams in the Rub' al-Khali. Large crude stone axes have been found on what were the shores of those lakes,

In The Arabian Gulf

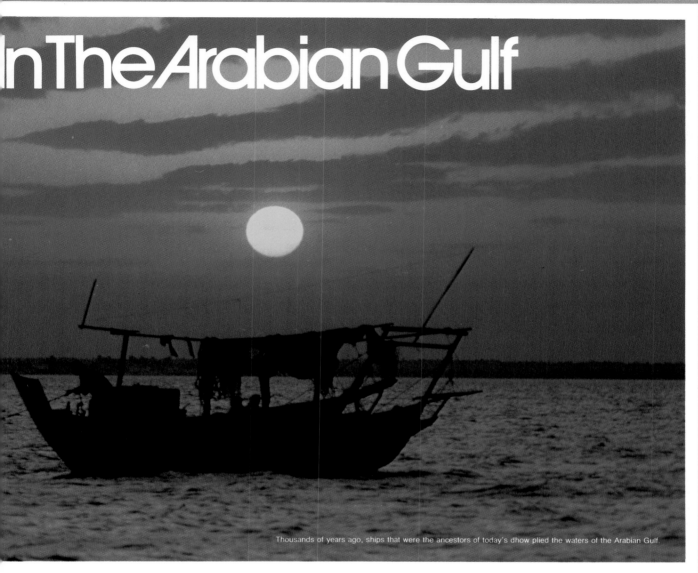

Thousands of years ago, ships that were the ancestors of today's dhow plied the waters of the Arabian Gulf.

and similar axes have been found on other parts of the peninsula.

In a later rainy age — between six and nine thousand years ago — the peoples of the time left hundreds of thousands of beautifully worked stone tools by the now vanished lakes and streams. And during the later centuries, when there were still lakes, people living beside a spring in what is now the northern edge of the al-Hasa oasis were using 'Ubayd pottery.

The discovery of 'Ubayd pottery in eastern Arabia was a definite surprise. This pottery, with its characteristic stripes, zigzags, and loops, is identical to pottery found primarily in Iraq, Iran, and Syria, and such early contacts between those areas and the Gulf had never been suspected. The subsequent excavation of three 'Ubayd sites in Saudi Arabia (two of them near what are now Jubail and Hofuf), as well as two in Qatar and one in Bahrain, showed that 'Ubayd culture extended nearly four hundred miles further south than archaeologists had believed. At some of these sites archaeologists also found sharp arrow heads and tools made from obsidian — natural glass

formed during volcanic eruptions; they had been imported by the 'Ubayd people from the Lake Van region of Turkey some nine hundred miles to the north.

By about 3000 B.C., a thousand years after the rise of Sumer, the earliest known civilization, eastern Arabia was widely settled and, as the Gulf by then had become an artery of ancient trade, the area was a prosperous one. Tarut Island, for example, was in direct or indirect contact with civilizations in what are now parts of Russia, Pakistan, Iran, Iraq, Syria, Kuwait, and Oman. Among the goods traded were copper, stone, wood, gold, ivory, carnelian, and lapis lazuli — which were exchanged for woven goods and foodstuffs. Among the popular luxury items were carved stone bowls and plaques. Designs on bowls found at Tarut Island — snakes, leopards, bulls, and various geometric patterns — are identical to those on bowls found in the other civilizations, but more different designs have been reported from Tarut than from any other place. One particularly attractive find on Tarut Island was a figure, about an inch and half tall, which was carved in lapis lazuli, a stone mined in northern Afghanistan.

(Continued on page 32)

Tomb excavated at Jawan on the Saudi Arabian mainland contained an alabaster statuette and jewelry of gold and precious stones dating from the first century A.D.

Early Times

The most famous Gulf civilization of this period — and therefore the focus of archaeological investigation — was Dilmun. Cuneiform texts found at Ur refer to a land called Ni-tuk-ki in Sumerian and Dilmun in Akkadian. In Sumerian myths it was a pure, bright place where "the lion kills not, the wolf snatches not the lamb." It was also the scene of certain incidents in the legend of Gilgamesh, the epic which fascinated Mesopotamian peoples for thousands of years.

Dilmun was also an actual country — with Bahrain as its center — that exported and transshipped goods into the Mesopotamian economy from such other lands as Oman and India. "Ships of Dilmun from the foreign lands brought me wood as a tribute," boasts a ruler of Lagash in the middle of the third millennium B.C. The expansionist empires of Mesopotamia often tried to draw Dilmun into their political and economic orbit, but it was not until about 600 B.C. that the Assyrians brought Dilmun's independence to an end.

To amend and amplify what was known about the Gulf in ancient times, a Danish archaeological expedition, sent by the Museum of Aarhus, began working in the Arabian Gulf in the 1950s. Most of the digging was in Bahrain, where, with the active support of the Bahrain Government,

archaeologists unearthed a large palace, and a town site going back to the third millennium. Within the palace complex they found the skeletons of snakes buried in covered pots — a practice that perhaps may be related to the "snake of immortality" referred to in the Epic of Gilgamesh. They also found weights suggesting a possible commercial tie with the Indus Valley, where weights of similar value were used. The expedition also unearthed a Dilmun town on Failaka Island in Kuwait, the remains of a people who lived in Abu Dhabi during the same period, and copper works in Oman — suggesting that it might be the lost land of Makan — which produced the copper on which the Bronze Age civilization of Mesopotamia was based.

The most notable archaeological feature of the western Gulf is the existence of large fields of burial mounds on Bahrain Island and on the mainland south of Dhahran. Over the years travelers who have seen them have advanced several theories about who were buried in the mounds. By the 1960s archaeologists were certain that the larger graves date back to Dilmun and the smaller ones to Hellenistic times — specifically to the successors of Alexander the Great. In the last years of his life Alexander, after reaching India, intended to add Arabia to his conquests. Although he died before he could do so, his successors in Syria and Mesopotamia, the Seleucids, occupied territory at the head of the Gulf and built cities there in the Hellenistic pattern. The Danish expedition has investigated two of them — one at Thaj in Saudi Arabia, the other on Failaka Island in Kuwait, where they unearthed typical Hellenistic temples, votive inscriptions to the Greek gods, and sherds of pottery from mainland Greece.

Archaeologists in the Gulf would also like to find the famous city called Gerrha, somewhere on the Arabian coast. Strabo, quoting earlier sources, reports that it was a Babylonian colony and that its merchants generally carried their merchandise, including incense, by land, a reference to the great caravans plodding north from what is now Yemen.

By this trade, Strabo adds, "both the Sabaeans and the Gerrhaei have become the richest of all tribes, and possess a great quantity of articles wrought in gold and silver, as couches, tripods, basins, drinking vessels, to which we must add the costly magnificence of their houses for the doors, walls and roofs are variegated with inlaid ivory, gold, silver and precious stones." Because of this wealth, the Seleucids under Antiochus III in 205 B.C. threatened to level Gerrha, and a leader of the city sent a

A tiny lapis lazuli figure and Dilmun pottery were found on Tarut Island.

large tribute of silver, pearls, and other precious gems along with a letter. This letter said, "Destroy not, O King, those two things which have been given of the gods, perpetual peace and freedom."

The exact location of Gerrha is still a mystery. Pliny described it as being opposite the island of Tylos, the classical name for Bahrain, "famous for the vast number of its pearls," and also refers to the region of Attene, fifty miles inland, possibly the oasis of al-Hasa. It is also possible that Gerrha is buried under the Jafurah sands where Seleucid coins have been found near the remains of an extensive irrigation system just inland from the Gulf. But these identifications are just conjecture; the location of Gerrha remains unknown.

There are other early sites. Jawan, for example, a tomb complex near the road from Dhahran to Ras Tanura, has been excavated by an Aramco archaeologist with the agreement of the Government of Saudi Arabia. Objects found in the tomb, some of gold, belong to the middle of the first century A.D. Many inhabitants of eastern Arabia along the Gulf became Christians in the first few centuries of the Christian era, and Church sources say Christian bishoprics existed there from the third century on — one of them, a Nestorian bishopric, located in Darin, the old port of Tarut Island. With the advent of Islam, however, all those Christian communities were absorbed into the Islamic state.

visited King Solomon. In the Quran she is described as ruling from "a magnificent throne" and in the Bible as coming to visit Solomon in a great caravan laden with "spices and very much gold and precious stones." This so-called Queen of Sheba was most probably the chieftain of the tribe of Saba, although she may have come from a Sabaean colony in the northern part of the peninsula rather than from the land of Saba in the south.

Other kingdoms in southern Arabia that later came to prominence around Saba were Ma'in, north of Saba; Awsan in the southwestern corner nearest Aden; Qataban, northeast of Awsan; and Hadhramaut, east of Qataban. This southern civilization in its later periods is often referred to as Himyaritic rather than Minaean or Sabaean, after the southwestern tribe of Himyar, which grew increasingly powerful.

The Sabaean civilization of southern Arabia, based on trade between India and the Mediterranean, produced works of art such as this relief of a ram.

To a great extent the prosperity of southern Arabia rested on trade — based largely on the sale of its own products (most notably aromatics) and on the transshipment of spices and other valuable cargoes from across the Arabian Sea. It is difficult today to grasp the importance of spices and aromatics in the ancient world. Spices were used to preserve food, or to flavor food preserved by smoking and drying and thus left tasteless. Aromatics were also important. They were used to adorn and perfume the body and were essential ingredients in the spiritual and political life of the times. They were used in religious rites, in the embalming and burial of the dead, in the consecration or "anointment" of the rulers, and — most importantly — as offerings in the great temples of Egypt and Canaan. In sum, spices and aromatics were valuable enough to justify the risks and costs of long trading voyages.

This inscription is in Himyaritic, a language of the pre-Islamic southern Arabians.

Some of the commodities that the people of southern Arabia traded in came from India and East Africa, but the most important — the rare and expensive aromatic gums called frankincense and myrrh — grew in Arabia Felix itself. In fact, although trade was of major importance, Sabaean prosperity rested to an even greater extent on agriculture, and to support this one of the engineering marvels of the age, the great dam of Marib, was built. Nearly two thousand feet across, the dam spanned the Wadi Adhanah in the black hills near Marib, the capital of Saba, deflecting and

CARTHAGE

THRACE

BLACK SEA

GREECE

PHRYGIA

Sardis

CILICIA

ARMENIA

CASPIAN SEA

Athens

Carchemish

MEDITERRANEAN SEA

Sidon

SYRIA

Tyre

Damascus

Tigris River

Euphrates River

Cyrene

Jerusalem

Memphis

Nile River

EGYPT

al-Qusayr

RED

Thebes

Aswan

FIRST CATARACT

SEA

Nile River

THE MIDDLE EAST IN THE FIFTH CENTURY B.C.

United under the Achaemenian kings, the Medes and Persians rapidly extend the boundaries of their empire. Reliefs in the fifth-century ceremonial capital of Persepolis graphically illustrate the cosmopolitan character of this empire, which extends from what is now Afghanistan and Pakistan through the Fertile Crescent to Egypt and northward through Asia Minor to the Danube. Only mainland Greece in the Age of Pericles successfully resists and obtains a peace agreement recognizing the independence of the city states and Greek colonies on the west coast of Asia Minor. The tolerant rule of the Persians encourages revival of the cities of the Levant, which have been successively occupied or destroyed by Assyrian and Babylonian forces.

The Roman Empire proclaimed its might in the East as elsewhere by raising temples and other public buildings of imposing size and presence. Opposite page: The columns of the Temple of Jupiter at Baalbek in Lebanon are the largest of the ancient world. This page, clockwise from above: A ceremonial gate at Palmyra, an oasis and caravan station in the Syrian Desert. A carved head gazes down from a wall in Leptis Magna, built by the Romans in what is now Libya. The so-called Temple of Bacchus at Baalbek, which has withstood the onslaught of time better than most. A curved colonnade of classical pillars graces the forum at Jerash in today's Jordan.

GAUL
ITALY
Rome
Carthage
SICILY Syracuse
MAURETANIA
MEDITERRANEAN SEA
GREECE Athens
Byzantium BLACK SEA
ANATOLIA
Pergamum
Tarsus
CRETE
CYPRUS
Antioch Palmyra Dura-Europus
Berytus Damascus
Sidon
Tyre Gerasa Bosra
Caesaria Philadelphia
PALESTINE Jerusalem
ARMENIA
CASPIAN SEA
P
Tigris River
Euphrates River
SYRIA
Hatra
Leptis Magna
Alexandria
LIBYA
Memphis
Nile River
Petra
ARABIA PETRAEA
SINAI
EGYPT
Tayma
Madain Salih
Thebes
Al-'Ula
Berenice
RED
Nile River
Jiddah Mecc
SEA

THE MIDDLE EAST AND THE ROMAN EMPIRE IN THE SECOND CENTURY A.D.

The Roman Empire achieves its maximum territorial extent, completely surrounding the Mediterranean. Expansion to the east is checked by the Parthians and the Syrian Desert. Conditions are chaotic in southern Arabia (known in classical times as Arabia Felix or "Happy Arabia"), since the overland trade routes on which it depended for its prosperity have been bypassed by the development of sea routes through the Red Sea to India. However, Gerrha on the Arabian Gulf and the caravan cities of the north continue to prosper. The caravan kingdom of the Nabataeans, which has extended its territory into north-central Arabia and established a city at Madain Salih, is annexed by the Roman Empire as Arabia Petraea or "Rocky Arabia."

The Nabataeans, who controlled trade routes in northwestern Arabia from the fourth to the first century B.C., carved their tombs into sandstone cliffs at Petra, now in Jordan.

At Madain Salih, the Nabataeans established another important center, possibly at the frontier shared with the southern Arabians.

Palmyra, an ancient caravan port on the edge of the Syrian Desert, was important in biblical times as a center of east-west trade.

retaining the waters of seasonal flash floods, and, through an elaborate system of sluices and canals, distributing the water to the cultivated areas. The dam, in fact, was a cornerstone of the economy of the kingdom.

THE NORTH ARABIANS: To reach the Fertile Crescent and the Mediterranean the south Arabian merchants had to enlist the help of the Arabians of the north, who were masters of the desert. Only they knew the great wadi systems, which provided not only easier terrain for travel but also water near the surface in the ancient stream beds. Only they knew the location of desert wells and pools, the oasis way stations, the best grazing, and the alliances and hostilities of the tribes. And only they were familiar with the efficient use of the camel, which alone made desert travel possible.

The northern Arabians developed a great network of routes for their caravans. The main route from the south led from Yemen along the western side of the peninsula through Mecca and Yathrib (now called Medina) and thence via different branches into Mesopotamia, Syria, Palestine, and across Sinai into Egypt. Other routes branched off from this at the oasis of Najran, in the southwestern part of what is now Saudi Arabia, and at Mecca, to run north and east to Babylon and the rest of Mesopotamia and to the port of Gerrha on the Arabian Gulf. They also organized the caravans, often made up of hundreds of camels, into joint stock companies and contributed to the development of important commercial centers. These centers grew up in the oases where the camel trains halted, where customs duties were charged for the passage of merchandise, and where goods were often sold or redistributed — in places like Gerrha, Mecca, Yathrib, and al-'Ula, a south Arabian colony in west-central Arabia. As a result the Arabians of the north gradually became equal partners with those of the south or even dominated them in the caravan trade.

Meanwhile, the isolation that had protected southern Arabia's commercial monopoly began to collapse. In the second century B.C. Hippalus, a Greek Egyptian, unlocked the secret of the monsoons and the ensuing increase in seaborne trade slowly but surely undermined and reduced the trade by caravan. The south also faced invasions from

Ethiopia, and once from Rome. About the same time, at the northern termini of the desert routes, other caravan cities had also been growing into centers of commercial importance to rival the established towns to the south. The most important of these were Petra and Palmyra.

Petra was the capital of a people called the Nabataeans, believed to be descended from the desert nomads. In the fourth century B.C. the Nabataeans had seized control of the northern portion of the rich trade routes running up the western coast of Arabia and, at their peak, extended their power from Madain Salih, north of Medina, to Damascus. But their main city was Petra in what is now Jordan. Both Petra and Madain Salih are remarkable for the beauty of their tombs. Rather than erecting buildings from separate structural elements, the Nabataeans carved their tombs out of sandstone cliffs, often imitating Egyptian, Greek, or Roman motifs. Petra — in the poet's phrase "a rose-red city half as old as time" — was hidden in an inaccessible valley in Wadi Musa and unknown to the West for centuries until rediscovered in 1812 by the Anglo-Swiss explorer John Burckhardt. Madain Salih, though close to the pilgrim route from Damascus to Mecca, was first seen and described by a Westerner, Charles Doughty, in 1876.

Palmyra — City of Palms — a desert port for caravans entering Mesopotamia, was known in the Bible as Tadmor, and that is its name in Arabic today. Inscriptions found there indicate that the population was mixed and that the inhabitants spoke Aramaic, Greek, and Latin. A large colony of merchants and caravaners from northern Arabia occupied a quarter of the city.

THE ROMANS: Because of their importance, both Petra and Palmyra were absorbed into the orbit of the Romans, who from the first century B.C. had been moving eastward in a series of campaigns that would eventually bring much of the Middle East under their control. Rome incorporated Petra into the Roman Province called Arabia Petraea, and absorbed Palmyra in the first century A.D.

For Petra, Rome's victory was in effect the end of its history. But Palmyra proved more difficult to digest. In the third century, Odenathus, a prince of Palmyra, built up a

40

strong autonomous state embracing all of Syria, northwestern Mesopotamia, and western Armenia. Odenathus' wife Zenobia, apparently of Arab stock to judge by her name (Zaynab), took the reins after his death and aggressively expanded Palmyrene power into Asia Minor, Mesopotamia, and Egypt and, declaring her son emperor, even had coins struck bearing his portrait and her own. This was too much for Rome — it meant the loss of the entire eastern empire — and in 272 Aurelian was sent to attack Palmyra. He destroyed Palmyrene power, captured Zenobia, and brought her to Rome decked in golden chains. She was then pensioned off and ended her days confined in a Roman villa.

If one Arab ruler went to Rome in chains, however, another became a Roman emperor. Called Philip the Arabian, he was a Syrian from Hawran who had served with the Roman legions against the Persians, was proclaimed emperor by his troops, and ruled the empire for years.

In the meantime, Christianity had become a potent force spreading through the Roman Empire and beyond. In the fourth century, for example, the kings of Ethiopia were converted and pockets of Christianity were established in southern Arabia. Najran became a Christian center and there were churches in Aden, San'a, Hadhramaut, and the island of Tarut near present-day Qatif. But there were also Judaic influences in the area and eventually they clashed. In the sixth century a Judaized king of Saba attacked Najran, in an attempt to impose Judaism on the area, and massacred the inhabitants in a place called al-Ukhdud ("The Ditch"), an event mentioned in the Quran: "destroyed were the inhabitants of The Ditch." In response Ethiopian forces crossed the Strait of Bab al-Mandab, crushed the army of Saba, and established a protectorate over southern Arabia.

At about the same time, from the third to sixth centuries, two other Arabian states had arisen to prominence — states whose wealth, culture, and martial exploits would be celebrated in Arabic verse for centuries. One was al-Hirah; the other was Ghassan, which rose from the ashes of Zenobia's ill-fated Palmyrene domains.

Ghassan was a client of Byzantium and its ally in the endless wars between Byzantium and Persia. The Ghassanids were Arabs of Yemeni stock and Christians of the Monophysite persuasion. Al-Hirah, in what is now southern Iraq, bore the same relation to Sassanid Persia as Ghassan did to Byzantium. The people were Nestorian Christians but the rulers — called Lakhmids — remained pagan in deference to their Persian master, who identified Christianity with the Byzantine enemy.

A third Arab power on the peninsula was little-known Kindah, centered in al-Yamamah in southern Najd. Nominally a client of Himyar in the south, it at one time attacked and imposed some sort of hegemony over al-Hirah and was predominantly polytheistic.

THE RISE OF MECCA: None of those states, however, had any political influence in the area called the Hijaz, where a number of caravan cities had not only continued to develop as mercantile centers but had also managed to remain independent. Indeed, the Hijaz had brought the desert tribes into its own orbit. Yathrib was one of the caravan towns; Tabuk and Khaybar were others. But the greatest, and the one destined to play the most important role in the future of the Muslim world, was Mecca.

Mecca grew up around a shrine, the Ka'bah, whose origins go back to antiquity, but its wealth was founded on trade. It was the "commercial republic" of Arabia in the sixth century.

Although Mecca, as one of the northern Arabs' caravan cities, had established commercial contacts with Syria and Yemen, it was nevertheless relatively isolated. In the sixth century, however, there occurred a series of events that would catapult it into prominence. One of the events was the collapse of the great dam at Marib — which confirmed the decline of southern Arabia as a power and left a vacuum in the peninsula. At about the same time an Ethiopian governor of southern Arabia sent an expedition to conquer Mecca — thus effectively involving the city in the events of the day. But the most important event was the rise to power in Mecca itself of the tribe of Quraysh, into which, in about the year 570, a child called Muhammad would be born. Together, these events set the stage for the most important single development in the history of the Middle East: the advent of Islam.

Remnants of the great dam at Marib in Yemen recall the vast water management system which for more than a millennium diverted floodwaters to irrigate some four thousand acres of the prosperous city-state.

ISLAM AND
ISLAMIC HISTORY

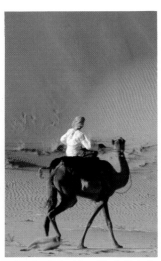

In the still solitude of desert life, the Bedouins learn harsh lessons of patience, endurance, and survival.

In or about the year 570 the child who would be named Muhammad and who would become the Prophet of one of the world's great religions, Islam, was born into a family belonging to a clan of Quraysh, the ruling tribe of Mecca, a city in the Hijaz region of northwestern Arabia.

Originally the site of the Ka'bah, a shrine of ancient origins, Mecca had with the decline of southern Arabia (see Chapter 1) become an important center of sixth-century trade with such powers as the Sassanians, Byzantines, and Ethiopians. As a result the city was dominated by powerful merchant families among whom the men of Quraysh were preeminent.

Muhammad's father, 'Abd Allah ibn 'Abd al-Muttalib, died before the boy was born; his mother, Aminah, died when he was six. The orphan was consigned to the care of his grandfather, the head of the clan of Hashim. After the death of his grandfather, Muhammad was raised by his uncle, Abu Talib. As was customary, Muhammad as a child was sent to live for a year or two with a Bedouin family. This custom, followed until recently by noble families of Mecca, Medina, Tayif, and other towns of the Hijaz, had important implications for Muhammad. In addition to enduring the hardships of desert life, he acquired a taste for the rich language so loved by the Arabs, whose speech was their proudest art, and learned the patience and forbearance of the herdsmen, whose life of solitude he first shared and then came to understand and appreciate.

About the year 590, Muhammad, then in his twenties, entered the service of a widow named Khadijah as a merchant actively engaged with trading caravans to the north. Sometime later Muhammad married Khadijah, by whom he had two sons — who did not survive — and four daughters.

During this period of his life Muhammad traveled widely. Then, in his forties he began to retire to meditate in a cave on Mount Hira outside of Mecca, where the first of the great events of Islam took place. One day, as he sat in the cave, he heard a voice, later identified as that of the Angel Gabriel, which ordered him to:

Recite: In the name of thy Lord who created, Created man from a clot of blood.

Three times Muhammad pleaded his inability to do so, but each time the command was repeated. Finally, Muhammad recited the words of what are now the first five verses of the 96th surah or chapter of the Quran — words which proclaim God the Creator of man and the Source of all knowledge.

At first Muhammad divulged his experience only to his wife and his immediate circle. But as more revelations enjoined him to proclaim the oneness of God universally, his following grew, at first among the poor and the slaves, but later also among the most prominent men of Mecca. The revelations he received at this time and those he did so later are all incorporated in the Quran, the Scripture of Islam.

Not everyone accepted God's message transmitted through Muhammad. Even in his own clan there were those who rejected his teachings, and many merchants actively opposed the message. The opposition, however, merely served to sharpen Muhammad's sense of mission and his understanding of exactly how Islam differed from paganism. The belief in the unity of God was paramount in Islam; from this all else followed. The verses of the Quran stress God's uniqueness, warn those who deny it of impending punishment, and proclaim His unbounded compassion to those who submit to His will. They affirm the Last Judgment, when God, the Judge, will weigh in the balance the faith and works of each man, rewarding the faithful and punishing the transgressor. Because the Quran rejected polytheism and emphasized man's moral responsibility, in powerful images, it presented a grave challenge to the worldly Meccans.

THE HIJRAH: After Muhammad had preached publicly for more than a decade, the opposition to him reached such a high pitch that, fearful for their safety, he sent some of his adherents to Ethiopia, where the Christian ruler extended protection to them, the memory of which has been cherished by Muslims ever since. But in Mecca the persecution worsened. Muhammad's followers were harassed, abused, and even tortured. At last, therefore, Muhammad sent seventy of his followers off to the northern town of Yathrib, which was later to be renamed Medina ("The City"). Later, in the early fall of 622, he learned of a plot to murder him and, with his closest friend, Abu Bakr al-Siddiq, set off to join the emigrants.

In Mecca the plotters arrived at Muhammad's home to find that his cousin, 'Ali, had taken his place in bed. Enraged, the Meccans set a price on Muhammad's head and set off in pursuit. Muhammad and Abu Bakr, however, had taken refuge in a cave where, as they hid from their pursuers, a spider spun its web across the cave's mouth. When they saw that the web was unbroken, the Meccans passed by and Muhammad and Abu Bakr went on to Medina, where they were joyously welcomed by a throng of Medinans as well as the Meccans who had gone ahead to prepare the way.

This was the *Hijrah* — anglicized as Hegira — usually, but inaccurately, translated as "Flight" — from which the Muslim era is dated. In fact, the Hijrah was not a flight but a carefully planned migration which marks not only a break in history — the beginning of the Islamic era — but also, for Muhammad and the Muslims, a new way of life. Henceforth, the organizational principle of the community was not to be mere blood kinship, but the greater brotherhood of all Muslims. The men who accompanied Muhammad on the Hijrah were called the *Muhajirun* — "those that made the Hijrah" or the "Emigrants" — while those in Medina who became Muslims were called the *Ansar* or "Helpers."

Muhammad was well acquainted with the situation in Medina. Earlier, before the Hijrah, the city had sent envoys to Mecca asking Muhammad to mediate a dispute between two powerful tribes. What the envoys saw and heard had impressed them and they had invited Muhammad to settle in Medina. After the Hijrah, Muhammad's exceptional qualities so impressed the Medinans that the rival tribes and their allies temporarily closed ranks as, on March 15, 624, Muhammad and his supporters moved against the pagans of Mecca.

The first battle, which took place near Badr, now a small town southwest of Medina, had several important effects. In the first place, the Muslim forces, outnumbered three to one, routed the Meccans. Secondly, the discipline displayed by the Muslims brought home to the Meccans, perhaps for the first time, the abilities of the man they had driven from their city. Thirdly, one of the allied tribes which had pledged support to the Muslims in the Battle of Badr, but had then proved lukewarm when the fighting started, was expelled from Medina one month after the battle. Those who claimed to be allies of the Muslims, but tacitly opposed them, were thus served warning: membership in the community imposed the obligation of total support.

A year later the Meccans struck back. Assembling an army of three thousand men, they met the Muslims at Uhud, a ridge outside Medina. After an initial success the Muslims were driven back and the Prophet himself was wounded. As the Muslims were not completely defeated, the Meccans, with an army of ten thousand, attacked Medina again two years later but with quite different results. At the Battle of the Trench, also known as the Battle of the Confederates, the Muslims scored a signal victory by introducing a new defense. On the side of Medina from which attack was expected they dug a trench too deep for the Meccan cavalry to clear without exposing itself to the archers posted behind earthworks on the Medina side. After an inconclusive siege, the Meccans were forced to retire. Thereafter Medina was entirely in the hands of the Muslims.

The Constitution of Medina — under which the clans accepting Muhammad as the Prophet of God formed an alliance, or federation — dates from this period. It showed that the political consciousness of the Muslim community had reached an important point; its members defined themselves as a community separate from all others. The Constitution also defined the role of non-Muslims in the community. Jews, for example, were part of the community; they were *dhimmis,* that is, protected people, as long as they conformed to its laws. This established a precedent for the treatment of subject peoples during the later conquests. Christians and Jews, upon payment of a yearly tax, were allowed religious freedom and, while maintaining their status as non-Muslims, were associate members of the Muslim state. This status did not apply to polytheists, who could not be tolerated within a community that worshipped the One God.

Ibn Ishaq, one of the earliest biographers of the Prophet, says it was at about this time that Muhammad sent letters to the rulers of the earth — the King of Persia, the Emperor of Byzantium, the Negus of Abyssinia, and the Governor of Egypt among others — inviting them to submit to Islam. Nothing more fully illustrates the confidence of the small

A colonnade of lofty arches surrounds the courtyard at the Prophet's Mosque in Medina, after Mecca the second holiest city of Islam.

The Holy Quran

Islam appeared in the form of a book: the Quran. Muslims, consider the Quran (sometimes spelled "Koran") to be the Word of God as transmitted by the Angel Gabriel, in the Arabic language, through the Prophet Muhammad. The Muslim view, moreover, is that the Quran supersedes earlier revelations; it is regarded as their summation and completion. It is the final revelation, as Muhammad is regarded as the final prophet — "the Seal of the Prophets."

In a very real sense the Quran is the mentor of millions of Muslims, Arab and non-Arab alike; it shapes their everyday life, anchors them to a unique system of law, and inspires them by its guiding principles. Written in noble language, this Holy Text has done more than move multitudes to tears and ecstasy; it has also, for almost fourteen hundred years, illuminated the lives of Muslims with its eloquent message of uncompromising monotheism, human dignity, righteous living, individual responsibility, and social justice. For countless millions, consequently, it has been the single most important force in guiding their religious, social, and cultural lives. Indeed, the Quran is the cornerstone on which the edifice of Islamic civilization has been built.

The text of the Quran was delivered orally by the Prophet Muhammad to his followers as it was revealed to him. The first verses were revealed to him in or about 610, and the last revelation dates from the last year of his life, 632. His followers at first committed the Quran to memory and then, as instructed by him, to writing. Although the entire contents of the Quran, the placement of its verses, and the arrangement of its chapters date back to the Prophet, as long as he lived he continued to receive revelations. Consequently, the Holy Text could only be collected as a single corpus — "between the two covers" — after the death of Muhammad.

This is exactly what happened. After the battle of al-Yamamah in 633, 'Umar ibn al-Khattab, later to become the second caliph, suggested to Abu Bakr, the first caliph, that because of the grievous loss of life in that battle, there was a very real danger of losing the Quran, enshrined as it was in the memories of the faithful and in uncollated fragments. Abu Bakr recognized the danger and entrusted the task of gathering the revelations to Zayd ibn Thabit, who as the chief scribe of the Prophet was the person to whom Muhammad frequently dictated the revelations in his lifetime. With great difficulty, the task was carried out and the first complete manuscript compiled from "bits of parchment, thin white stones — ostracae — leafless palm branches, and the memories of men." Later, during the time of 'Uthman, the third caliph, a final, authorized text was prepared and completed in 651, and this has remained the text in use ever since.

The contents of the Quran differ in substance and arrangement from the Old and New Testaments. Instead of presenting a straight historical narrative, as do the Gospels and the historical books of the Old Testament, the Quran treats, in allusive style, spiritual and practical as well as historical matters.

The Quran is divided into 114 *surahs,* or chapters, and the surahs are conventionally assigned to two broad categories: those revealed at Mecca and those revealed at Medina. The surahs revealed at Mecca — at the beginning of Muhammad's mission — tend to be short and to stress, in highly moving language, the eternal themes of the unity of God, the necessity of faith, the punishment of those who stray from the right path, and the Last Judgment, when all man's actions and beliefs will be judged. The surahs revealed at Medina are longer, often deal in detail with specific legal, social, or political situations, and sometimes can only be properly understood with a full knowledge of the circumstances in which they were revealed.

All the surahs are divided into *ayahs* or verses and, for

purposes of pedagogy and recitation, the Quran as a whole is divided into thirty parts, which in turn are divided into short divisions of nearly equal length, to facilitate study and memorization.

The surahs themselves are of varying length, ranging from the longest, Surah 2, with 282 verses, to the shortest, Surahs 103, 108, and 110, each of which has only three. With some exceptions the surahs are arranged in the Quran in descending order of length, with the longest at the beginning and the shortest at the end. The major exception to this arrangement is the opening surah, "al-Fatihah," which contains seven verses and which serves as an introduction to the entire revelation:

> In the Name of God, the Merciful, the Compassionate.
> Praise be to God, Lord of the Worlds;
> The Merciful, the Compassionate;
> Master of the Day of Judgment;
> Thee only do we worship, and Thee alone we ask for help.
> Guide us in the straight path,
> The path of those whom Thou hast favored; not the path of those who earn Thine anger nor of those who go astray.

Non-Muslims are often struck by the range of styles found in the Quran. Passages of impassioned beauty are no less common than vigorous narratives. The sublime "Verse of the Throne" is perhaps one of the most famous:

> God — There is no god but He,
> The Living. the Everlasting;
> Slumber seizes Him not, neither sleep;
> To Him belongs all that is
> In the heavens and the earth;
> Who is there that can intercede with Him
> Save by His leave?
> He knows what lies before them
> And what is after them,
> Nor do they encompass anything of His knowledge
> Except such as He wills;
> His Throne extends over the heavens and earth;
> The preserving of them wearies Him not;
> He is the Most High, the All-Glorious.

Muslims regard the Quran as untranslatable; the language in which it was revealed — Arabic — is inseparable from its message and Muslims everywhere, no matter what their native tongue, must learn Arabic to read the Sacred Book and to perform their worship. The Quran of course is available in many languages, but these versions are regarded as interpretations rather than translations — partly because the Arabic language, extraordinarily concise and allusive, is impossible to translate in a mechanical, word-for-word way. The inimitability of the Quran has crystallized in the Muslim view of i'jaz or "impossibility," which holds that the style of the Quran, being divine, cannot be imitated: any attempt to do so is doomed to failure.

It must also be remembered that the Quran was originally transmitted orally to the faithful and that the Holy Text is not meant to be read only in silence. From the earliest days it has always been recited aloud or, more accurately, chanted. As a result, several traditional means of chanting, or intoning, the Quran were found side by side. These methods carefully preserved the elaborate science of reciting the Quran — with all its intonations and its cadence and punctuation. As the exact pronunciation was important — and learning it took years — special schools were founded to be sure that no error would creep in as the traditional chanting methods were handed down. It is largely owing to the existence of these traditional methods of recitation that the text of the Quran was preserved without error. As the script in which the Quran was first written down indicated only the consonantal skeleton of the words, oral recitation was an essential element in the transmission of the text.

Because the circumstances of each revelation were thought necessary to correct interpretation, the community, early in the history of Islam, concluded that it was imperative to gather as many traditions as possible about the life and actions of the Prophet so that the Quran might be more fully understood. These traditions not only provided the historical context for many of the surahs — thus contributing to their more exact explication — but also contained a wide variety of subsidiary information on the practice, life, and legal rulings of the Prophet and his companions.

This material became the basis for what is called the *sunnah,* or "practice" of the Prophet — the deeds, utterances, and *taqrir* (unspoken approval) of Muhammad. Together with the Quran, the sunnah, as embodied in the canonical collections of traditions, the *hadith,* became the basis for the *shari'ah,* the sacred law of Islam.

Unlike Western legal systems, the shari'ah makes no distinction between religious and civil matters; it is the codification of God's Law, and it concerns itself with every aspect of social, political, economic, and religious life. Islamic law is thus different from any other legal system; it differs from canon law in that it is not administered by a church hierarchy; in Islam there is nothing that corresponds to a "church" in the Christian sense. Instead, there is the *ummah* — the community of the believers — whose cohesion is guaranteed by the sacred law. Every action of the pious Muslim, therefore, is determined by the Quran, by precedents set by the Prophet, and by the practice of the early community of Islam as enshrined in the shari'ah.

No description, however, can fully capture the overwhelming importance of the Quran to Muslims. Objectively, it is the central fact of the Islamic faith, the Word of God, the final and complete revelation, the foundation and framework of Islamic law, and the source of Islamic thought, language, and action. It is the essence of Islam. Yet it is, in the deeply personal terms of a Muslim, something more as well. In innumerable, almost indescribable ways, it is also the central fact of Muslim life. To a degree almost incomprehensible in the West it shapes and colors broadly, specifically, and totally the thoughts, emotions, and values of the devout Muslim's life from birth to death.

THE MIDDLE EAST AND THE MEDITERRANEAN IN THE SIXTH CENTURY A.D.

The Byzantine Empire, successor to the defunct Roman Empire to the west, reaches an accommodation with the Sassanian Empire, its archrival to the east, and recovers much of the territory of the Romans. The Ghassanids, a Christian Arab tribe in Syria, are clients of the Byzantine Empire while the pagan Lakhmid Dynasty, rulers of the Christian state of al-Hirah, are clients of Sassanid Persia. The Kingdom of Kindah encompasses central Arabia from the Nafud to the borders of Hadhramaut, while Mecca and

other mercantile centers of the Hijaz in western Arabia remain independent. The Aksumite Empire of Ethiopia, which has acquired great prosperity from the maritime traffic through the Red Sea, dominates the languishing kingdoms of southern Arabia, which are further impoverished by the collapse of the great dam at Marib in 575. The strategic location of the Arabian Peninsula athwart the trade routes between eastern and western civilizations is the basis for its early development and continuing prominence.

TRADE ROUTES ·········

community, as its military power, despite the Battle of the Trench, was still negligible. But its confidence was not misplaced. Muhammad so effectively built up a series of alliances among the tribes — his early years with the Bedouins must have stood him in good stead here — that by 628 he and fifteen hundred followers were able to demand access to the Ka'bah during negotiations with the Meccans. This was a milestone in the history of the Muslims. Just a short time before, Muhammad had had to leave the city of his birth in fear of his life. Now he was being treated by his former enemies as a leader in his own right. A year later, in 629, he reentered and, in effect, conquered Mecca without bloodshed and in a spirit of tolerance which established an ideal for future conquests. He also destroyed the idols in the Ka'bah, to put an end forever to pagan practices there. At the same time Muhammad won the allegiance of 'Amr ibn al-'As, the future conqueror of Egypt, and Khalid ibn al-Walid, the future "Sword of God," both of whom embraced Islam and joined Muhammad. Their conversion was especially noteworthy because these men had been among Muhammad's bitterest opponents only a short time before.

The Ka'bah, spiritual axis of the Muslim world, stands in the courtyard of Mecca's Sacred Mosque.

In one sense Muhammad's return to Mecca was the climax of his mission. In 632, just three years later, he was suddenly taken ill and on June 8 of that year, with his third wife 'Aishah in attendance, the Messenger of God "died with the heat of noon."

The death of Muhammad was a profound loss. To his followers this simple man from Mecca was far more than a beloved friend, far more than a gifted administrator, far more than the revered leader who had forged a new state from clusters of warring tribes. Muhammad was also the exemplar of the teachings he had brought them from God: the teachings of the Quran, which, for centuries, have guided the thought and action, the faith and conduct, of innumerable men and women, and which ushered in a distinctive era in the history of mankind. His death, nevertheless, had little effect on the dynamic society he had created in Arabia, and no effect at all on his central mission: to transmit the Quran to the world. As Abu Bakr put it: "Whoever worshipped Muhammad, let him know that Muhammad is dead, but whoever worshipped God, let him know that God lives and dies not."

Devout Muslims from all over the world gather for the pilgrimage to Mecca, for nearly fourteen centuries one of the most impressive religious gatherings in the world.

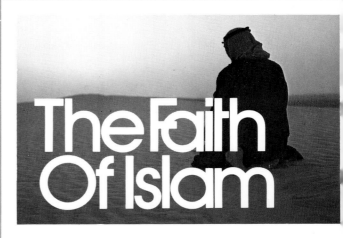

The Faith Of Islam

Islam, in Arabic, means "submission" — submission to the will of God. Faithful Muslims, therefore, submit unreservedly to God's will and obey His precepts as set forth in the Quran and transmitted to mankind by Muhammad, His Messenger.

Muslims believe that theirs is the only true faith. Islam, they say, was revealed through a long line of prophets inspired by God. Among them are Ibrahim (Abraham), patriarch of the Arabs through his first son Isma'il (Ishmael); Musa (Moses), who received the Torah (Tawrah); Dawud (David), who spoke through the Psalms (Zabur); and 'Isa (Jesus), who brought the Gospels (Injil). But the full and final revelation came through Muhammad, the last of all prophets, and was embodied in the Quran, which completes and supersedes all previous revelations.

As the chief source of Islamic doctrine and practice, the Quran is the main foundation of the shari'ah, the sacred law of Islam, which covers all aspects of the public and private, social and economic, religious and political lives of all Muslims. In addition to the Quran the shari'ah has three sources: the sunnah, the practice of the Prophet; ijma', the consensus of opinion; and qiyas, reasoning by analogy. The sunnah — which supplements and complements the Quran, the Word of God, and is next to it in importance — embodies the meticulously documented acts and sayings of the Prophet recorded in a body of writings called the hadith. Ijma' is the consensus of qualified jurists on matters not specifically referred to in the Quran or the sunnah. Qiyas is the application of human reasoning to extend the principles found in the two primary sources — the Quran and the sunnah — to cases involving matters unknown in the early years of Islam.

Systematized in the second and third centuries of the Muslim era (the eighth and ninth centuries A.D.), the shari'ah later developed into four major schools of jurisprudence: the Hanafi School, founded by Abu Hanifah; the Maliki School, founded by Malik ibn Anas; the Shafi'i School, founded by Muhammad al-Shafi'i; and the Hanbali School — the principal system of law governing Saudi Arabia today — founded by Ahmad ibn Hanbal. Each of these men, all exceptional scholars, wrote or dictated long and learned commentaries upon which their schools of law were founded. Based on one or the other of these schools, learned officials called qadis administer the law in shari'ah courts. Despite the great body of tradition and law, however the practice of Islam is essentially personal — a direct relationship between individuals and God. Although there are *imams,* who lead prayers and deliver sermons, there are no priests or ministers.

To practice their faith, Muslims must accept five primary obligations which Islam imposes. Called the Five Pillars of Islam, they are: the profession of faith *(shahadah),* devotional worship or prayer *(salah),* the religious tax *(zakah),* fasting *(sawm),* and the pilgrimage to Mecca *(hajj).*

The first pillar, the profession of faith, is the repetition of the statement, "There is no god but God; Muhammad is the Messenger of God" — in Arabic the euphonious *"La ilaha illa Allah; Muhammadun rasul Allah."* It is a simple statement, yet also profound, for in it a Muslim expresses his complete acceptance of, and total commitment to, the message of Islam.

The second pillar, devotional worship or prayer, requires Muslims to pray five times a day — the dawn prayer, the noon prayer, the afternoon prayer, the sunset prayer, and the evening prayer — while facing toward the Ka'bah, the House of God, in Mecca. Like all Islamic ceremonies, prayer is simple and personal, yet also communal, and the wording of the prayers, the ablutions which are required before prayers, the number of bows, and other parts of the ritual are set out in detail.

The religious tax, the third pillar, is *zakah* in Arabic, a word that in the Prophet's lifetime came to suggest an obligatory religious tax. Like prayer, zakah is considered a form of worship. It enshrines the duty of social responsibility by which well-to-do Muslims must concern themselves about those less fortunate. The zakah prescribes payments of fixed proportions of a Muslim's possession for the welfare of the community in general and for its needy members in particular, whether Muslims or non-Muslims. This tax is often levied and disbursed by the state, but in the absence of a government collecting system it must be disbursed by the taxable Muslims themselves. In addition, all Muslims are encouraged to make voluntary contributions to the needy called *sadaqah.*

The fourth pillar is fasting during Ramadan, the ninth month of the Muslim year. Ordained in the Quran, the fast is an exacting act of deeply personal worship in which Muslims seek a richer perception of God and in which, as one writer puts it, Muslims assert that "man has larger needs than bread."

Ramadan begins with the sighting of the new moon, a moment usually signaled by cannon fire, after which abstention from eating and drinking, as well as physical continence, is obligatory every day between dawn and sunset. It is a rigorous fast, but its object is not mere abstinence and deprivation; it is, rather, the subjection of the passions and the purification of one's being so that the soul is brought nearer to God. Fasting is also an exercise in self-control and self-denial whereby one learns to appreciate the pangs of hunger that the poor often feel. The exercise of self-control extends far beyond refraining from food and drink; to make one's fast acceptable to God, one must also refrain from cursing, lying, cheating, and abusing or harming others.

Although rigorous, however, the fast, by Quranic injunction, also admits of a warm compassion. Those who are ill, or on an arduous journey, for example, may fast the

prescribed number of days at another time; those for whom fasting is impossible may forego it if they give stipulated alms to the needy.

The month of fasting is also joyous. In Muslim regions, in modern times, the faithful — at the sound of the sunset cannon or the call of the muezzin — break their fast, perform voluntary nocturnal worship *(tarawih),* and throng the streets in moods that are at once festive and, in the spirit of Ramadan, communal. For those who retire and rest after the day's fast there are, in some areas, men called *musahhirs* who, in the silent, predawn darkness beat muted drums and call the faithful to awake and eat before the long day's fast begins again.

The Ramadan cannon signals the time for sunset prayers and the breaking of the fast.

The last ten days of Ramadan are particularly sacred because they include the anniversary of the night on which Muhammad received his first revelation from God — "the Night of Power" — and the appearance, on the final day, of the thin edge of the new moon announcing the end of Ramadan. At that moment the favor of God descends upon Muslims and, in a spirit of joyous achievement, they begin the three days of celebration called *'Id al-Fitr,* the Feast of the Breaking of the Fast. To cement social bonds further, Islam has instituted *zakat al-fitr,* an obligatory levy in the form of provisions or money for the poor, so that they can share in the joy of 'Id al-Fitr.

The fifth pillar of Islam is the pilgrimage to Mecca — the *hajj.* One of the most moving acts of faith in Islam, the hajj is, for those Muslims who can get to Mecca, the peak of their religious life, a moment when they satisfy a deep yearning to behold at least once the Ka'bah — the House of God and the physical focus of a lifetime of prayer. The hajj is at once a worldwide migration of the faithful and a remarkable spiritual happening that, according to Islamic tradition, dates back to Abraham, was affirmed by Muhammad, and then, by Muhammad's own pilgrimage, systematized into rites which are simple in execution but rich in meaning.

The hajj proper must be made between the eighth and thirteenth days of the 12th month — Dhu al-Hijjah — of the Muslim year, but in one sense it begins when a Muslim

(Continued on page 52)

The Faith Of Islam

approaches Mecca, bathes, trims his nails and hair, discards jewelry and headgear, and puts on the *ihram* dress. This consists of two simple white seamless garments symbolizing a state of purity; in donning it pilgrims make a declaration of pilgrimage and pronounce a devotional utterance called the *talbiyah:* "Here I am, O God, at Thy Service" — in Arabic the joyous cry *"Labbayk!"* After donning the ihram dress, the pilgrims may enter the *haram,* the sacred precinct surrounding Mecca, and then Mecca itself, where they perform the *tawaf* — the circling of the Ka'bah — and the *sa'y* — the running between two hills at al-Mas'a in Mecca. All this can be part of the *'umrah* or "lesser pilgrimage," often a prelude to the hajj but not an integral part of it. One of the main distinctions between the hajj and the 'umrah is that the 'umrah can be done at any time of the year, while the hajj must be performed on specified dates.

The major rites of the hajj begin on the eighth day of Dhu al-Hijjah when, with thunderous cries of *"Labbayk!"* the pilgrims pour out of Mecca to Mina, where, as the Prophet did, they meditate overnight. On the next day they proceed en masse to 'Arafat, even farther outside Mecca, and pray and meditate in what is the central rite of the pilgrimage: "the standing" — a few precious hours of profound self-examination, supplication, and penance in which, many say, a Muslim comes as close to God as he can on earth.

A pillar marks the Mount of Mercy, the rocky hill rising from the plain of 'Arafat.

Sacrifice during which the pilgrims sacrifice animals — partly to commemorate Abraham's willingness to sacrifice his son and partly to symbolize a Muslim's willingness to sacrifice what is dearest to him. As Muslims throughout the world perform identical sacrifices on the same day, the Muslims at Mina in effect share their pilgrimage with Muslims everywhere.

As the pilgrims have now completed much of the hajj, Muslim men now clip their hair or shave their heads and women clip a symbolic lock to mark partial deconsecration. The pilgrims may also, at this point, remove the ihram dress and bathe.

In Mecca the rites are concluded by the tawaf of the return, the Circling of the Ka'bah seven times on foot, an act implying that all human activity must have God at the center. After the last circuit the pilgrims worship in the courtyard of the Mosque at the Place of Abraham, where the Patriarch himself offered prayer and, with Ishmael, stood while building the Ka'bah. The tawaf of the return is the last essential devotion of the pilgrimage; now the pilgrims have become *hajjis* — those who have completed the hajj. Most pilgrims also attempt to kiss, touch, or salute the *Hajar al-Aswad,* the Black Stone of the Ka'bah, a fragment of polished stone revered as a sign sent by God and a remnant of the original structure built by Abraham and Ishmael. Many also make the *sa'y* or running, a reenactment of a frantic search for water by Hagar when she and Abraham's son Ishmael were stranded in the valley of Mecca until the Angel Gabriel led them to water in the Well of Zamzam.

Dressed in their simple *ihram* garments, all pilgrims are equal in the eyes of God.

At 'Arafat many actually do stand — from just after noon to just before sunset — but some also visit other pilgrims or the Mount of Mercy, where Muhammad delivered his farewell sermon. The standing is not the end of the hajj, but is the culmination of a Muslim's devotional life. As the Prophet said, "The best of prayers is the prayer of the Day of 'Arafat."

After sunset the pilgrims move to a place called Muzdalifah, where they gather stones for the "throwing of the pebbles" or "stoning of the pillars," and then pray and sleep. The third day of the pilgrimage, back at Mina, they enact a repudiation of evil by throwing the pebbles at a pillar held by many to represent Satan. According to one tradition it was in this area that Satan urged Abraham to perform God's command to sacrifice his son Ishmael. At Mina too, begins *'Id al-Adha,* the great worldwide Feast of

It is also customary for pilgrims to return to Mina between the eleventh and thirteenth days and cast their remaining pebbles at the three pillars there and then, in Mecca, make a farewell circling of the Ka'bah. Some may also visit the Mosque of the Prophet in Medina before returning to their homes throughout the world in the "sudden, glad stillness" of those who have stood at 'Arafat.

THE RIGHTLY GUIDED CALIPHS: With the death of Muhammad, the Muslim community was faced with the problem of succession. Who would be its leader? There were four persons obviously marked for leadership: Abu Bakr al-Siddiq, who had not only accompanied Muhammad to Medina ten years before, but had been appointed to take the place of the Prophet as leader of public prayer during Muhammad's last illness; 'Umar ibn al-Khattab, an able and trusted Companion of the Prophet; 'Uthman ibn 'Affan, a respected early convert; and 'Ali ibn Abi Talib, Muhammad's cousin and son-in-law. To avoid contention among various groups, 'Umar suddenly grasped Abu Bakr's hand, the traditional sign of recognition of a new leader. Soon everyone concurred and before dusk Abu Bakr had been recognized as the *khalifah* of Muhammad. *Khalifah* — anglicized as caliph — is a word meaning "successor" but also suggesting what his historical role would be: to govern according to the Quran and the practice of the Prophet.

Abu Bakr's caliphate was short but important. An exemplary leader, he lived simply, assiduously fulfilled his religious obligations, and was accessible and sympathetic to his people. But he also stood firm when, in the wake of the Prophet's death, some tribes renounced Islam; in what was a major accomplishment, Abu Bakr swiftly disciplined them. Later, he consolidated the support of the tribes within the Arabian Peninsula and subsequently funneled their energies against the powerful empires of the East: the Sassanians in Persia and the Byzantines in Syria, Palestine, and Egypt. In short, he demonstrated the viability of the Muslim state.

The second caliph, 'Umar — appointed by Abu Bakr in a written testament — continued to demonstrate that viability. Adopting the title *Amir al-Muminin,* "Commander of the Believers," 'Umar extended Islam's temporal rule over Syria, Egypt, Iraq, and Persia in what from a purely military standpoint were astonishing victories. Within four years after the death of the Prophet the Muslim state had extended its sway over all of Syria and had, at a famous battle fought during a sandstorm near the River Yarmuk, blunted the power of the Byzantines — whose ruler Heraclius had shortly before disdainfully rejected the letter from the unknown Prophet of Arabia.

Even more astonishingly, the Muslim state administered the conquered territories with a tolerance almost unheard of in that age. At Damascus, for example, the Muslim leader Khalid ibn al-Walid signed a treaty which read as follows:

> This is what Khalid ibn al-Walid would grant to the inhabitants of Damascus if he enters therein: he promises to give them security for their lives, property and churches. Their city wall shall not be demolished, neither shall any Muslim be quartered in their houses. Thereunto we give them the pact of Allah and the protection of His Prophet, the caliphs and the believers. So long as they pay the poll tax, nothing but good shall befall them.

This tolerance was typical of Islam. A year after Yarmuk, 'Umar, in the military camp of al-Jabiyah on the Golan Heights, received word that the Byzantines were ready to surrender Jerusalem and rode there to accept the surrender in person. According to one account, he entered the city alone and clad in a simple cloak, astounding a populace accustomed to the sumptuous garb and court ceremonials of the Byzantines and Persians. He astounded them still further when he set their fears at rest by negotiating a generous treaty in which he told them:

> In the name of God ... you have complete security for your churches which shall not be occupied by the Muslims or destroyed.

This policy was to prove successful everywhere. In Syria, for example, many Christians who had been involved in bitter theological disputes with Byzantine authorities — and persecuted for it — welcomed the coming of Islam as an end to tyranny. And in Egypt, which 'Amr ibn al-'As took from the Byzantines after a daring march across the Sinai Peninsula, the Coptic Christians not only welcomed the Arabs, but enthusiastically assisted them.

This pattern was repeated throughout the Byzantine Empire. Conflict among Greek Orthodox, Syrian Monophysites, Copts, and Nestorian Christians contributed to the failure of the Byzantines — always regarded as intruders — to develop popular support, while the tolerance which Muslims showed toward

To many people in the early years of Islam, this Byzantine noble warrior was a symbol of tyranny.

Symbol of the oneness and centrality of God, the Ka'bah stands in the courtyard of Mecca's Sacred Mosque where at the season of the hajj the faithful gather for rituals that precede and end their pilgrimage. Facing page: Pakistani youth in the pilgrim's simple robe reads his Quran; above him are pilgrims at the climax of their hajj, "standing" before God at 'Arafat near the spot where Muhammad delivered his farewell sermon. Below: Crowds at the small town of Mina cast pebbles at pillars that symbolize evil. This page, top: Hajjis spend one night camped at Muzdalifah between 'Arafat and Mina. Above: In the ceremony of sa'y they reenact the search for water by Hagar, wife of the patriarch Abraham.

Christians and Jews removed the primary cause for opposing them.

'Umar adopted this attitude in administrative matters as well. Although he assigned Muslim governors to the new provinces, existing Byzantine and Persian administrations were retained wherever possible. For fifty years, in fact, Greek remained the chancery language of Syria, Egypt, and Palestine, while Pahlavi, the chancery language of the Sassanians, continued to be used in Mesopotamia and Persia.

'Umar, who served as caliph for ten years, ended his rule with a significant victory over the Persian Empire. The struggle with the Sassanid realm had opened in 687 at al-Qadisiyah, near Ctesiphon in Iraq, where Muslim cavalry had successfully coped with elephants used by the Persians as a kind of primitive tank. Now with the Battle of Nihavand, called the "Conquest of Conquests," 'Umar sealed the fate of Persia; henceforth it was to be one of the most important provinces in the Muslim Empire.

His caliphate was a high point in early Islamic history. He was noted for his justice, social ideals, administration, and statesmanship. His innovations left an enduring imprint on social welfare, taxation, and the financial and administrative fabric of the growing empire.

After the death of 'Umar an advisory council composed of Companions of the Prophet selected as the third caliph 'Uthman, during whose rule the first serious strains on Islamic unity would appear. 'Uthman achieved much during his reign. He pushed forward with the pacification of Persia, continued to defend the Muslim state against the Byzantines, added what is now Libya to the empire, and subjugated most of Armenia. 'Uthman also, through his cousin Mu'awiyah ibn Abi Sufyan, the governor of Syria, established an Arab navy which fought a series of important engagements with the Byzantines.

Of much greater importance to Islam, however, was 'Uthman's compilation of the text of the Quran as revealed to the Prophet. Realizing that the original message from God might be inadvertently distorted by textual variants, he appointed a committee to collect the canonical verses and destroy the variant recensions. The result was the text that is accepted to this day throughout the Muslim world.

These successes, however, were qualified by serious administrative weaknesses. 'Uthman was accused of favoritism to members of his family — the clan of Umayyah. Negotiations over such grievances were opened by representatives from Egypt but soon collapsed and 'Uthman was killed — an act that caused a rift in the community of Islam that has never entirely been closed.

This rift widened almost as soon as 'Ali, cousin and son-in-law of the Prophet, was chosen to be the fourth caliph. At issue, essentially, was the legitimacy of 'Ali's caliphate. 'Uthman's relatives — in particular Mu'awiyah, the powerful governor of Syria, where 'Ali's election had not been recognized — believed 'Ali's caliphate was invalid because his election had been supported by those responsible for 'Uthman's unavenged death. The conflict came to a climax in 657 at Siffin, near the Euphrates, and eventually resulted in a major division between the Sunnis or Sunnites and the Shi'is (also called Shi'ites or Shi'ah), the "Partisans" of 'Ali — a division that was to color the subsequent history of Islam.

Actually the Sunnis and the Shi'is are agreed upon almost all the essentials of Islam. Both believe in the Quran and the Prophet, both follow the same principles of religion and both observe the same rituals. However, there is one prominent difference, which is essentially political rather than religious, and concerns the choice of the caliph or successor of Muhammad.

The majority of Muslims support the elective principle which led to the choice of Abu Bakr as the first caliph. This group is known as *ahl al-sunnah wa-l-jama'ah*, "the people of custom and community," or Sunnis, who consider the caliph to be Muhammad's successor only in his capacity as ruler of the community. The main body of the Shi'is, on the other hand, believes that the caliphate — which they call the imamate or "leadership" — is nonelective. The caliphate, they say, must remain within the family of the Prophet — with 'Ali the first valid caliph. And while Sunnis consider the caliph a guardian of the *shari'ah*, the religious law, the Shi'is see the imam as a trustee inheriting and interpreting the Prophet's spiritual knowledge.

After the battle of Siffin, 'Ali — whose chief strength was in Iraq, with his capital at Kufa — began to lose the support of many of

A great horned headdress was the Sassanid symbol of royalty.

This eighth-century manuscript from Mecca or Medina is one of the two oldest known existing copies of the Quran.

his more uncompromising followers and in 661 he was murdered by a former supporter. His son Hasan was proclaimed caliph at Kufa but soon afterward deferred to Mu'awiyah, who had already been proclaimed caliph in Jerusalem in the previous year and who now was recognized and accepted as caliph in all the Muslim territories — thus inaugurating the Umayyad dynasty which would rule for the next ninety years.

The division between the Sunnis and the Shi'is continued to develop, however, and was widened in 680 when 'Ali's son Husayn tried to win the caliphate from the Umayyads and, with his followers, was killed at Karbala in Iraq. His death is still mourned each year by the Shi'is.

THE UMAYYADS: The shift in power to Damascus, the Umayyad capital city, was to have profound effects on the development of Islamic history. For one thing, it was a tacit recognition of the end of an era. The first four caliphs had been without exception Companions of the Prophet — pious, sincere men who had lived no differently from their neighbors and who preserved the simple habits of their ancestors despite the massive influx of wealth from the conquered territories. Even 'Uthman, whose policies had such a divisive effect, was essentially dedicated more to the concerns of the next world than of this. With the shift to Damascus much was changed.

In the early days of Islam, the extension of Islamic rule had been based on an uncomplicated desire to spread the Word of God. Although the Muslims used force when they met resistance they did not compel their enemies to accept Islam. On the contrary, the Muslims permitted Christians and Jews to practice their own faith and numerous conversions to Islam were the result of exposure to a faith that was simple and inspiring.

With the advent of the Umayyads, however, secular concerns and the problems inherent in the administration of what, by then, was a large empire began to dominate the attention of the caliphs, often at the expense of religious concerns — a development that disturbed many devout Muslims. This is not to say that religious values were ignored; on the contrary, they grew in strength for centuries. But they were not always at the forefront and from the time of Mu'awiyah the caliph's role as

"Defender of the Faith" increasingly required him to devote attention to the purely secular concerns which dominate so much of every nation's history.

Mu'awiyah was an able administrator, and even his critics concede that he possessed to a high degree the much-valued quality of *hilm* — a quality which may be defined as "civilized restraint" and which he himself once described in these words:

> I apply not my sword where my lash suffices, nor my lash where my tongue is enough. And even if there be one hair binding me to my fellowmen, I do not let it break: when they pull I loosen, and if they loosen I pull.

Nevertheless, Mu'awiyah was never able to reconcile the opposition to his rule nor resolve the conflict with the Shi'is. These problems were not unmanageable while Mu'awiyah was alive, but after he died in 680 the partisans of 'Ali resumed a complicated but persistent struggle that plagued the Umayyads at home for most of the next seventy years and in time spread into North Africa and Spain.

Medieval Muslims regarded the Great Mosque built by the Umayyads in Damascus as one of the wonders of the world.

The Umayyads, however, did manage to achieve a degree of stability, particularly after 'Abd al-Malik ibn Marwan succeeded to the caliphate in 685. Like the Umayyads who preceded him, 'Abd al-Malik was forced to devote a substantial part of his reign to political problems. But he also introduced much-needed reforms. He directed the cleaning and reopening of the canals that irrigated the Tigris-Euphrates Valley — a key to the prosperity of Mesopotamia since the time of the Sumerians — introduced the use of the Indian water buffalo in the riverine marshes, and minted a standard coinage which replaced the Byzantine and Sassanid coins, until then the sole currencies in circulation. 'Abd al-Malik's organization of government agencies was also important; it established a model for the later elaborate bureaucracies of the 'Abbasids and their successor states. There were specific agencies charged with keeping pay records; others concerned themselves with the collection of taxes. 'Abd al-Malik established a system of postal routes to expedite his communications throughout the far-flung empire. Most important of all, he

Facing al-Gharbiyah, the western minaret, a muezzin at the Umayyad Mosque calls believers to prayer.

KINGDOM OF THE FRANKS

ANDALUSIA
Cordoba
Malaga Toledo
Granada
Tangier
MAGHRIB
Tours
Toulouse
KINGDOM OF THE LOMBARDS
Constantinople BLACK SEA
Tunis
Kairouan
BYZANTINE EMPIRE
Sinope
Dabil
Tabriz
CASPIAN SEA
ARMENIA
Mosul
Tigris River Bag
MEDITERRANEAN SEA
CYPRUS
Tripoli
Beirut
Antioch Aleppo
Hama SYRIA
Homs
Damascus
Rakkah
Euphrates River
Karb

Tripoli
LIBYA
Barqa
Alexandria
PALESTINE
Jerusalem
Gaza

Fustat
SINAI
FEZZAN
EGYPT
Tabuk

al-Qusayr
Kha

Aswan
Medir

Yanbu

Nile River
Jiddah
Mecca

RED

SEA

Aksum

ETHIOPIA

THE WORLD OF ISLAM IN THE EIGHTH CENTURY A.D.

The map has been completely transformed in the brief span of a hundred years by a new force in world affairs, the Arabs. Inspired by the newly revealed religion of Islam, they have crushed the Byzantines and other successors of the Roman Empire as they push west across North Africa and into Spain and have defeated the Sassanid Persians as they sweep eastward to the borders of China. Religious and administrative leadership is provided by the caliphate at Damascus under the Umayyads and at Baghdad under the 'Abbasids, who in 750 displace the Umayyad Dynasty (a branch of which continues to flourish for another three hundred years in Spain). At a time when urban life and culture have virtually disappeared in Europe, society prospers and civilization flowers in the lands under the administration and protection of the Muslim caliphate.

introduced Arabic as the language of administration, replacing Greek and Pahlavi.

Under 'Abd al-Malik, the Umayyads expanded Islamic power still further. To the east they extended their influence into Transoxania, an area north of the Oxus River in today's Soviet Union, and went on to reach the borders of China. To the west, they took North Africa, in a continuation of the campaign led by 'Uqbah ibn Nafi' who founded the city of Kairouan — in what is now Tunisia — and from there rode all the way to the shores of the Atlantic Ocean.

These territorial acquisitions brought the Arabs into contact with previously unknown ethnic groups who embraced Islam and would later influence the course of Islamic history. The Berbers of North Africa, for example, who resisted Arab rule but willingly embraced Islam, later joined Musa ibn Nusayr and his general, Tariq ibn Ziyad, when they crossed the Strait of Gibraltar to Spain. The Berbers later also launched reform movements in North Africa which greatly influenced the Islamic civilization. In the East, Umayyad rule in Transoxania brought the Arabs into contact with the Turks who, like the Berbers, embraced Islam and, in the course of time, became its staunch defenders. Umayyad expansion also reached the ancient civilization of India, whose literature and science greatly enriched Islamic culture.

In Europe, meanwhile, the Arabs had passed into Spain, defeated the Visigoths, and by 713 had reached Narbonne in France. In the next decades, raiding parties continually made forays into France and in 732 reached as far as the Loire Valley, only 170 miles from Paris. There, at the Battle of Tours, or Poitiers, the Arabs were finally turned back by Charles Martel.

One of the Umayyad caliphs who attained greatness was 'Umar ibn 'Abd al-'Aziz, a man very different from his predecessors. Although a member of the Umayyad family, 'Umar had been born and raised in Medina, where his early contact with devout men had given him a concern for spiritual as well as political values. The criticisms that religious men in Medina and elsewhere had voiced of Umayyad policy — particularly the pursuit of worldly goals — were not lost on 'Umar who, reversing the policy of his predecessors, discontinued the levy of a poll tax on converts.

The minaret of the Great Mosque at Kairouan in Tunisia became the prototype for the majority of North African minarets.

Charles Martel checked Muslim expansion into Frankish territory.

Arabic Writing

The intricate pattern of the Quranic "Verse of the Throne" (see page 47) written in angular kufic characters in the form of a square seems almost like a maze.

Another maze-like ornamental square of angular kufic is made up of the names of the ten most revered Companions of Muhammad.

The Arabs gave to a large part of the world not only a religion — Islam — but also a language and an alphabet. Where the Muslim religion went, the Arabic language and Arabic writing also went. Arabic became and has remained the national language — the mother tongue — of North Africa and all the Arab countries of the Middle East.

Even where Arabic did not become the national language, it became the language of religion wherever Islam became established, since the Quran is written in Arabic, the Profession of Faith is to be spoken in Arabic, and five times daily the practicing Muslim must say his prayers in Arabic. Today, therefore, one can hear Arabic spoken — at least for religious purposes — from Mauritania on the Atlantic, across Africa and most of Asia, and as far east as Indonesia and the Philippines. Even in China (which has a Muslim population of some forty million) and the Central Asian republics of the USSR, Arabic can be heard in the *shahadah*, in prayer, and in the chanting of the Quran.

Of those people who embraced Islam but did not adopt Arabic as their everyday language, many millions have taken the Arabic alphabet for their own, so that today one sees the Arabic script used to write languages that have no basic etymological connection with Arabic. The languages of Iran, Afghanistan, and Pakistan are all written in the Arabic alphabet, as was the language of Turkey until some fifty years ago. It is also used in Kashmir and in some places in the Malay Peninsula and the East Indies, and in Africa it is used in Somalia and down the east coast as far south as Tanzania.

The *basmalah* ("In the name of God, the Merciful, the Compassionate" — the opening words of the Quran) is here done in an elaborate thuluth script with the letters joined so that the entire phrase is written without lifting the pen from the paper.

It is generally accepted that the Arabic alphabet developed from the script used for Nabataean, a dialect of Aramaic used in northern Arabia and what is now Jordan during roughly the thousand years before the start of the Islamic era. It seems apparent that Syriac also had some influence on its development. The earliest inscription that has been found that is identifiably Arabic is one in Sinai that dates from about A.D. 300. Another Semitic script which was in use at about the same time and which is found on inscriptions in southern Arabia is the origin of the alphabet now used for Amharic, the official language of Ethiopia.

The Arabic alphabet has twenty-eight letters (additional letters have been added to serve the needs of non-Arabic languages that use the Arabic script, such as those of Iran and Pakistan), and each of the letters may have up to four different forms. All of the letters are strictly speaking consonants, and unlike the Roman alphabet used for English and most European languages Arabic writing goes from right to left.

Another significant difference is that the Arabic script has been used much more extensively for decoration and as a means of artistic expression. This is not to say that the Roman alphabet (and others such as the Chinese and Japanese, for instance) are not just as decorative and have not been used just as imaginatively. Since the invention of printing from type, however, calligraphy (which means literally "beautiful writing") has come to be used in English and the other European languages only for special documents and on special occasions and has declined to the status of a relatively minor art.

Another basmalah in ornamental thuluth script is written in the shape of an oval.

In the countries that use the Arabic alphabet, on the other hand, calligraphy has continued to be used not only on important documents but for a variety of other artistic purposes as well. One reason is that the cursive nature of the Arabic script and certain of its other peculiarities made its adaptation to printing difficult and delayed the introduction of the printing press, so that the Arab world continued for some centuries after the time of Gutenberg to rely on handwriting for the production of books (especially the Quran) and of legal and other documents. The use of Arabic script has therefore tended to develop in the direction of calligraphy and the development of artistically pleasing forms of hand lettering, while in the West the trend has been toward printing and the development of ornamental and sometimes elaborate type faces.

Another and perhaps more important reason was a religious one. The Quran nowhere prohibits the representation of humans or animals in drawings or paintings, but as Islam expanded in its early years it inherited some of the prejudices against visual art of this kind that had already taken root in the Middle East. In addition, the early Muslims tended to oppose figural art (and in some cases all art) as distracting the community from the worship of God and hostile to the strictly unitarian religion preached by Muhammad, and all four of the schools of Islamic law banned the use of images and declared that the painter of animate figures would be damned on the Day of Judgment.

Wherever artistic ornamentation and decoration were required, therefore, Muslim artists, forbidden to depict human or animal forms, for the most part were forced to resort either to what has since come to be known as "arabesque" (designs based on strictly geometrical forms or patterns of leaves and flowers) or, very often, to calligraphy. Arabic calligraphy therefore came to be used not only in producing copies of the Quran (its first and for many centuries its most important use), but also for all kinds of other artistic purposes as well: on porcelain and metalware, for carpets and other textiles, on coins, and as architectural ornament (primarily on mosques and tombs but also, especially in later years, on other buildings as well).

(Continued on page 62)

Arabic Writing

At the start of the Islamic era two types of script seem to have been in use — both derived from different forms of the Nabataean, alphabet. One was square and angular and was called *kufic* (after the town of Kufa in Iraq, though it was in use well before the town was founded). It was used for the first, handwritten copies of the Quran, and for architectural decoration in the earliest years of the Islamic Empire. The other, called *naskhi,* was more rounded and cursive and was used for letters, business documents, and wherever speed rather than elaborate formalism was needed. By the twelfth century kufic was obsolete as a working script except for special uses and in northwest Africa, where it developed into the *maghribi* style of writing still used in the area today. Naskhi, the rounded script, remained in use and from it most of the many later styles of Arabic calligraphy have been developed.

The basmalah is here written in ornamental "floriated" kufic (above) and in naskhi (below).

Calligraphy flourished during the Umayyad era in Damascus. During this period scribes began the modification of the original thick and heavy kufic script into the form employed today for decorative purposes, as well as developing a number of new scripts derived from the more cursive naskhi. It was under the 'Abbasids, however, that calligraphy first began to be systematized. In the first half of the tenth century the 'Abbasid vizier Ibn Muqlah completed the development of kufic, established some of the rules of shape and proportion that have been followed by calligraphers since his time, and was first to develop what became the traditional classification of Arabic writing into the "six styles" of cursive script: naskhi (from which most present day printing types are derived), *thuluth* (a more cursive outgrowth of naskhi), *rayhani* (a more ornate version of thuluth), *muhaqqaq* (a bold script with sweeping diagonal flourishes), *tawqi'* (a somewhat compressed variety of thuluth in which all the letters are sometimes joined to each other), and *ruq'ah* (the style commonly used today for ordinary handwriting in most of the Arab world). It was from these six, and from kufic, that later calligraphers, not only in the Arab world but in Iran, Turkey, and elsewhere as well, developed and elaborated other scripts.

The ruq'ah script is used for headlines and titles and is the everyday written script of most of the Arab world.

In Iran, for example, there came into use a particularly graceful and delicate script called *ta'liq,* in which the horizontal strokes of the letters are elongated and which is often written at an angle across the page. From ta'liq, in turn, another script called *nasta'liq* was derived which combines the Arabic naskhi and the Persian ta'liq into a beautifully light and legible script.

The graceful Persian ta'liq script is used in a sentence which starts "Beauty is a spell which casts its splendor upon the universe..."

It was in Ottoman Turkey, however, that calligraphy attained the highest development once the early creative flowering had faded elsewhere in the Middle East. So renowned were Ottoman calligraphers, in fact, that a popular saying was that "The Quran was revealed in Mecca, recited in Egypt, and written in Istanbul." The Ottomans were not content merely to improve and develop the types of script that they inherited from the Arabs and Persians but also added a number of new styles to the calligrapher's repertoire.

The diwani script (top) and the so-called "royal" diwani (below) were developed by Ottoman calligraphers for use on state documents.

One important addition by the Ottoman calligraphers was the script called *diwani,* so called from the word *diwan* (meaning state council or government office) since it was at first used primarily for documents issued by the Ottoman Council of State. It is an extremely graceful and very decorative script, with strong diagonal flourishes, though less easy to read than some other styles. After its development in Turkey, it spread to the Arab countries and is in use today for formal documents and also as architectural decoration.

This tughra (monogram or insignia) of the Ottoman Sultan Abdul-Hamid shows the three elongated vertical strokes which are characteristic of this style.

Examples of more or less standard types of script such as these do not by any means exhaust the number of styles. Islamic calligraphers have experimented endlessly and have been extremely imaginative. Another distinctive Turkish contribution is the *tughra,* an elaborate and highly stylized rendering of the names of the Ottoman sultan, originally used to authenticate imperial decrees. The tughra later came to be used both in Turkey and by rulers of the Arab countries as a kind of royal insignia or emblem, on coins and stamps and wherever a coat of arms or royal monogram would be used by European governments.

In the muthanna or "doubled" style of calligraphy shown on the left each half of the design is a mirror image of the other. The basmalah in the thuluth script on the right has been written in the shape of an ostrich.

Another unusual variation of calligraphy, not often used nowadays, is the style called *muthanna* (Arabic for "doubled"). This is not really a type of script in itself but consists of a text in one of the standard scripts such as naskhi worked into a pattern in which one half is a mirror image of the other. Even more imaginative is what may be called pictorial calligraphy, in which the text (usually the profession of faith, a verse from the Quran, or some other phrase with religious significance) is written in the shape of a bird, animal, tree, boat, or other object. A Quranic verse in the kufic script, for example, may be written so that it forms the picture of a mosque and minarets.

The angular kufic script is here used to put a well-known religious expression into the form of a mosque with four minarets.

The art of calligraphy is still very much alive in the Arab world and wherever the Arabic alphabet is used. The list of everyday uses is almost endless: coins and paper money bear the work of expert calligraphers, wall posters and advertising signs in every town show the calligrapher's art, as do the cover and title page of every book, and the major headlines in every newspaper and magazine have been written by hand. Calligraphy — the art of "beautiful writing" — continues to be something that is not only highly prized as ornament and decoration but is immensely practical and useful as well.

This move reduced state income substantially, but as there was clear precedent in the practice of the great 'Umar ibn al-Khattab, the second caliph, and as 'Umar ibn 'Abd al-'Aziz was determined to bring government policy more in line with the practice of the Prophet, even enemies of his regime had nothing but praise for this pious man.

The last great Umayyad caliph was Hisham, the fourth son of 'Abd al-Malik to succeed to the caliphate. His reign was long — from 724 to 743 — and during it the Arab empire reached its greatest extent. But neither he nor the four caliphs who succeeded him were the statesmen the times demanded when, in 747, revolutionaries in Khorasan unfurled the black flag of rebellion that would bring the Umayyad Dynasty to an end.

Although the Umayyads favored their own region of Syria, their rule was not without accomplishments. Some of the most beautiful existing buildings in the Muslim world were constructed at their instigation — buildings such as the Umayyad Mosque in Damascus, the Dome of the Rock in Jerusalem, and the lovely country palaces in the deserts of Syria, Jordan, and Iraq. They also organized a bureaucracy able to cope with the complex problems of a vast and diverse empire, and made Arabic the language of government. The Umayyads, furthermore, encouraged such writers as 'Abd Allah ibn al-Muqaffa' and 'Abd al-Hamid ibn Yahya al-Katib, whose clear, expository Arabic prose has rarely been surpassed.

For all that, the Umayyads, during the ninety years of their leadership, rarely shook off their empire's reputation as a *mulk* — that is, a worldly kingdom — and in the last years of the dynasty their opponents formed a secret organization devoted to pressing the claims to the caliphate put forward by a descendant of al-'Abbas ibn 'Abd al-Muttalib, an uncle of the Prophet. By skillful preparation, this organization rallied to its cause many mutually hostile groups in Khorasan and Iraq and proclaimed Abu al-'Abbas caliph. Marwan ibn Muhammad, the last Umayyad caliph, was defeated and the Syrians, still loyal to the Umayyads, were put to rout. Only one man of importance escaped the disaster — 'Abd al-Rahman ibn Mu'awiyah al-Dakhil, a young prince who with a loyal servant fled to Spain and in 756 set up an Umayyad Dynasty there.

The shrine of the Dome of the Rock in Jerusalem, built in an area revered by Muslims, Christians, and Jews alike, covers the rock from which Muhammad is believed to have ascended to heaven with the Angel Gabriel.

Preeminent among artists of the Muslim world is the calligrapher, as it is his privilege to adorn the word of God. Opposite page: Ornamental kufic is used on a Quranic page that typifies the marriage of calligraphy and illumination, an art that reached its zenith in the fourteenth century. Cursive scripts on this page, clockwise from left: Fourteenth-century manuscript of a pharmaceutical text translated from Greek. Quran stand of wood, dated 1360, a fine example of Mongol art from western Turkestan. Section of the gold-embroidered *kiswah,* the black cloth covering of the Ka'bah, which is renewed each year at the time of the pilgrimage. Detail from a fourteenth-century Persian tile. Miniature from the *Shah-Nameh* (Book of Kings), illustrating the epic by the Persian poet Firdausi.

ISLAM IN SPAIN: By the time 'Abd al-Rahman reached Spain, the Arabs from North Africa were already entrenched on the Iberian Peninsula and had begun to write one of the most glorious chapters in Islamic history.

After their forays into France were blunted by Charles Martel, the Muslims in Spain had begun to focus their whole attention on what they called al-Andalus, southern Spain (Andalusia), and to build there a civilization far superior to anything Spain had ever known. Reigning with wisdom and justice, they treated Christians and Jews with tolerance, with the result that many embraced Islam. They also improved trade and agriculture, patronized the arts, made valuable contributions to science, and established Cordoba as the most sophisticated city in Europe.

A forest of eight hundred and fifty pillars connected by Moorish arches lines the great mosque of Cordoba.

By the tenth century, Cordoba could boast of a population of some 500,000, compared to about 38,000 in Paris. According to the chronicles of the day, the city had 700 mosques, some 60,000 palaces, and 70 libraries — one reportedly housing 500,000 manuscripts and employing a staff of researchers, illuminators, and book binders. Cordoba also had some 900 public baths, Europe's first streetlights and, five miles outside the city, the caliphal residence, Madinat al-Zahra. A complex of marble, stucco, ivory, and onyx, Madinat al-Zahra took forty years to build, cost close to one-third of Cordoba's revenue, and was, until destroyed in the eleventh century, one of the wonders of the age. Its restoration, begun in the early years of this century, is still under way.

By the eleventh century, however, a small pocket of Christian resistance had begun to grow, and under Alfonso VI Christian forces retook Toledo. It was the beginning of the period the Christians called the Reconquest, and it underlined a serious problem that marred this refined, graceful, and charming era: the inability of the numerous rulers of Islamic Spain to maintain their unity. This so weakened them that when the various Christian kingdoms began to pose a serious threat, the Muslim rulers in Spain had to ask the Almoravids, a North African Berber dynasty, to come to their aid. The Almoravids came and crushed the Christian uprising, but eventually seized control themselves. In 1147, the Almoravids were in turn defeated by another coalition of Berber tribes, the Almohads.

Pool in the Patio de los Arrayanes reflects the grandeur of the incomparable Alhambra.

Although such internal conflict was by no means uncommon — the Christian kingdoms also warred incessantly among themselves — it did divert Muslim strength at a time when the Christians were beginning to negotiate strong alliances, form powerful armies, and launch the campaigns that would later bring an end to Arab rule.

The Arabs did not surrender easily; al-Andalus was their land too. But, bit by bit, they had to retreat, first from northern Spain, then from central Spain. By the thirteenth century their once extensive domains were reduced to a few scattered kingdoms deep in the mountains of Andalusia — where, for some two hundred years longer, they would not only survive but flourish.

It is both odd and poignant that it was then, in the last two centuries of their rule, that the Arabs created that extravagantly lovely kingdom for which they are most famous: Granada. It seems as if, in their slow retreat to the south, they suddenly realized that they were, as Washington Irving wrote, a people without a country, and set about building a memorial: the Alhambra, the citadel above Granada that one writer has called "the glory and the wonder of the civilized world."

The Alhambra was begun in 1238 by Muhammad ibn al-Ahmar who, to buy safety for his people when King Ferdinand of Aragon laid siege to Granada, once rode to Ferdinand's tent and humbly offered to become the king's vassal in return for peace.

It was a necessary move, but also difficult — particularly when Ferdinand called on him to implement the agreement by providing troops to help the Christians against Muslims in the siege of Seville in 1248. True to his pledge, Ibn al-Ahmar complied and Seville fell to the Christians. But returning to Granada, where cheering crowds hailed him as a victor, he disclosed his turmoil in that short, sad reply that he inscribed over and over on the walls of the Alhambra: "There is no victor but God."

Over the years, what started as a fortress slowly evolved under Ibn al-Ahmar's successors into a remarkable series of delicately lovely buildings, quiet courtyards, limpid pools, and hidden gardens. Later, after Ibn al-Ahmar's death, Granada itself was rebuilt and became, as one Arab visitor wrote, "as a silver vase filled with emeralds."

Science And Scholarship In Al-Andalus

For Europe and Western civilization the contributions of Islamic Spain were of inestimable value. When the Muslims entered southern Spain — which they called al-Andalus — barbarians from the north had overrun much of Europe and the classical civilization of Greece and Rome had gone into eclipse. Islamic Spain then became a bridge by which the scientific, technological, and philosophical legacy of the 'Abbasid period, along with the achievements of al-Andalus itself, passed into Europe.

In the first century of Islamic rule in Spain the culture was largely derived from that of the flourishing civilization being developed by the 'Abbasids in Baghdad. But then, during the reign of 'Abd al-Rahman III (912-961), Islamic Spain began to make its own contributions.

'Abd al-Rahman III was passionately interested in both the religious and the secular sciences. He was also determined to show the world that his court at Cordoba equaled in greatness that of the caliphs at Baghdad. Sparing neither time nor expense, he imported books from Baghdad and actively recruited scholars by offering handsome inducements. Soon, as a result, scholars, poets, philosophers, historians, and musicians began to migrate to al-Andalus. Soon, too, an infrastructure of libraries, hospitals, research institutions, and centers of Islamic studies grew up, establishing the intellectual tradition and educational system which made Spain outstanding for the next four hundred years.

One of the earliest of the scholars drawn to al-Andalus was 'Abbas ibn Firnas, who came to Cordoba to teach music (then a branch of mathematical theory) and to acquaint the court of 'Abd al-Rahman with the recent developments in this field in Baghdad. Not a man to limit himself to a single field of study, however, Ibn Firnas soon began to investigate the mechanics of flight. He constructed a pair of wings out of feathers on a wooden frame and made the first attempt at flight, anticipating Leonardo da Vinci by some six hundred years. Later, having survived the experiment with a back injury, he also constructed a famous planetarium. Not only was it mechanized — the planets actually revolved — but it simulated such celestial phenomena as thunder and lightning.

As in the 'Abbasid centers of learning, Islamic Spain's interest in mathematics, astronomy, and medicine was always lively — partly because of their obvious utility. In the tenth century Cordoban mathematicians began to make their own original contributions. The first original mathematician and astronomer of al-Andalus was Maslamah al-Majriti, who died in 1008. He had been preceded by competent scientists — men like Ibn Abi 'Ubaydah of Valencia, a leading astronomer in the ninth century. But al-Majriti was in a class by himself. He wrote a number of works on mathematics and astronomy, studied and elaborated the Arabic translation of Ptolemy's *Almagest,* and enlarged and corrected the astronomical tables of the famous al-Khwarazmi. He also compiled conversion tables in which the dates of the Persian calendar were related to Hijrah dates, so that for the first time the events of Persia's past could be dated with precision.

Al-Zarqali, known to the West as Arzachel, was another leading mathematician and astronomer who flourished in Cordoba in the eleventh century. Combining theoretical knowledge with technical skill, he excelled at the construction of precision instruments for astronomical use and built a water clock capable of determining the hours of the day and night and indicating the days of the lunar months. He also contributed to the famous Toledan Tables, a highly accurate compilation of astronomical data. Arzachel was famous as well for his *Book of Tables.* Many "books of tables" had been compiled before then, but his is an almanac containing tables which allow one to find the days on which Coptic, Roman, lunar, and Persian months begin, other tables which give the position of planets at any given time, and still others facilitating the prediction of solar and lunar eclipses. He also compiled valuable tables of latitude and longitude.

Another important scholar was al-Bitruji, who developed a new theory of stellar movement, based on Aristotle's thinking, in his *Book of Form,* a work that was later popular in the West. The names of many stars are still those given them by Muslim astronomers, such as Altair (from *al-tair,* "the flier"), Deneb (from *dhanab,* "tail"), and Betelgeuse (from *bayt al-jawza,* "the house of the twins" or "Gemini"). Other terms still in use today such as zenith, nadir, and azimuth are also derived from Arabic and so reflect the work of the Muslim astronomers of al-Andalus and their impact on the West.

Scientists of Islamic Spain also contributed to medicine, the Muslim science par excellence. Interest in medicine goes back to the very earliest times (the Prophet himself stated that there was a remedy for every illness),

(Continued on page 68)

Al-Andalus

and although the greatest Muslim physicians practiced in Baghdad, those in al-Andalus made important contributions too. Ibn al-Nafis, for example, discovered the pulmonary circulation of blood.

During the tenth century in particular, al-Andalus produced a large number of excellent physicians, some of whom studied Greek medical works translated at the famous House of Wisdom in Baghdad. Among them was Ibn Shuhayd, who in a fundamental work recommended drugs be used only if the patient did not respond to diet and urged that only simple drugs be employed in all cases but the most serious. Another important figure was Abu al-Qasim al-Zahrawi, the most famous surgeon of the Middle Ages. Known in the West as Abulcasis and Albucasis, he was the author of the *Tasrif,* a book that, translated into Latin, became the leading medical text in European universities during the later Middle Ages. Its section on surgery contains illustrations of surgical instruments of elegant, functional design and great precision.

Tongue depressor and tooth extractors were illustrated in a surgical treatise by al-Zahrawi.

Other chapters describe amputations, opthalmic and dental surgery, and the treatment of wounds and fractures. Ibn Zuhr, known as Avenzoar, was the first to describe pericardial abcesses and to recommend tracheotomy when necessary as well as being a skilled practical physician, and Ibn Rushd wrote an important book on medical theories and precepts. The last of the great Andalusian physicians, Ibn al-Khatib, also a noted historian, poet, and statesman, wrote an important book on the theory of contagion in which he said: "The fact infection becomes clear to the investigator, whereas he who is not in contact remains safe," and described how transmission is effected through garments, vessels, and earrings.

Islamic Spain made contributions to medical ethics and hygiene as well. One of the most eminent theologians and jurists, Ibn Hazm, insisted that moral qualities were mandatory in a physician. A doctor, he wrote, should be kind, understanding, friendly, and able to endure insults and adverse criticism. Furthermore, he went on, a doctor should keep his hair and fingernails short, wear clean clothes, and behave with dignity.

As an outgrowth of medicine, Andalusian scientists also interested themselves in botany. Ibn al-Baytar, for example, the most famous Andalusian botanist, wrote a book called *Simple Drugs and Food,* an alphabetically arranged compendium of medicinal plants, most of which were native to Spain and North Africa, and which he had spent a lifetime gathering. In another treatise Ibn al-'Awwam lists hundreds of species of plants and gives precise instructions regarding their cultivation and use. He writes, for example, of how to graft trees, produce hybrids, stop blights and insect pests, and make perfume.

Another important field of study in al-Andalus was the study of geography. Partly out of economic and political considerations, but mostly out of an all-consuming curiosity about the world and its inhabitants, the scholars of Islamic Spain started with works from Baghdad and went on to add such contributions as a basic geography of al-Andalus by Ahmad ibn Muhammad al-Razi and a description of the topography of North Africa by Muhammad ibn Yusuf al-Warraq. Another contributor to geography was al-Bakri, an important minister at the court of Seville but also an accomplished linguist and litterateur. One of his two important geographical works is devoted to the geography of the Arabian Peninsula, with particular attention to the elucidation of its place-names. It is arranged alphabetically, and lists the names of villages, towns, wadis, and monuments which he culled from the hadith and from histories. The other was an encyclopedia of the entire world, arranged by country, with each entry preceded by a short historical introduction. It included descriptions of the people, customs, and climate of each country, the principal features, the major cities, and even anecdotes.

In the study of geography such figures as Ibn Jubayr, an Andalusian traveler, and the most famous traveler of all, Ibn Battutah, also made important contributions. Born in North Africa, then in the cultural orbit of Islamic Spain, Ibn Battutah traveled extensively for twenty-eight years and produced a travel book that proved to be a rich source for both historians and geographers. It included invaluable information on people, places, navigation, caravan routes, roads, and inns. But the most famous geographer of the period was al-Idrisi, who studied in Cordoba. After traveling widely, al-Idrisi settled in Sicily and wrote a systematic geography of the world, usually known as the *Book of Roger* after his patron Roger II, the Norman King of Sicily. The information contained in the *Book of Roger* was also engraved on a silver planisphere, a disc-shaped map that was one of the wonders of the age.

Al-Idrisi's planisphere is considered the first scientific map of the world.

Innumerable scholars in al-Andalus also devoted themselves to the study of history and linguistic sciences, the prime "social sciences" cultivated by the Arabs, and brought them to a high level. Ibn al-Khatib, for example, who distinguished himself in almost all branches of learning, produced more than fifty works on travel, medicine, poetry, music, politics, and theology, as well as writing the finest history of Granada that has survived. The most original mind of the period, however, was undoubtedly Ibn Khaldun, the first historian to develop and explicate general laws governing the rise and decline of civilizations. In the *Prolegomena,* an introduction to a huge, seven-volume universal history — an introduction longer than some of the volumes — Ibn Khaldun approached history as a science and challenged the logic of many accepted historical accounts. In a sense, he was the first modern philosopher of history.

Another great area of Andalusian intellectual activity was philosophy, where an attempt was made to deal with intellectual problems posed by the introduction of Greek philosophy into the context of Islam. One of the first to deal with this was Ibn Hazm, who as the author of more than four hundred books has been described as "one of the giants of the intellectual history of Islam." There were other philosophers too, such as Ibn Bajjah, known to the West as Avempace, who was also a physician and Ibn Tufayl, the author of *Hayy ibn Yaqzan,* the story of a child growing up in complete solitude on a desert island who, entirely by his own intellectual efforts, discovers for himself the highest physical and metaphysical realities. It was however, Averroes — Ibn Rushd — who earned the greatest reputation. He was an ardent Aristotelian and his works had a lasting effect, in their Latin translation, on the development of Western philosophy.

The list of Islamic Spain's contributions to the West, in fact, is almost endless. In addition to Islamic Spain's contributions in mathematics, economy, medicine, botany, geography, history, and philosophy, al-Andalus also developed and applied important technological innovations: the windmill and new techniques in the crafts of metalworking, weaving, and building.

Meanwhile, outside Granada, the Christian kings waited. In relentless succession they had retaken Toledo, Cordoba, and Seville. Only Granada survived. Then, in 1482, in a trivial quarrel, the Muslim kingdom split into two hostile factions and, simultaneously, two strong Christian sovereigns, Ferdinand and Isabella, married and merged their kingdoms. As a result, Granada fell ten years later. On January 2, 1492 — the year they sent Columbus to America — Ferdinand and Isabella hoisted the banner of Christian Spain above the Alhambra and Boabdil, the last Muslim king, rode weeping into exile with the bitter *envoi* from his aged mother, "Weep like a woman for the city you would not defend like a man!"

In describing the fate of Islam in Spain, Irving suggested that the Muslims were then swiftly and thoroughly wiped out. Never, he wrote, was the annihilation of a people more complete. In fact, by emigration to North Africa and elsewhere, many Muslims carried remnants of the Spanish era with them and were thus able to make important contributions to the material and cultural life of their adopted lands.

Much of the emigration, however, came later. At first, most Muslims simply stayed in Spain; cut off from their original roots by time and distance they quite simply had no other place to go. Until the Inquisition, furthermore, conditions in Spain were not intolerable. The Christians permitted Muslims to work, serve in the army, own land, and even practice their religion — all concessions to the importance of Muslims in Spain's still prosperous economy. But then, in the period of the Inquisition, all the rights of the Muslims were withdrawn, their lives became difficult, and more began to emigrate. Finally, in the early seventeenth century, most of the survivors were forcibly expelled.

THE 'ABBASIDS: In the Middle East, during these centuries, the 'Abbasids, after their victory over the Umayyads, had transformed the Umayyads' Arab empire into a multinational Muslim empire. They moved the capital of the empire from Syria to Iraq, where they built a new capital, Baghdad, from which, during the next five centuries, they would influence many of the main events of Islamic history.

A Moorish-built tower soars above the Guadalquivir River in Seville.

Astride the Tigris, present-day Baghdad stands in the vicinity of the 'Abbasid capital, a fabulous city of mosques, mansions and libraries.

UMAYYAD CALIPHATE
Cordoba Toledo
Tangier Malaga Granada
Kairouan
Tunis
Palermo
SICILY
MEDITERRANEAN SEA
CRETE
Constantinople BLACK SEA
Sinope Trapezus Tiflis Tabriz CASPIAN SEA
BYZANTINE EMPIRE ARMENIA AZERBALJAN
Athens Smyrna RUM Tarsus Mosul
Antioch Aleppo HAMDANIDS
CYPRUS Damascus SYRIA Euphrates River
Tripoli Barqa
FATIMID
Alexandria
Jerusalem
Cairo
SINAI Aqaba
FATIMID
CALIPHATE
Nile River
Yanbu
Aswan
Jiddah Mecca
Nile River
RED
SEA

THE 'ABBASID CALIPHATE AND RIVAL STATES AT END OF THE TENTH CENTURY A.D.

Although most of Islam still acknowledges the religious authority of the 'Abbasid caliphate, political power is dispersed among a number of independent states. The largest of these is controlled by the Fatimids who, starting out from Tunisia early in the century, have advanced across North Africa to Egypt and Palestine and down the west coast of Arabia to Hadhramaut. Persian culture has revived under the Samanids. The Hamdanids dominate Syria and northern Mesopotamia. But the center of culture and learning has shifted from Baghdad to the caliphate of Cordoba, where an Umayyad Dynasty still flourishes.

The Great Mosque of the Umayyads in Damascus dates from the early eighth century, and numerous works of rebuilding have not changed its fundamental character.

Golden domes and gold-topped minarets highlight the mosque of al-Kazimayn in Baghdad, built in the early sixteenth century.

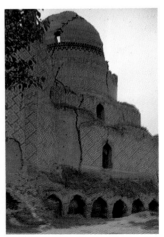

The mosque of Bibi Khanum, named for Tamerlane's favorite wife, was once the most imposing building of Samarkand.

In the early period of 'Abbasid rule, al-Mansur, the second caliph of the dynasty, continued the reorganization of the administration of the empire along the lines that had been laid down by his Umayyad predecessor, 'Abd al-Malik. Much of the 'Abbasid administration, for example, was left in the hands of well-educated Persian civil servants, many of whom came from families that had traditionally served the Sassanid kings. The important office of *wazir* or vizier, chief counselor, may well have developed from Sassanid models. The vizier was much more than an advisor; indeed, when the caliph was weak, a capable vizier became the most powerful man in the empire.

The creation of the office of the vizier was only one of the innovations the 'Abbasids brought to statecraft. Another was the development of the Umayyad postal system into an efficient intelligence service; postmasters in outlying provinces were the eyes and ears of the government, and regular reports were filed with the central government on everything from the state of the harvest to the doings of dissident sects. Under the 'Abbasids too a whole literature was created for the use and training of the clerical classes that had come into being. Since all government business was by now transacted in Arabic, manuals of correct usage were written for the instruction of non-Arabic speakers who had found government employment. There was also a vast literature on the correct deportment of princes, as well as anthologies of witty sayings and anecdotes with which to enliven one's epistolary style.

In some ways the 'Abbasids were more fortunate than the Umayyads. When, for example, al-Mansur died in 775 after a reign of twenty years, his son, al-Mahdi, inherited a full treasury and an empire that was more devoted to trade than war.

The developments in trade, indeed, are among the achievements of the 'Abbasids that are too often overlooked. Because Islamic rule unified much of the Eastern world, thus abolishing many boundaries, trade was freer, safer, and more extensive than it had been since the time of Alexander the Great. Muslim traders, consequently, established trading posts as far away as India, the Philippines, Malaya, the East Indies, and China.

From the eighth to the eleventh centuries this trade was largely concerned with finding and importing basic necessities — grain, metals, and wood. To obtain them, of course, the Muslims had to export too, often using the imports from one region as exports to another: pearls from the Gulf, livestock from the Arabian Peninsula (particularly Arabian horses and camels), and — one of the chief products — cloth. The Muslims also traded medicines, an offshoot of 'Abbasid advances in medical science, as well as paper and sugar.

This expansion of commercial activity led to other developments too. One was a system of banking and exchange so sophisticated that a letter of credit issued in Baghdad could be honored in Samarkand in Central Asia or Kairouan in North Africa. The demands of trade also generated development of crafts. From Baghdad's large urban population, for example, came craftsmen of every conceivable sort: metalworkers, leatherworkers, bookbinders, papermakers, jewelers, weavers, druggists, bakers, and many more. As they grew in importance to the economy, these craftsmen eventually organized themselves into mutual-benefit societies which in some ways were similar to later Western guilds and which offered many social services: lodging travelers, engaging in pious works such as caring for orphans, and endowing schools. Because of this growth in commerce the 'Abbasids also developed a system by which a *muhtasib,* an inspector, made sure that proper weights and measures were given and that dishonest practices of all sorts were avoided.

THE GOLDEN AGE: The early 'Abbasids were also fortunate in the caliber of their caliphs, especially after Harun al-Rashid came to the caliphate in 786. His reign is now the most famous in the annals of the 'Abbasids — partly because of the fictional role given him in *The Thousand and One Nights* (portions of which probably date from his reign), but also because his reign and those of his immediate successors marked the high point of the 'Abbasid period. As the Arab chronicles put it, Harun al-Rashid ruled when the world was young, a felicitous description of what in later times has come to be called the Golden Age of Islam.

The Golden Age was a period of unrivaled intellectual activity in all fields: science, technology, and (as a result of intensive study of the Islamic faith) literature — particularly biography, history, and linguistics. Scholars, for example, in collecting and reexamining the *hadith,* or "traditions" — the sayings and actions of the Prophet — compiled immense biographical detail about the Prophet and other information, historic and linguistic, about the Prophet's era. This led to such memorable works as *Sirat Rasul Allah,* the "Life of the Messenger of God," by Ibn Ishaq, later revised by Ibn Hisham; one of the earliest Arabic historical works, it was a key source of information about the Prophet's life and also a model for other important works of history such as al-Tabari's *Annals of the Apostles and the Kings* and his massive commentary on the Quran.

'Abbasid writers also developed new genres of literature such as *adab,* the embodiment of sensible counsel, sometimes in the form of animal fables; a typical example is *Kalilah wa-Dimnah,* translated by Ibn al-Muqaffa' from a Pahlavi version of an Indian work. Writers of this period also studied tribal traditions and wrote the first systematic Arabic grammars.

During the Golden Age Muslim scholars also made important and original contributions to mathematics, astronomy, medicine, and chemistry. They collected and corrected previous astronomical data, built the world's first observatory, and developed the astrolabe, an instrument that was once called "a mathematical jewel." In medicine they experimented with diet, drugs, surgery, and anatomy, and in chemistry, an outgrowth of alchemy, isolated and studied a wide variety of minerals and compounds.

Important advances in agriculture were also made in the Golden Age. The 'Abbasids preserved and improved the ancient network of wells, underground canals, and waterwheels, introduced new breeds of livestock, hastened the spread of cotton, and, from the Chinese, learned the art of making paper, a key to the revival of learning in Europe in the Middle Ages.

The Golden Age also, little by little, transformed the diet of medieval Europe by introducing such plants as plums, artichokes, apricots, cauliflower, celery, fennel, squash, pumpkins, and eggplant, as well as rice, sorghum, new strains of wheat, the date palm, and sugarcane.

Many of the advances in science, literature, and trade which took place during the Golden Age of the 'Abbasids and which would provide the impetus for the European Renaissance reached their flowering during the caliphate of al-Mamun, son of Harun al-Rashid and perhaps the greatest of all the 'Abbasids. But politically the signs of decay were already becoming evident. The province of Ifriqiyah — North Africa west of Libya and east of Morocco — had fallen away from 'Abbasid control during the reign of Harun al-Rashid, and under al-Mamun other provinces soon broke loose also. When, for example, al-Mamun marched from Khorasan to Baghdad, he left a trusted general named Tahir ibn al-Husayn in charge of the eastern province. Tahir asserted his independence of the central government by omitting mention of the caliph's name in the mosque on Friday and by striking his own coins — acts which became the standard ways of expressing political independence. From 821 onward Tahir and his descendants ruled Khorasan as an independent state, with the tacit consent of the 'Abbasids.

Al-Mamun died in 833, in the town of Tarsus, and was succeeded by his brother, al-Mu'tasim, under whose rule the symptoms of decline that had manifested themselves earlier grew steadily worse. As he could no longer rely on the loyalty of his army, al-Mu'tasim recruited an army of Turks from Transoxania and Turkestan. It was a necessary step, but its outcome was dominance of the caliphate by its own praetorian guard. In the years following 861, the Turks made and unmade rulers at will, a trend that accelerated the decline of the central authority. Although the religious authority of the 'Abbasid caliphate remained unchallenged, the next four centuries saw political power dispersed among a large number of independent states: Tahirids, Saffarids, Samanids, Buwayhids, Ziyarids, and Ghaznavids in the east; Hamdanids in Syria and northern Mesopotamia; and Tulunids, Ikhshidids, and Fatimids in Egypt.

Some of these states made important contributions to Islamic culture. Under the Samanids, the Persian language, written in the Arabic alphabet, first reached the level of a literary language and poets like Rudaki, Daqiqi, and Firdausi flourished. The Ghaznavids

Persian miniature depicts students with a teacher of astronomy — one of the sciences to which scholars of the Golden Age made great contributions.

Muslim scientists developed the astrolabe, an instrument used long before the invention of the sextant to observe the position of celestial bodies.

Books of fables, often illustrated, served a dual purpose — to instruct and to entertain.

Artisans in far reaches of the Muslim world, born to differing traditions but united in service of a common faith, wove the rich fabric of Islamic art with a common repertory of motifs. Above: Calligraphy, itself an art, decorates a tenth-century bowl from Samarkand. Right: Geometric interlacings in a detail from a wooden pulpit in a twelfth-century Moroccan mosque. Facing page, beginning below: Ivory horn made in Sicily, late eleventh century, when Fatimid influence reached Italy. Gold pendant with cloisonné inlay from Egypt, twelfth century. The seventeenth-century bottle from Kirman in Persia combines Chinese-inspired elements with Islamic arabesque. Sixteenth-century crimson brocade reflects the opulence of the Ottoman court.

patronized al-Biruni, one of the greatest and most original scholars of medieval Islam, and the Hamdanids, a purely Arab dynasty, patronized such poets as al-Mutanabbi and philosophers like the great al-Farabi, whose work kept the flame of Arab culture alive in a difficult period. But in historical terms, only the Fatimids rivaled the preceding dynasties.

THE FATIMIDS: The most stable of the successor dynasties founded in the ninth and tenth centuries was that of the Fatimids, a branch of the Shi'is. The Fatimids won their first success in North Africa, where they established a rival caliphate at Raqqadah near Kairouan and, in 952, embarked on a period of expansion that within a few years took them to Egypt.

For a time the Fatimids aspired to be rulers of the whole Islamic world, and their achievements were impressive. At their peak they ruled North Africa, the Red Sea coast, Yemen, Palestine, and parts of Syria. The Fatimids built the Mosque of al-Azhar in Cairo — from which developed al-Azhar University, now the oldest university in the world and perhaps the most influential Islamic school of higher learning. Fatimid merchants traded with Afghanistan and China and tried to divert some of Baghdad's Arabian Gulf shipping to the Red Sea.

Founded in 970, the mosque of al-Azhar in Cairo is one of the earliest and finest examples of the Egyptian style in Islamic architecture.

But the Fatimids' dreams of gaining control of the Islamic heartland came to nothing, partly because many of the other independent states refused to support them and partly because they, like the 'Abbasids in Baghdad, lost effective control of their own mercenaries. Such developments weakened the Fatimids, but thanks to a family of viziers of Armenian origin they were able to endure until the Ayyubid succession in the second half of the twelfth century — even in the face of the eleventh-century invasion by the Seljuk Turks.

THE SELJUK TURKS: Although individual Turkish generals had already gained considerable, and at times decisive, power in Mesopotamia and Egypt during the tenth and eleventh centuries, the coming of the Seljuks signaled the first large-scale penetration of Turkish elements into the Middle East. Descended from a tribal chief named Seljuk,

The Quran, the primary document of the Islamic faith, is the first Arabic book. Its style, at once vigorous, allusive, and concise, deeply influenced later compositions in Arabic, as it continues to color the mode of expression of native speakers of Arabic, Christian as well as Muslim, both in writing and in conversation.

The Quran also largely determined the course of Arabic literature. The earliest Arabic prose came into being not from literary motives, but to serve religious and practical needs, above all the need to fully understand the Islamic revelation and the circumstances of the first Muslim community in the Hijaz. The sayings and actions of the Prophet and his Companions were collected and preserved, at first by memory and then by writing, to be finally collected and arranged by such men as al-Bukhari and Muslim in the ninth century. This material, the *hadith*, not only provided the basic texts from which Islamic law was elaborated, but also formed the raw material for historians of the early Muslim community. Since each hadith, or "saying," is a first-person narrative, usually by an eyewitness of the event described, they have an immediacy and freshness that has come down unimpaired through the centuries. The personalities of the narrators — Abu Bakr, 'Umar, 'Aishah, and a host of others — are just as vivid as the events described, for the style of each hadith is very personal.

The hadith also determined the characteristic form of such works as Ibn Ishaq's *Life of the Messenger of God*, originally written in the middle of the eighth century. In this book, hadith dealing with the life of the Prophet are arranged in chronological order, and the comments of the author are kept to a minimum. Events are seen through the eyes of the people who witnessed them; three or four versions of the same event are often given, and in each case the "chain of transmission" of the hadith is given, so that the reader may judge its authenticity.

During Umayyad times, a number of historians wrote monographs on specific historical, legal, and religious questions, and in each case these authors seem to have adhered to the hadith method of composition. Although few of the works of these writers have survived in their entirety, enough has been preserved by later incorporation in such vast works as the *Annals* of al-Tabari to give us an idea not only of their method of composition, but also of their wide-ranging interests.

The practice of prefacing a chain of authorities to each hadith led to the compilation of vast biographical dictionaries, like the *Book of Classes* of the early ninth century author Ibn Sa'd, which includes a biography of the Prophet and a great deal of information on notable personalities in Mecca and Medina during his lifetime. Works such as this allowed readers to identify and judge the veracity of transmitters of hadith; later, the content of biographical dictionaries was broadened to include poets, writers, eminent reciters of the Quran, scientists, and the like. These biographical dictionaries are often lively reading, and are a mine of information about social and political circumstances in the Islamic world.

The spread of Islam naturally found chroniclers, such as al-Waqidi, who wrote in the late eighth and early ninth centuries, and al-Baladhuri, who composed his well-known *Book of the Conquests* in the ninth century. These books, like the hadith, were written for practical motives

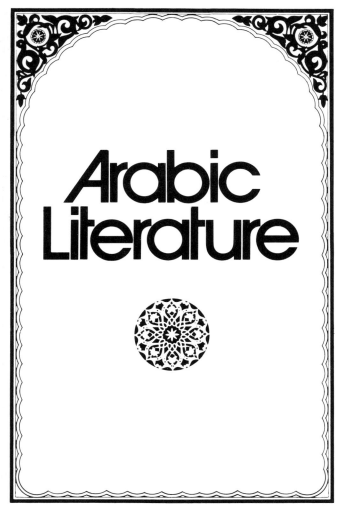

Arabic Literature

Al-Waqidi was interested in establishing the exact chronology of the spread of Islam in the Arabian Peninsula and adjoining areas, while al-Baladhuri was interested in legal and tax problems connected with the settlement of new lands. Their books nevertheless are classics of their kind and, aside from containing much interesting information, they have passages of great descriptive power.

By the ninth century, the method of compiling history from hadith and carefully citing the authorities for each tradition — a process which had resulted in books of unwieldy length — was abandoned by some authors, like al-Dinawari and al-Ya'qubi, who omitted the chains of transmitters and combined hadith to produce a narrative. The result was greater readability and smaller compass, at the sacrifice of richness and complexity. The works of al-Dinawari and al-Ya'qubi, unlike those of their predecessors, aimed to entertain as well as instruct; they are "literary" productions. This form of light history reached its apogee in the tenth century in al-Mas'udi's brilliant and entertaining *Meadows of Gold and Mines of Gems,* a comprehensive encyclopedia of history, geography, and literature. The literary productions of these men would not, however, have been possible without the careful collections of historical hadith made by their predecessors.

Just as the writing of history began from practical rather than literary motives, so the collection and preserva-

tion of Arabic poetry was undertaken by scholars with, at first, little interest in its artistic merit. The linguists and exegetes of Kufa and Basra began collecting this poetry in the eighth century because of the light it threw on unusual expressions and grammatical structures in the Quran and the hadith. Editions and commentaries were prepared of the poems of 'Antarah, Imru al-Qays, and many others, and thus the works of the early poets were preserved for later generations.

The Quran apart, poetry has always been considered the highest expression of literary art among the Arabs. Long before the coming of Islam, Bedouin poets had perfected the forms of panegyric, satire, and elegy. Their poetry obeys strict conventions, both in form and content, which indicates that it must have had a long period of development before it was finally committed to writing by scholars.

The principal form used by the desert poets was the *qasidah* or ode, a poem of variable length rhyming in the last syllable of each line. The qasidah begins with a description of the abandoned encampment of the poet's beloved and goes on to an account of his anguish at her absence and his consuming love for her. The poet then describes an arduous journey across the desert and ends the qasidah with an appeal to the generosity of his host. Although the subject matter is almost invariable, the language is very complex and of great precision.

In the Hijaz during the first century of Islam, contemporary with the first hadith scholars, a group of poets broke with the past and introduced new forms and subjects. Men like 'Umar ibn Abi Rabi'ah wrote realistic and urbane verse, and a school of poetry which expressed the themes of Platonic love grew up around the poet Jamil ibn Mu'ammar, better known as Jamil al-'Udhri. The lives and works of these poets of the Umayyad period are preserved in the entertaining tenth-century anthology by Abu al-Faraj al-Isfahani, the *Book of Songs.*

The Umayyad court in Damascus patronized poets and musicians. It was also the scene of the development of the type of Arabic literature called *adab.* Adab is usually translated as "belles-lettres," which is slightly misleading. This literature, at least in its inception, was created to serve the practical end of educating the growing class of government ministers in the Arabic language, manners and deportment, history, and statecraft. Works in Sanskrit, Pahlavi, Greek, and Syriac began to find their way into Arabic at this time. 'Abd al-Hamid ibn Yahya al-Katib, an Umayyad official, and the creator of this genre, defined its aims as follows: "Cultivate the Arabic language so that you may speak correctly; develop a handsome script which will add luster to your writings; learn the poetry of the Arabs by heart; familiarize yourself with unusual ideas and expressions; read the history of the Arabs and the Persians, and remember their great deeds." 'Abd Allah ibn al-Muqaffa', a contemporary of 'Abd al-Hamid ibn Yahya, translated the history of the ancient kings of Persia into Arabic, as well as *Kalilah wa-Dimnah,* an Indian book of advice for princes cast in the form of animal fables. His works are the earliest surviving examples of Arabic art prose and are still used as models in schools throughout the Middle East.

By the ninth century, Arabic literature had entered its

(Continued on page 78)

Arabic Literature

classical age. The various genres had been defined — adab, history, Quranic exegesis, geography, biography, poetry, satire, and many more. Al-Jahiz was perhaps the greatest stylist of the age, and one of the most original personalities. He wrote more than two hundred books, on every conceivable subject; he was critical, rational, and always amusing. His *Book of Animals* is the earliest Arabic treatise on zoology and contains very modern-sounding discussions of such things as animal mimetism and biological adaptation. He wrote one of the earliest and best treatises on rhetoric and a large number of amusing essays. By the time of his death at the age of ninety-six he had shown that Arabic prose was capable of handling any subject with ease. The most gifted of al-Jahiz's contemporaries was probably Ibn Qutaybah, also a writer of encyclopedic learning and an excellent stylist. His *Book of Knowledge,* a history of the world beginning with the creation, is the earliest work of its kind and later had many imitators.

The tenth century witnessed the creation of a new form in Arabic literature, the *maqamat.* This was the title of a work by al-Hamadhani, called Badi' al-Zaman, "The Wonder of the Age." His *Maqamat* ("Sessions") is a series of episodes written in rhymed prose concerning the life of Abu al-Fath al-Iskandari, a sort of confidence trickster, who takes on a different personality in each story and always succeeds in bilking his victims. These stories are witty and packed with action, and were immediately popular. Al-Hamadhani was imitated by al-Hariri a hundred years later. Al-Hariri was a linguistic virtuoso, and his *Maqamat* is filled with obscure words, alliteration, puns, and wild metaphors. He too was extremely popular, and many learned commentaries were written on his *Maqamat.* This purely Arab form can most closely be compared with the Spanish picaresque novels, which it may have influenced.

Rhymed prose, which had come to be used even in government documents, was employed by Abu al-'Ala al-Ma'arri in his *Message of Forgiveness,* one of the best known of Arabic prose works. Al-Ma'arri lived in the eleventh century, leading an ascetic life in his native Syrian village. Blind from the age of four, he possessed a prodigious memory and great intellectual curiosity and skepticism. *The Message of Forgiveness* is cast in the form of a journey to paradise; the narrator there interrogates the scholars and poets of the past regarding their lives and works, receiving surprising and often ironic responses. The book is an extended critique of literature and philology, and represents a high point of classical Arabic culture.

One of the other great figures of late classical literature was the poet al-Mutanabbi, whose skill in handling the complex meters of Arabic poetry was probably unsurpassed. His verbal brilliance has always been admired by Arab critics, although it is difficult for those whose native tongue is not Arabic to appreciate it fully.

The period between the fall of Baghdad to the Mongols in 1258 and the nineteenth century is generally held to be a period of literary as well as political decline for the Arabs. It is true that during these five hundred years

Arabic writers were more preoccupied with the preservation of their literary heritage than with the development of new forms and ideas. This is the age of encyclopedias, commentaries, and lexicons. Faced with the massive destruction of books by the invasions of Genghis Khan and Hulagu and later of Tamerlane, scholars compiled digests and abridgments of works that had survived in order to ensure their continued existence.

There were also some original works, however. Ibn Battutah, the greatest traveler of the Middle Ages, lived in the fourteenth century, and his *Travels* provide a fascinating picture of the Muslim world, from the islands of the Indian Ocean to Timbuktu. Ibn Khaldun, like Ibn Battutah a native of North Africa, lived in the later fourteenth and early fifteenth centuries. His *Prolegomena* is a work of brilliance and originality; the author analyzes human society in terms of general sociological laws and gives a lucid account of the factors that contribute to the rise and decline of civilizations. Ibn Khaldun's style is innovative, simple, and very personal, and perfectly suited to the expression of his often difficult ideas.

This postclassical period also saw the composition of popular romances, such as the *Romance of 'Antar,* based on the life of the famous pre-Islamic poet; the *Romance of the Bani Hilal,* a cycle of stories and poems based on the migration of an Arabian tribe to North Africa in the eleventh century; and many more. These romances could be heard recited in coffee shops from Aleppo to Marrakesh until very recently. The most famous popular work of all, *The Thousand and One Nights,* assumed its present form during the fifteenth century.

A revival of Arabic literature began in the nineteenth century, and coincided with the first efforts of Arabic-speaking nations to assert their independence of Ottoman rule. Napoleon, during his brief occupation of Egypt in the late eighteenth century, introduced a printing press with fonts of Arabic type, and Muhammad 'Ali, ruler of Egypt from 1805 to 1848, initiated a series of projects to modernize Egypt. He encouraged the use of Arabic in schools and government institutions, and established a printing press. Selected Egyptian students were sent to study in France, and on their return assigned to undertake translations of Western technical manuals on agriculture, engineering, mathematics, and military tactics. These works, together with many of the classics of Arabic literature, were printed at the government press at Bulaq and had a profound impact on intellectuals in the Arab East.

Another factor in the literary revival was the swift growth of journalism in Lebanon and Egypt. Starting in the late 1850s, newspapers were soon available through the Middle East. By 1900 well over a hundred and fifty newspapers and journals were being published. These journals had a great influence on the development and modernization of the written Arabic language; their stress on substance rather than style did much to simplify Arabic prose and bring it within the comprehension of everyone.

One of the first leaders of the Arabic literary renaissance was the Lebanese writer and scholar Butrus al-Bustani, whose dictionary and encyclopedia awakened great interest in the problems of expressing modern

Western ideas in the Arabic language. His nephew Sulayman translated Homer's *Iliad* into Arabic, thus making one of the first expressions of Western literature accessible to the Arabic-reading public. Other writers, such as the Egyptian Mustafa al-Manfaluti, adapted French romantic novels to the tastes of the Arab public, as well as writing elegant essays on a variety of themes.

The historical novel, in the hands of Jurji Zaydan, proved immensely popular, perhaps because of the intense interest Arabs have always had in their past, and because of the novelty of a new form. But the first Arabic novel that can rank with European productions is Muhammad Husayn Haykal's *Zaynab*, set in Egypt and dealing with local problems.

Perhaps the greatest figure in modern Arabic literature is Taha Husayn. Blind from an early age, Taha Husayn wrote movingly of his life and beloved Egypt in his autobiography, *al-Ayyam*, "The Days." Taha Husayn was a graduate of both al-Azhar and the Sorbonne, and his voluminous writings on Arabic literature contributed a new critique of this vast subject.

The novel was not the only new form introduced to the Arabic-reading public. The drama, first in the form of translations of Western work, then of original compositions, was pioneered by Ahmad Shawqi and came to maturity in the hands of Tawfiq al-Hakim. Tawfiq al-Hakim's long career and devotion to the theater did much to make this one of the liveliest arts of the Middle East.

The history of modern Arabic poetry, with its many schools and contending styles, is almost impossible to summarize. Traditional forms and subjects were challenged by 'Abbas Mahmud al-'Aqqad, Mahmud Shukri, and Ibrahim al-Mazini, who strove to introduce nineteenth-century European themes and techniques into Arabic, not always with success. Lebanese poets were in the forefront of modernist verse, and one of them, Gibran Kahlil Gibran, proved very popular in the West. Poets are now experimenting with both old and new techniques, although discussions of form have given way to concern for content. The exodus of Palestinians from their native land has become a favorite theme, often movingly handled.

In Saudi Arabia, it was not until well into the twentieth century that literary movements in neighboring lands made themselves felt. Poetry, of course, has been cultivated in Arabia since the pre-Islamic period, and it has lately been influenced by new forms and subjects. Hasan al-Qurashi, Tahir Zamakhshari, Hasan Faqi, and Mahrum (the pen name of Amir 'Abd Allah al-Faysal) have won renown for their poetry throughout the Arab world. Hasan Faqi's poetry is introspective and philosophical, while the verse of the three others is lyrical and romantic. Ghazi al-Gosaibi is distinguished by a fresh, fecund imagination that expresses itself in both Arabic and English verse. Two novels by the late Hamid al-Damanhuri have been well received. They are *Thaman al-Tadhiyah*, "The Price of Sacrifice," and *Wa-Marrat al-Ayyam*, "And the Days Went By." With the rapid increase in education and communications in the kingdom, Saudi presses are now beginning to publish more and more works by Saudi writers, and it can certainly be expected that the great social changes that are taking place in Saudi Arabia will eventually be reflected in equally far-reaching developments in the literature of the country.

whose homeland lay beyond the Oxus River near the Aral Sea, the Seljuks not only developed a highly effective fighting force but also, through their close contacts with Persian court life in Khorasan and Transoxania, attracted a body of able administrators. Extending from Central Asia to the Byzantine marches in Asia Minor, the Seljuk state under its first three sultans — Tughril Beg, Alp-Arslan, and Malikshah — established a highly cohesive, well-administered Sunni state under the nominal authority of the 'Abbasid caliphs at Baghdad.

One of the administrators, the Persian Nizam-al-Mulk, became one of the greatest statesmen of medieval Islam. For twenty years, especially during the rule of Sultan Malikshah, he was the true custodian of the Seljuk state. In addition to having administrative abilities, he was an accomplished stylist whose book on statecraft, *Siyasat-Namah*, is a valuable source for the political thought of the time. In it he stresses the responsibilities of the ruler: for example, if a man is killed because a bridge is in disrepair, it is the fault of the ruler, for he should make it his business to apprise himself of the smallest negligences of his underlings. Nizam-al-Mulk, furthermore, was a devout and orthodox Muslim who established a system of *madrasahs* or theological seminaries (called *nizamiyah* after the first element of his name) to provide students with free education in the religious sciences of Islam, as well as in the most advanced scientific and philosophical thought of the time. The famous theologian al-Ghazali whose greatest work, the *Revival of the Sciences of Religion*, was a triumph of Sunni theology taught for a time at the nizamiyah schools at Baghdad and at Nishapur. Nizam-al-Mulk was the patron of the poet and astronomer 'Umar al-Khayyam (Omar Khayyam), whose verses, as translated by Edward FitzGerald in the nineteenth century, have become as familiar to English readers as the sonnets of Shakespeare.

The *Rubaiyat* of Omar Khayyam owes its popularity in the West to the translation by FitzGerald.

After the death of Malikshah in 1092, internal conflict among the young heirs led to the fragmentation of the Seljuks' central authority into smaller Seljuk states led by various members of the family, and still smaller units led by regional chieftains, no one of whom was able to unite the Muslim world as still another force appeared in the Middle East: the Crusaders.

Tangier · ALMORAVIDS · Cordoba · Algiers · Kairouan · Tunis · SICILY · Palermo · MEDITERRANEAN SEA · CRETE · BYZANTINE EMPIRE · Constantinople · BLACK SEA · Smyrna · Sinope · Trapezunt · Kayseri · ARMENIA · AZERBAIJAN · Tiflis · CASPIAN SEA · Rayy · Tabriz · Tarsus · Mosul · Antioch · Aleppo · AL JAZIRAH · CYPRUS · SYRIA · Damascus · Euphrates · Tigris River · Bagh

Tripoli · Barqa · Alexandria · Jerusalem · Ashkelon · Aqaba · Cairo · FATIMIDS · Nile River · Aswan · Yanbu · S · E · H · I · J · Med · Jiddah · Mecca

RED · SEA

THE MIDDLE EAST AND THE MEDITERRANEAN ON THE EVE OF THE CRUSADES

The Seljuks from beyond the Oxus, the first Turkic people to penetrate the Middle East in force, have adopted Islam and quickly overrun most of the 'Abbasid lands east of the Mediterranean, including Oman and the Hijaz, and have wrested most of Anatolia from the Byzantine Empire. The Fatimids have successfully resisted the Seljuks and retain control in Egypt and Sinai. In the west, Berber nomads, the Almoravids, have established themselves in Morocco and succeed the Umayyads in a reduced area in Spain. To the east, Transoxania under the Qarakhanids is a Seljuk vassal state and the Ghaznavids of Khorasan and Afghanistan are expanding Muslim rule in India. At the end of the eleventh century, as the Seljuk central authority is being eroded by internal conflict, the initially successful invading forces of the Crusaders arrive on the scene.

THE CRUSADERS: To Arab historians, the Crusaders were a minor irritant, their invasion one more barbarian incursion, not nearly as serious a threat as the Mongols were to prove in the thirteenth and fourteenth centuries.

The First Crusade began in 1095 after the Byzantines — threatened by Seljuk power — appealed to Pope Urban II for military aid. Pope Urban, hoping to divert the Christian kings and princes from their struggles with each other, and perhaps also seeing an opportunity to reunite the Eastern and Western churches, called for a "Truce of God" among the rulers of Europe and urged them to take the Holy Land from the Muslims.

Considered dispassionately, the venture was impossible. The volunteers — a mixed assemblage of kings, nobles, mercenaries, and adventurers — had to cross thousands of miles of unfamiliar and hostile country and conquer lands of whose strength they had no conception. Yet so great was their fervor that in 1099 they took Jerusalem, establishing along the way principalities in Antioch, Edessa, and Tripoli. Although unable to fend off the Crusaders at first — even offering the Crusaders access to Jerusalem if they would come as pilgrims rather than invaders — the Muslims eventually began to mount effective counterattacks. They recaptured Aleppo and besieged Edessa, thus bringing on the unsuccessful Second Crusade.

In the meantime the Crusaders — or Franks, as the Arabs called them — had extended their reach to the borders of Egypt, where the Fatimids had fallen after two hundred years. There they faced a young man called Salah al-Din (Saladin) who had founded still another new dynasty, the Ayyubids, and who was destined to blunt the thrust of the Crusaders' attack. In 1187 Saladin counterattacked, eventually recapturing Jerusalem. The Europeans mounted a series of further crusading expeditions against the Muslims over the next hundred years or so, but the Crusaders never again recovered the initiative. Confined to the coast, they ruled small areas until their final defeat at the hands of the Egyptian Mamluks at the end of the thirteenth century.

Although the Crusades achieved no lasting results in terms of military conquest, they were important in the development of trade, and their long-range effects on Western society — on everything from feudalism to fashion

The most imposing of the many fortresses built by the Crusaders, the elegant Krak des Chevaliers in Syria (top) held out against the Muslims for over a century and a half. The Crusader castle at Sidon in Lebanon (below) was abandoned after the final defeat of the Crusader Kingdom of Jerusalem.

— are inestimable. Ironically, they also put an end to the centuries-old rivalry between the Arabs and Byzantines. By occupying Constantinople, the capital of their Christian allies, in the Fourth Crusade, the Crusaders achieved what the Arabs had been trying to do from the early days of Islam. Although the Byzantine Empire continued until 1453, when Constantinople fell to the Ottoman Turks, it never recovered its former power after the Fourth Crusade, and subsisted only in the half-light of history during its remaining years.

For the West, however, the Crusaders' greatest achievement was the opening of the eastern Mediterranean to European shipping. The Venetians and Genoese established trading colonies in Egypt, and luxury goods of the East found their way to European markets. In the history of the Middle Ages, this was far more important than ephemeral conquests. Control of the Eastern trade became a constantly recurring theme in later relations between the European countries and the East, and in the nineteenth century was to lead to widespread Western intervention.

THE MONGOLS AND THE MAMLUKS: In the thirteenth century still another threat to the Muslim world appeared in the land beyond the Oxus: the Mongols. Led by Genghis Khan, a confederation of nomadic tribes which had already conquered China now attacked the Muslims. In 1220 they took Samarkand and Bukhara. By mid-century they had taken Russia, Central Europe, northern Iran, and the Caucasus, and in 1258, under Hulagu Khan, they invaded Baghdad and put an end to the remnants of the once-glorious 'Abbasid Empire. The ancient systems of irrigation were destroyed and the devastation was so extensive that agricultural recovery, even in the twentieth century, is still incomplete. Because a minor scion of the dynasty took refuge with the Mamluks in Egypt, the 'Abbasid caliphate continued in name into the sixteenth century. In effect, however, it expired with the Mongols and the capture of Baghdad. From Iraq the Mongols pressed forward into Syria and then toward Egypt where, for the first time, they faced adversaries who refused to quail before their vaunted power. These were the Mamluks, soldier-slaves from the Turkish steppe area north of the Black and Caspian Seas with a later infusion of Circassians from the region of the Caucasus Mountains.

The Mamluks had been recruited by the Ayyubids and then, like the Turkish mercenaries of the 'Abbasid caliphs, had usurped power from their enfeebled masters. Unlike their predecessors, however, they were able to maintain their power, and they retained control of Egypt until the Ottoman conquest in 1517. Militarily formidable, they were also the first power to defeat the Mongols in open combat when, in 1260, the Mongols moved against Palestine and Egypt. Alerted by a chain of signal fires stretching from Iraq to Egypt, the Mamluks were able to marshal their forces in time to meet, and crush, the Mongols at 'Ayn Jalut near Nazareth in Palestine.

In the meantime, the Mongols, like so many of the peoples who had come into contact with Islam, had begun to embrace it. At the dawn of the fourteenth century, Ghazan Khan Mahmud officially adopted Islam as the religion of the state, and for a time peace descended on the eastern portion of the Mongol empire. During this period the Mongols built mosques and schools and patronized scholarship of all sorts. But then, in 1380, a new Turko-Mongol confederation was hammered together by another world conqueror: Tamerlane, who claimed descent from Genghis Khan. Under Tamerlane, the Mongol forces swept down on Central Asia, India, Iran, Iraq, and Syria, occupying Aleppo and Damascus and threatening — but not defeating — the Mamluks. Once again, however, the Muslims survived their invaders. Tamerlane died on his way to conquer China, and his empire melted away.

Politically and economically, the Mongol invasions were disastrous. Some regions never fully recovered and the Muslim empire, already weakened by internal pressures, never fully regained its previous power. The Mongol invasions, in fact, were a major cause of the subsequent decline that set in throughout the heartland of the Arab East. In their sweep through the Islamic world the Mongols killed or deported numerous scholars and scientists and destroyed libraries with their irreplaceable works. The result was to wipe out much of the priceless cultural, scientific, and technological legacy that Muslim scholars had been preserving and enlarging for some five hundred years.

THE LEGACY: The foundation of this legacy was the astonishing achievements of Muslim scholars, scientists, craftsmen, and traders during the two hundred years or so that are called the Golden Age. During this period, from 750 to 950, the territory of the Muslim Empire encompassed present-day Iran, Syria, Iraq, Egypt, Palestine, North Africa, Spain, and parts of Turkey and drew to Baghdad peoples of all those lands in an unparalleled cross-fertilization of once isolated intellectual traditions.

Geographical unity, however, was but one factor. Another was the development of Arabic, by the ninth century, into the language of international scholarship as well as the language of the Divine Truth. This was one of the most significant events in the history of ideas.

A third important factor was the establishment in Baghdad of a paper mill. The introduction of paper, replacing parchment and papyrus, was a pivotal advance which had effects on education and scholarship as far-reaching as the invention of printing in the fifteenth century. It made it possible to put books within the reach of everyone.

The Mamluks, originally a class of soldier-slaves, seized power in Egypt in the thirteenth century and stood fast against the Mongols.

Unlike the Byzantines, with their suspicion of classical science and philosophy, the Muslims were enjoined by the Prophet to "seek learning as far as China" — as, eventually, they did. In the eighth century, however, they had a more convenient source: the works of Greek scientists stored in libraries in Constantinople and other centers of the Byzantine empire. In the ninth century the Caliph al-Mamun, son of the famous Harun al-Rashid, began to tap that invaluable source. With the approval of the Byzantine emperor, he dispatched scholars to select and bring back to Baghdad Greek scientific manuscripts for translation into Arabic at *Bayt al-Hikmah,* "the House of Wisdom."

Bayt al-Hikmah was a remarkable assemblage of scholar-translators who undertook a Herculean task: to translate into Arabic all of what had survived of the philosophical and scientific tradition of the ancient world and incorporate it into the conceptual framework of Islam.

As the early scholars in the Islamic world agreed with Aristotle that mathematics was the basis of all science, the scholars of the House of Wisdom first focused on mathematics. Ishaq

The fierce Tamerlane, one of history's greatest conquerors, is also remembered as a patron of architecture and the arts.

ANDALUSIA
Tangier
Granada
Cartagena
Barcelona
Marseilles
Genoa
Venice
Rome
BULGARIA
Constantinople
BLACK SEA
EMPIRE OF
Angora
Sinope
TRAPEZUNT
Trapezunt
Tiflis
Tabriz
Sultaniya
CORSICA
SARDINIA
Tunis
SICILY
BYZANTINE
EMPIRE
Athens
Smyrna
SELJUKS
Konya
Kayseri
CILICIAN
ARMENIA
ARMENIA
AZERBAIJAN
ALMOHADS
Kairouan
MEDITERRANEAN   SEA
CRETE
SYRIA
Aleppo
Mosul
Tigris River
Euphrates River
AL-JAZIRAH
Tripoli
Benghazi
Cyrene
CYPRUS
Homs
Damascus

Alexandria
Jerusalem
Cairo
M A M L U K S
EGYPT
Nile River
M A M L U K S

Aswan

Nile River

RED

Jiddah
Mecca

SEA

ETHIOPIA

THE MUSLIM WORLD IN THE MONGOL PERIOD

At the end of the thirteenth century the Mongols have swept across Asia, leaving devastation in their wake and creating for a brief time the greatest empire in history, stretching from Korea to Poland. Their advance has finally been checked by the Mamluks in Egypt, and the Mongol Empire starts to break up almost immediately, with Mesopotamia and Persia being ruled by the Il Khanid Dynasty of Mongols. In the west a Berber dynasty, the Almohads, rules in Morocco, and the Nasrids rule in the Kingdom of Granada, all that remains of the once extensive Umayyad domains in Spain. The Byzantine Empire never recovers after being occupied by the Crusaders in 1202, but the tiny Empire of Trapezunt, an offshoot of the Byzantine Empire, prospers from trade, having been bypassed by both the Seljuks and the Mongols. At the end of the century the Mamluks take Acre, ending Christian rule in the Levant and the era of the Crusades. Although Europeans no longer occupy territory in the eastern Mediterranean, its waters are open to their shipping and provide access to eastern trade.

A sophisticated water clock featured trumpeters, half life-size, who sounded the hour.

ibn Hunayn and Thabit ibn Qurrah, for example, prepared a critical edition of Euclid's *Elements,* while other scholars translated a commentary on Euclid originally written by a mathematician and inventor from Egypt, and still others translated at least eleven major works by Archimedes, including a treatise on the construction of a water clock. Other translations included a book on mathematical theory by Nichomachus of Gerasa, and works by mathematicians like Theodosius of Tripoli, Apollonius Pergacus, Theon, and Menelaus, all basic to the great age of Islamic mathematical speculation that followed.

The first great advance on the inherited mathematical tradition was the introduction of "Arabic" numerals, which actually originated in India and which simplified calculation of all sorts and made possible the development of algebra. Muhammad ibn Musa al-Khwarazmi seems to have been the first to explore their use systematically, and wrote the famous *Kitab al-Jabr wa-l-Muqabalah,* the first book on algebra, a name derived from the second word in his title. One of the basic meanings of *jabr* in Arabic is "bone-setting," and al-Khwarazmi used it as a graphic description of one of the two operations he uses for the solution of quadratic equations.

The scholars at *Bayt al-Hikmah* also contributed to geometry, a study recommended by Ibn Khaldun, the great North African historian, because "it enlightens the intelligence of the man who cultivates it and gives him the habit of thinking exactly." The men most responsible for encouraging the study of geometry were the sons of Musa ibn Shakir, al-Mamun's court astronomer. Called Banu Musa — "the sons of Musa" — these three men, Muhammad, Ahmad, and al-Hasan, devoted their lives and fortunes to the quest for knowledge. They not only sponsored translations of Greek works, but wrote a series of important original studies of their own, one bearing the impressive title *The Measurement of the Sphere, Trisection of the Angle, and Determination of Two Mean Proportionals to Form a Single Division between Two Given Quantities.*

The Banu Musa also contributed works on celestial mechanics and the atom, helped with such practical projects as canal construction, and in addition recruited one of the greatest of the ninth-century scholars, Thabit ibn Qurrah.

Mechanical figures atop a bloodletting device recorded the amount drawn from a patient.

During a trip to Byzantium in search of manuscripts, Muhammad ibn Musa happened to meet Thabit ibn Qurrah, then a money changer but also a scholar in Syriac, Greek, and Arabic. Impressed by Thabit's learning, Muhammad personally presented him to the caliph, who was in turn so impressed that he appointed Thabit court astrologer. As Thabit's knowledge of Greek and Syriac was unrivaled, he contributed enormously to the translation of Greek scientific writing and also produced some seventy original works — in mathematics, astronomy, astrology, ethics, mechanics, music, medicine, physics, philosophy, and the construction of scientific instruments.

Although the House of Wisdom originally concentrated on mathematics, it did not exclude other subjects. One of its most famous scholars was Hunayn ibn Ishaq, Ishaq's father — known to the West as Joanitius — who eventually translated the entire canon of Greek medical works into Arabic, including the Hippocratic oath. Later a director of the House of Wisdom, Hunayn also wrote at least twenty-nine original treatises of his own on medical topics, and a collection of ten essays on ophthalmology which covered, in systematic fashion, the anatomy and physiology of the eye and the treatment of various diseases which afflict vision. The first known medical work to include anatomical drawings, the book was translated into Latin and for centuries was the authoritative treatment of the subject in both Western and Eastern universities.

Others prominent in Islamic medicine were Yuhanna ibn Masawayh, a specialist in gynecology, and the famous Abu Bakr Muhammad ibn Zakariya al-Razi — known to the West as Rhazes. According to a bibliography of his writings, al-Razi wrote 184 works, including a huge compendium of his experiments, observations, and diagnoses with the title *al-Hawi,* "The All-Encompassing."

A fountainhead of medical wisdom during the Islamic era, al-Razi, according to one contemporary account, was also a fine teacher and a compassionate physician, who brought rations to the poor and provided nursing for them. He was also a man devoted to common sense, as the titles of two of his works suggest: *The Reason Why Some Persons and the Common People Leave a Physician Even If He Is Clever,*

Modern Arabic (western)	1	2	3	4	5	6	7	8	9	0
Early Arabic (western)										
Arabic letters used as numerals										
Modern Arabic (eastern)										
Early Arabic (eastern)										
Early Devanagari (Indian)										
Later Devanagari (tenth-century Sanskrit)										

ArabicNumerals

The system of numeration employed throughout the greater part of the world today was probably developed in India, but because it was the Arabs who transmitted this system to the West the numerals it uses have come to be called Arabic.

After extending Islam throughout the Middle East, the Arabs began to assimilate the cultures of the peoples they had subdued. One of the great centers of learning was Baghdad, where Arab, Greek, Persian, Jewish, and other scholars pooled their cultural heritages and where in 771 an Indian scholar appeared, bringing with him a treatise on astronomy using the Indian numerical system.

Until that time the Egyptian, Greek, and other cultures used their own numerals in a manner similar to that of the Romans. Thus the number 323 was expressed like this:

Egyptian	999	∩∩	III
Greek	HHH	△△	III
Roman	CCC	XX	III

The Egyptians actually wrote them from right to left, but they are set down above from left to right to call attention to the similarities of the systems.

The Indian contribution was to substitute a single sign (in this case meaning "3" and meaning "2") indicating the number of signs in each cluster of similar signs. In this manner the Indians would render Roman CCC XX III as:

CCC XX III
3 2 3

This new way of writing numbers was economical but not flawless. The Roman numeral CCC II, for instance, presented a problem. If a 3 and a 2 respectively were substituted for the Roman clusters CCC and II, the written result was 32. Clearly, the number intended was not thirty-two but three hundred and two. The Arab scholars perceived that a sign representing "nothing" or "nought" was required because the place of a sign gave as much information as its unitary value did. The place had to be shown even if the sign which showed it indicated a unitary value of "nothing." It is uncertain whether the Arabs or the Indians filled this need by inventing the zero, but in any case the problem was solved: now the new system could show neatly the difference between XXX II (32) and CCC II (302).

If the origin of this new method was Indian, it is not at all certain that the original shapes of the Arabic numerals also were Indian. In fact, it seems quite possible that the Arab scholars used their own numerals but manipulated them in the Indian way. The Indian way had the advantage of using much smaller clusters of symbols and greatly simplifying written computations. The modern forms of the individual numbers in both eastern Arabic and western Arabic, or European, appear to have evolved from letters of the Arabic alphabet.

The Semites and Greeks traditionally assigned numerical values to their letters and used them as numerals. This alphabetical system is still used by the Arabs, much as Roman numerals are used in the West for outlines and in enumerating kings, emperors, and popes.

The new mathematical principle on which the Arabic numerals were based greatly simplified arithmetic. Their adoption in Europe began in the tenth century after an Arabic mathematical treatise was translated by a scholar in Spain and spread throughout the West.

Architectural monuments spanning a thousand years bear witness to the spread of Islam. Seen at left is a unique fusion of Roman and Asian elements, Jerusalem's Dome of the Rock, built in 691-692. Continuing clockwise, facing page: Purity of line characterizes the late twelfth-century Kutubiyah Mosque of the Berbers in Marrakesh. Sixteenth-century Sultan Selim Mosque at Edirne is the apogee of Ottoman Turkish architecture, soaring space enclosed with a massive dome. Persia's greatest contribution to ornament, gloriously colored enameled tile, faces the dome and stalactite portal of Shaykh Lutf Allah Mosque, built in the early 1600s on Isfahan's vast royal plaza. The peak of Mogul architecture and possibly the most famous work of all times and cultures is the dazzling Taj Mahal mausoleum built at Agra in 1629. Above: Water courses and fountains make an oasis of the Alhambra palace built at Granada in the fourteenth century. Here incredibly light and elegant elements of Islamic decoration find their highest realization.

and *A Clever Physician Does Not Have the Power to Heal All Diseases, for That is Not within the Realm of Possibility.*

The scholars at the House of Wisdom, unlike their modern counterparts, did not "specialize." Al-Razi, for example, was a philosopher and a mathematician as well as a physician and al-Kindi, the first Muslim philosopher to use Aristotelian logic to support Islamic dogma, also wrote on logic, philosophy, geometry, calculation, arithmetic, music, and astronomy. Among his works were such titles as *An Introduction to the Art of Music, The Reason Why Rain Rarely Falls in Certain Places, The Cause of Vertigo,* and *Crossbreeding the Dove.*

Another major figure in the Islamic Golden Age was al-Farabi, who wrestled with many of the same philosophical problems as al-Kindi and wrote *The Perfect City,* which illustrates to what degree Islam had assimilated Greek ideas and then impressed them with its own indelible stamp. This work proposed that the ideal city be founded on moral and religious principles from which would flow the physical infrastructure. The Muslim legacy included advances in technology too. Ibn al-Haytham, for example, wrote *The Book of Optics,* in which he gives a detailed treatment of the anatomy of the eye, correctly deducing that the eye receives light from the object perceived and laying the foundation for modern photography. In the tenth century he proposed a plan to dam the Nile. It was by no means theoretical speculation; many of the dams, reservoirs, and aqueducts constructed at this time throughout the Islamic world still survive.

Muslim engineers also perfected the waterwheel and constructed elaborate underground water channels called *qanats.* Requiring a high degree of engineering skill, *qanats* were built some fifty feet underground with a very slight inclination over long distances to tap underground water and were provided with manholes so that they could be cleaned and repaired.

Agricultural advances are also part of the Muslim legacy. Important books were written on soil analysis, water, and what kinds of crops were suited to what soil. Because there was considerable interest in new varieties — for nutritive and medicinal purposes — many new plants were introduced: sorghum, for example, which had recently been discovered in Africa.

The introduction of numerous varieties of fruits and vegetables and other plants to the West via the Islamic empire was, however, largely the result of the vast expansion of trade during the Golden Age. This trade was vital; in the central lands of the 'Abbasid empire natural resources such as metals and wood were scarce, and increases in urban populations had outstripped the capacity of the agricultural system to support them. The 'Abbasids, therefore, were forced to develop extensive and complicated patterns of trade. To obtain food, for example, Baghdad had to import wheat from Syria and Egypt, rice from the Fayyum in Egypt, southern Morocco, and Spain, and olive oil from Tunisia. Called "a forest of olive trees," Tunisia exported so much olive oil that its port of Sfax was called "the port of oil."

To obtain scarce metals the 'Abbasids had to turn elsewhere. They imported the technologically advanced "ondanique" steel from India, for example, and then processed it at such famous centers of weapons manufacture as Damascus and Toledo, both of which cities won fame for their blades. The 'Abbasids also imported iron from Europe, tin from the British Isles and Malaya, and silver from northern Iran, Afghanistan, and the Caucasus. For gold, once the vast quantities in the treasuries of the conquered countries were exhausted, they turned to several sources. One was the gold mines of the Hijaz which were reopened around 750, reworked for about four hundred years, and then, in 1931, explored again by Karl Twitchell, who was searching for minerals in that area on behalf of King 'Abd al-'Aziz of Saudi Arabia.

For these necessities the 'Abbasid traders exchanged a wide variety of products: pearls, livestock, paper, sugar, and (a specialty of the Islamic world) luxurious cloth. The traditional cloths were wool and linen — the latter an Egyptian specialty since ancient times — but cotton, which was introduced into upper Iraq about the time of the Prophet, later spread with Islam around the Mediterranean, to Syria, North Africa, Spain, Sicily, Cyprus, and Crete.

The cloth trade produced a number of auxiliary exports: gold and silver thread for

At Hama in Syria, antique wooden wheels still lift the waters of the Orontes to gardens, baths, and cooling fountains.

embroidery, gum from the Sudan for glazing, and needles, looms, and dyestuffs. Closely connected with the trade in dyestuffs was the trade in medicines, an offshoot of 'Abbasid advances in medicine and the spread of hospitals in all major Islamic cities. As scientific research and translation of medical texts from India and possibly even China expanded the earlier pharmacopoeia, ingredients for medicines were brought from all over the known world and also reexported.

Because the religious, political, and military achievements of the Islamic period loom so large in the history of the world, the extraordinary cultural, scientific, technological, and commercial achievements are frequently obscured or overlooked. Yet these advances were, in fact, of enduring significance to mankind as a whole. The destruction by the Mongols of many of these achievements and of much of what the Muslims had accomplished by the end of the Golden Age was a tragic loss for the West and for the world as a whole.

THE OTTOMANS: During the second Mongol invasion, Tamerlane had met and very nearly annihilated another rising power: the Ottomans. Under a minor chieftain named Othman, groups of Turkish-speaking peoples in Anatolia were united in the Ottoman confederation which, by the second half of the fourteenth century, had conquered much of present-day Greece and Turkey and was threatening Constantinople.

The Ottoman state was born on the frontier between Islam and the Byzantine Empire. Turkish tribes, driven from their homeland in the steppes of Central Asia by the Mongols, had embraced Islam and settled in Anatolia on the battle lines of the Islamic world, where they formed the Ottoman confederation. They were called *ghazis,* warriors for the faith, and their highest ambition was to die in battle for their adopted religion.

In addition to their military abilities the Turks seem to have been endowed with a special talent for organization. Towards the end of the Ottoman Empire, this talent fossilized into bureaucracy — and a moribund bureaucracy at that. But at the beginning, when its institutions were responsive to the needs of the people and the state, the Ottoman Empire was a model of administrative efficien-

cy. This, together with a series of brilliant sultans — culminating in the redoubtable Suleiman the Magnificent — established the foundations of an empire that at its height was comparable to that of the Romans.

The first important step in the establishment of this empire was taken in 1326 when the Ottoman leader Orhan captured the town of Bursa, south of the Sea of Marmara, and made it his capital.

It was probably during the reign of Orhan that the famous institution of the Janissaries, a word derived from the Turkish *yeni cheri* ("new troops"), was formed. An elite corps of slave soldiers conscripted from the subject population of the empire, they were carefully selected on the basis of physique and intelligence, educated, trained, introduced to Islam, and formed into one of the most formidable military corps ever known. At a later period the Janissaries became so powerful that they made and unmade sultans at their will, and membership in the corps was a sure road to advancement.

Orhan's successor, Murad I, who launched naval attacks upon the Aegean coasts of Europe, established himself on the European shores of the Bosporus, and crushed a Balkan coalition. The next Ottoman leader was Bayazid I, who besieged Constantinople and routed the armies dispatched by an alarmed Europe to raise the siege.

It was at this point in history that Tamerlane and his Mongols advanced into Anatolia and very nearly crushed the Ottomans forever. They recovered, however, and later, under the leadership of a new sultan, Murad II, besieged Constantinople for the second time. They were repulsed, but by 1444 they had advanced into Greece and Albania, leaving Constantinople isolated though unconquered. Murad II was succeeded by Mehmed (Muhammad) II, called "The Conqueror" because on May 29, 1453, after his artillery finally breached Constantinople's massive walls, the city fell.

After the fall of Constantinople, and during the sixteenth century, the Ottoman system evolved the centralized administrative framework by which the sultans maintained effective control over the extraordinarily diverse peoples in the vast empire.

An important part of this framework was the *millet* system — essentially a division of the

The Janissaries, soldiers of an elite force organized by the Turks in the fourteenth century, were famed as the world's best-disciplined infantry.

The mosque at Kyustendil in Bulgaria was founded during Ottoman rule.

Vienna   Budapest HUNGARY   ROMANIA
                                                    CRIMEA   Azov
BOSNIA   Belgrade   Bucharest   CASPIAN SEA
Venice   Sarajevo SERBIA   BULGARIA   Istanbul   BLACK SEA   Tiflis   Baku
Algiers   Tunis   Arta   Izmir   Ankara   Sinope   Trebizond   Tabriz
                              Athens GREECE   Bursa   Konya   Kayseri   Sivas   Marash   ARMENIA
              MEDITERRANEAN   SEA   CRETE   CYPRUS   Antioch   Aleppo   Mosul
Tripoli   Tripoli   Hama   MESOPOTAMIA
        Benghazi   Haifa   Beirut   Homs   SYRIA   Euphrates R.
                                                    Jerusalem Damascus   Tigris River   Bag
        LIBYA   Alexandria   Port Said   Gaza
                O T T O M A N   Cairo   E M P I R E
                                        Suez
                                        SINAI   Aqaba
                                Nile River   al-Qusayr
                EGYPT
                                                                Yanbu   Med

                                Nile River   Jiddah   Mecca

                                                                RED

                                                                SEA

                                                        E T H I O P I A

THE OTTOMAN EMPIRE AT ITS GREATEST EXTENT

In the sixteenth century three Muslim empires are at or close to the pinnacle of their power and brilliance: the Ottomans under Suleiman the Magnificent, Safavid Persia under Shah Abbas the Great, and Mogul India under Akbar the Great. The Ottoman Turks have conquered and maintain effective control over diverse peoples in a vast empire stretching from Persia almost to the gates of Vienna and along the north coast of Africa to Algiers. In the Arabian Peninsula the Ottomans penetrate to al-Hasa on the Arabian Gulf and to Mocha on the Red Sea. However, the sharifs of Mecca and Medina are virtually independent. Throughout this period the Ottomans contest control of the Arabian Gulf and the Red Sea with the Portuguese, who establish themselves in Bahrain, Muscat, and Hormuz and assist Ethiopia in repulsing the Turks from the coast of East Africa.

Suleiman the Magnificent, his sovereignty stretching from Budapest to Baghdad and from Mesopotamia to Morocco, was the leading sovereign of the sixteenth century.

The Hijaz Railway, completed by the Turks in 1908, linked Damascus with Medina, eight hundred miles to the south.

Mustafa Kemal, also known as "Ataturk," was leader of the nationalist movement that established the secular Turkish Republic.

empire into a communal system based upon religious affiliation. Each *millet* was relatively autonomous, was ruled by its own religious leader, and retained its own laws and customs. The religious leader, in turn, was responsible to the sultan or his representatives for such details as the payment of taxes. There were also, however, organizations which united the diverse peoples. Particularly important were the guilds of artisans which often cut across the divisions of religion and location.

There was also a territorial organization of the empire, at the upper levels of which was a unit called the *muqata'ah* under the control of a noble or administrator who could keep some portion of the state revenues derived from it. The amount varied with the importance of the individual noble or administrator, and he could use it as he saw fit. Such rights were also given to some administrators or governors in place of, or in addition to, salaries, thus insuring a regular collection of revenues and reducing record keeping.

The Ottoman Empire reached its peak in size and splendor under the sultan called Suleiman the Magnificent, who ruled from 1520 to 1566 and was known to the Turks as Suleiman the Law-Giver. But from the middle of the sixteenth century on the empire began to decline. This process got under way as the office of the Grand Vizier gradually assumed more power and indifferent sultans began to neglect administration. Another factor was that the Janissaries became too strong for the sultans to control. The sultans were further weakened when it became customary to bring them up and educate them in isolation and without the skills necessary to rule effectively.

Some sultans later regained power through political maneuverings and by playing off factions against one another, but as a result administration was paralyzed. When Europe found a new route to India — thus eliminating the traditional transshipment of goods through the Arab regions of the empire, revenues began to fall, triggering inflation, corruption, administrative inefficiency, and fragmentation of authority.

Temporary reforms under various sultans, and the still formidable, if weakened, military prowess of the Ottomans helped maintain their empire. As late as 1683, for example, they besieged Vienna. Nevertheless,

the decline continued. Because of the increasingly disruptive part played by the Janissaries, the empire, in a series of eighteenth-century wars, slowly lost territory. Because of administrative paralysis, local governors became increasingly independent and, eventually, revolts broke out. Even the various reform movements were balked, and with the invasion of Egypt in 1798 by France it became obvious that the once powerful empire was weakening.

In 1824 Mahmud II finally broke the power of the Janissaries, brought in German advisers to restructure the army, and launched a modernization program. He also brought the semiautonomous rulers in various provinces under control, with the exception of the defiant and able Muhammad 'Ali in Egypt. On the death of Mahmud, his sons continued his efforts with a series of reforms called the *tanzimat*. Some of these were no more than efforts to placate European powers — which by then had great influence on the empire's policies — but others, in education and law, were important. Again, however, the effects were temporary and the empire continued to lose territory through rebellion or foreign intervention.

By the early years of the twentieth century the Ottoman Empire was clearly in decline and was referred to as the "Sick Man of Europe." There were, however, some positive accomplishments in this period, such as the Hijaz Railway. Building the railway was undertaken in 1900 by Sultan Abdul-Hamid, as a pan-Islamic project. Completed in 1908, it permitted thousands of Muslims to make the pilgrimage in relative comfort and safety. It also helped to give the Ottoman government more effective control over its territories in western Arabia.

During the early twentieth century too, a group called the Young Turks forced the restoration of the constitution (which had been suspended by Abdul-Hamid), eventually deposed the sultan, and again attempted to modernize the Ottoman state. The Turkish defeat in the First World War (in which the Ottoman Empire sided with Germany and the Central Powers) finally discredited the Young Turks, however, and paved the way for the success of a new nationalist movement under the leadership of an army officer named Mustafa Kemal, later known as Ataturk or "Father of the Turks." The nationalist government under Ataturk, dedicated to leading

Turkey in the direction of secularism and Westernization, abolished the sultanate, declared a republic, and eventually (in 1924) abolished the caliphate as well.

THE COMING OF THE WEST: The Western world had for centuries been gradually penetrating most of the areas that had once been part of the Muslim empire, and in the latter part of the nineteenth century, in the vacuum left by the long decay and decline of the Ottoman Empire, European powers came to dominate the Middle East.

Among the first Europeans to gain a foothold in the Middle East were the Venetians who, as early as the thirteenth century, had established trading posts in what are now Lebanon, Syria, and Egypt, and who controlled much of the shipping between Arab and European ports. Then, in 1497, five years after Ferdinand and Isabella ended Islamic rule in Spain, Vasco da Gama led a fleet of four Portuguese ships around Africa and in 1498 found a new sea route to India from Europe. Dutch, British, and French frigates and merchantmen followed and began establishing trading outposts along the shores of the Indian Ocean, eventually undercutting both Venetian shipping and the Mediterranean trade on which the Middle East had thrived for millennia.

The process of European penetration was gradual and complex; but there were, nevertheless, clearly identifiable turning points. In the sixteenth century, for example, the Ottoman Empire voluntarily granted a series of concessions called the "Capitulations" to European powers — concessions which gave the Europeans decided advantages in foreign trade in the empire. Another turning point was the invasion of Egypt in 1798 by Napoleon Bonaparte. Hoping to cut Britain's lines to India and cripple its maritime and economic power, Napoleon crushed the Mamluks (who governed Egypt under Ottoman suzerainty) and briefly occupied the country. By defeating Egypt, then still part of the Ottoman Empire, Napoleon exposed the inner weaknesses, both military and administrative, of the sultans, shattered the myth of Ottoman power, and inaugurated more than 150 years of direct political intervention by the West.

Europe's worldwide nineteenth-century search for raw materials, markets, military bases, and colonies eventually touched most of what had been the Arab empire. In 1820 Great Britain imposed a pact on Arab tribes on the coast of the Arabian Gulf; in the 1830s France occupied Algeria; in 1839 Britain occupied Aden, at the strategic entrance to the Red Sea; and in 1869 Ferdinand de Lesseps, with the backing of the French emperor, completed what would become, and still is, one of the key shipping arteries of the world, the Suez Canal.

Western culture spread with Western economic and political control. In Lebanon missionaries from several countries founded a network of schools and universities. By introducing modern Western ideas these fostered the growth of Arab nationalism, contributed to the revival of Arabic literature, and provided a powerful impulse toward modernization. In addition to education, contact with the West led to improvements in medical care and the introduction of Western techniques in agriculture, commerce, and industry. For the most part, however, Western domination tended to benefit the nations of Europe at the expense of the Arab world. Although the Suez Canal, for example, has been of immense value to Egypt, the profits for nearly a century went to European shareholders in the company that managed the canal. Western and Western-stimulated efforts to modernize parts of the Middle East, moreover, often led Middle Eastern rulers to incur debts which led to European financial control and then to European political domination. It was such a series of steps that ended with France occupying Tunisia in 1881 and Britain taking control of Egypt in 1882. Later, in emulation, Italy in 1911 seized Libya.

Resistance to European penetration took several forms. In the cities, Arab intellectuals debated whether modernization or a return to their roots would be the more effective path to the removal of foreign dominance and, consequently, to independence. Elsewhere, Muslim leaders such as the Mahdi in the Sudan and 'Abd al-Qadir al-Jazairi in Algeria took direct action. These struggles were later romanticized and distorted in a wave of books and films on, for example, Gordon of Khartoum and the French Foreign Legion. Still other intellectuals, such as the Egyptian Muhammad 'Abduh and his Syrian disciple Rashid Rida, undertook to reform the Muslim educational

When Vasco da Gama sailed a new sea route from Europe to India, he was guided by an illustrious Arab navigator.

Charles George Gordon, earlier nicknamed "Chinese Gordon," died while leading British forces in the Sudan.

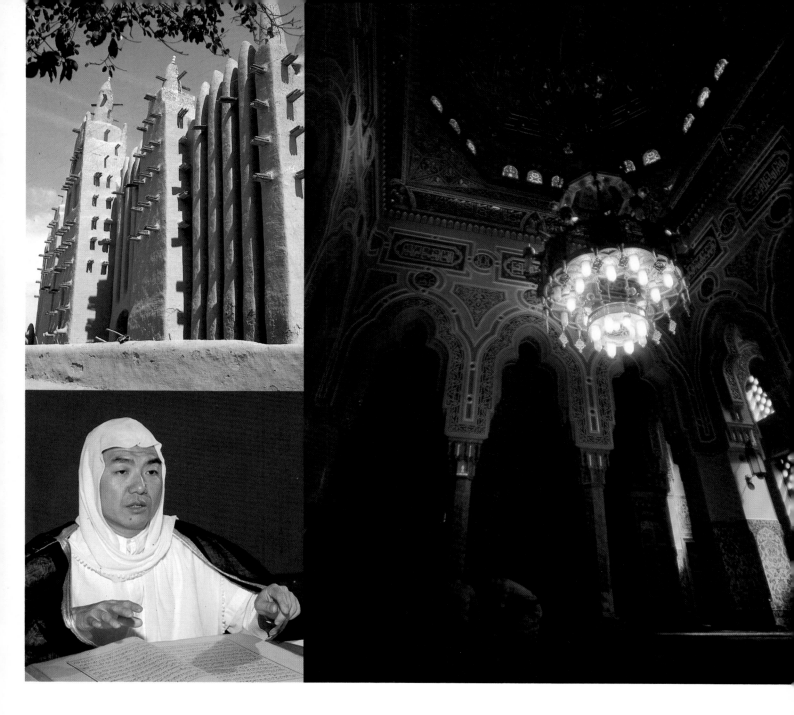

Islam numbers many millions of adherents outside the Middle Eastern countries. At top, this page, is the Mopti Mosque in the West African republic of Mali. The religious teacher directly above is Taiwanese. At top right is the mosque in Washington, D.C., a landmark for the two million Muslims of North America. Right: Sunset silhouettes a minaret in Sarajevo, Yugoslavia, a city of some eighty mosques that bear witness to the long Islamic heritage of Bosnia and Herzegovina. Facing page: One of the largest mosques of the Far East is in Bandar Seri Bagawan, capital of the Sultanate of Brunei in Southeast Asia.

system and to restate Islamic values in terms of modern concepts — needs deeply felt by most Muslim thinkers of the nineteenth and twentieth centuries.

Western penetration also drew the Middle East into the First World War, when the Ottoman Empire sided with Germany, and Great Britain, in response, encouraged and supported the Arab Revolt against the Turks. By promising aid — and ultimate independence from the Ottomans — Great Britain encouraged the Arabs to launch a daring guerrilla campaign against Turkish forces, a campaign widely publicized in press coverage of T. E. Lawrence ("Lawrence of Arabia") and in Lawrence's own writings.

Arab attacks against the Turks, in which the British soldier-scholar known as "Lawrence of Arabia" played a well-publicized role, were a valuable contribution to the victory of the Allied forces in the Middle East in World War I.

Lord Balfour, British Foreign Secretary in 1917, issued the historic declaration which promised British support for a Jewish "national home."

By diverting Turkish strength and blocking the Turkish-German route to the Red Sea and India, the Arab Revolt contributed substantially to the Allied victory, but it did not result in full independence for the Arab lands. Instead, France and Great Britain secretly agreed to partition most of the Arab provinces of the Ottoman Empire between them and eventually obtained mandates from the League of Nations: Britain over Iraq, Palestine, and Transjordan; France over Syria and Lebanon. The mandates were inconsistent with British promises to the Arabs and, furthermore, contrary to the recommendations of President Wilson's King-Crane Commission, a group sent to the Middle East in 1919 specifically to ascertain the wishes of the Arab peoples.

The mandates, however, were granted, thus extending Western control of the Middle East and also setting the stage for one of the most tragic and intractable conflicts of modern times: the conflict over Palestine which has, since 1948, ignited four wars, sent masses of Palestinian Arabs into exile, contributed to the energy crisis of 1973, and, from 1975 on, fueled the civil war in Lebanon.

The conflict over Palestine actually goes back to 1896, when Theodor Herzl published a pamphlet called *Der Judenstaat* ("The Jewish State"), in which he advocated British-backed Jewish colonization in Argentina or Palestine — with the hope of eventually creating a sovereign Jewish state. Herzl's writings and personal advocacy led to the formal development of Zionism, a political movement dedicated to the creation of such a state, and eventually focusing on Palestine. The Zionist

claim to Palestine was mainly based on the fact that there had been periods of Hebrew rule in Canaan and the land west of the Jordan River between 1300 B.C. and A.D. 70.

The Arabs considered this claim to be without substance. Palestine, they pointed out, had been part of the Islamic world almost continually for twelve centuries; from 636 to the First World War. In 1917, however, Lord Balfour, the British Foreign Secretary, issued the Balfour Declaration, which promised British support for the establishment of a "national home for the Jewish people" in Palestine providing that "nothing shall be done which may prejudice the civil and religious rights of existing non-Jewish communities" — a reference to the Arabs, who then were 92 percent of the population. The declaration was interpreted by key Zionist leaders as support for a sovereign Jewish state, but this interpretation has been disputed. Both Winston Churchill and Lord Balfour himself later said publicly that "a national home" meant a cultural or religious center, a view that America's King-Crane Commission independently presented. Establishment of a national home did not imply a Jewish state, the commission said.

In the wake of the Balfour Declaration, and during the British mandate, Jewish immigration increased. So, in proportion, did sporadic strife between Arabs and Jews. Immigration nevertheless continued and in the 1930s — with the rise of Adolf Hitler — and after World War II, Jewish immigration increased still further. As British efforts to control it generated widespread disapproval in the West and stimulated underground warfare by militant Zionist units against British forces, Britain eventually placed the problem in the hands of the United Nations, which in 1947 voted to partition Palestine into Jewish and Arab States.

Fighting then flared up in Palestine. Six months later, when Britain withdrew and formation of the State of Israel was proclaimed, the Arabs went to war against the newly declared nation. As Jewish forces were victorious — and as stories spread that some 250 Arab civilians had been massacred in a village called Deir Yassin — thousands of Palestinians fled, among the first of today's 3.4 million refugees and exiles. Eventually the United Nations negotiated a truce, but fighting became endemic and war broke out again in 1956, 1967, and 1973. The 1967 war triggered underground warfare by Palestinian militants, whose attacks were primarily aimed at Israel, but also included strikes in Europe and hijackings on international air routes.

In order to settle the conflict, numerous United Nations Resolutions have been passed calling for peace, the return of the refugees to their homes, Israeli withdrawal from occupied territories, and the establishment of permanent boundaries. Several Western nations have attempted mediation, a Palestinian spokesman has argued the matter before the General Assembly of the UN, and in 1977 President Sadat of Egypt traveled to Jerusalem and appeared before the Israeli parliament in an unprecedented peace initiative. President Carter of the United States brought the leaders of Egypt and Israel together in the United States and himself traveled to the Middle East in an attempt to persuade at least these two countries to conclude a peace treaty, and in March 1979 Egypt and Israel signed a treaty to which the United States was also a signatory. Although it led to an improvement in Egyptian-Israeli relations which resulted in Israeli evacuation of some occupied Egyptian territory and the opening of the Suez Canal to Israeli ships, however, this separate peace treaty did nothing to bring about withdrawal of Israeli occupation forces from East Jerusalem, the West Bank, and the Golan Heights of Syria and left untouched the root cause of the entire problem — that is, the status of the Palestinians. The immediate net result of the treaty, in fact, was a general increase in tension in the Middle East which manifested itself in an apparent increase in Israeli intransigence in the occupied territories and the isolation of Egypt from the rest of the Arab world, including those countries on which it has been most heavily dependent for economic and political backing and which were opposed to the separate treaty because it failed to achieve a permanent and comprehensive peace.

REVIVAL IN THE ARAB EAST: Elsewhere in the Arab world, meanwhile, the last vestiges of European political dominance were being eliminated. Egypt, for example, after ousting in 1952 a royal dynasty going back to the 1800s and installing Gamal Abdel Nasser as president, forced the British to relinquish control of the Suez Canal and withdraw from the country. Algeria, ten years later, won its independence from France after six years of bitter warfare. Even earlier, Iraq, Syria, and Lebanon had broken their ties with Britain and France.

This tumultuous period also saw an increase in the influence of the United States and the Soviet Union in the Middle East. Neither power had played a major role in the early phases of penetration, but this changed as they developed conflicting interests with regard to the Arab-Israeli dispute, the construction of the Aswan Dam in Egypt, the rise of a number of radical governments in the area, and the emergence of the Arab world as a pivotal supplier of oil to the world.

Inaugurated in 1971 amid hopes it would revolutionize the life of Egypt, the Aswan High Dam is, in its own way, a monument as great as any left by the pharaohs.

In the same period, the Arab countries themselves, voluntarily and pragmatically, continued to adopt Western techniques, forms, and to some extent concepts. Most Arab countries, for example, have embraced the concept of the sovereign nation-state and Western patterns of political administration: parliaments, political parties, and constitutions. Many, too, have adopted Western legal codes, have accepted international and regional organizations and international courts as means of dealing with other nations, and have organized and equipped their armed forces along Western lines. In recent years, most Arab countries have also adopted the modern industrial economy as a national goal and introduced modern techniques of agriculture and modern methods of transport and mass communications, and invested vast sums in education. Even in recreation and amusement, Western influences are strong.

If Western influences are important in the Middle East, however, they are by no means paramount. Western forms have been adapted as much as they have been adopted, and healthy hybrid forms and concepts abound. More importantly, traditional values are still deeply cherished and promoted. In sum, modernization has not been entirely synonymous with Westernization. By the end of the 1970s the Arabs, having assumed control of their own destinies, had emerged as full and independent participants in the affairs of the world. In the forefront was Saudi Arabia, the heartland of Islam, and the site of the momentous events which initiated Islamic history fourteen centuries ago.

Chronological Chart

	600	622	700	800	900	1000	1100	1200
al-Andalus		VISIGOTHS		UMAYYAD AMIRATE		CALIPHATE OF CORDOBA	MANY SMALL DYNASTIES	
Morocco				IDRISIDS			ALMORAVIDS	ALMOHADS
Algeria			KHARIJIS			HAMMADIDS		
Tunisia		BYZANTINES		AGHLABIDS		ZIRIDS		
Libya						FATIMIDS		
Egypt		CALIPHS	'ABBASIDS		TULUNIDS			AYYUB
Arabian Peninsula		RIGHTLY GUIDED	UMAYYADS			QARMATIANS	SELJUKS	
Greater Syria					TULUNIDS	IKHSHIDIDS FATIMIDS	CRUSADERS FATIMIDS	
						HAMDANIDS		
Iraq	SASSANIANS			'ABBASIDS			SELJUKS	'ABBA
Persia				SAFFARIDS	BUWAYHIDS			GHURIDS
Transoxania				TAHIRIDS	SAMANIDS		QARAKHANIDS KHWARAZM-SHAHS	
						SELJUKS		GHURIDS
Afghanistan						GHAZNAVIDS		
India					PRE-ISLAMIC RULERS			
Asia Minor				BYZANTINES				SELJUKS
Balkans				PRE-ISLAMIC RULERS				

622, BEGINNING OF THE ISLAMIC ERA

100

Of Islamic History

	1300	1400	1500	1600	1700	1800	1900	1980

CHRISTIAN SPAIN AND PORTUGAL . *

NASRID KINGDOM OF GRANADA

MARINIDS — WATTASIDS — SA'DIS — 'ALAWIS — SPANISH

PORTUGUESE

ABD AL-WADIDS — FRENCH

HAFSIDS — OTTOMANS — ITALIAN — INDEPENDENT

MAMLUKS — MUHAMMAD 'ALI'S LINE — BRITISH — M.A. LINE

RASULIDS
LOCAL SHAYKHS AND AMIRS — AL SA'UD — AL SA'UD — AL SA'UD

MAMLUKS — OTTOMANS — FR.

AQ QOYUNLU — OTTOMANS — BRITISH

MAMLUKS

MONGOLS — SAFAVIDS — SHAH — INDEPENDENT

UZBEK AND KAZAK KHANATES — RUSSIAN

TIMURIDS — SAFAVIDS — NADIR — AFGHAN DYNASTIES

DELHI SULTANS — DELHI SULTANS — MOGULS — BRITISH — INDPT
BAHMANIDS

OTTOMANS — TURKISH REPUBLIC

INDEPENDENT

	1300	1400	1500	1600	1700	1800	1900	1980

STRIPING INDICATES AREA OF PARTIAL OR INTERMITTENT CONTROL

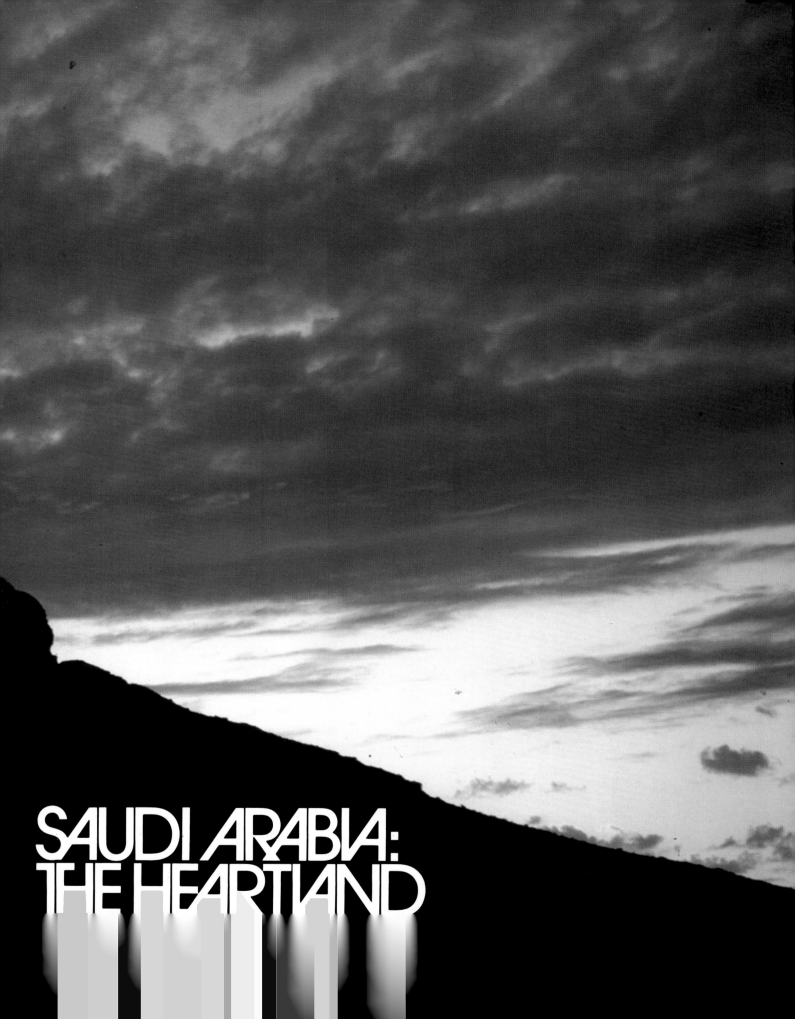

SAUDI ARABIA: THE HEARTLAND

Salt flats called *sabkhahs* — sometimes partly covered by encroaching sand — are a common sight in low-lying areas.

Hummocks of sand held by desert shrubs characterize *dikakah* terrain.

Massive sand dunes of the Rub' al-Khali.

In the history of Saudi Arabia, location, terrain, and climate have all been significant factors. Because the peoples of the Arabian Peninsula were cut off from Africa and Iran by narrow seas and separated from the northern civilizations by difficult terrain, and because they lived, to a large extent, in or by forbidding deserts, they developed cultures in relative isolation from those of the Tigris, Euphrates, and Nile river valleys. Coupled with a harsh climate and the peninsula's particularly demanding terrain, this isolation substantially affected what is now Saudi Arabia. Nevertheless Arabia belongs to and is part of a huge and relatively uniform geographical unit stretching from the west coast of Africa across six thousand miles to the Indus Valley.

The Arabian Peninsula is shaped like the head of an axe, the butt attached to the Asian continent in the north and the edge facing the Arabian Sea, an arm of the Indian Ocean. In the west the Red Sea divides the peninsula from Africa and in the east the Arabian Gulf divides it from Iran.

Close to the Red Sea coast, a range of mountains drops sharply toward the sea on the west, while eastward the land slopes gradually across the greater part of the peninsula to the Arabian Gulf. Near the center of Arabia the slope is interrupted by a series of parallel escarpments, like folds in a piece of cloth, with steep western faces; but on the eastern side the land again assumes a gentle slope until, on the shores of the Arabian Gulf, it merges almost imperceptibly with the sea. There are local mountains, gravel plains, buttes and mesas, great stretches of sand, lava fields, oases, and a network of great and small wadis — river beds that are usually dry. There are mountains too along the southern coast, in southern Yemen, and in Hadhramaut and Oman farther to the east.

Geographically the Arabian Peninsula may be divided into a number of regions, each characterized by distinctive terrain: the coasts, the sand deserts, the plateaus, the escarpments, and the mountains.

ARABIAN GULF COASTAL REGIONS: The strip of land bordering the western and southern parts of the Arabian Gulf is low and sandy — no part of it is more than a few hundred feet above sea level — and the configuration of the coast is extremely irregular. For some distance from the coast the sea is shallow and full of shoals and in many places the waterfront shifts back and forth over several miles at the whim of tide and wind. Shallow fords connect some islands with the mainland at low tide, while under some conditions coastal flats are covered by the sea for miles inland. Sand spits often change their form as a result of wind and waves.

One feature commonly found in this area is the salt flat — called *sabkhah* in Arabic. Salt flats occur in depressions in which water, a few feet below the surface, evaporates and leaves a deposit of salt. This salt, mixed with sand, forms a crust a few inches deep which, above the moisture level, dries into a flat surface. In dry weather the surface, sometimes cracked into irregular shapes, provides excellent driving for automobiles. But when rain falls the sabkhahs turn into impassable morasses; after a short period of drying they form a thin, deceptively dry crust hiding the mud below.

The northeastern coast of Arabia, from Jubail to Kuwait Bay, consists primarily of low, rolling plains covered with a thin mantle of sand which supports bushes and grass — sparse in some places, dense in others. The roots hold the sand in hummocks forming terrain called in Arabic 'afjah or dikakah. West of Kuwait this bumpy terrain merges with the gravel plains of the Dibdibah through which the broad valley called al-Batin runs northeast to the channels of the Tigris and Euphrates. In early days al-Batin was a main route between Iraq and the heart of Arabia.

From Jubail southward lies a fairly wide belt of drifting sand piled up into large dunes. Widening to the south, this belt merges with the sand area known as the Jafurah, which in turn runs into the great sand desert of the Rub' al-Khali, "the Empty Quarter" — the region of the highest and most impressive dunes in the peninsula and one of the great sand areas of the world.

The sands of the Jafurah lie upon flat gravel plains called *hadabahs*, which emerge east of the sands near al-'Uqayr, an old port of the Gulf. To the west of the sands, the plains spread out in broad, gravelly sheets from the oasis of al-Hasa in the north to an area some distance south of Yabrin. Scrub palms, and green oases such as Qatif and al-Hasa, break the monotony of the barren land and show the presence of water under the sand.

West of the coastal strip sands extends a barren plateau called the Summan, 50 to 150 miles wide, where old stream channels and other forms of erosion have cut the hard rock plain into irregular terrain. From this plateau isolated buttes and mesas as well as extensive tablelands project into the coastal lowlands.

THE GREAT NAFUD AND THE DAHNA:
In the north of the peninsula lies an expanse of reddish sand, known as the Nafud, covering approximately 22,000 square miles and reaching almost to the Jordan border. *Nafud* is the term used for a sand region in the northern part of Saudi Arabia, and what is known to Westerners as the Great Nafud is called simply *al-Nafud* by the Bedouins. It contains a few watering places and affords good grazing for camels, sheep, and goats in winter and spring.

From the Great Nafud in the north a great arc of sand, one of the distinctive geographical features of Saudi Arabia, sweeps down to the Rub' al-Khali in the south. The middle of this arc, a long narrow belt of sand called the Dahna, is approximately 800 miles long. The sands here are from medium to fine in grain, and the color, because of iron oxide (hematite) stain, approaches a deep orange, especially in the morning and late afternoon light. Trailing off to the south of the Great Nafud and generally parallel to the Dahna are other large stretches of sand lying west of the Tuwayq Escarpment.

THE EMPTY QUARTER:
In the southern part of Saudi Arabia is the immense body of sand known as the Rub' al-Khali or Empty Quarter. Occupying a basin bordered by the mountains of Oman on the east, the plateau behind the coastal escarpments on the south, and the foothills of the mountains of Yemen and 'Asir on the southwest, the Rub' al-Khali is approximately 750 miles long and has a maximum width of nearly 400 miles. It covers an area of about 250,000 square miles (bigger than France, Belgium, and Holland together) and is the largest continuous body of sand in the world.

The sands of the Empty Quarter are not all of one type. Some areas are covered by comparatively stabilized sand sheets. Across other areas mobile dunes move with the prevailing winds and are shaped by the winds into varying forms. Dunes may be star-shaped, dome-shaped, or crescent-shaped. Masses of sand sometimes form long single or parallel veins or ridges — 'uruq in Arabic — and sand mountains of complex arrangement attain heights of from 500 to 800 feet.

Most of the Rub' al-Khali is uninhabited except during the infrequent rains, when Bedouins move in to take advantage of the pasturage. A few parts support scattered nomads, especially along the regular north-south crossing which follows a string of water wells between longitudes 50° and 52° east. Bedouins also frequent the northeastern section, which contains many wells of salty water satisfactory for the watering of camels. The Bedouins call the area *al-Ramlah* or *al-Rimal*, the words for sandy areas. The Rub' al-Khali, formerly crossed only by hardy Bedouins, was one of the last regions on earth to be explored by Westerners. Bertram Thomas, the first such explorer, made a trip in 1931 from Salalah on the Arabian Sea to the peninsula of Qatar on the Arabian Gulf. In 1932 H. St. John Philby explored the central and northwestern portions, which he described in his book *The Empty Quarter*. Yet another Englishman, Wilfred Thesiger, made several trips through unexplored parts of the Rub' al-Khali from 1945 onward.

NORTHERN SAUDI ARABIA:
The northern region of Saudi Arabia, lying between the Great Nafud and the Jordan and Iraq borders, is geographically part of the great Syrian Desert. It is made up of rock, gravel plains, and lava beds.

The plateau between the northern extremity of the Great Nafud and the junction of the borders of Saudi Arabia, Jordan, and Iraq attains an elevation of 2,900 feet and forms the divide between the drainage east to the Euphrates and west to Wadi al-Sirhan, a great depression 200 miles long, 20 to 30 miles wide, and 1,000 feet below the level of the plateau. For thousands of years one of the most important trade routes connecting the Mediterranean and central Arabia passed through Wadi al-Sirhan and the oasis of al-Jawf.

ESCARPMENT REGION:
West of the sands of the Dahna lies Najd, the heartland of Saudi

The rocky Summan plateau parallels the coastal lowlands.

The narrow Dahna sand belt stretches in a long arc from the Great Nafud southward to the Rub' al-Khali.

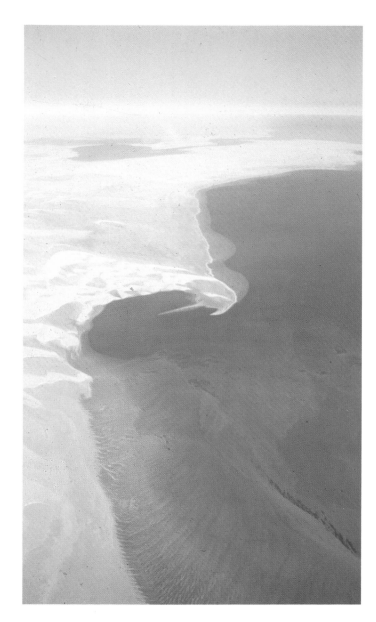

Saudi Arabia, while arid for the most part, exhibits a varied geography that in places belies its sand desert image. Rugged on the western side, with stark peaks rising boldly from a narrow coastal plain, the land tilts roughly eastward until, sandy and low, its soft edge merges almost imperceptibly with the waters of the Gulf. Most spectacular are the southwestern coastal highlands of 'Asir, seen at left above, where bare mountains of jagged igneous rock some 10,000 feet high plunge to terraced green fields and cultivated lowland valleys. Below, far left: Sinuous dunes of the Rub' al-Khali often interconnect in a network of overlapping sand ridges to form a nearly impenetrable barrier to the south; not until this century was the region crossed by travelers other than hardy Bedouins. Center: Eroded limestone formations break the monotony of the central plateau region as several parallel escarpments curve through central Arabia in a generally north-south direction; most prominent is the Tuwayq Escarpment, whose cliffs seen here rise an average of 2,800 feet above sea level. Left: Lines of deep-rooted tamarisk trees keep dunes from engulfing farmland at the oasis town of Buraydah in northern Najd, where fingers of sand project south from the Great Nafud desert. Directly above: Sea, sand, and shallow shoals blend into graceful patterns along the eastern shore of the peninsula where, from the air, it is sometimes difficult to tell where the land ends and the water begins.

Arabia. About 200 miles wide, this region is dominated by several escarpments which are steep on the western side with gentle eastern slopes; among them are the 500-mile-long Tuwayq Escarpment and the 'Aramah Escarpment. The Tuwayq Escarpment has an average elevation of 2,800 feet above sea level with a maximum of 3,500 feet. The top of the escarpment is about 800 feet above the level of the plains to the west. Sedimentary formations that outcrop along the eastern watershed of the Tuwayq Escarpment include the water-bearing strata that support irrigation works of important agricultural areas on the plains to the east, such as al-Kharj. The 'Aramah Escarpment, about 1,800 feet above sea level, is less imposing; it is only about 400 feet higher than the plain to the west of it.

Water from deep springs supports rich agricultural development in the al-Kharj area.

The remaining escarpments, which are roughly parallel to the two dominant ones, are lower and not so long. Some, however, appear to be major elevations when contrasted with the adjacent featureless plains.

CENTRAL PLATEAU REGION: Within the arc formed by the Great Nafud and the Tuwayq Escarpment, and reaching as far as the western coastal mountains, lies a broad central plateau about three hundred miles wide. Most of this area is part of the ancient land mass of Arabia and was not covered by the sea which deposited layers of sediment that make up the surface of eastern Saudi Arabia. The rocks of the central plateau are largely of igneous and metamorphic origin, and over its western half there are extensive lava beds of comparatively recent date.

The elevation of the central plateau ranges from 3,500 to 4,500 feet, although there are depressions as low as 3,000 feet and ridges higher than 6,000 feet. The plateau has a gentle, gradual slope eastward from the coastal mountains. Short streams of high gradient have carved deep gorges in the steep-walled western flanks of the coastal range. Longer patterns of drainage have developed on the gentler eastern slopes. Of the latter, the greatest is Wadi al-Rumah, which through its extension, al-Batin, runs northeast to the vicinity of Basra in Iraq. Three large valleys, Ranyah, Bishah, and Tathlith, join to flow in times of flood into Wadi al-Dawasir, which trends eastward to the Rub' al-Khali.

Wildlife

The Arabian Peninsula is the habitat of a surprising variety of mammals, insects, reptiles, and birds; and the Arabian Gulf, as a five-year marine biology survey in the 1970s showed, plays host to possibly four thousand species of marine life.

MAMMALS: Some of the peninsula's more beautiful mammals, unfortunately, now exist only in the most isolated areas and others survive only in zoos. Once, for example, three species of gazelles — called in Arabic, the *rim*, the *'ifri*, and the *idm* — roamed the plains and sands of Arabia in large herds and the oryx *(Oryx leucoryx)* — the antelope which may have given rise to the unicorn legends — ranged widely through the Rub' al-Khali and the Great Nafud deserts. By the mid-1950s, however, hunters using trucks and cars had almost exterminated the gazelle, and few, if any, oryx now exist outside the zoos or private herds in Qatar and other Gulf states and in Arizona and California. Jackals and two species of desert fox still survive, as do the ibex, or mountain goat, the wolf, the striped hyena, the baboon, the leopard, and possibly the cheetah, though all of these except the jackal and the fox are rare. The list of the peninsula's larger mammals also includes a unique wild goat known as the Arabian tahr; it inhabits cliff faces in the mountains of Oman where a national park is being planned to preserve it from extinction. There are still occasional sightings of leopards in the highlands of southwestern Arabia and Oman.

The desert hedgehog is well protected with a coat of sharp spines.

Arabia's smaller mammals include the strikingly patterned black-and-white ratel or honey badger; the hyrax — a plump, furry, rodent-like vegetarian the size of a beaver; the mongoose; the porcupine; and the desert hedgehog. There are small hedgehog populations in some Aramco communities and they make charming, if shy, pets. Hares, smaller than American jackrabbits, are found throughout the country and are still often hunted in the traditional way — with falcons and salukis.

One of the most interesting desert mammals is the

ubiquitous jerboa, which resembles the American kangaroo rat and is its ecological equivalent. Described by Charles Doughty in his classic *Arabia Deserta* as "a small white aery creature... of a pitiful beauty," it is also one of the most highly adapted desert mammals; at least two species of jerboa can move about and survive in true sand desert, hopping on their hind legs. Sand cats, two species of spiny mouse, gerbils, *jirds* (sand rats), and bats also inhabit the deserts.

BIRDS: Bird life is also surprisingly extensive. Vultures, partridges, and ravens are common in Arabia, as is the owl — which some Bedouins say was originally a wailing woman, seeking her lost child in the wilderness. Along the coasts there are flamingos, egrets, pelicans, cormorants, and many smaller shore birds. In the oases the most common bird is the white-cheeked bulbul, a songbird with a sulfur-yellow bottom. There is also an occasional ring-necked parakeet, with its raucous screech and distinctive long tail. The hoopoe — cinnamon-colored, with a handsome black-and-white crest — is broadly accepted as a harbinger of the rainy winter season, and the plaintive voice of *Umm Salim,* the two-striped lark, is familiar to desert travelers, as are sightings of the crested lark and desert lark.

Until he moves, this winter visitor is nearly invisible against the brush.

Altogether, more than two hundred and fifty non-native bird species from all over the Palearctic region winter in Arabia or pass across the peninsula on their way to wintering grounds in Africa, and their seasonal presence brightens the watered localities of the kingdom. Cuckoos, thrushes, warblers, swallows, wagtails, and wheatears, along with hordes of shore birds and waterfowl, are among the seasonal migrants.

Eagles, hawks, and falcons — especially kestrels — fly wild in many parts of Saudi Arabia, and falcons are trapped and trained for hunting, which is still to some extent the sport of the ordinary Bedouin as well as of the rich and noble in Arabia. As a conservation measure, the Government of Saudi Arabia has outlawed hunting of game birds and most animals with firearms, thus limiting hunting to falconry.

Typically, a falcon's quarry includes the houbara bustard *(Chlamidotis undulata;* Arabic *hubara),* the hare, sand grouse, doves, quail, and the stone curlew. Once

common in Saudi Arabia, the ostrich was last reported shot in the north of the kingdom in 1938; it weighed three hundred pounds and covered the ground in nine-foot strides. Though fragments of ostrich-egg shells are still sometimes found in the desert, it seems certain that the bird is extinct on the Arabian Peninsula.

REPTILES: Arabia also has some forty species of land snakes, most of which are harmless. In the Eastern Province the sand boa, Gray's whip snake, the Arabian leaf-nosed snake, the variable sand snake, and the diademed sand snake are common varieties. Also harmless, if alarming to see, is the Moila snake, a rear-fanged species *(Malpolon moilensis)* that is sometimes mistaken for a hooded cobra. Although it belongs to a different family altogether, the Moila snake spreads its neck and raises its head in the way a cobra does. But although its venom is effective against the small rodents, the snake is not considered dangerous to man.

The sand boa is common in sandy areas of the Eastern Province.

There are some venomous snakes in Saudi Arabia, however. One, fairly common in the Eastern Province, is the sand viper *(Cerastes cerastes).* Its bite, however, is rarely fatal; nearly all victims recover without special medical attention. This snake is also called the horned viper, but less than half of them actually have "horns" — raised scales above the eyes. Desert travelers occasionally see this viper's distinctive track in the sand; the trace is discontinuous and consists of series of evenly spaced J-like marks, for the snake is a sidewinder. Because it is a nocturnal reptile, the viper itself is rarely seen.

One highly venomous reptile is the black cobra *(Walterinnesia aegyptia).* A hoodless variety of cobra, this six-foot, blue-black to tar-black snake is dangerous, but fortunately it is also very rare or very shy and only seven specimens have been reported from Saudi Arabia. Bedouin folklore has it that the black cobra can change itself at will into any other shape it chooses — a camel, a woman, a horse — and does so in order to lure humans to their doom. The true cobra, the hooded variety, has been reported in the western parts of Saudi Arabia along with the puff adder. Another venomous reptile is the sea snake, common to the warm waters of the Arabian Gulf. Sea snake venom is potentially lethal, but sea snakes, although sometimes

(Continued on page 110)

Wildlife

curious, are shy and tend to avoid swimmers and skin divers. Furthermore, the snake's mouth is too small, and its gape too narrow, to bite humans effectively.

Sea snakes, fortunately not aggressive, are often seen in the Gulf.

Because Saudi Arabia is an arid land, many lizards can also be found there. None are poisonous. One common type is the *dabb* or spiny-tailed lizard, a heavy-bodied plant-eating species that grows to a length of twenty inches. Usually lethargic, but cantankerous when disturbed, it can run very fast and uses its armored tail like a club to defend itself. To avoid capture, the dabb runs to its deep, spiral burrow or sometimes wedges itself into a rock crevice and inflates its body with deep breaths. According to the Bedouins, dabb meat tastes like chicken.

Another type of lizard is the longer but slimmer *waral,* or desert monitor, a carnivore related to the Komodo dragon. The waral is aggressive and very agile, with relatively long legs. Although Bedouins eat the dabb, they will not eat the waral. There is also the fascinating *tuhayhi,* a small agamid lizard which, if chased, can disappear almost magically into the sand by vibrating its body and sinking under the surface, leaving only a faint line in the sand. Its blocky head, like that of an American horned toad, and its black-tipped tail identify him. Lacertid lizards are common too, especially *Acanthodactylus;* with rows of scales projecting from its toes like oars, this six-inch long lizard can move with the speed of an arrow as it darts from bush to bush.

With a nearly translucent body, the gecko has a natural camouflage.

Another interesting Arabian lizard is the five-inch long sand-swimming skink whose smooth submarine-shaped body and tapering snout enable it to swim through the sand as a fish does in water — and with similar movements of its body. It inhabits sand desert, particularly the steep slip-faces of active dunes. The sand skink is called *dammusah* in Arabic and the scientific name of one species, *Scincus philbyi,* commemorates H. St. John B. Philby, the British explorer of Arabia.

Other lizards are the pale beige or pink, almost translucent geckos, soft-bodied small lizards with fleshy tails and adhesive toes — welcome guests in some houses in Arabia because of their efficiency in hunting insects; and the *nadus,* a reddish, legless lizard, which lives under the sand surface, its eyes reduced to nearly functionless dots. The nadus is harmless, and may die in a few minutes if exposed to direct desert sun.

AQUATIC ANIMALS: As there are virtually no rivers or lakes and few swamps in lowland Saudi Arabia, freshwater animals are not many and are largely limited to the Caspian turtle and the frog — both seen frequently in oasis irrigation ditches — and the four-inch killifish *(Aphanius dispar),* which is found in springs in the Qatif and al-Hasa oases and in small ponds formed by water from the springs. Recently a smaller African freshwater fish was introduced into local irrigation ditches because it feeds on mosquito larvae. Several species of other freshwater fish are found in highland streams and pools in 'Asir.

Streamlined, fast-swimming jacks frequent the Gulf coastal reefs.

Life in the seas around the Arabian Peninsula, however, is rich and varied; sports fishing and spearfishing, as a result, are popular pastimes. One of the most common of the Arabian Gulf gamefish is the *hamur,* a dark-colored grouper, slightly speckled and similar in form to a bullhead and weighing up to thirty pounds. Its meat is like that of the sea bass and it lives under rock ledges near the coasts. Another is the *kan'ad,* a silver-colored king mackerel which reaches twenty pounds and is a hard fighter on the line. The meat resembles that of the halibut in color. Others are the *qidd,* the barracuda — which attains a length of four feet and a weight of twenty pounds — and the *sayyafi,* the sawfish. Increasingly rare, the sawfish weighs up to several hundred pounds and is caught near the shore during the spawning season.

Other fish commonly caught by trolling are the *jihabah,* a variety of tuna; and the *subayti,* sometimes caught with a hook but more often by spearing. Scuba divers can sometimes pick up quantities of delicious spiny lobsters or sea crayfish.

Whales and dolphin are occasionally seen in the Gulf too; they enter from the Indian Ocean. There are also several species of sharks that are relatively common.

Altogether, according to a recent study of the Gulf's marine biology, there are in the Gulf some four thousand species of marine life — including fish, echinoderms, mollusks, and algae. The study, made over approximately five years by four marine biologists, was sponsored by Aramco as part of a continuing audit of the environment in its area of operations. Its results were published in 1977 under the title *Biotopes of the Western Arabian Gulf: Marine Life and Environments of Saudi Arabia*. Among the findings were some fifteen hundred species of marine life previously unreported in the Gulf.

INSECTS: Few of the peninsula's insects have economic importance. Wild bees exist in the 'Asir province and some farmers of the Eastern Province keep hives. Some of the most common insects are either pests or plagues. Locusts, for example, periodically devastated crops and wild vegetation over huge areas until the Government of Saudi Arabia, in cooperation with international agencies, began to monitor the growth of locust populations and suppress incipient swarms. Mosquitoes, which spread malaria, and swarms of flies were also major problems until, after World War II, the government launched extensive pesticide-spraying programs in the Eastern Province. Perhaps the insect most commonly encountered in the deserts of Arabia is the dung beetle. Barely able to fly, it is very industrious on the ground, collecting balls of dung in which to lay its eggs. There is also a variety of arachnids: the scorpion, the velvety red rain mite, small jumping spiders, and the hairy *shabath*, a sun spider or solifuge, also known as the camel spider. A nocturnal arachnid, it is harmless but as it is also aggressive and large — up to six-inches in diameter — it is often mistaken for a tarantula.

The fat-tailed scorpion, like other species, moves primarily by night

Scorpion stings are painful but rarely, except perhaps in cases of very young children, pose a threat to life. The black "fat-tailed scorpion," *Androctonus crassicauda*, is one of the more common species seen in eastern Saudi Arabia. Several other species, yellow or yellow-green in color, may also be encountered. Scorpions are nocturnal and are seldom seen until their sand burrows or under-stone haunts are disturbed. Avoiding barefoot walking at night eliminates most of the risk of being stung.

Watering places in the central plateau are few and far between, though the high elevation draws more rainfall than comes to the regions to the east. The area is sparsely populated except in the north between the depression of Wadi al-Rumah and the southern edge of the Great Nafud. In the region of the mountain ranges of Jabal Shammar lies the great oasis of Hayil with its many dependent towns and villages.

The oasis of Hayil lies just south of the Great Nafud.

THE MOUNTAINS: Along the eastern shore of the Red Sea stretches a coastal plain confined by mountains dropping sharply toward the sea; it is called Tihamah, sometimes divided into Tihamat al-Hijaz, Tihamat 'Asir, and Tihamat al-Yaman. The abrupt western drop of the coastal range is the result of a break or fault in the crust of the earth, between the land masses of what are now Arabia and Africa, into which poured the Red Sea. The Red Sea, as a result, is deep, but as there are numerous shoals near the Arabian shore the coast affords few good natural harbors. The best are at Jiddah, which is the port of Mecca, Yanbu' and al-Wajh in the north, and Jaizan in the south. In southern Yemen the best ports are Aden on the southern coast of the peninsula and, further east, Mukalla in Hadhramaut.

Between the Gulf of Aqaba to the north and Mecca, the coastal mountains are seldom higher than 7,000 feet and generally do not exceed 4,000 feet. But in 'Asir and Yemen they are much higher. Southeast of Mecca several peaks are more than 8,000 feet high and elevations continue to rise in the south, reaching their highest point — about 12,000 feet — west of San'a, the capital of Yemen. Continuing on, to fringe the southwestern margin of the peninsula, the mountains average 6,000 to 8,000 feet, while eastward the elevations decrease to 3,000 feet in Dhufar, except for a peak 4,800 feet high north of the port of Mirbat. The mountains of southern Arabia are composed essentially of sedimentary rock dipping gently northward into the Rub' al-Khali basin, with the southern slopes irregular and precipitous.

Terraced fields are cultivated in the mountain valleys of 'Asir.

Between the eastern extension of the mountains of Dhufar and the southern part of the ranges of Oman, there is a plateau some hundred and fifty miles long that averages 500 feet in height. Then come the mountains of Oman, known as al-Hajar, with conspicuously

The prince of Arabian wildlife is the falcon, trapped and trained for the centuries-old art of hunting in which these spectacular aerial performers catch their prey by sheer speed and often in a power dive. The Saker species above, *Falco cherruq,* is prized for its keen eyesight; next to it is the bustard called hubara, *Chamydotis undulata,* a plump wide-winged game bird conspicuous in flight but nearly invisible on the ground. Directly above: Tree frog, *Hyla savignyi,* and a colorful species of beetle. At left: Waral, *Varanus griseus,* a powerful, predatory thirty-inch monitor lizard. Opposite page: Red Sea coral reef, world famous for the variety of its undersea life; starfish, *Pentaceraster mammillatus,* a gaudy species with no two members quite the same color; green sea turtle, *Chelonia mydas,* which breeds on Arabian Gulf islands; "sand bubbler" crab, *Scopimera scabricauda,* found in millions on tidal sandbanks. Drawings depict the graceful gazelle and larger oryx, both members of the antelope family now rarely seen, and a tiny hedgehog.

Steep north face of the Omani mountains presents a formidable barrier.

rugged topography; elevations reach 10,000 feet in the central massif of the Jabal al-Akhdar (the Green Mountain). Sweeping westward and northward roughly parallel to the Gulf of Oman, the mountains in the area, with steep slopes both seaward and toward the inland plateau, are very unlike the mountains on the western and southern sides of the Arabian Peninsula, which are characterized by steep slopes on the seaward side and gentle slopes toward the interior.

CLIMATE: Weather conditions in Arabia vary almost as much as the terrain. In the mountains that fringe the peninsula on the west, south, and southeast, annual rainfall is about twenty inches and there are often torrential downpours and destructive flash floods; yet the Rub' al-Khali may receive no rain for as long as ten years. In the interior the air is dry while on the coast summer humidity is excessive, particularly at night. In summer, temperatures in some areas may exceed 120°F in the shade, but in the spring the days are balmy and the nights are clear, and in winter temperatures drop below freezing in the central and northern regions and snow sometimes falls in the mountains, the northern plateau, and even on rare occasions in the capital, Riyadh. There are also strong winds such as the prevailing northwest winds along the eastern coast — the winds called the *shamal* — which frequently whip up dust and sandstorms.

The climate of the peninsula, nevertheless, is largely characterized by aridity and heat. As a result the vegetation, wild life, and domesticated animals of the peninsula share one distinctive feature: a high degree of adaptability to the special demands of life in the desert. The ability of men to adapt and survive in this harsh environment has had important effects on the history of the peninsula and Saudi Arabia.

ARABIA IN THE ISLAMIC ERA: Because of the outward impetus of Islamic expansion in the seventh and eighth centuries, and the overshadowing historical importance of the brilliant civilizations that were established in Syria, Iraq, al-Andalus, and elsewhere, the history of much of the Arabian Peninsula between the death of the Prophet and the rise

Plants

Most of Saudi Arabia is part of the great desert biome that stretches eastward six thousand miles from the Atlantic coast of North Africa to the Indus Valley. Within this zone, which plant geographers call the "North African-Indian desert floristic region," the terrain and climate are relatively uniform — and so, as a result, is the plant life. The extreme south of the Arabian Peninsula, Yemen, the mountains of Oman, and the highlands of 'Asir, because of their higher altitude and different climate, host a different range of species.

Some areas, such as the central and western deserts, support scattered acacia trees, and in the southwestern highlands there are true forests of juniper and wild olive trees — now under government protection. There are also oases and other areas where man has planted such trees as tamarisks for windbreaks. Most plants, however, are small annual herbs or low shrubs that have adapted to the hot, usually dry climate.

Plants have adapted to the Arabian climate in various ways. Some have "learned" to store water in fleshy stems or in roots buried deep in cooler sands. Most limit their surface area by seasonally restricting the number and size of leaves — through which water would evaporate — and some, additionally, secrete a waxy covering to stems or leaves to reduce evaporation. Others have leaf surfaces covered with fine hairs which both reflect heat and cut down on water losses. Some species, known generally as halophytes or saltplants, have evolved a tolerance to salty soils and mineral-rich water that would kill their unadapted relatives.

Many plants produce well-protected seeds that, in some cases, can remain dormant for years if necessary, and then germinate and sprout rapidly. Most of them live out their entire life cycle in one rainy season that may be only a few weeks long.

Another characteristic of Saudi Arabia's vegetation is the small number of species that exist. The Eastern Province, for example, has only about four hundred and fifty native plants, while the considerably smaller Lebanon-Palestine area — which borders on several different floristic regions and where the landforms are very varied — has over thirty-five hundred species. This small number of desert species reflects the difficulties faced by plants in adapting to such a harsh environment. A third feature of Arabian desert vegetation is the rarity of what botanists call "endemic species": plants that are peculiar to the area and are found nowhere else. Most of the species apparently did acacia • rhanterium • broomrape • calligonum • horwoodia • Thompson

not arise in the area but gradually migrated to it, as they adapted, from neighboring regions.

Of the plants that have adapted to conditions in the Arabian desert, those common enough to be conspicuous are few. In eastern Arabia, a sedge *(Cyperus conglomeratus)* and a perennial grass *(Panicum turgidum)* are common in the coastal sands. Further inland, the 'arfaj shrublet *(Rhanterium epapposum)* is the dominant species over hundreds of square miles, while a saltbush called *rimth (Haloxylon salicornicum)* covers the ground in poorly drained areas where the groundwater is salty. Both 'arfaj and rimth provide important pasturage to camels, with the saltbush supplying the salt that grazing animals need.

Southwestern Arabia has native cactus-like plants, but these are euphorbias and stapelias, not true cacti, which are not native to the Old World. The few species of prickly pear *(Opuntia)* that are now found in the Middle East — and sometimes in the flowerbeds of the Aramco oil communities — were introduced by travelers.

Although some Bedouins formerly ate a score or more different wild herbs in times of famine, none are now important as food. *Samh,* the seeds of a fleshy leaved *Mesembryanthemum,* are still sometimes collected and ground into flour for making bread in northern Arabia, while desert truffles, not identical with the European species, are considered a delicacy by Saudi Arabs and Westerners alike during their brief season.

Some desert plants have scientifically proved medicinal value, though claims made for many other folk remedies are yet to be confirmed. *Boswellia* and *Commiphora* trees, whose frankincense and myrrh were transported to the West more than two thousand years ago from southern Arabia, still grow in Dhufar and Hadhramaut. But the chief economic value of the desert vegetation is as pasturage for grazing livestock.

As if to compensate for the harsh conditions they must survive, many desert plants have flowers of a beauty out of all proportion to their modest numbers and small size. Fragrant bright yellow spikes of broomrape — a root-parasitic plant sometimes called "desert candle" — color the spring roadsides in eastern Arabia, and the delicate desert camomile grows in scattered carpets on the sand. Further north and west, on the rocky steppes, dense growths of wild iris brighten the depressions where rain

pools have lain; elsewhere tiny yellow lilies grow, and the mauve *khuzama (Horwoodia dicksoniae),* a member of the mustard family whose scientific name commemorates the botanical work of Dame Violet (Mrs. H. R. P.) Dickson of Kuwait. The fruiting of the *'abal* bush *(Calligonum comosum)* marks the height of the spring flowering season on the deep sands. This leafless woody shrub is valued as firewood by desert travelers, but the winter rains bring out pale pink flowers and by late spring the bush is covered with a brilliant trimming of scarlet fruits.

The small annual but woody *kaftah,* or *kaff Maryam* (Mary's hand), known to botanists as *Anastatica hierochuntica,* figures in Arabian folklore. Its small branches drop their leaves at the end of the spring and roll inwards like closing fingers, enclosing and protecting the seeds in a firm brown ball. With the first rain, or when placed in water, the ball opens completely and drops the seeds for germination. It is likened in Arab tradition to the hand of Christ's mother, clenched in the pains of childbirth.

What is probably the most familiar, and valuable, plant on the peninsula, however, is the date palm *(Phoenix dactylifera),* traditionally the most important single cultivated plant of the entire North African-Indian desert region. The limits of distribution of this tree, like those of the single-humped camel, coincide almost exactly with the boundaries of the desert biome. Throughout this zone it provides a staple food as well as valuable wood and fiber by-products still sometimes used for weaving and thatching. It is so much a part of life in Saudi Arabia that it is included as part of the royal emblem.

Other domesticated plants include wheat, barley, sorghum, and millet — the chief grains grown in Arabia — and alfalfa, a common oasis crop grown for feed. Cotton, rice, melons, grapes, pomegranates, oranges, and other tree fruits are also cultivated, and in recent years adapted varieties of a wide range of vegetable crops have been introduced and enthusiastically accepted. On the high terraces of 'Asir, the once profitable coffee plant has virtually disappeared. Coffee is still grown in the mountains of Yemen, but it has been supplanted there to some extent by the more profitable *qat (Catha edulis)* whose leaves, when chewed, are mildly narcotic. In southern Arabia there is also some cultivation of the dyestuffs henna, safflower, and indigo.

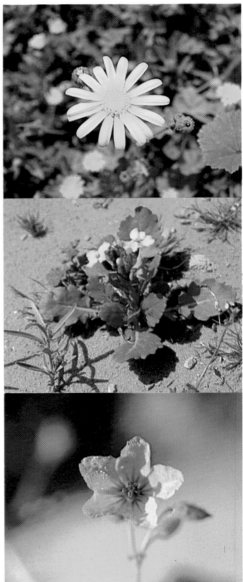

Essentially all of a given year's rain in Saudi Arabia —
except in the mountainous southwest — falls between November and May and not infrequently in a
few violent downpours that may be the season's sum
total. After such rains in early springtime, wadis,
depressions, and flat sandy areas suddenly burst
into color with the bloom of wild annuals in remarkable variety. Directly above, from top: The daisy-like
Senecio desfontainae; lavender *Diplotaxis acris,* the
flower seen in profusion in the adjacent field; a dainty
pink cranesbill from the same family as the geranium.
Facing page, far right: The fragrant mauve *Harwoodia
dicksoniae,* one of the few flowering plants endemic
to Arabia, and the striped *Onoborychis ptolemaica.*
The most important cultivated plant is the date palm,
Phoenix dactylifera, numbering probably three million in the Eastern Province alone. At left: A lone
acacia tree stands amid miles of a summer-blooming
bush of the family *Compositae,* which in several
varieties is characteristic of silt basins of the interior.

in the eighteenth century of the reform movement headed by Muhammad ibn 'Abd al-Wahhab is not adequately chronicled. Yet Arabia continued to play an important role during this long period.

In the course of expansion, many tribesmen flocked to the banner of Islam. Soon men born and raised in the peninsula could be found stationed from the borders of China to the shores of the Atlantic. As many tribes moved to the new lands, the political center of the Muslim world shifted from Medina to Damascus and later to Baghdad (see Chapter 2), and the Arabian Peninsula, relatively isolated from the great events occurring in Syria and Iraq, receded in political importance. Mecca and Medina, however, continued to play a paramount role in the life and culture of the Islamic community. Mecca, of course, had been an important entrepôt in the pre-Islamic period. Now, as the goal of the hajj, the Muslims' holy pilgrimage, it also became important in the spread of ideas. Inevitably, pilgrims from every province of the new Islamic empire would discuss recent developments and establish contacts in faraway lands. Medina, first capital of the empire, adopted home of Muhammad after the Hijrah and site of the Mosque of the Prophet, naturally drew thousands of new Muslims eager to see the scene of Muhammad's activities and those of his successors.

White headdress of a Muslim in the Philippines identifies him as a *hajji*, one who has made the pilgrimage to Mecca.

Medina, consequently, became a center of learning in which the early Muslim scholars gathered and organized the vast body of traditions — the hadith — going back to the Prophet himself. It was a natural impulse to seek as much information as possible about every aspect of life in the city of the Prophet in order to comprehend fully the language and content of the traditions. These gave invaluable testimony on the known practices of the Prophet, and formed the sunnah, which together with the Quran provided the main bases of the shari'ah, the sacred law of Islam (see Chapter 2).

The heartland of the Islamic faith, therefore, did not lose its importance during the Umayyad and 'Abbasid periods. Umayyad caliphs rebuilt the Mosque of the Prophet and the 'Abbasids devoted a great deal of time and money to providing civic amenities in Mecca and Medina and along the pilgrimage route from Baghdad to the Hijaz. The Caliph Harun al-Rashid and his wife Zubaydah made nine pilgrimages, and Zubaydah saw to the construction of an aqueduct to bring drinking water to Mecca. She also constructed a series of wells and caravanserais along the route from Baghdad to Mecca, which has been known ever since as *Darb Zubaydah* or "the Road of Zubaydah."

The Arabs of the peninsula continued to play an important role in the spread of Islam. Merchants from southern Arabia for example, brought the new faith into East Africa and islands of the Indian Ocean. Even today, in the tranquil backwaters of Quilon and Cochin on the Malabar coast of India, small communities of Muslims may be found — many proudly tracing their genealogies back to families originally from Oman, Hadhramaut, Yemen, or the Hijaz.

Islam spread to Java and the Philippines in similar fashion. According to tradition, the first Muslims arrived at Jolo Island in the Sulu Archipelago in 1380 on a Chinese junk bound for Canton and began to spread the teachings of the Prophet.

In the intervening centuries, meanwhile, the sharifs of Mecca, direct descendants of the Prophet, had established themselves in Mecca and made this city, rather than Medina, politically dominant in the Hijaz. In their early years the sharifs were independent rulers, but from the twelfth century on they became to a degree dependent upon the rulers of Egypt to keep the pilgrimage routes to Mecca and the trade routes of the Red Sea and across the peninsula secure. As a result, Mecca continued to be not only the holiest city of Islam but also a prosperous center of trade, especially during the pilgrimage season. The well-known twelfth-century Andalusian traveler Ibn Jubayr visited it and reported that "from all parts produce is brought to it, and it is the most prosperous of countries in its fruits, useful requisites, commodities, and commerce.... Not on the face of the world are there any goods or products but that some of them are in Mecca...."

Such prosperity, however, also attracted the attention of the Crusaders, who by then had established themselves at the eastern end of the Mediterranean. In 1181 Reynaud de Châtillon, master of the castle of Karak near the Dead Sea, attacked a pilgrim caravan in northern Arabia. The following year he sent a fleet into the Red Sea, intending to attack Medina. Ibn Jubayr, who arrived in Mecca shortly after this event, says:

> They had then sailed forth to harass (Muslim) pilgrims … went on to 'Aydhab where they caught a ship coming with pilgrims from Jiddah. On the land they seized a large caravan journeying from Qass to 'Aydhab and killed all in it, leaving none alive. They captured two ships bringing merchandise from the Yemen and burnt many foods prepared on the beaches as provisions for Mecca and Medina — God exalt them. Many infamous acts they committed …. The worst, which shocks the ears for its impiousness and profanity, was their aim to enter the City of the Prophet — may God bless and preserve him — and remove him from the sacred tomb ….

The Crusaders, as it turned out, were repulsed by a Muslim fleet and the raiders were captured. But the expedition, nevertheless, was of greater significance than it might seem. For although the attack was essentially part of the religious conflict of the period, it was also a faint distant harbinger of the coming age of Western colonial expansion.

In 1256 Hulagu Khan, a grandson of Genghis Khan, crossed the Oxus River and entered the lands of Islam. Two years later Baghdad fell before the Mongol hordes and the caliph was put to death. For several years there were no pilgrim caravans from Iraq, but as peace settled over the land the caravans to Mecca resumed.

In succeeding years, Mecca continued to receive visits from the various rulers who came to hold power in the Islamic world. One was Mansa Musa of Mandingo, a new Muslim kingdom far away in West Africa, whose arrival in Mecca in 1325 caused a sensation. His baggage train, it was said, contained a hundred camel-loads of gold, each weighing three hundred pounds, and his arrival in Mecca reminded Muslim pilgrims from other lands that despite the Mongols and the Crusades, Islam was still expanding.

Muslim rulers also continued to give financial support for the maintenance of the Holy Places. In the late fifteenth century Qait-Bay, a Mamluk sultan of Egypt, helped the sharifs of Mecca repair and restore the mosques and public buildings of Mecca and Medina. The aqueduct built earlier by Zubaydah was cleaned and repaired, the inner chamber of the Ka'bah was faced with marble, and four centers — one for each of the four canonical schools of Islamic law — were opened, along with a new almshouse for the relief of indigent pilgrims.

CARAVANS TO MECCA: It was during this period too that the organization of the caravans to Mecca took its classical form. The caravans were highly organized, for in those days nothing could be left to chance in the deserts of Arabia. They were led by an official called *Amir al-Hajj*, the commander of the pilgrimage, who had the absolute authority of a ship's captain at sea. Under him were a troop of soldiers, outriders, and guides, who were charged with defending the pilgrims from attack; notaries, a judge and secretary; an official charged with the care of the animals and another in charge of provisions; a saddler, a chef with a full staff of cooks, and even an inspector of weights and measures to make sure no pilgrim was cheated along the way.

The caravans marched at night, traveling until sunrise, in order to avoid the heat of the day. During the cooler months they would then rest and set off again later, riding until it was time to say the evening prayer. But during the summer, when travel in the afternoon was impossible, the caravans would move only at night.

The caravan was divided into three parts — an advance guard, the main body, and a rear guard. As many as eight outriders who knew the lay of the land would precede the advance guard, and at night each man in the advance guard carried a torch to guide those who came behind. In the main body of the caravan — which usually traveled a quarter of a mile behind the advance guard — there would be physicians, spare camels for carrying the sick and infirm, and next, a camel carrying an elaborate litter covered with silk, in which rested a beautifully inscribed Quran, a gift to Mecca. In one of the caravans this was followed by fifteen more camels carrying the various sections of the *kiswah*, the embroidered silk covering for the Ka'bah, renewed each year. These camels with their precious burdens were accompanied by a group of

Painting by a Damascus artist depicts pilgrim caravans from Egypt and Syria meeting at 'Arafat in 1905. The sumptuously decorated litters carried equally sumptuous gifts for the Holy Mosque in Mecca.

musicians, who played marching songs throughout the journey.

There were several main caravan routes to Mecca. Pilgrims from Turkey assembled in Istanbul and slowly marched across the Anatolian plateau, gathering pilgrims from every town through which they passed. In Damascus they joined the pilgrims from Syria, then crossed northern Arabia and angled south to Medina and Mecca. This was the same route later followed by the Hijaz Railway from Damascus to Medina, which after its completion in 1908 carried thousands of pilgrims from Turkey and Syria to the Hijaz.

Pilgrims from Iraq assembled in Baghdad and followed "the Road of Zubaydah," which passed near the present pump station of Rafha on the Trans-Arabian Pipe Line (Tapline), crossed Najd directly to Medina, and picked up the main road to Mecca.

A third route, used by pilgrims from Egypt, ran along the Red Sea coast of Arabia, which was more plentifully supplied with water than the routes across north-central Arabia.

The pilgrims coming by these routes converged on Mecca where they joined other pilgrims who had traveled overland across Africa or sailed west from India and the East Indies, thus linking Arabia, the religious heartland of Islam, with Muslims in the rest of the Islamic world.

Until the nineteenth century, the main routes of the pilgrim caravans to Mecca were overland from Cairo, Damascus, and Baghdad.

THE FOREIGN INTRUSION: In the early sixteenth century the Muslims of Arabia were feeling a new impact of Western intrusion into the Middle East: by then Vasco da Gama had pioneered the new ocean route from Europe to India (see Chapter 2) and other European powers were beginning to build trading stations and otherwise establish themselves along the Arabian Gulf and the Red Sea.

In Arabia the effect of the European expansion was at first slight. But the Portuguese were well aware of the commercial importance of Jiddah, the port of Mecca. As one traveler wrote to Portugal, "Jiddah... is the most prosperous commercial center in the whole of the Red Sea." They tried, therefore, to secure a foothold on the Red Sea and, when that failed, turned to the far side of Arabia, where in 1507 they captured Hormuz, at the mouth of the Arabian Gulf, and Muscat — and then Bahrain in 1521. Close on the heels of the

High above the bay at Muscat stands the fort built by the Portuguese in the sixteenth century.

Portuguese came the Dutch, the English, and the French, all attempting to establish trading posts and to control ports. In 1649 the Omanis expelled the Portuguese from Muscat, built up a fleet of their own, and restored a degree of Arab control over the Gulf.

The Ottomans (see Chapter 2), who had become the major power in the Islamic world, spared neither money nor pains to beautify Mecca and Medina, and the sister of Suleiman the Magnificent financed another renovation and repair of Mecca's always precarious water supply. Later, under Selim II, the architect Sinan — considered by some authorities to have been as creative an architect as Michelangelo — renovated the Sacred Mosque in an undertaking that would endure until the Kings of Saudi Arabia, Sa'ud and Faysal, commissioned still more extensive renovations in the twentieth century.

MUHAMMAD IBN 'ABD AL-WAHHAB: In the early eighteenth century, in Najd, the central region of Arabia, the man was born who would in alliance with the House of Sa'ud pave the way for the establishment of the modern Kingdom of Saudi Arabia. His name was Muhammad ibn 'Abd al-Wahhab. The son of a *qadi*, a religious judge versed in the shari'ah law (see Chapter 2), Muhammad ibn 'Abd al-Wahhab was born and grew up in a town called al-'Uyaynah north of Riyadh. Later he studied in Mecca and Medina and then spent some time in Basra and in al-Hasa before returning to Najd. At the end of this period of study Shaykh Muhammad ibn 'Abd al-Wahhab had become familiar with the currents of religious thought and the great political and social problems of his time. By then too he had concluded, from his observations of the world and his wide reading, that reforms were imperative.

Muhammad ibn 'Abd al-Wahhab, on his return, was particularly appalled by the superstitions of both the town dwellers and tribesmen of Najd and their devotion to the cult of local saints, which had grown up in many areas of the Islamic world — encouraged perhaps by the isolation of many outlying regions from the centers of Islamic orthodoxy. He began to call for a return to basic principles of Islam as contained in the Quran and the sunnah.

Shaykh Muhammad was the very opposite of an innovator. He was a *salafi*, a traditionalist, and certainly did not intend to found a new sect of Islam, or even to make a new interpretation of its basic teachings. He believed in a return to Islam as presented in the Quran, a perception of the unimpaired and inviolate oneness of God. Anything that conflicted with that unity was to be denounced as *shirk*, polytheism — that is, unlawful association of anyone or anything with God.

Muhammad ibn 'Abd al-Wahhab followed the Hanbali School of Islamic law. The chief influence on him was the thirteenth-century theologian Ibn Taymiyah who, as a modern interpreter has put it, "bowed to no authority higher than the Quran, tradition and the practice of the community and lifted his voice high against innovation, saint worship, vows, and pilgrimages to shrines."

Like most reformers Shaykh Muhammad ran into opposition. He was driven from al-'Uyaynah and forced to take refuge in the town of al-Dir'iyah very close to present-day Riyadh. In ruins today, the old town of al-Dir'iyah was located on high ground above Wadi Hanifah. The ruler of al-Dir'iyah, Muhammad ibn Sa'ud, met him and welcomed him.

THE HOUSE OF SA'UD: It was, for the future Kingdom of Saudi Arabia, a fateful meeting. The two men — one an idealistic reformer bent on bringing the Islamic community back to the purity of its origins, the other an astute chieftain — formed an immediate warm regard for one another's qualities, and established a relationship that links their descendants to the present day.

As Shaykh Muhammad was an eloquent and sincere preacher, his uncompromising reaffirmation of the basic beliefs of Islam soon won many followers. It also alarmed many leaders in Najd, especially those in independent Riyadh, so near al-Dir'iyah. The nascent movement, whose followers called themselves *al-Muwahhidun*, "those who affirm the Unity of God," or "Unitarians," was seen as a threat to established authority.

Muhammad ibn Sa'ud, the friend and protector of Shaykh Muhammad, died in 1765, but under his very able son and successor, 'Abd al-'Aziz, who had been carefully nurtured in the reformist tradition of the Muwahhidun, the movement continued. In 1773 — three years before the American

Declaration of Independence — 'Abd al-'Aziz captured Riyadh and within fifteen years controlled all of Najd. Then, in the winter of 1789-90, the Muwahhidun crushed the paramount tribe of al-Hasa, the Bani Khalid, at a famous battle at the hill of Ghuraymil just southwest of present-day Abqaiq. As the Bani Khalid had opposed the rise of the House of Sa'ud from the beginning, the victory at Ghuraymil was very important.

Two years after that battle, Shaykh Muhammad ibn 'Abd al-Wahhab died at the age of ninety and was buried, as he would have wished and in accordance with the sunnah of the Prophet, in an unmarked grave in the town of al-Dir'iyah. But the movement which he had founded — which is sometimes referred to as "Wahhabism" — did not die with him. On the contrary, it continued, under the leadership of the House of Sa'ud, to win adherents. In 1801 the reform forces were strong enough to strike inside Iraq and destroy the tombs of the saints at the Shi'i pilgrimage center of Karbala.

In 1803 'Abd al-'Aziz was succeeded by his son Sa'ud, but again the movement lost no ground by the death of a leader. By the early years of the nineteenth century, Saudi power extended over most of the Arabian Peninsula, including much of Oman, parts of Yemen, and the Holy Cities of Mecca and Medina in the Hijaz. Raids were made into Syria and in 1811 a campaign against Baghdad was contemplated.

The town of al-Dir'iyah, now in ruins, provided refuge for the eighteenth-century reformer Muhammad 'Abd al-Wahhab.

By then too, the territory controlled by the House of Sa'ud or Al Sa'ud, as it is known in Arabic, was so vast that the peninsula was divided into twenty districts, with a loyal member of the reform movement as governor of each, and a qadi in charge of religious matters and public education. Part of the revenue of each district was consigned to the construction of forts and mosques, and many towns were provided with a simple, unpretentious mosque and a fort.

In Constantinople, meanwhile, the Ottoman sultan had been alarmed at these incursions into what were, nominally, territories of the Ottoman Empire. He therefore ordered Muhammad 'Ali, the governor of the Ottoman province of Egypt, to undertake a punitive expedition against the Saudis and to re-establish Ottoman authority over the Holy Cities.

Muhammad 'Ali delegated the task to his

Muhammad 'Ali Pasha governed the province of Egypt for the Ottoman Empire.

Family Tree Of The House Of Sa'ud (simplified)

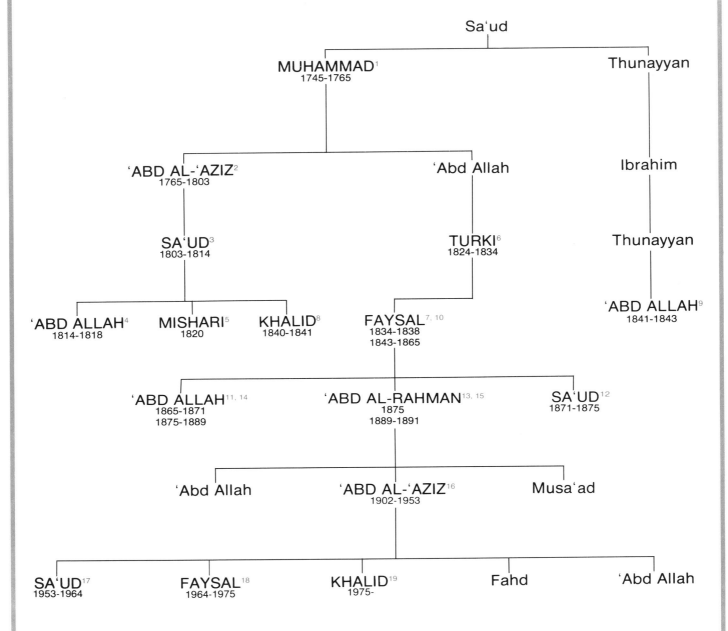

Sa'ud

MUHAMMAD[1]
1745-1765

Thunayyan

'ABD AL-'AZIZ[2]
1765-1803

'Abd Allah

SA'UD[3]
1803-1814

TURKI[6]
1824-1834

Ibrahim

Thunayyan

'ABD ALLAH[4]
1814-1818

MISHARI[5]
1820

KHALID[8]
1840-1841

FAYSAL[7, 10]
1834-1838
1843-1865

'ABD ALLAH[9]
1841-1843

'ABD ALLAH[11, 14]
1865-1871
1875-1889

'ABD AL-RAHMAN[13, 15]
1875
1889-1891

SA'UD[12]
1871-1875

'Abd Allah

'ABD AL-'AZIZ[16]
1902-1953

Musa'ad

SA'UD[17]
1953-1964

FAYSAL[18]
1964-1975

KHALID[19]
1975-

Fahd

'Abd Allah

Capital letters denote rulers of the Saudi state and numerals indicate the sequence in which they ruled.

King 'Abd al-'Aziz, the founder of the modern Kingdom of Saudi Arabia, was in the sixth generation in direct descent from Sa'ud ibn Muhammad ibn Muqrin, who died in 1725 and from whom Al Sa'ud and Saudi Arabia derive their names. The simplified family tree shown here extends only as far as the sons of King 'Abd al-'Aziz, and of these it includes only those who have ruled as king or who have held one of the top positions in the government of the state, that is, have served as Vice Presidents of the Council of Ministers.

son Tusun Pasha. His forces were badly defeated, although they did succeed in taking Mecca, and Muhammad 'Ali, exasperated by his son's considerable losses of men — both to disease and to the enemy — finally took charge himself. He went to Arabia and initially had considerable success against the redoubtable foe. Then, forced to return to Egypt for political reasons, he sent his second son Ibrahim Pasha into Arabia at the head of a more powerful army.

In 1818 Ibrahim arrived in Najd with the full power of the Egyptian army behind him. Besieging the Saudi ruler 'Abd Allah, who had succeeded Sa'ud, Ibrahim captured al-Dir'iyah, sent 'Abd Allah as prisoner to Constantinople, and leveled al-Dir'iyah. He destroyed forts and other defense works, encouraged local rivalries, and a year later, thinking he had destroyed Al Sa'ud forever, returned to the Hijaz and then to Egypt.

After the departure of the Egyptian forces, a number of mutually antagonistic local amirs in Najd tried to profit from the disruption of the Saudi state. These ambitions, however, were thwarted by Turki ibn 'Abd Allah, a close relative (though not the son) of the dead 'Abd Allah.

TURKI IBN 'ABD ALLAH: During the siege of al-Dir'iyah Turki had taken refuge at a nearby town, but in 1823 he felt the time was ripe for a counterattack. Entering al-Dir'iyah without a fight, he immediately moved against Riyadh, which he took as well. He was the first member of the House of Sa'ud to make Riyadh his capital and it has remained the capital of the dynasty ever since.

Turki reigned for eleven years and by the time of his death had largely restored the boundaries of the Saudi state to what they were before the Egyptian invasion, though he did not recover the Holy Cities. Having expelled the invaders from Najd, he was, to his compatriots, a heroic defender of Saudi independence in the face of foreign aggression. But he was also firmly committed to good government in accordance with the Quran and the sunnah of the Prophet, and was concerned about the level of religious education in the provinces. When he captured al-Hasa, he enforced the performance of the five daily prayers, ordered all to follow the precepts of Islam meticulously, and exhorted his people to fear God, to pray, and to pay the *zakah* (the religious tax). He also stressed the responsibility of the individual not only for his own behavior, but for that of his community, and urged people to avoid the practice of usury — always regarded as contrary to the teachings of Islam. In a letter setting forth his views, he ordered his district governors to standardize all weights and measures to prevent cheating and misunderstandings, stated that any bargain once made was inviolable, forbade the use of tobacco, encouraged study, and ended by asserting that any injustices should be referred to him personally.

Ibrahim Pasha of Egypt led a campaign into central Arabia to subdue the House of Sa'ud.

The genre of the instructive epistle addressed to the entire community, as in the example just summarized, was very popular during this period. A number of historical works were composed as well — principally chronicles of the Unitarian movement — by scholars such as Ibn Bishr, Ibn Ghannam, Ibn 'Isa, and others. This led, under Turki's successor, to a sharpening of interest in religious literature in Arabia. This revival certainly did not achieve the sophisticated levels of other literary periods although Taha Husayn, one of the foremost twentieth-century critics of Arabic literature, was struck by the poetry written at this time:

> They returned in their poetry to the ancient style and gave us ... that sweet Arabic song, which had not been heard in the memory of living men. This song, whose authors did not imitate the city folk nor force themselves to search for new and strange expressions, was conceived in liberty and borne along by all the greatness, the yearning for the highest ideal, and the strong longing for the revival of ancient glory, which filled its soul.

Turki was succeeded as head of the Saudi state by his son Faysal, who previously had been captured and then had escaped from the Egyptians. Faysal was faced with yet another Egyptian attempt to establish control over Najd. In 1838 he was captured once again, bravely giving himself up to the enemy rather than see his loyal followers slaughtered, and for the second time was taken to Egypt and imprisoned.

For the second time, however, he escaped and made his way back to Najd in 1843, an

Lewis Pelly described Saudi leaders of his day in an account of his trip to central Arabia in 1865.

First exported in number in the mid-1800s, the Arabian horse grew increasingly popular abroad.

Pearling was once an important means of livelihood along the shores of the Gulf.

exploit that added to his popularity among the tribes and also marked the end for a while of Ottoman efforts to quell the House of Sa'ud. Muhammad 'Ali was growing old and the Ottomans, distracted by wars in Moldavia and Wallachia, eventually had to content themselves with exercising titular control of the Hijaz.

Faysal, a just, stern man, continued to reign until his death in 1865. He was described by Lewis Pelly, the British Resident in the Gulf, as generous to the poor and a scholar who held regular discussions on the works of Ibn Taymiyah and Muhammad ibn 'Abd al-Wahhab. According to Pelly, Faysal was also interested in the economic problems of Arabia. Pelly said that Faysal spoke "very sensibly on the physical and political position of Arabia; explaining its great want to be that of rain. If only rain would fall agriculture would be possible, and the tribes might then be rendered sedentary." He was also, Pelly went on, "successful in curbing the predatory habits of his tribes; and . . . was desirous of inculcating among them more settled habits, and turning their minds towards agriculture and trade."

Both agriculture and trade were limited at that period, but during Faysal's rule a market for Arabian horses developed in British India. For centuries Arabia had bred fine horses, but in the 1860s demand picked up and exports soared. Horses bred by the famous Shammar tribe were exported through Kuwait and such Saudi ports as Qatif; according to one estimate, six hundred horses were exported through Kuwait in 1863. The demand, in fact, eventually exhausted the supply and a moratorium was placed on the export of horses for four years. Other than Arabian horses, however, the only exports of any consequence were dates and pearls. According to one estimate some 750,000 tons of dates a year were exported during this period — two thirds of which came from the oasis of al-Hasa and the rest from Qatif. The trade of the period, although limited, still required some form of currency, and there were several to choose from: coins minted by the Ottomans, the British, and the Indians, and the commonest currency — the Maria Theresa thaler or dollar. There were also at that time coins called in Arabic *tawilahs* ("long ones"). Minted in al-Hasa, they were made of silver, copper, or

lead and consisted of a strip of the metal folded in half to form what looked like tweezers and stamped on the side with an Arabic inscription in kufic script. At one time tawilahs — called *larins* outside Arabia — were accepted as currency from the Gulf to Ceylon.

THE BIRTH OF 'ABD AL-'AZIZ AL SA'UD: With the death of Faysal in 1865, this relatively brief period of peace and prosperity came to an end. First, rivalry over the succession weakened Saudi unity. Then, taking advantage of the Saudis' internal conflict, the Ottomans occupied much of the eastern seaboard and the oasis of al-Hasa. Landing in 1871 at Ras Tanura, the present site of Aramco's oil refinery and major shipping terminal, the Turks took Qatif, then marched a hundred miles to Hofuf, the main town of al-Hasa, where they overcame stubborn resistance put up by the Saudi governor and occupied the fortress. The Turkish commander was awarded a sword, studded with diamonds, with the word "Najd" engraved on the blade — although no Turkish troops had entered the central region of Arabia.

In the story of the House of Sa'ud, however, two other events overshadow the Turkish invasion. One was the birth of a son to 'Abd al-Rahman ibn Faysal, the man who had emerged as the reigning head of the House of Sa'ud. The son — who would later create the Kingdom of Saudi Arabia — was named 'Abd al-'Aziz ibn 'Abd al-Rahman Al Faysal Al Sa'ud, known to the West as Ibn Sa'ud and to his subjects simply as 'Abd al-'Aziz. The other event was the rise to power of a dynasty called Al Rashid or the House of Rashid, which led to a conflict that would occupy the Saudis, and young 'Abd al-'Aziz, for decades.

Based in north-central Arabia, with the town of Hayil as capital, the House of Rashid had taken advantage of the uncertainties over the Saudi succession to install a deputy governor in Riyadh in Saudi territory. In response, 'Abd al-Rahman, when he emerged as head of the House of Sa'ud, attacked Riyadh and recaptured it. Muhammad ibn Rashid, in turn, marched on Riyadh and, finding the defense too strong for a direct assault, besieged it. During the siege he cut down a large number of date palms on which the townspeople depended for sustenance, a common practice in Arabian warfare in that period. After forty days of this harsh but indecisive activity, Ibn Rashid proposed negotiations with the defenders. In the Saudi delegation was the young boy 'Abd al-'Aziz, making his debut on the stage of history.

The truce that was arranged as a consequence of these negotiations was short-lived. Muhammad ibn Rashid soon led his men to the area of the Qasim, in northern Najd, where he attacked and routed the Saudis at the battle of al-Mulayda on January 21, 1891. Isolated and bereft of allies, 'Abd al-Rahman sent his women and children to the protection of his friend the ruler of Bahrain, while he himself, with no hope of returning to Riyadh, took to the desert in the south where he had friends among the tribes. For a time 'Abd al-Rahman and a handful of loyal followers roamed the fringes of the Rub' al-Khali, but later they moved on to Qatar and then to Bahrain. Finally they took refuge in Kuwait, where they spent the better part of a decade.

For 'Abd al-'Aziz the years he and his father spent in Kuwait as guests of the ruler, Mubarak al-Sabah, provided valuable insights into international politics. Mubarak was an able politician and Kuwait, strategically placed at the head of the Arabian Gulf, was then the focus of Western activity in the area. The British had special treaty relations with Kuwait, Bahrain, Oman, and the shaykhdoms on the Trucial Coast; the Russians, as part of their centuries-old search for a warm-water port, were probing for outlets in the Arabian Gulf; and both the Germans and the Turks were looking toward Kuwait as the possible terminus for the Berlin-to-Baghdad railway, an attempt to challenge Britain's hegemony in the Gulf.

As he observed the international negotiations of Mubarak al-Sabah, however, 'Abd al-'Aziz also kept an intent eye on the Rashidis, now allied with the Turks in al-Hasa and led by a nephew of Muhammad ibn Rashid whose name was also 'Abd al-'Aziz and who had a reputation for being weaker and more rash than his formidable uncle.

In 1901 'Abd al-'Aziz Al Sa'ud, then about twenty years old, decided that it was time for the House of Sa'ud to win back the lands wrested from it by the Turks and Ibn Rashid. As the entire force the Saudis could muster at this time consisted of only forty men, 'Abd al-Rahman tried to dissuade him. But 'Abd al-'Aziz would not be dissuaded; the House of Rashid had just mounted an attack on Kuwait and Shaykh Mubarak was willing to let 'Abd al-'Aziz create a diversion. Toward the end of 1901 therefore, 'Abd al-'Aziz set off for Najd with his forty men in the first phase of a campaign to rebuild the fortunes of the House of Sa'ud.

THE ATTACK ON RIYADH: The Saudi force did not attack immediately. Instead, it spent several months on the northern fringes of the Rub' al-Khali, hoping to win reinforcements from the tribes camped near the wells of Yabrin and Haradh — the latter became a government agricultural station. 'Abd al-'Aziz was able to recruit only twenty more warriors but, reluctant to wait any longer, he decided to attack Riyadh anyway, and with only sixty men behind him he set off.

At a distance of one and a half hour's march from Riyadh, 'Abd al-'Aziz left one-third of his force with the camels, instructing them to return to Kuwait if no message was received from him within twenty-four hours. Then, with the rest of his men, he advanced on foot — to be less conspicuous — until he reached the outskirts of the city. There 'Abd al-'Aziz waited for night to fall.

At last it was time. 'Abd al-'Aziz stationed his brother Muhammad in the groves with thirty-three men to act as a back-up force and quietly scaled the walls with the others. Inside the walls, they knocked on the door of the house of a cattle dealer, who fled. His daughters, recognizing 'Abd al-'Aziz, were gagged and locked up. Next 'Abd al-'Aziz sent a messenger back to tell Muhammad, waiting outside the walls, to advance with all possible stealth into the city. Finally, by standing on one another's shoulders, 'Abd al-'Aziz and his men entered the house of 'Ajlan, Ibn Rashid's governor, silenced the servants, and searched the house. Learning that 'Ajlan was in the custom of spending his nights in the fort of al-Masmak in the city, they decided to wait for morning when the gates of the fort would be opened.

It was difficult to wait. As 'Abd al-'Aziz recalled in later years, they "slept a little while … prayed the morning prayer and sat thinking about what we should do." But at last the dark desert sky lightened and they prepared for action.

Mubarak al-Sabah, ruler of Kuwait, was host to the young exiled member of the House of Sa'ud.

Modern architecture distinguishes Saudi Arabia's major cities, for example Jiddah, the bustling Red Sea port and commercial metropolis seen at top. Directly above: Eastern Province night scene in al-Khobar, shopping center for thousands living nearby, and an international hotel designed to blend into the desert landscape at Riyadh. Right: Luxury-hotel construction approaches the Gulf shore at Dammam. Opposite page: Patterned, curved facade of King Faysal Specialist Hospital has become a Riyadh landmark, as has its awning-striped water tower, far corner. Far right: Minarets of the Sacred Mosque loom behind modern apartment buildings in Mecca, hub of all Islam.

'Abd al-'Aziz reestablished the Saudi Dynasty in the heartland of Arabia with a daring assault on Riyadh, whose city walls, seen at left above, he with a small band of men scaled stealthily by night, using a palm trunk for their ladder. As al-Masmak fort came to life at dawn, the outnumbered attackers sprang towards its entrance and with gunfire and rocks hurtling about them pursued the Rashidi governor through the postern gate seen above — killed him, captured the garrison, and sent criers forth to proclaim that the House of Sa'ud had retaken the town.

Originally they had planned to take 'Ajlan prisoner as soon as he left the fort and entered the house. But as the sun rose and the gates of the fort opened, they saw that 'Ajlan was not alone; he walked out of the gate accompanied by ten bodyguards. Instantly 'Abd al-'Aziz and his followers sprang to the attack, leaving four men in the house to cover them with rifles.

At the sudden appearance of 'Abd al-'Aziz, 'Ajlan's bodyguards bolted, leaving 'Ajlan facing the Saudi onslaught alone, with only a sword for defense. Darting forward, 'Abd Allah ibn Jiluwi, a cousin of 'Abd al-'Aziz, threw a spear at 'Ajlan but missed; the spear went into the gate of the fort where the steel point, imbedded in the wood, can still be seen today.

No coward, 'Ajlan lunged at 'Abd al-'Aziz, who later reminisced: "He made at me with his sword, but its edge was not good. I covered my face and shot at him with my gun. I heard the crash of the sword upon the ground and knew that the shot had hit 'Ajlan, but had not killed him. He started to go through the postern gate, but I caught hold of his legs. The men inside caught hold of his arms while I still held his legs. His company were shooting their firearms at us and throwing stones upon us. 'Ajlan gave me a powerful kick in the side so that I was about to faint. I let go of his legs and he got inside. I wished to enter, but my men would not let me. Then 'Abd Allah ibn Jiluwi entered with the bullets falling about him. After him ten others entered. We flung the gate wide open, and our company ran up to reinforce us. We were forty and there before us were eighty. We killed half of them. Then four fell from the wall and were crushed. The rest were trapped in a tower; we granted safe-conduct to them and they descended. As for 'Ajlan, Ibn Jiluwi slew him."

Such is the epic story, as related by King 'Abd al-'Aziz, of how Riyadh was taken on January 16, 1902, as the sun was rising over the desert and the city was just coming to life. The capture of Riyadh marked the dawn of a new era in the history of Arabia and a turning point in the fortunes of the House of Sa'ud.

In Riyadh, as the news swiftly spread, the people welcomed the new ruler joyfully; they had suffered under the harsh rule of Ibn Rashid. 'Abd al-'Aziz, knowing his small band could never hold the city if the Rashidis were

to counterattack, immediately set about repairing the defenses of Riyadh. The Rashidis did not attack, however, and during the next six months 'Abd al-'Aziz completed his defenses, sent for his father in Kuwait, and handed over the city to him while he took the field. This close relationship between father and son was to last until the death of 'Abd al-Rahman nearly thirty years later. It was a relationship of mutual respect, of profitable consultation on all important matters, of willingness on the part of the son to cede to his father the place of highest honor on every public occasion.

Meanwhile, the inhabitants of the area south of Riyadh, learning that the House of Sa'ud had retaken the city, hastened to acknowledge the suzerainty of 'Abd al-'Aziz; his exploit in capturing Riyadh with so small a force had won the admiration of the Bedouins, who rode into Riyadh from the desert to join him.

Simultaneously 'Abd al-'Aziz began to prepare for a large-scale offensive against the Rashidis. For although the taking of Riyadh was a master stroke, he knew that his situation was still precarious and that he still faced a long, arduous campaign against the House of Rashid and its Turkish allies. 'Abd al-'Aziz had demonstrated his daring with the capture of Riyadh. Now, as he would for the next quarter of a century, he would demonstrate the rarer qualities of knowing when to advance and when to retreat, when to conciliate and when to punish.

'Abd Allah ibn Jiluwi in later life became Governor of the Eastern Province.

Riyadh in 1950, with its flat-topped roofs and crenelated parapets, looked much as it did in the early days of 'Abd al-'Aziz.

COUNTERATTACK: At Hafar al-Batin, meanwhile, Ibn Rashid continued to plan his campaign against Kuwait. He apparently regarded the young Saudi as no great threat to his power and felt he could deal with him at a later date. Knowing that 'Abd al-'Aziz Al Sa'ud had few resources, he assumed that he could offer few tangible advantages to the villagers and tribesmen of Najd, wholly absorbed as they were in their hard struggle for existence.

Ibn Rashid's assumption turned out to be wrong. In another of the shrewd moves for which 'Abd al-'Aziz later would be famous, he and his brother Sa'ud set about winning the hearts of the people of al-Kharj, al-Aflaj, and Wadi al-Dawasir — all regions over which the authority of the House of Rashid had been at best nominal.

The Rashidis finally struck back. In the fall of 1902 Ibn Rashid headed south. Bypassing Riyadh, now strongly fortified, he made a raid into al-Kharj hoping to subdue the district before 'Abd al-'Aziz had prepared for its defense. Again, he miscalculated. 'Abd al-'Aziz, by means of a forced night march, had reached the village and date groves of al-Dilam earlier and had prepared an ambush. It caught the Rashidis unaware, and after a fierce, daylong battle Ibn Rashid was forced to retreat all the way to his northern capital of Hayil.

This second victory gave another tremendous boost to the prestige of 'Abd al-'Aziz Al Sa'ud and consolidated his popularity with the people. He had proved himself in battle and could now count on the support of the inhabitants of Najd from Riyadh to Wadi al-Dawasir.

THE STRUGGLE FOR NAJD: Ibn Rashid, however, was not going to let Najd slip from his fingers without a fight, and for the next few years the two sides battled almost continually for mastery. 'Abd al-'Aziz attacked the heartlands of Al Rashid in the area of Jabal Shammar and in 1904 attacked the province of the Qasim, capturing the two key towns of 'Unayzah and Buraydah. He won over to his cause the people of the Washm and Sudayr as well. By the spring of the year he was master of central Najd.

At that point Ibn Rashid, unable to contain the Saudi advance himself, appealed to his Turkish allies for help and when he renewed the contest towards the end of May 1904 he was accompanied by eight battalions of Turkish troops equipped with artillery.

The Saudi forces confronted the combined troops of Ibn Rashid and the Turks in the province of the Qasim, outside the town of Buraydah. The battle was running in favor of the Saudis when 'Abd al-'Aziz was wounded by shrapnel from a Turkish cannon shot and forced to retire. It was, of course, a defeat, but by the time he had recovered from his wounds and returned to the fray some months later, the fierce heat of an Arabian summer had taken its toll of the Turkish troops. In the next encounter, 'Abd al-'Aziz, seeing some of his men begin to waver, personally led an attack on the Turkish artillery. The Turks gave ground, Ibn Rashid's Shammar forces broke,

Buraydah, a trading center in Najd, was seized by 'Abd al-'Aziz Al Sa'ud at an early stage.

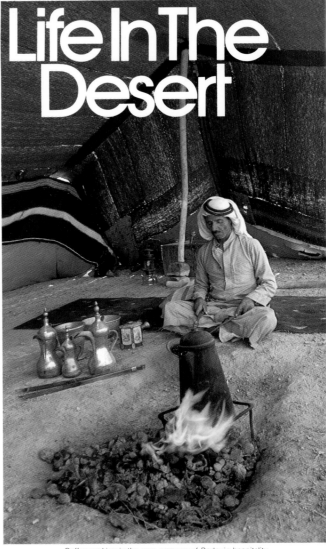

Life In The Desert

Coffee-making is the very essence of Bedouin hospitality.

In the arid lands which make up most of Saudi Arabia men, as well as plants and animals, have adapted to the stringent conditions imposed by terrain and climate. This is particularly true of the Bedouins, the nomadic people who have inhabited large regions of the peninsula for centuries.

The word "Bedouin" comes from the French version of the Arabic word *badawi* (plural, *badu*) which means simply desert dweller. It is an accurate term but used only by townsmen. They refer to themselves, simply and proudly, as "Arabs." Bedouin life evolved from the demands of a harsh environment. The constant and compelling need for water and pasturage, for example, led the tribes to divide much of the Arabian Peninsula into tribal areas — called *dirahs* or ranges — some of which were very large. Within each dirah were the wells used by the tribe, often marked with the tribe's camel brand. Use of another tribe's wells without permission was forbidden, and unlawful crossing of another tribe's dirah could lead to war.

The need for water and pasturage, indeed, shaped every aspect of Bedouin life. When, for example, desert

A Bedouin's life is one of independence and self-reliance.

Wool from Bedouin's animals goes into heavy tent fabric, woven by women of the tribe.

thunderstorms lighted the horizon in the evening, the tribe would head for the area that had received the downpour so that they could pasture their herds on the quick-growing vegetation that resulted. When little or no rain fell, the tribes would cluster about their wells, drawing water — often from considerable depths — to keep their animals alive. And when there was a drought, the desert would often erupt in tribal clashes, as tribes were forced to move from their own dirahs to those of others. Until the introduction of firearms, the conflicts — often swift raids on enemy encampments — were fought with swords, daggers, and long cane spears. Raiding parties sometimes rode by camel to enemy territory, then mounted their horses for the attack.

The demands of life in the desert also shaped codes of hospitality. As any traveler would die without water, food, and shelter, every man — even an enemy — could claim three days of hospitality from any other man. It would not, furthermore, be granted grudgingly; the host might find himself in the same predicament as his guest at another time. Similarly the host would offer travelers not only hospitality, but also protection.

The shaykhs or leaders of Bedouin tribes were usually chosen from a few specific families, but as tribal society was basically democratic their authority was derived from the consent of their fellow tribesmen, who were free to oppose it at any time. Sometimes, it is true, large tribes split into factions because of opposition to a shaykh, but these factions would almost always unite against a common enemy; collective responsibility was a powerful force for order within the tribe.

Bedouin society accorded women a position somewhat superior to that of many women in towns. Married women were often consulted on important decisions, and in the old days some women accompanied the tribes to the battlefield and cheered on the warriors. Their work, furthermore, was vital: to raise the children, to gather fuel — a time-consuming occupation in itself — fetch water, milk the animals, cook, spin yarn, and weave the tent cloths and blankets that constitute a good part of the wealth of most Bedouin families. As a result they were accorded great respect.

One of the jobs given women was to pitch the tent, the "house of hair," which is symbolic of Bedouin life and which suggests the adaptability of the Bedouin to his demanding environment. The black tents had to fulfill stringent requirements. They had to be easy to erect and dismantle, light and portable, easy to maintain and repair, airy, and resistant to wind and rain, yet provide insulation from the sun and protection against the cold.

Essentially, the black tent consists of long strips of cloth woven from black or brown wool and goat's hair, which are sewn together to provide a roof and to make sides, which are attached to the roof with wood or pins, all of this being supported by ropes and poles and pegged to the ground. The open side faces away from the winds, and the interior is usually separated by vertical curtains into three sections: the men's section, where guests are received, the family section, and the kitchen. The floor area is covered with rugs, either woven by the women of the tribe or purchased in market towns, and the owner's sword or rifle is hung from the tentpole in the men's section, in front of which is the hearth, with coffeepots and other coffee-making implements ranged around.

To settled Arabs, the Bedouins have traditionally been regarded as the repositories of manly virtues: they were proud, independent, resourceful, courageous, loyal, hospitable, and generous. In addition, they were thought to speak the purest Arabic, uncontaminated by contact with foreign elements in the cities. These views, no doubt, were and are often exaggerated; but Bedouins nonetheless did develop a distinctive way of life and their contributions, historically, have been important as well as interesting. In the perpetual hunt for scarce meat (their herds were kept primarily for milk) the Bedouins painstakingly developed the art of falconry and bred the saluki, a handsome greyhound. Bedouins also developed the Arabian horse, one of the more famous breeds in the world, and learned to make use of the camel, the animal which enabled them to master the desert and control overland trade routes for millennia.

The camel, curiously, seems to have originated in North America as a small Eocene mammal which probably migrated and eventually made its way to central Asia, the Middle East, North Africa, and the Sahara Desert, evolving into today's one-hump and two-hump camels. Another group of ancestral camels migrated to Central and South America where they evolved into today's llamas, alpacas, guanacos, and vicuñas.

(Continued on page 132)

Life In The Desert

The camel, despite its awkward appearance, is a remarkable example of successful adaptation to environment. It can traverse arid lands in which no other large mammal can survive and has enabled man to penetrate into and survive in these regions as well.

Domesticated centuries ago, the camel enabled nomadic peoples to conquer the desert.

The most striking adaptation of the camel to desert life is its ability to conserve water — although not, as was once believed, in its hump or stomach. Instead, the camel has evolved a number of mechanisms which allow it to absorb and retain large quantities of water. Its drinking capacity naturally varies with the seasons of the year, weather conditions, and the level of the animal's dehydration, but is truly large. It may range from only some sixteen gallons to as many as fifty in a drinking session of two watering episodes separated by only a few hours. Fifty gallons would be the equivalent of about one-half of the animal's dehydrated weight. The camel's body temperature, moreover, can rise as much as six degrees Fahrenheit during the day without its losing precious body moisture in wasteful cooling through sweating. The camel can also eat low-protein desert shrubs and convert them to body tissue and drink water high in salts and minerals and convert it, along with salty desert shrubs, into milk (a primary element in the Bedouins' diet). The camel's peculiar kidney physiology, finally, allows it to recycle its own urea, a process which not only provides an additional source of protein but also assists in water conservation.

The camel has remarkable eyelashes — two sets for each eye — which effectively screen its eyes from sand and dust. It also possesses large, soft, padded feet which work on the snowshoe principle and allow it to walk over drift sand without sinking in. The long neck of the camel allows it to nibble low-growing desert herbs comfortably as well as leaves from trees, and also serves to balance the animal's rather unwieldy body as it runs.

During the winter, camels are ordinarily not watered at all; they receive enough moisture from what they eat. As the weather grows warmer, however, they are watered every seven to nine days and in full summer every two days. The top speed of a good riding camel is around fourteen miles an hour. They are capable of many different paces: from a walk that covers about four miles an hour to a long-distance stride with which a camel can, relatively easily, cover a hundred miles in a day.

When, and exactly how, the camel was domesticated is not precisely known but it is easily conceivable that the process of domestication got under way between 3000 and 2500 B.C. in south Arabia. In due course men started riding camels — the stage of development that allowed the Bedouins to venture deeper, and for longer periods, into the large areas of arid land of the Middle East.

As a beast of burden, the camel had no peer in the arid regions; it was less expensive to maintain, had a longer working life, and could carry loads in areas where oxen or donkeys could not. For all these reasons, the early Arabs were able to monopolize the ancient trade routes between the East and the civilized towns of Mesopotamia, Egypt, and the Mediterranean and were able to establish mercantile cities and kingdoms in northern and central Arabia. The camel's efficiency, in fact, impeded the development of roads; wheeled vehicles drawn by oxens, for example, could not compete with the low cost of camel transport.

As a means of transport, the camel is no longer as important as it used to be in Saudi Arabia. Statistics are scarce but the age of the camel seems to have passed into history. Traditional caravan routes are falling into disuse and many wells on these routes, untended for years, are filling up with sand and vanishing. The camel is still used for milk and meat, but rarely for transport.

The days of the camel caravan are fading into history.

The life of the Bedouin has been changing too. Even the Bedouins who cling to the nomadic, pastoral way of life are relying increasingly on trucks to haul water to their herds and are abandoning some of the Spartan ways of the past for the more comfortable ways of an industrialized world. Many Bedouins still range through the deserts but today they are more often than not at the wheel of 25-ton trailer trucks rather than at the head of a column of camels. Others have left herding to work in factories and oil installations and not a few, under Saudi Arabia's extensive educational program, have enrolled and been graduated from universities abroad. In short, present-day Bedouins are adapting to the exigencies of modern life as, millennia ago, they adapted to the demands of the arid steppes and deserts.

the retreat became a rout, and the Saudis captured stores of equipment and a large sum of Turkish gold.

A few months later, while 'Abd al-'Aziz was dealing with problems in the south, Ibn Rashid tried yet once more to reassert his authority over the province of the Qasim. The people of the province, however, sent a delegation to 'Abd al-'Aziz in Riyadh, pleading with him to return. He did so, and caught Ibn Rashid by surprise. While Ibn Rashid was desperately trying to rally his troops, he was shot down in his camp near Buraydah in April 1906. The contest between 'Abd al-'Aziz of the House of Rashid and 'Abd al-'Aziz of the House of Sa'ud, which had lasted since the capture of Riyadh four years and three months before, was at an end.

CONSOLIDATION: After the defeat of the Rashidis, 'Abd al-'Aziz began the difficult task of consolidating his victory. But within two years he was confronted with still another adversary: the Sharif Husayn ibn 'Ali.

In 1908 the Sharif Husayn, appointed by the Ottoman Government, became Amir of the Hijaz. Husayn had been born in Mecca, but had spent most of his life in Istanbul and was nearly sixty years old. He was a man of great culture, charm, and integrity, but also extremely ambitious and committed to the preservation of the Hijaz as a fief of his family, the Hashimites.

Husayn, therefore, was delighted when, in 1908, the Turks completed the Hijaz Railway linking Damascus to Medina. The Hijaz was now tied to the Ottoman Empire by a more substantial bond than the formal recognition of Ottoman suzerainty by the sharifs. The Turks could move troops expeditiously toward the very heart of Arabia if need be.

To make matters worse, Husayn had apprehended 'Abd al-'Aziz Al Sa'ud's brother Sa'd during a mission to enlist the aid of the 'Utaybah tribe against the Rashidis. Husayn offered to release Sa'd if 'Abd al-'Aziz would recognize his hegemony over the Qasim and pay him tribute. Although torn between his political aims and his love for his brother, 'Abd al-'Aziz agreed to meet Husayn's terms and Sa'd was released.

Another difficulty was the continual shifting of allegiances by the Bedouin tribes. Depending on the personality of their shaykhs, tribal feuds, and complex family relationships, the Bedouins would support first one ruler and then his opponent. To 'Abd al-'Aziz this seemed to be an even greater stumbling block to the unification of his realm than the threat of outside intervention.

In pondering this problem, 'Abd al-'Aziz concluded that until order had been established in Najd, his ambition to unite the provinces of Arabia into a single kingdom would be doomed to failure. He concluded too that order would depend on providing security for his subjects and a better life for the tribes; in 1910 a drought had killed thousands of camels and sheep and spawned unrest in both Najd and Kuwait. After long consultation with the members of his family and his religious advisors, therefore, 'Abd al-'Aziz decided upon a plan to settle the Bedouins in agricultural communities, while still preserving their ability as fighting men. At the same time he dispatched teachers to the tribes, summoning them to take part in a revival of pure Islam.

Those who answered the call were called *Ikhwan* — "Brethren" — and grouped into settlements which were at first based primarily upon common beliefs and practices, though later they came to be associated with particular tribes or tribal groups. The settlers were given land, agricultural implements, seeds, money for their everyday needs, and arms for defense. They were also given money for the construction of mosques to which religious teachers were assigned.

The first of the Ikhwan settlements was started at the wells of al-Artawiyah in northern Najd in 1912 and in a very short time numbered ten thousand men. Soon there were scores of Ikhwan settlements with thousands of men at strategic points throughout Najd, the most famous being at Ghatghat at no great distance west of Riyadh. These settlers would become the elite troops in 'Abd al-'Aziz's growing forces.

EXPANSION: 'Abd al-'Aziz now turned his attention toward eastern Arabia where the Turks, who had occupied much of it in 1871, were still in control. At this time — 1913 — the Ottomans were plagued with difficulties both in Turkey itself, where the Young Turks were agitating for much-needed reforms (see Chapter 2), and in their European provinces, where

Securing the loyalty of the Bedouins was a critical task facing the young 'Abd al-'Aziz.

Ikhwan settlements established by the future King became the backbone of his forces.

al-Qurayyat

Sakaka
al-Jawf

Tayma

Khaybar

Medina

Yanbu'al-Nakhl
Yanbu'al-Bahr

Rabigh

Jiddah   al-Hawiyah
            Mec

RED   al-Lith

SEA

GROWTH OF THE MODERN SAUDI STATE

Having recaptured Riyadh from the Rashidis in 1902, 'Abd al-'Aziz Al Sa'ud spends the next thirty-odd years dealing with threats to his position and in reestablishing, consolidating, and extending Saudi control. The first few years bring expansion to the south toward Wadi al-Dawasir and to the north and west into Sudayr and the Qasim as far as the towns of Buraydah and 'Unayzah. In 1913 the Turks are expelled from al-Hasa and the coastal towns on the Arabian Gulf, and 'Abd al-'Aziz gains control of most of what is now the

Eastern Province of Saudi Arabia. The next great period of expansion comes after World War I when the Saudis come into conflict with the Hashimites, expel them from Mecca, Medina, Jiddah, and the rest of the Hijaz, and drive to the northwest as far as the borders of Trans-Jordan. The final period of growth comes in the following decade when the Saudis move south to establish control over Jaizan and the district of Najran.

The fort at Hofuf was the first of the Turkish garrisons to surrender as 'Abd al-'Aziz pushed his authority into the eastern areas.

Ruins of the fort at al-'Uqayr on the Gulf recall the days of Ottoman occupation.

British recognition of 'Abd al-'Aziz followed contacts with the Saudis by Captain Shakespear, British political agent in Kuwait.

independence movements were challenging their supremacy. It seemed a propitious time for action and 'Abd al-'Aziz, with his newly formed corps of Ikhwan behind him, struck on a moonless night in April 1913. At the head of six hundred men, he crept up to the fortifications of Hofuf, the Turkish headquarters in al-Hasa, scaled the wall on ropes and the trunks of palm trees, and, before the sleeping garrison could gather its wits, captured the inner fortress and accepted the Turkish governor's surrender. To press his advantage, 'Abd al-'Aziz moved quickly on other Turkish garrisons in al-'Uqayr and Qatif, chivalrously allowing the Turks to depart without surrendering their weapons.

The consolidation of al-Hasa completed, 'Abd al-'Aziz then sought an agreement with the Turks to stabilize the situation in the Arabian Gulf. The Turks, however, while negotiating with 'Abd al-'Aziz, made an agreement to deliver arms to the supporters of the House of Rashid, who were still hostile. 'Abd al-'Aziz, therefore, laid the groundwork for an understanding with the British, and in the winter of 1913 Captain W. H. I. Shakespear, the British Political Agent in Kuwait, visited 'Abd al-'Aziz in Riyadh. The discussions between 'Abd al-'Aziz and Shakespear laid the foundations of the Anglo-Saudi treaty of 1915 whereby Britain recognized Ibn Sa'ud as hereditary ruler of Najd, al-Hasa, Qatif, Jubail, and their dependencies in return for support in World War I.

In Europe, by then, the war had begun. One of the many causes of the conflict was international rivalry for control of the Middle East — partly because, with the opening of the Suez Canal (see Chapter 2), the Middle East had become a key link between Britain and her Indian Empire, between France and Indo-China, and between the Dutch and the East Indies. Other European nations, furthermore, had strategic and commercial interests in the Middle East which they wished to expand, and many European governments hoped to profit from what they regarded as the inevitable dismemberment of the Ottoman Empire.

In the Middle East, at the same time, national movements for independence from the Ottomans were growing, while sentiments of pan-Arabism were everywhere in evidence. The Arab world, after centuries of Turkish rule, was rediscovering its identity.

When the powers of Europe went to war in 1914, control of the Middle East was divided between two of the greatest colonial powers in the world: Great Britain and the Ottoman Empire. The Ottomans still exerted a form of authority over most of the Red Sea coast as far south as Yemen, and still actively ruled Palestine, Syria, and Mesopotamia. The British controlled Egypt and the Suez Canal, their lifeline to India, as well as Aden. As they considered the Arabian Gulf lay within their sphere of influence, they had announced in 1903 that the establishment of a naval base or fortified port in the Gulf by any other power would be regarded as "a very grave menace to British interests" and one which Britain would certainly resist with all the means at its disposal.

Britain's first objective, after the outbreak of war, was to wrest control of Mesopotamia — now Iraq — from the Turks. As part of their campaign, they sought Saudi help against the House of Rashid, an ally of the Ottomans, while at the same time encouraging the Sharif Husayn to expel the Turks from the Hijaz.

'Abd al-'Aziz did not take a decisive part in World War I. He had domestic troubles enough; first, as always, with the House of Rashid, and second with a rebellion by the tribe of the 'Ujman during which he was twice severely wounded and lost his beloved brother Sa'd, whom he had ransomed from his captivity by the Sharif Husayn.

Toward the end of World War I, however, 'Abd al-'Aziz found himself faced with the open hostility of the Sharif Husayn, whom he had refrained from attacking during the war, despite provocations, because of their common wish to see the last of the Turks leave the peninsula. But now Husayn was armed and supported by the British, with whom he had concluded a secret agreement under which they committed themselves to support the establishment of an independent Arab state comprising most of the Arab lands east of Egypt.

At the end of the war, the Allies recognized Husayn not as King of the Arab Countries — the title he chose for himself — but only as King of the Hijaz. Britain and France themselves, by mandates, took over a large part of the territories the sharif thought he had been promised: Palestine, Iraq, and Syria.

If disappointed by the Allies' betrayal, however, Husayn was still determined to retain at least the Hijaz, and launched three attacks upon the oasis of al-Khurmah, which was strategically located on the route between the Hijaz and Najd. In the first attacks the people of al-Khurmah succeeded in holding off Husayn's troops, but as the situation became desperate they appealed to 'Abd al-'Aziz for help. At first 'Abd al-'Aziz simply warned Husayn to desist, but when the sharif, ignoring the warning, sent four thousand men armed with machine guns and artillery against al-Khurmah, 'Abd al-'Aziz sent his troops into action. In May 1919, in the middle of a dark night, the Saudi Ikhwan attacked from all sides and inflicted a crushing defeat upon the sharif's expedition at the nearby town of Turabah.

With al-Khurmah and Turabah safely attached to the Saudi realm, the ways to the Hijaz and to 'Asir, the mountainous region south of Mecca, were now open and in 1920 the Saudis captured Abha, the capital of 'Asir. Two years later 'Abd al-'Aziz's son Faysal, later to become the third king of Saudi Arabia, led an army to 'Asir to suppress a serious rebellion there. Since then 'Asir has remained a tranquil part of the Saudi state.

Meanwhile, the Rashidis were once again at war with Al Sa'ud and to end this constant threat to stability 'Abd al-'Aziz besieged the Rashidi headquarters in Hayil, long a thorn in the Saudi side. This time his efforts met with success, and after three months Hayil capitulated and the surviving members of the House of Rashid were brought to Riyadh, where they remained his honored guests. The long rivalry between the two houses was finally at an end.

In 1922 'Abd al-'Aziz extended his expanding domains to the west and north by annexing the oases of Khaybar and Tayma. On his northern frontiers, he took the important Wadi al-Sirhan and the oasis of al-Jawf.

Events were moving towards a climax. The last act of the drama began in September 1924, when a detachment of the Ikhwan appeared before the city of Tayif, in the highlands above Mecca. The force probably had no intention of attacking the town, for the commander of the detachment was a few hours' march in the rear. But the sight of the Ikhwan created a panic, and 'Ali, a son of the Sharif Husayn, withdrew with his troops towards Mecca. The townsmen, left defenseless, agreed to surrender the town peaceably.

When the gates were swung open, however, the Ikhwan were reported fired upon. Thinking themselves betrayed, they attacked, and fierce fighting ensued before their commander arrived and restored order. This was the only time during the Hijaz campaign when the Saudi forces lost their heads; normally, they kept strict discipline.

With the Saudis in Tayif, the days of the Sharif Husayn were obviously numbered, and prominent citizens of the Hijaz began to bring pressure to bear on him to abdicate in favor of his son 'Ali. For a long time the aged ruler refused, but finally he yielded, and in October 1924 he boarded a ship in Jiddah and sought refuge in Transjordan, from which the British later moved him to Cyprus, where he spent his last years.

One of the first acts of his son 'Ali, now king, was to evacuate Mecca, considered indefensible once Tayif had fallen, and to concentrate his troops in Jiddah. In October 1924, therefore, after Saudi advance forces had entered Mecca, 'Abd al-'Aziz entered the Holy City — not as a conqueror but in the humble garb of a pilgrim.

For the sharifs of Mecca the end was now in sight, and in 1925 it came. In the first days of December Medina surrendered, and two weeks later Jiddah capitulated. 'Ali boarded a ship for Iraq, where his brother Faysal reigned, and on January 6, 1926, the leading citizens of Mecca offered allegiance to 'Abd al-'Aziz as successor to the title King of the Hijaz. Soon after, in a ceremony of investiture in the Sacred Mosque of Mecca, the new King swore that he would rule his new domains in accordance with the sacred law of Islam.

REORGANIZATION: These domains were now extensive. Reaching from the borders of Iraq in the north to the far side of the Rub' al-Khali in the south, and from the Arabian Gulf in the east to the Red Sea in the west, they comprised an area three times the size of France and included the Holy Cities of Mecca and Medina.

Fully aware that the addition of the Hijaz to his dominions brought unprecedented responsibilities as protector of the Holy Cities, 'Abd al-'Aziz convened an Islamic Congress in Mecca after the pilgrimage in the summer of

Tayif, summer resort from pre-Islamic times, still attracts local tourists with well-appointed hotels.

Countless pilgrims once passed through the old Mecca Gate, now demolished, in Jiddah.

The foundations of this mosque at al-Jawf, an important center on the caravan route, reportedly go back to the Caliph 'Umar ibn al-Khattab.

Much of Saudi Arabia's land is cultivable and with added nutrients can be productive wherever water can be made available. Deep, prolific aquifers make agriculture by irrigation profitable in many areas, and water-management studies enhanced by experimentation with new crops, machinery, and farming techniques continue to add to the success of new ventures. At left: Vegetable production is increased with use of hydroponic greenhouses and, in the field, by plastic sheeting to help retain soil moisture. Continuing clockwise: Fat-tailed sheep, once the Bedouins' traditional source of meat, milk, and wool. Government farm in al-Hasa oasis, scene of experiments with crops and livestock. Citrus grove in Tayif, a major supplier of many varieties of fruit for both local consumption and export. Al-Hasa water project where hundreds of miles of concrete irrigation and drainage channels web across 50,000 acres. Directly above: Field of barley, an important grain crop along with wheat, millet, and sorghum, adjacent to a view of a project at Wadi al-Sahba where 10,000 acres of reclaimed desert have been turned over to a commercial firm for production of meat, poultry, and dairy products.

1926. The purpose of the congress was to reassure Muslim opinion throughout the world and to give all Muslims an opportunity to suggest measures regarding the pilgrimage and regulate other religious matters of common interest. Thus reassured, Muslims from all over the world during the following years flocked to the Holy Cities for the hajj season.

Remaining in the Hijaz for a time, 'Abd al-'Aziz devoted his attention to organizing the administration of the province and to finding a way of controlling the fiercely independent Bedouins. This was not a simple problem; historically the Bedouin tribes had opposed the imposition of any central authority. But the King's solution was simplicity itself: the chief of every tribe was told that he was responsible for any crime committed by his people and that if for any reason he failed to control them the King would intervene. As 'Abd al-'Aziz (who understood the Bedouins well) dealt with tribal problems with tact and firmness, his system was successful. In talking to the various shaykhs, he made it clear that the land could only resist foreign intervention if it were united under one rule and that the alternative was the anarchy he had spent much of his lifetime bringing to an end. By assisting the tribes in periods of drought and distress, he removed the basic incentive for raids upon neighboring tribes and passing caravans.

In January 1927 'Abd al-'Aziz was officially proclaimed King of the Hijaz and Najd and its Dependencies, with Riyadh and Mecca as his two capitals, and in May of the same year Great Britain in the Treaty of Jiddah formally recognized the kingdom as a fully sovereign state. On September 22, 1932, the country was renamed the Kingdom of Saudi Arabia.

In 1928, however, as 'Abd al-'Aziz was still organizing his kingdom, some of the Ikhwan leaders who had helped him conquer the Hijaz attacked an Iraqi border fort, in defiance of his express orders. As this was in direct violation of the boundary agreement he had concluded with the British at al-'Uqayr in 1922, 'Abd al-'Aziz was, reluctantly, forced to take action; he could not tolerate insubordination which threatened the existence of his young state.

The Ikhwan were motivated by a number of factors in their rebellion. First of all, they were disturbed by 'Abd al-'Aziz's political realism; they saw no reason to honor arrangements with any powers that did not belong to

Every Bedouin chief was made accountable to the King for the actions of his tribe.

'Abd al-'Aziz Al Faysal Al Sa'ud was to become famous in the West simply as King Ibn Sa'ud.

Stamps

Saudi Arabia has been a member of the Universal Postal Union since 1927 and of the Arab Postal Union since 1948, and through arrangements sponsored or supervised by these organizations it maintains regular postal contact with almost all countries of the world. During the period of the first five-year Development Plan (1970-75) the Saudi Arabian Ministry of Telegraphs, Posts, and Telephones more than doubled the number of post offices in the kingdom (from 108 to 228) and as of the late 1970s the national airline, Saudia, and other carriers provided daily service between Saudi Arabia and other countries in Europe, Asia, Africa, and America. Further expansion and improvement of the country's postal services is one of the goals of the government's development plans.

In the 1930s when the first geologists of the California Arabian Standard Oil Company (later to be renamed Aramco) came ashore at Jubail, however, postal services were very limited, especially in the eastern part of the kingdom. The only international mail service in what was then called al-Hasa Province was by boat between al-'Uqayr and Bahrain, and the small post office at al-Khobar was unable to handle the quantities of mail involved in the oil operations. The mail pouches, accordingly, were taken down to al-Khobar pier and put aboard a company launch, accompanied by a Saudi postal official, and sent to Bahrain. Saudi stamps were not used; Bahraini stamps were applied, and return addresses in this period show "CASOC, Bahrain Island." Late in 1941 the al-Khobar post office was expanded and supplied with the large quantities of stamps required, and from this time on the company's mail began to show Saudi stamps. The first mail-carrying commercial airline flight (flown by TWA) landed in Dhahran on July 6, 1946, and in 1962 the first jet air service to and from Dhahran was inaugurated — an event the Saudi Post Office marked with the issue of a commemorative set of five stamps.

First Saudi air stamps appeared in 1949; set issued in 1963 marks first jet service.

The postage stamps of the Kingdom of Saudi Arabia and its forerunners offer a fascinating field for the stamp collector, from the sometimes crude provisional issues of the early days before the establishment of the kingdom to the colorful and professionally produced issues of recent times. The first stamps issued for use in what is now Saudi Arabia date back only to 1916, but the postal history of Arabia goes back well before that. In fact the first postal service in the modern sense was provided by an Egyptian post office which operated in Jiddah from June 1865 until it was closed at the end of June 1881. This service was maintained principally for the use of Egyptian businessmen in Jiddah and for Egyptian pilgrims on their way to or from the Holy Cities, but it was available to all who wished to make use of it, and the records of the Egyptian post office indicate that the Jiddah office was a successful and profitable one. Egyptian stamps used in Jiddah can be identified by the cancellation, which reads "Gedda" or "Djeddah."

Postmark indicates Egyptian stamp showing Sphinx and Pyramids was used in Jiddah.

The Hijaz at this time was under the suzerainty of the Ottoman Empire, and more or less contemporaneously with the operation of the Egyptian post office the Turks began to extend their postal system into the Hijaz and southward into Yemen. Turkish post offices were opened in Jiddah and Mecca in 1871 and by 1892 had reached at least as far south in what is now Saudi Arabia as the town of al-Qunfudhah. Stamps used at these offices were the contemporary Turkish issues, and here again collectors can identify them by their cancellations. Most of the Ottoman post offices in the Hijaz closed in 1916 when the Sharif Husayn, with British backing, declared himself King of the Hijaz, but Turkish forces held out in Medina until January 1919, and the Turkish post office in that city was the last to close. The Turks also maintained post offices in Qatif, al-Hasa, and Jubail in eastern Arabia; these offices were closed when Saudi forces captured this area and expelled the Turks in 1913. Collectors know that stamps bearing cancellations from these three offices are very scarce.

Letter bearing Turkish stamps was mailed from Ottoman post office in the Hijaz.

The first adhesive postage stamps of Arabia appeared in 1916-1917 under the auspices of the Sharif Husayn and were inscribed "Hijazi Postage" and "Mecca." The designs, selected by Colonel T. E. Lawrence ("Lawrence of Arabia") and Sir Ronald Storrs of the British High Commission in Cairo, were based on decorative carvings on mosques and other historical buildings in Cairo and on pages from famous copies of the Quran.

This 1/8-qirsh stamp of 1917 was one of the first postage stamps of the Hijaz.

In 1921-1922 Husayn, relying on secret commitments given him by the British during World War I and wishing to indicate that his domains were not restricted to the Hijaz alone, reissued these stamps with an Arabic overprint reading "Hashimite Arab Government" and the Hijrah date 1340. A short time later a set of locally printed stamps appeared with the same inscription as well as the arms of the Hashimite family, and in 1924 this set was reissued with an overprint commemorating the proclamation of King Husayn as caliph.

Arms of the ruling Hashimite family are shown on this 1/8-qirsh Hijaz stamp.

In July 1925, after the abdication of Husayn, a further set of stamps was issued, based on stylized arabesque designs and inscribed "Hijazi Arab Government." The central feature of each design was an elaborate calligraphic rendering of the name 'Ali ibn al-Husayn, and these were the last stamps issued by the Hashimites; five months after they appeared the Saudi forces captured Jiddah and the Hashimites withdrew from the Hijaz.

Stamps issued in 1925 bear the name of 'Ali as King of the Hijaz.

The Saudi Government in Najd and eastern Arabia at first had no formal apparatus of public postal services, and individuals who had a need to correspond with the world outside had to arrange for private travelers to carry letters either westward to the Hijaz and Egypt or eastward to Bahrain or Kuwait. As the Saudis moved into the Hijaz in 1924 and 1925 and took over the existing postal system, however, there was a need for new stamps to represent the

(Continued on page 142)

Stamps

new status quo. The immediate solution was to improvise by using a series of overprints reading variously "Najdi Postage" or "Najdi Sultanate Postage" which were applied to whatever stamps the retreating Hashimites had left behind them — including not only regular Hashimite postage issues but also Hijaz Railway tax stamps and various other Hijazi revenue stamps and even a few Turkish stamps left over from a still earlier period.

Saudi forces entering the Hijaz issued overprinted Hashimite and Turkish stamps.

The first definitive issue of Saudi stamps, printed in Egypt and consisting of five denominations from one-quarter to five qirsh inscribed "Hijaz and Najd," appeared in February 1926, shortly after 'Abd al-'Aziz was named King of the Hijaz and Sultan of Najd. These have been followed by a number of later issues. The first regular issue with which Aramco employees became familiar as they moved into the eastern part of the kingdom was the so-called *tughra* or monogram issue (so named after the main feature of the design, a highly stylized monogram of King 'Abd al-'Aziz) which appeared piecemeal between 1934 and 1957. Between 1960 and 1975 there appeared a very long series of over 225 stamps in three designs depicting the dam across Wadi Hanifah near Riyadh, Aramco's Buqqa gas-oil separator plant in the Abqaiq oil field, and an airplane of Saudi Arabian Airlines. A so-called "tourist" issue showing various local scenes such as the Ka'bah in Mecca, an Arab horse, and the rock tombs of Madain Salih appeared between 1968 and 1975; and another definitive pictorial set depicting the Ka'bah, a drilling rig in the offshore Khafji oil field, and other scenes began to appear in 1976.

Regular Saudi postage stamps show King's monogram, Aramco GOSP, and the Ka'bah.

Commemoratives mark world anti-malaria campaign and Dammam-Jiddah highway project.

The commemorative stamp issues of Saudi Arabia form a fascinating and often colorful and attractive record of some of the major events in the kingdom's history. The first Saudi commemoratives consisted of a set of five stamps overprinted and issued in July 1925 to mark the first pilgrimage to take place after the reestablishment of Saudi rule over Mecca, and other overprinted issues appeared later in the same year to commemorate the extension of Saudi authority to Medina and Jiddah after the withdrawal of the Hashimites.

Thirtieth year of Saudi national airline was marked by commemorative set of stamps.

A set of commemoratives issued in January 1934 to mark the proclamation of 'Abd al-'Aziz's eldest son, Sa'ud, as Crown Prince was the first set of Saudi stamps to be inscribed "Saudi Arabia" instead of the earlier "Hijaz and Najd," and these have since become some of the scarcest and most valuable stamps of Saudi Arabia. Later commemoratives have honored various international events and anniversaries, such as World Refugee Year, the centennial of the World Meteorological Organization, and the hundredth anniversary of the invention of the telephone, as well as milestones in the history and development of Saudi Arabia including the fiftieth anniversary of the capture of Riyadh, the expansion of Dammam port, the completion of the Dammam-Jiddah highway, and the thirtieth anniversary of Saudia, the national airline. The handsomest of all the commemorative stamps of Saudi Arabia is probably the set issued in July 1975 as a memorial to King Faysal and showing a classically simple portrait of the late King in the act of performing his prayers.

The memorial set issued in 1975 shows King Faysal at prayer.

the reform movement of the Muwahhidun. After the conquest of the Hijaz, furthermore, many of them had come in contact with a more worldly urban life than they had previously known, and they looked with suspicion and mistrust on 'Abd al-'Aziz's readiness to accept some aspects of this life. In 1925, during the siege of Jiddah, for example, the more fanatical among the Ikhwan had opposed the use of the telephone, and 'Abd al-'Aziz had hesitated for some weeks before installing a line between Mecca and his headquarters at the front. At that time he reportedly had won over the Ikhwan by having them listen to verses from the Quran read over the telephone, thus convincing them that "the devil had fled" from this suspicious instrument.

Doubters remained, however, and at a conference of the Ikhwan in 1926 at al-Artawiyah, the first and greatest of the Ikhwan settlements, 'Abd al-'Aziz was criticized for making use of the telegraph, the telephone, the radio, and the motor car — all of them described as "inventions of the devil." In January 1927, therefore, 'Abd al-'Aziz convened a conference of Ikhwan leaders and ulema or religious leaders in Riyadh to discuss these and other matters. During the conference the ulema issued a *fatwa* or religious opinion declining to make a decision on the telegraph, since there was no precedent either for it or against it in the shari'ah (Islamic law), but refrained from taking a stand on the radio, the telephone, and other modern means of communications.

Faced now, in the attack on the Iraqi border, with outright disobedience of his orders on the part of the Ikhwan, 'Abd al-'Aziz moved against them. As they were, by the King's own design, elite forces, the fighting lasted for a year and a half. Finally, at a battle near al-Artawiyah in the spring of 1929, 'Abd al-'Aziz defeated them, brought the rebel leaders to Riyadh, and eventually broke the power of all the rebellious Ikhwan settlements.

In the 1930s the King was confronted with another, less tractable, problem: the economy of the kingdom was still based on stock rearing and traditional subsistence farming in the fertile areas. As more than 40 percent of the population was engaged in agriculture, Saudi Arabia's revenues, essentially, stemmed from customs duties and levies on pilgrims. Now, however, as the worldwide

depression of 1930s worsened, the numbers of pilgrims dropped drastically: in 1929 a hundred thousand pilgrims visited Mecca; in 1931, only forty thousand.

In 1931, at the request of 'Abd al-'Aziz, an American mining engineer named Karl Twitchell came to visit the King in Jiddah and to discuss a survey of the potential resources of the kingdom — particularly untapped sources of water in the Hijaz. Twitchell was unable to discover new water sources there, but he did find the ancient tailings of five gold mines (one of which may have been worked during the time of King Solomon) and in 1934 the Saudi Arabian Mining Syndicate, Ltd., was formed to work Mahd al-Dhahab, "the Cradle of Gold," fifty miles south of Medina.

Karl Twitchell spearheaded early efforts to tap Saudi Arabia's natural resources.

The originally controversial radio system proved its usefulness in a brief war against Yemen which broke out in 1934 when the Imam Yahya of Yemen disputed the Saudi title to the 'Asir region north of Najran, and encouraged local tribes to revolt. 'Abd al-'Aziz sent his oldest sons, Sa'ud and Faysal — both later to become kings — to deal with the threat and kept in touch with them via radio. Sa'ud led a column into the mountains, while Faysal followed the coast and captured the port of Hodeida in Yemen. Yahya abandoned his claim to the disputed area and signed a peace treaty with the Government of Saudi Arabia in May 1934, at Tayif. 'Abd al-'Aziz's terms were moderate — an adjustment of the borders to the south and the exaction of an indemnity of £100,000 in gold to compensate the Saudi Government for expenses incurred during the campaign.

The Saudi victory and 'Abd al-'Aziz's generous terms to his defeated foe — he made no attempt to add Yemen to his kingdom — created a favorable impression throughout the Arab world. The war also led to an ambitious road-building project — a response to the introduction of modern vehicles to transport troops.

In the meantime 'Abd al-'Aziz, still in need of funds to finance the development he thought necessary, had opened discussions with respect to petroleum exploration in Saudi Arabia. In economic terms it was the most important decision of his reign. In 1933, after a concession had been granted to the Standard Oil Company of California, two American geologists landed at Jubail on the east coast to

Protruding stone slabs prevent rainwater from dissolving the characteristic mud-brick buildings in 'Asir.

Rabat Tangier
MOROCCO
A L G E R I A   T U N I S I A
Algiers   Tunis
Tripoli
Benghazi

M E D I T E R R A N E A N   S E A

Istanbul BLACK SEA
Ankara   T U R K E Y
Antioch
Beirut
CYPRUS LEBANON   S Y R I A   Euphrates River
Haifa   Damascus
Alexandria   Port Said Jerusalem
Gaza   TRANS-
Cairo   JORDAN
Suez
SINAI   Aqaba
Mosul
Tigris River   Bagh
CASPIAN SEA
U · S
ISR

L I B Y A

E G Y P T

Nile River

Medin
Yanbu

Nile River

Jiddah   Mecca

R E D

S E A

A N G L O -

E G Y P T I A N

S U D A N

Omdurman
Khartoum

White Nile

Blue Nile

E T H I O P I A

THE MIDDLE EAST AFTER THE FIRST WORLD WAR

With the final defeat of the House of Rashid and the expulsion of the Hashimites from the Hijaz, the Saudi state under King 'Abd al-'Aziz has reestablished itself and extends its control over much of the Arabian Peninsula, and its independence is given *de jure* recognition by Great Britain with the Treaty of Jiddah in May 1927. Simultaneously, however, European colonial control over the other lands of the Middle East and North Africa has reached its peak. Algeria is ruled as a part of metropolitan France, Morocco and Tunisia are French protectorates, and Libya is an Italian colony. The British protectorate over Egypt has been formally ended in 1922, but British influence remains strong and British troops are stationed in the country. Except for Yemen and the territories under 'Abd al-'Aziz, all of the Arabian Peninsula is under some degree of British influence or control. To the north, Iraq is a British mandate, France has been given control over Syria and Lebanon, and the British have mandates over Palestine and Transjordan.

BRITAIN   FRANCE   ITALY

begin a search for petroleum that would eventually lead to the discovery of some of the world's largest oil reserves (see Chapter 4) and transform Saudi Arabia from a simple desert kingdom into a power in world economics and politically one of the most important countries in the Middle East.

These effects, of course, were not felt until after World War II; for although oil in commercial quantities was found in 1938, the war held back the development of production facilities. In the interim, because the war prevented many pilgrims from reaching Mecca, and because severe drought decimated the Bedouins' herds, economic conditions worsened.

At first 'Abd al-'Aziz met his essential expenditures by advances against future oil royalties. Later Great Britain assumed responsibility for aid to Saudi Arabia (since existing U.S. legislation precluded direct American financial aid to the kingdom), and eventually in the last years of the war Saudi Arabia became eligible for lend-lease and other assistance from the United States.

Prince Faysal headed his country's delegation to the founding of the United Nations in San Francisco.

FOREIGN RELATIONS: During most of World War II, the King maintained a position of benevolent neutrality towards Britain and the United States. In return for U.S. military aid, however, he allowed the Americans to construct and use an airfield at Dhahran for maintenance, repair, and other technical services for Allied planes. In 1942 an American legation was opened in Saudi Arabia and in 1944 a Saudi Arabian legation was opened in Washington — both later raised to the rank of embassies.

In February 1945 the King agreed to go to Egypt, where he met first with President Franklin D. Roosevelt aboard an American cruiser anchored in the Great Bitter Lake in the Suez Canal Zone, and then with British Prime Minister Winston Churchill and Foreign Minister Anthony Eden at the Fayyum oasis south of Cairo.

This historic meeting between the American President and the Saudi King confirmed Saudi Arabia's adherence to the Allied cause and in March 1945 Saudi Arabia entered the war on the Allied side. 'Abd al-'Aziz and Roosevelt also exchanged letters in which the King stated that all countries should help and receive the Jewish victims of Nazi Germany,

The Suez Canal Zone was the setting for a historic wartime meeting between King 'Abd al-'Aziz and President Roosevelt.

and that Palestine could not be expected to do this alone. Roosevelt, for his part, recalled in his letter the assurance he had personally given the King at their meeting that the U.S. Government would make no change in its policy toward the Palestine question without full consultation with both the Arabs and the Jews and that he would undertake no actions which might prove hostile to the Arab people. Two weeks later, President Roosevelt reported to the American Congress on his meeting with the King of Saudi Arabia in these words: "Of the problems of Arabia, I learned more about the whole problem, the Muslim problem, the Jewish problem, by talking with Ibn Sa'ud for five minutes than I could have learned in the exchange of two or three dozen letters."

In March 1945 Saudi Arabia joined Egypt, Iraq, Lebanon, Syria, Transjordan, and a representative of the Palestinian people in signing a Pact of Union of Arab States, the foundation of the Arab League.

During the war, too, a number of the King's sons visited the United States and one of them, Prince Faysal, later headed the Saudi delegation at the founding of the United Nations in San Francisco — the first of several assignments he was to undertake as his role in forming the foreign policy of Saudi Arabia expanded.

INTERNAL DEVELOPMENT: At the end of the war Saudi Arabia's situation in the world had already begun to change. As its oil resources had attracted U.S. Government support, oil revenues were starting to mount at a gratifying rate, and at last 'Abd al-'Aziz could begin to move more rapidly toward fulfilling his dream of transforming a tribal and regional society into a modern, centrally administered state.

One of the country's vital needs was, and still is, education. Immediately upon unifying Saudi Arabia in 1926, 'Abd al-'Aziz founded a new school in Mecca. In 1945 he instituted an extensive program of school construction and by 1951 had raised the number of schools in the kingdom to 226, with 1,217 teachers and a combined enrollment of 29,887 pupils, all supplied with free books and tuition. This was the beginning of a long campaign that reached a climax with the government devoting one-sixth of its $143-billion second five-year Development Plan to education.

Another need to which the Saudi Government gave attention was agriculture, a reflection of 'Abd al-'Aziz's earlier perception that agricultural settlements were vital to a country where less than one percent of the land is arable, and where the food supply, as a result, was in earlier years sometimes problematical. Agriculture, in fact, has always been important in Arabia. Throughout the kingdom the evidence of ancient expertise in the arts of irrigation and water conservation is unmistakable, and remains of ancient dams that once spanned wadis in the western part of the country can still be seen today. Near Tayif, one of the best preserved — which today looks like the wall of a giant terrace — displays on its downstream face an inscription dating it to the first century of Islam.

During the long years of decline and tribal warfare, unfortunately, much of the ancient knowledge of irrigation techniques had been lost, and 'Abd al-'Aziz therefore invited a U.S. agricultural mission to visit the country in 1942 and report on its agricultural potential. He also laid the groundwork for pilot projects set up in al-Kharj and elsewhere — projects that became the nucleus of the later government farms and breeding stations. Lastly, the King strongly backed development of the vast underground supplies of water of the eastern part of the kingdom which, today, are being tapped for government irrigation projects.

In July 1947 the government announced that it intended to spend some $270 million to build roads, schools, and hospitals, to install electrical power generation plants, and to foster agricultural irrigation projects. In the early 1950s as state revenues from the postwar boom in oil production approached the $100 million mark, Saudi Arabia was able, with American technical assistance, to launch these and other development programs. Construction was begun of a system of paved roads tying together the major cities of the kingdom, an air service linking the two coasts was established, and modern harbor facilities were built in Jiddah so that the ancient port could take larger ships. A powerful radio station was put into operation in Jiddah, and authorization was given for development of plans for a telephone network which culminated in the 1970s with the construction of a cross-country telephone and telex communications system

based on coaxial cable, microwave transmission stations, and satellite ground stations. The year 1951 saw the completion of a project begun in the late 1940s which was of particular importance to 'Abd al-'Aziz — a railroad linking his capital, Riyadh, with the port of Dammam on the east coast.

Health and medicine were other interests close to the King's heart. On conquering the Hijaz one of his first acts was to improve medical facilities for the pilgrims to Mecca, an act which earned the gratitude of Muslims everywhere; and in 1947, even as plans for hospitals were being discussed, he ordered four surplus field hospitals from the American Army to be used in the inevitable interim between the planning and construction of permanent ones.

These hospitals were actually the first elements in a building program that, in the mid-1970s, brought forth the King Faysal Specialist Hospital and Research Center in Riyadh — one of the most modern medical facilities in the world — and scores of other hospitals throughout the country. As a result of the King's interest in health and medicine, each administrative district in the kingdom was helped to establish its own medical infrastructure, and today there are over seven hundred dispensaries and health centers, as well as mobile medical units which periodically visit the more isolated parts of the country. Another result is that such diseases as malaria, trachoma, and smallpox, all once endemic, have been virtually eliminated.

King 'Abd al-'Aziz established the basis of the country's present administration. In 1953 he sanctioned the formation of a Council of Ministers to act under the presidency of his son, Crown Prince Sa'ud. King 'Abd al-'Aziz, however, did not live to see the profound effect that such projects were to have on his kingdom. On November 9, 1953, with many of them barely launched, he died after fifty-one years as leader and king of a country from which he had been exiled as a youth but later had reconquered, pacified, and finally developed. His life, by any standards, was remarkable. In 1900, when he was about twenty years old, the Arabian Peninsula was one of the least known and most isolated areas in the world. When he died Saudi Arabia, because of his efforts, was well on the way to becoming a world power. His achievements indeed were

Steady growth and industrialization have stimulated today's use of modern cargo-handling techniques at Dammam port.

A specialist works with an electron microscope at King Faysal Specialist Hospital and Research Center, a superbly equipped institution for high-technology medicine.

Jiddah's bustling harbor is the largest on the Red Sea coast.

Saudi Arabia's commitment to education suited to the Kingdom's specific needs is evidenced in institutions across the country. Above left: The pink-domed Royal Technical Institute of Riyadh, said to be the best-equipped of its kind in the Middle East. Facing page, top and center: The University of Petroleum and Minerals atop the jabal at Dhahran, an architectural masterpiece as well as a source of graduates for the professional needs of the country's main industry. Directly above: Professor and students at King 'Abd al-'Aziz University in Jiddah. At left: Pupils at an intermediate boys school and, at far left, opposite page, in an elementary girls school classroom.

almost unparalleled, and due, by common consent, to a powerful intelligence, unflagging courage, exceptional vision, and above all a profound faith in God.

KING SA'UD IBN 'ABD AL-'AZIZ: 'Abd al-'Aziz was succeeded by his son Sa'ud who, twenty years before, had been designated as his successor. Sa'ud was born in Kuwait in 1902, the year his father captured Riyadh. After the conquest of the Hijaz in 1925, he was put in charge of the affairs of Najd, with a special responsibility for tribal affairs. While President of the Council of Ministers he also worked with his younger brother Faysal in extending the administrative structure of the state — through establishment of ministries and autonomous agencies which eventually modified or eliminated most elements of the direct, personal rule that had characterized the reign of 'Abd al-'Aziz. In 1933 he was proclaimed his father's heir and in November 1953, in accordance with the established procedure for the succession, he became king.

During his reign, King Sa'ud broadened Saudi Arabia's relations with its neighbors by undertaking a series of trips and official visits to friendly states. But his reign covered troubled years. On October 17, 1955, he signed a treaty of defense and friendship with Egypt and in the following year, when the French and British attacked Egypt following the nationalization of the Suez Canal Company, Saudi Arabia broke its diplomatic relations with Britain and France. In 1958, with the creation of the United Arab Republic, and Saudi concern over the growing influence of the Soviet Union in the Middle East, relations with Egypt cooled swiftly and did not improve significantly until the early 1970s.

Relations with Jordan, still ruled by the descendants of 'Abd al-'Aziz's former opponents the sharifs of Mecca, improved, and Saudi Arabia also supported Kuwait, its small neighbor to the north, against external threats. In 1958 Sa'ud and the ruler of Bahrain agreed on a boundary in the waters between their two countries.

During Sa'ud's reign, too, the kingdom was plagued with financial difficulties. Despite increasing oil revenues, spending had outstripped income and, in order to finance development projects, large loans against future oil income had been drawn and the

Food

The Bedouins have a saying that translates to "He makes coffee day and night." Among a people justifiably famous for their hospitality, it is a way of describing a generous man. In the old custom, the preparation of Arab coffee — flavored with aromatic cardamom seed but unsweetened — was indeed man's work, and the ring of the brass mortar in which he pounded fresh-roasted beans to powder was music to the ears of expectant guests. If the guest was a man of standing, the host would be obliged to kill a sheep, and the coffee would be followed by an offering of trays heaped high with rice and chunks of mutton or, on rare occasion, rice-stuffed baby lamb rubbed with spice and roasted whole — all surrounded by circles of flat, unleavened bread. The guest would know it was time to go when his host passed the censer trailing the filmy smoke of frankincense or scented wood, for by tradition this signaled the end of the "Arab feast."

Loyalty to custom and tradition is the essence of all Middle East food and feasting, and many of the finest dishes of the Arabs' heritage are centuries old. Arab poets of the Middle Ages celebrate some — like the Damascene sweets still relished today — in detailing the banquets of the caliphs of Baghdad, and both peasant fare and court cuisine spread with the marching armies of Islam. Part of the table of present-day Saudi Arabia comes from the traditions developed by the peninsular Arabs themselves, part from this age-old culinary pool.

Typically Levantine, for instance, are two purees eaten with bread as appetizers: *hummus* made from ground chickpeas, and baba ghannouj *(baba ghannuj)* made from mashed eggplant, both mixtures rich with tahini *(tahinah),* or sesame-seed paste, and pungent with lemon juice and garlic. Typically Turkish are tomatoes, peppers, zucchini, or eggplant stuffed with a spicy mixture of rice, pine nuts, and currants that may also be the center for a wrapping of grape leaves in a version more typically Greek. *Burghul,* or cracked wheat, mixed with finely chopped parsley, onions, tomatoes, and mint, is the main ingredient for the well-known salad called tabbouleh *(tabbulah)* in Lebanon and Syria; mixed with ground lamb and baked in a variety of shapes it is the basis for a meat dish called kibbeh *(kubbah).* The wheat is *jarish* in Saudi Arabia, where it is a

Thompson

favorite rice substitute in central Najd and the oases of the Eastern Province. Everywhere one finds members of that vast family of skewered meats and ground-meat kebabs. And everywhere there is *laban,* the yoghurt of the Middle East, and labneh *(labnah),* the rich cream cheese made from *laban* drained through cheesecloth.

For centuries the date was the Arabs' universal staple. Today in Saudi Arabia dates and coffee may still be offered to a caller; dates stuffed with almonds are a popular confection; dates baked into tiny, sugared cookies known as *ma'mul* are essential to the proper celebration of 'Id al-Fitr, the festival that comes with the close of Ramadan. Dates are the basis for *hunaynah,* a hearty, nearly stiff porridge of ground dates cooked with butter and semolina and flavored with cardamom that is a classic breakfast dish of Najd.

Cardamom is the flavoring, too, for *saliq,* the best known evening rice dish of the country — a hot pudding for which the rice is first half-cooked with meat or chicken broth, then usually simmered with milk until soft. Essential here is a hint of *mustaka,* gum arabic, the aromatic resin of the mastic tree which, like frankincense, recalls the ancient incense trade. A spice mixture of cumin, cinnamon, turmeric, and black pepper which the housewife buys ready mixed flavors a favorite dish of the Eastern Province made with the tender trout-size *subayti,* a local fish that abounds in the Arabian Gulf along with fat-fleshed grouper, king mackerel, and succulent shrimp.

To sample the food of Saudi Arabia in its greatest variety, one must look to the Hijaz, where trade and pilgrim caravans have long lent a cosmopolitan air. Paradoxically, the best time to sample this rich table is during Ramadan when, after the dawn-to-sunset fast, the evening meal is lavish.

The Ramadan fast is broken with a few sips of water, then a few dates and a thick drink prepared from sheets of dried, pressed apricots chopped and pureed with water. The meal itself begins — invariably, in the Hijaz — with a thick, nourishing soup made from soaked wheat and lamb stock, rich with chunks of lamb and spices: cinnamon, cardamom, and the dry, curled leaf of tree wormwood.

Then come the brown Egyptian *ful,* broad beans cooked with tomato, onion, and oil, and next the much-loved *sanbusak,* paper-thin pastry made up in triangular shapes stuffed with ground meat, onion, the pungent leaf of coriander, or the long, spike-like local member of the garlic family called *kurrath.*

The meal may continue with eggs gently cooked on a bed of fried onion, green pepper, and tomato, followed by one or two main dishes. There might be *kabsah* — chicken or lamb sauteed with garlic, onion, tomato, grated carrot, and grated orange rind, served atop rice that has simmered in the meat sauce and all garnished with raisins and almonds. *'Aysh abu lahm* is a local speciality the Hijazis describe as "something like pizza." A leavened dough, egg-rich and flavored with seeds of fennel and black caraway, is baked in the shape of a thick-bottomed pie shell, filled with fried mutton and chopped kurrath or spring onion, and topped with a sauce made from tahinah. There might be a large grouper laid open and covered with onion, tomato, garlic, hot pepper, and cumin, baked and served with lemon, or fish baked with a sweet-sour sauce made from dried tamarind.

The customary way to end such a banquet is with a sweet, preferably one that is soft and cold like the elegant *muhallabiyah,* a delicate pudding of rice flour and milk, lightly flavored with orange blossom or rose water and decorated with almonds and pistachios. For special guests many sweets would be served, and there are many identified especially with the Ramadan season: *luqmat al-qadi,* spoonfuls of soft, light dough sometimes lightly spiced with cardamom and saffron, fried and then dipped in syrup; *qatayif,* store-bought pancakes stuffed at home with nuts and cheese, then fried and covered with syrup; *basbusah,* semolina cooked with sugar syrup, baked into squares and sometimes served with a topping of *qishtah,* the local answer to an Englishman's clotted cream; or *kunafah,* top and bottom layers of pastry that resembles shredded wheat with a middle layer of goat cheese, butter, and pine nuts, and over all, once again, a sweet syrup scented with rose water. The well-known sweet tooth of the Arabs is indulged in Ramadan, and never are rewards better earned.

country was plunging deep into debt. In 1958, therefore, Sa'ud granted his brother, Crown Prince Faysal, full executive powers in financial, internal, and foreign affairs.

In view of the gravity of the problems, Prince Faysal moved with dispatch. He introduced political and economic reforms, developed the cabinet system of government, granted greater freedom to the Saudi press, and, in addressing the financial crisis, insisted on strict austerity, reducing both government expenditures and those of the Royal Family. He also published a state budget for the first time.

Sa'ud's reign was characterized by many positive achievements, particularly in the field of education. The University of Riyadh was founded, government girls' schools were opened, the number of students sent to study abroad was increased, and within the kingdom many schools and religious institutes were established. In the field of social welfare, the government set up a grievance board to insure impartial hearings on citizen complaints, granted interest-free loans to farmers, and in accordance with Islamic law devoted proceeds from the zakah to helping the poor and needy. During Sa'ud's reign, the government built a huge housing complex in Jiddah for pilgrims to use free of charge during the hajj, renovated and extended the Sacred Mosque in Mecca and the Prophet's Mosque in Medina, and paved roads used by the pilgrims.

Sa'ud reigned until November 1964, when, because the King's health was declining, the Royal Family and religious leaders persuaded Faysal to replace him.

KING FAYSAL IBN 'ABD AL-'AZIZ: Born in Riyadh in 1906, Faysal was educated by his maternal grandfather, 'Abd Allah ibn 'Abd al-Latif Al al-Shaykh, a noted religious scholar and a descendant of Muhammad ibn 'Abd al-Wahhab. In 1918 at the age of twelve he accompanied his father on his military campaign against Hayil and in 1922 he led the campaign in 'Asir. Later, in 1934, he also commanded one of the Saudi columns in the war with Yemen.

In 1926, after the conquest of the Hijaz, Faysal was appointed Viceroy of the Hijaz as well as Chairman of the new Consultative Council (the forerunner of the Council of Ministers) and in 1930 he became Minister of

The Natural History Museum of the University of Riyadh belongs to the oldest and largest university of the kingdom.

Saudi Arab women have their own well-equipped institutions of higher learning.

Dress

As in all countries, dress in Saudi Arabia is influenced by climate, utility, and custom. With a few minor regional exceptions (usually slight variations or additions to the basic garment) traditional clothing is uniform across the peninsula, both among residents of towns and cities and among those who dwell in the oases, mountains, and deserts. Differences tend to be found only in the quality of materials used and in the fineness of tailoring; and fashion, for the most part, exercises an influence only on small details, although it does play a role in women's clothing and in the dress of some young men in urban areas.

Boys and men wear the *thawb*, a loose-fitting, ankle-length, usually white shirt which allows free circulation of air though covering almost the entire body. This was traditionally made of cotton, but today artificial fibers are also frequently used. The thawb is slightly more close fitting than the similar garment, called the *dishdashah*, worn in neighboring Gulf states. Both differ from the extremely full galabiya (*jallabiyah*) of Egypt, which is often of polished cotton and has broad, open sleeves, and the similar garment — usually of wool and less frequently of cotton — which is called djellaba (*jallabah*) in North Africa. The sleeves of the thawb close at the wrist. It also buttons at the collar, and matching sets of decorated buttons and cuff links are worn for formal occasions. Breast or side pockets are individual options.

In the cool months, warmer cloth, including wool worsted, is used for the thawb and the color may vary from white and cream to subdued shades of light gray, brown, and sometimes blue or green. It is not at all unusual to see a dark Western-style suit jacket worn over the thawb during the winter, but the more traditional, flowing floor-length cloak called the *bisht* in the eastern and western provinces and *mishlah* elsewhere in the kingdom is still more common. Extremely handsome, with a sweeping air of dignity, the cloak is made of finely woven wool or camel hair, and is worn over the shoulders like a cape, enclosing the arms but open in the front. Small slits in the seams allow the hands to extend when desired. It comes in natural colors of black, brown, and more rarely tan or cream, and is trimmed or edged in black cord or even — usually in the more expensive versions — in gold braid.

Worn on the head are the ubiquitous *ghutrah* and *'iqal,* the headcloth and double ring of black rope or cord to hold it, which to many in the West and elsewhere most represent the image of the adult Arab male. Today the ghutrah and 'iqal are seen worn not only with the thawb, but also with work clothes, military and boy scout uniforms, and even academic gowns.

The square headcloth comes in plain white and in red-and-white or black-and-white checks. The color is a matter of personal or regional preference, although the checks seem to be somewhat more common in the interior and rural regions of the peninsula and the white in the more urbanized areas. Folded diagonally to make a triangle, the headdress is draped with the fold across the forehead and the points hanging down the back of the head and shoulders. One or both ends or the tail of the

triangle can also be casually tossed forward over the shoulders, or wrapped loosely around the neck, across the ears and lower face, or even around the top of the head, offering the wearer varying degrees of protection from wind, dust, smoke, sun, heat, or cold. The way in which the cloth is wrapped and the angle or position in which the cord sits on the head are very much a matter of the wearer's personal preference.

Further north, in the Arab countries of the Eastern Mediterranean, the ghutrah is called *hattah* or *kufiyah* by those who wear it. In Saudi Arabia kufiyah is the name for the small, brimless, usually white cap worn by younger boys and by many men in informal situations, and frequently worn beneath the ghutrah to help position the 'iqal.

Sandals complete the traditional male dress, although today Western-style shoes are equally common. All kinds of sandals are worn, but the traditional type has a broad, oval-shaped natural leather strap decorated with geometric patterns of colored or metallic stitching across the top of the foot.

Other variations in the national dress are few. In the winter, herdsmen in the northern plateau regions along the Jordanian and Iraqi frontiers may wear very heavy cloaks, or *farwahs,* lined with sheepskin and covered in thick red, brown, or black canvas decorated on the back with bold open diamond patterns in black braid. Tribesmen or travelers in remote areas sometimes belt the usually

(Continued on page 154)

Dress

free-falling thawb with a wide leather strap in which they can carry a knife or money. In the extreme southwest, both men and women sometimes wear broad-brimmed conical straw hats.

In the coastal regions, workers in traditional jobs requiring freedom of movement, such as sailors, or farmers climbing date palms or planting rice, often wear a thin knit T-shirt with a brightly patterned cotton sarong called *izar* or *futah* tucked around the waist and reaching to mid-calf. In modern industries where men work close to heavy vehicles or machines with moving parts, Western-style trousers, shirts, safety shoes, and hard hats are replacing flowing thawbs, sandals, and ghutrahs, at least during working hours.

Little girls may wear frilly party dresses much like their counterparts in Europe and America, while their older sisters and their mothers slip the floor-length 'abayah over their heads and around their shoulders when going out in public, drawing it closed in front with their hands. Beneath the somber black 'abayah or when it comes off at home or at school or while visiting female friends, dresses are invariably bright and cheerful. Traditional dresses are basically colorful versions of the thawb, often decorated with glittering sequins or metallic thread. Many women in the larger towns today wear the latest Western fashions

beneath their 'abayahs and watch the rise and fall of the hemline as closely as their sisters abroad. Both women and girls, even those from families of modest income, often wear great amounts of gold or silver jewelry — which doubles both as ornament and as investment. Traditional wedding dresses are known for their intricate and colorfully embroidered fronts.

Like the 'abayah, the veil is generally worn by women and older girls outside the immediate family circle. Bedouin women and farm women of the 'Asir mountains have traditionally not worn the veil while performing daily chores, and tend rather to pull their 'abayahs modestly across their faces when strangers approach. This custom is also seen more frequently today in the larger cities. Veil styles range from a stiff fabric, cut mask-like with narrow eye slits, to a sheer piece of black chiffon or an ornamental draping with embroidery, beads, or rows of coins. But throughout the peninsula, and certainly among older women, the veil in some form is as typical and ubiquitous as is the ghutrah of the men.

On Thursdays and Fridays in the marketplaces of the major cities these days, one sees national costumes from the world over. Western expatriates in Saudi Arabia dress much as they would for similar climate and circumstances at home except that clothing, both in offices and on social occasions, is usually somewhat more casual. Revealing or tight-fitting clothing is considered inappropriate for either men or women, however, and even in sports situations a degree of modesty is a thoughtful sign of consideration and respect for local tradition.

Foreign Affairs. While holding those posts, Faysal traveled extensively in Europe, including the Soviet Union in 1934, and the Middle East. In 1939 he attended a conference on Palestine in London, and in 1943, with his brother the present King Khalid, he made a state visit to President Roosevelt in Washington. He also represented Saudi Arabia at the United Nations Conference of 1945 and, during the 1947 UN debate on the Palestine problem, delivered a historic speech opposing partition. Later, when King Sa'ud succeeded his father, Faysal was appointed President of the Council of Ministers and then, in 1964, became king.

As he had before his accession, King Faysal devoted much of his attention to foreign affairs, particularly, in the first years of his reign, to the problems arising from civil war in Yemen. To strengthen ties among the Muslim states of the world, he also traveled widely, particularly in Africa and the Middle East. As the spokesman and interpreter for Muslims everywhere, he was a spiritual force as well as a political leader.

On the domestic front Faysal continued to press forward with fiscal and administrative reforms. In keeping with his own expressed views on development — "change, but change slowly" — the reforms came gradually. The effect, nevertheless, was more centralization of government and administration.

ADMINISTRATIVE CHANGES: Originally the Kingdom of Saudi Arabia was divided into geographical regions. The main divisions were Najd, which covers a large part of the interior and includes the capital Riyadh; the Hijaz, which contains the Holy Cities of Mecca and Medina and also Jiddah, the kingdom's main port on the Red Sea; 'Asir, a mountainous district ruled from Abha and including Najran, a fertile valley close to the border with Yemen; and al-Hasa (later called the Eastern Province), named after the oasis of al-Hasa but also including Dammam, the Qatif oasis, Tarut Island, Jubail, the principal oil fields, and the major oil company communities of Dhahran, Abqaiq, and Ras Tanura.

Today, however, the kingdom has been subdivided into fourteen administrative districts which do not necessarily correspond with the geographical divisions. Of the fourteen districts five are considered major

amirates or provinces — the Eastern Province, Riyadh, Mecca, Hayil, and the Amirate of the Northern Frontiers. Two other principal provincial areas are those of Medina and the Qasim.

During the reign of 'Abd al-'Aziz the amirs, or governors, of the provinces — because of the size of the country and the absence of modern communication facilities — governed their areas semiautonomously, although in the King's name. Generally, even local officials of the central government were subordinates of the amirs. Under Faysal's gradual centralization of administration, however, this changed: most of the amirs of the provinces report to the Ministry of the Interior, and local representatives of the central government report to their respective ministries. Local leaders such as the heads of municipalities, towns, and villages report to the Ministry of Municipal and Rural Affairs in Riyadh.

The composition and procedures of the central government itself also changed in this period. Earlier, in 1953, King 'Abd al-'Aziz, recognizing that the simple direct methods of tribal administration would not suffice in a kingdom the size of Saudi Arabia, established the Council of Ministers under a president who was in effect the prime minister. Faysal, who had served as President of the Council, now began to modernize the kingdom's administrative machinery. One step was to invite experts from such institutions as the United Nations and the Ford Foundation to help with administrative organization and training. Another was to invest heavily in education and send thousands of young Saudi students to colleges and universities, both at home and abroad, in an effort to meet the country's need for trained personnel.

LAW IN MODERN SAUDI ARABIA: While Faysal pressed for changes in administration, however, he continued to adhere strictly to the fundamental law of the kingdom. This was, and is today, the shari'ah, the sacred law of Islam. Rooted in the Quran and the practices and sayings of the Prophet, it is the shari'ah, rather than a written constitution and man-made legislative acts, that is the heart of the legal system of the kingdom. Although essentially religious in nature, the shari'ah extends far beyond religious matters. In Saudi Arabia,

King Faysal, monarch from 1964 until 1975, earned renown as a spiritual as well as political leader.

Three Saudi PhD candidates attend a symposium sponsored by Georgetown University's new Center for Contemporary Arab Studies.

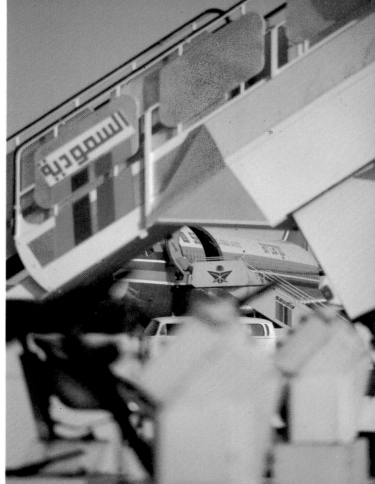

Thousands of miles of modern transportation lines today link the provinces of Saudi Arabia and help the kingdom cope with its growing commercial traffic and the increasing mobility of its people. This page, above: New port installations on the Gulf at Jubail, fast-developing industrial site in the Eastern Province. Top: Tri-Star of the fleet owned by Saudia, the national airline of Saudi Arabia and the biggest carrier in the Middle East. Opposite page, beginning at top: LPG tanker *Al-Berry*, the first vessel of this type to fly the Saudi flag. Terminal buildings at an entirely new Jiddah airport, successor to an outgrown facility. The Jiddah-Tayif highway, a showpiece of modern road-building techniques, cuts through the mountains of the Hijaz, while the Saudi Government railroad carries passengers and freight across 360 miles of desert between Riyadh and Dammam.

Turaif
al-Qurayyat
Badanah
Ar'ar
Sakaka
al-Jawf
JORDAN
Haql
Tabuk
Tayma
Duba
Madain Salih
al-'Ula
al-Wajh
Khaybar
Medina
Yanbu' al-Nakhl
Yanbu' al-Bahr
Rabigh
Jiddah
Me
RED
al-Li
SEA

SAUDI ARABIA: ROADS, PORTS, AND AIRPORTS

From its early days the Saudi Arab Government has seen the development of internal transportation as one of the most effective ways of unifying and thus strengthening the kingdom. When George Sadlier, probably the first Westerner to cross the Arabian Peninsula from coast to coast, made his journey in 1819, it took him almost three months to travel from Qatif to Yanbu', and when Philby made the trip from al-'Uqayr to Jiddah a century later it took him almost a month. Today the coasts of Saudi Arabia are only hours apart, and its towns and villages are linked by a network of 21,000 miles of paved major highways. Moreover, the country is served by a national airline that in 1979 carried nearly five million passengers on its domestic routes alone, a railroad running between Dammam and Riyadh, and ports that have been enlarged and modernized to handle the huge volumes of cargo needed to support its development plans.

—————— PIPELINES   —————— MAJOR ROADS   --------- UNDER CONSTRUCTION   ✈ AIRPORTS   ⚓ SEAPORTS as it once did throughout the Islamic world, the shari'ah regulates virtually all matters covered in Western countries by civil and criminal law. Because, furthermore, the shari'ah is considered as divine law, it is interpreted and administered by the qadis and ulema, a body of learned religious men; as a result the judiciary system in the kingdom has a considerable degree of independence from other branches of government.

In matters not expressly prohibited or enjoined by the shari'ah, however, the King, through the Council of Ministers and a number of commissions and councils, administers a relatively large body of regulations covering such areas as public health, customs, commerce, and labor — all increasingly important as the process of modernization moves ahead.

MODERNIZATION OF THE KINGDOM:
Under Faysal, the efforts of 'Abd al-'Aziz continued to bear fruit in all fields and particularly in transportation, communications, and industry.

Cars and trucks were introduced into Saudi Arabia in the 1920s and perhaps even earlier. Because of the nature of much of the terrain, and because of the lack of adequate roads, their use was at first largely restricted to the bigger towns (though Twitchell and geologists of Aramco crossed the peninsula by car a number of times in the early 1930s). Road construction on a large scale did not get under way until after World War II, but by 1979 the government had built about 12,500 miles of paved main highways including the 950-mile transpeninsular highway linking Dammam with Riyadh and Jiddah and the 880-mile road running from Dammam to the frontier with Jordan, as well as over 2,000 miles of feeder roads. In the late 1940s 'Abd al-'Aziz had also pushed construction of a 360-mile railroad from Dammam to Riyadh, completed in 1951.

To link the distant provinces of a country the size of all of Western Europe, Saudi Arabia also established a national airline in the 1940s. Now called Saudia, the airline grew rapidly into one of the major airlines of the Middle East. By the late 1970s its fleet of jets provided domestic flights daily throughout Saudi Arabia and international flights to many Middle East terminals as well as to India, Pakistan, North Africa, Europe, and North America.

Aramco geological parties were first to use cars in the Eastern Province.

Saudi pilot flies for the national airline of Saudi Arabia, the largest in the Middle East.

During Faysal's reign too, the government encouraged private development of agriculture and those sectors of the economy other than petroleum. In earlier times the pillars of the economy were date farming, livestock, pearling, and the export of such simple goods as *bishts* (handwoven woolen cloaks) and jewelry. In the 1960s the kingdom's entrepreneurs began to turn to the processing of plastics, steel, cement, and tiles. As encouragement the government began to provide low-cost industrial sites and special tax and customs incentives.

Many of these steps forward in the development of the resources and economic infrastructure of the kingdom were achieved under the first five-year Development Plan, inaugurated in 1970, under which the economy of the country grew very rapidly, with real national income increasing at a rate of almost 45 percent per year.

In 1969-1970, when the plan was being drawn up, Saudi Arabia's oil production was relatively low (less than 3.5 million barrels a day), the financial resources of the kingdom were limited, and there were definite restrictions on government spending. The plan was drawn up with these restrictions and limitations in mind.

The unforeseen rise in oil production in the years immediately after the plan went into effect (see Chapter 4) and the subsequent very large rise in government income meant that these restraints were no longer required. The period 1970-1975 turned out to be one with a very high rate of economic growth and accomplishment in which many of the goals of the Development Plan were reached or even surpassed, although not all of its objectives were achieved. For example, among the most important of the general goals of the plan was reducing the country's dependence on the oil industry for its income, but although there was a very substantial absolute increase in the importance of the non-oil sectors of the economy, their contribution to the gross national product was actually reduced in proportionate terms because of the very great increase in income from the oil industry. Nevertheless, the kingdom's planners gained valuable experience which they were subsequently able to put to good use in drawing up and implementing the second five-year Development Plan.

Money

These quarter-, half-, and one-riyal silver coins of Saudi Arabia appeared in 1936.

The first money of the House of Sa'ud was issued shortly after the capture of Mecca in 1924 and consisted of copper half-qirsh and quarter-qirsh coins bearing the *tughra* or monogram of 'Abd al-'Aziz and inscribed "Minted in the Mother of Villages" (a traditional name for Mecca). These coins circulated along with the gold dinar, silver riyal, and copper qirsh struck by the Hashimite government of the Hijaz as well as the Turkish silver majidi, the Austrian Maria Theresa dollar, and various other foreign coins. They were followed a year later by quarter-, half-, and one-qirsh coins issued in the name of 'Abd al-'Aziz as King of the Hijaz and Sultan of Najd.

Gold Hashimite dinar and silver Maria Theresa dollar circulated before Saudi coinage.

On January 24, 1928, 'Abd al-'Aziz established an independent monetary system based on the Saudi riyal, a silver coin about the size of a U.S. silver dollar and valued at one-tenth of a British sovereign. In 1936 a new riyal coin about the size of a U. S. half dollar was issued. This coin weighed 11.66 grams and was eventually valued at approximately 3.75 Saudi riyals to the U. S. dollar. New half-riyal and quarter-riyal silver coins and one-qirsh, half-qirsh, and quarter-qirsh cupronickel coins were issued. By the late 1950s the value of the silver content of the silver coins had become considerably more than their face value, and they disappeared from circulation. They were officially demonetized in December 1959. The cupronickel coins were

Large silver riyal of 'Abd al-'Aziz was inscribed "King of the Hijaz and Najd"

withdrawn from circulation in 1958 and demonetized in the following year. They were replaced by new cupronickel coins in one-qirsh, two-qirsh, and four-qirsh denominations.

For many years Saudi Arabia issued no paper currency. Major transactions had to be carried out with gold or large quantities of silver riyals and occasionally foreign banknotes such as Indian rupees, U. S. dollars, and Egyptian pounds. The expansion of oil production, with its impact on payments of all kinds, so increased the demands for cash, however, that the handling of silver and gold coins in the quantities needed became almost impossible. To pay oil royalties to the government, for example, Aramco for many years had to arrange for kegs of foreign gold coins to be flown to Jiddah for delivery to the Ministry of Finance. To pay its employees (whose bi-weekly wages in silver coins might weigh as much as ten pounds) the company had to transport, guard, and count some forty tons of silver coins every month.

In 1951, therefore, the government, realizing that it needed a more workable monetary system, invited a team of foreign financial experts to draw up a program of monetary reform. Out of the recommendations of the experts came the formation in the following year of the Saudi Arabian Monetary Agency (SAMA), a form of central bank established to strengthen and stabilize the country's currency, to centralize government receipts and payments, and to control disbursements authorized under the government's budget.

Saudi Arabia issued these gold sovereigns in 1952 (left), and 1958.

The monetary agency was forbidden by its charter to issue paper money, but in the year it was established it issued the Saudi sovereign, a gold coin of the same weight and approximate fineness as the British sovereign and with a par value of forty Saudi riyals. Following the discovery of a large number of counterfeit Saudi sovereigns, a new sovereign of the same size and weight but of a different design was issued in January 1958. Both types of sovereigns were later demonetized.

(Continued on page 162)

Money

Despite the explicit prohibition in its charter against the issue of paper money, SAMA in 1953 won government permission to issue "pilgrim receipts," a sort of traveler's check designed to meet the seasonal needs of foreign pilgrims for riyals. It was announced that the receipts were issued primarily to relieve pilgrims of the necessity of carrying large sums in heavy silver coins, but the receipts (fully backed by silver riyals and eventually issued in ten-, five-, and one-riyal denominations) were an immediate success and soon circulated throughout the kingdom. Within a short time more than 150 million riyals worth were in circulation, rapidly replacing both gold sovereigns and silver riyals, and they soon gained the virtual status of official paper currency. A new series of pilgrim receipts was issued beginning in 1954.

Pilgrim receipts, first issued in 1953, were forerunners of official paper currency.

In 1953 the financially cautious King 'Abd al-'Aziz died and government spending, previously held in check by him, began to increase substantially. Before long foreign exchange payments were exceeding income and debts had begun to accumulate. At the same time, the government abandoned the requirement that the receipts must have 100 percent hard-money backing — a move that proved disastrous when, between 1956 and 1958, severe inflation swept the country and the value of the riyal sank in relation to both goods and foreign currencies.

In 1956 additional problems developed. In the wake of the second Arab-Israeli war, oil production fell sharply and government revenues dropped from $341 million in 1955 to $290 million. On top of unchecked government spending, excessive borrowing, and the flight of capital, this drop in revenues weakened the riyal even more and by early 1958 the country was facing uncontrolled inflation, exhaustion of its foreign exchange reserves, and nearly half a billion dollars in debts.

At this point Crown Prince Faysal asked two financial experts, Anwar Ali of Pakistan and Ahmad Zaki Saad of Egypt (both on loan from the International Monetary Fund), to design and implement a program of fiscal and monetary reform. The objectives — to balance spending and income, pay the national debt, curb inflation, and stabilize the riyal — were challenging, particularly as the decisive measures needed had to be introduced cautiously and without imposing unenforceable controls. Yet the experts, with Faysal's firm and active backing, succeeded. By clamping

curbs on unessential imports, establishing a dual rate of exchange for the riyal, reducing government expenditures drastically, and devaluating the riyal, they reversed the decline in a year and a half.

At the beginning of 1960, the Government of Saudi Arabia revalued the riyal, fixing its value in terms of gold at the equivalent of 4.5 riyals to the U. S. dollar and insuring stability of the riyal by providing 100 percent backing in gold and foreign currency. At the same time it was announced that henceforth the riyal would contain twenty qirsh rather than twenty-two and that the qirsh would be divided into five halalah. Thus the currency, in effect, was put on a decimal basis for the first time.

By the end of 1960 the inflationary spiral had been stopped, the international exchange value of the riyal had been stabilized, and a start had been made on retiring the national debt. Saudi Arabia had joined the International Monetary Fund in 1957, and in March 1961 it accepted the Fund's obligation to make the Saudi riyal a fully convertible currency. Two years later the kingdom became, and has since remained, one of the few countries in the world without a national debt.

In June 1961 the Monetary Agency issued an official Saudi paper currency in denominations of one, five, ten, fifty, and a hundred riyals. The pilgrim receipts remained in circulation alongside the new paper money until 1963. Since 1976 Saudi banknotes (printed in Arabic on one side and English on the other) have borne not only crossed swords and a palm tree, the national emblem, but also portraits of King 'Abd al-'Aziz and King Faysal. The coinage consists of 5, 10, 25, and 50 halalah and one riyal (100 halalah) cupronickel coins. There is also a bronze 1 halalah coin, but this is rarely seen in circulation.

New coins in halalah denominations appeared after decimalization of Saudi currency.

By the mid-1970s Saudi Arabia had developed a sophisticated and responsible fiscal system capable of handling both the country's expanded internal money supply and its very large international reserve holdings. The kingdom, furthermore, was financing its enormous development program and other projects out of current income rather than from loans, was a key contributor to multi-million-dollar international aid programs, and had become an important source of capital for the World Bank and the International Monetary Fund. In 1978 it became entitled to appoint its own director to represent Saudi Arabia on the Executive Board of the IMF, a reflection of its position as one of the largest creditors of that organization.

During the period of the first Development Plan, Saudi Arabia emerged as a pivotal source of the world's petroleum supplies (see Chapter 4) and King Faysal's government was faced with a financial problem that was the reverse of his father's. Instead of worrying about how to make ends meet, the government had to cope with a monetary surplus that some Western economists said could upset finances and currencies around the world. The economists were quickly proven wrong. Although Saudi Arabia invested a good share of its surplus funds abroad, a substantial percentage was earmarked for aid to other, less fortunate, nations and in addition the kingdom began to channel billions of dollars into the ambitious second five-year Development Plan to expand the industrial infrastructure of the country.

THE DEATH OF FAYSAL: In March 1975 King Faysal was assassinated by a deranged young relative as he sat in his office in Riyadh. To the world at large his death was a shocking development and a serious loss; for Faysal, to the West as well as to the East, to Christians as well as to Muslims, had emerged in his last years as a moderating influence politically and economically throughout the Middle East. At a time when the political and economic impact of the Middle East was increasingly affecting the entire industrialized world, it was Faysal more than any other leader who spoke for balance and reason.

In Saudi Arabia, of course, the loss of Faysal was felt even more deeply. Like his father, he had ruled with the consent and blessings of his subjects, had governed them in the spirit of Islam, and had devoted his rule to providing a better life for his people and a better future for his country.

To some foreign observers the smooth transition of power and the lack of hysteria surrounding Faysal's death were surprising; to those who knew the country, however, they were not. Although Faysal had been an exceptional man and an effective leader, the Kingdom of Saudi Arabia, for which he so deeply cared, was not dependent for its stability on the rule of any one man.

KING KHALID IBN 'ABD AL-'AZIZ: Born in 1912 in Riyadh, Faysal's successor King

Khalid was exposed to the problems of the country at an early age. After the conflict with Yemen in 1934 he was his country's representative at the peace negotiations at Tayif. With Faysal, he had attended a number of international meetings on behalf of Saudi Arabia—in particular, the 1939 conference on Palestine held in London, the official visit to President Roosevelt in 1943, and the founding of the U.N. in 1945. In October 1962 Khalid was named Vice President of the Council of Ministers and in 1965 he was designated Crown Prince.

When Khalid assumed the responsibilities of the kingdom, the senior members of Al Sa'ud chose Fahd, a younger brother, to be Crown Prince. Assisted by Fahd, Khalid began to address himself to the problems of a kingdom that had changed almost beyond recognition since 'Abd al-'Aziz became King of the Hijaz almost fifty years before.

To a large extent the change in the country had come about because of Saudi Arabia's emergence as the single most important source of petroleum in the world. With oil reserves equal to about one-fourth the combined reserves of the entire world, Saudi Arabia at the time of Khalid's accession was playing a decisive role in world affairs economically and politically.

Internally the kingdom had changed too. In place of the relatively simple tribal rule of 'Abd al-'Aziz, Saudi Arabia's government and administrative system had grown into a huge, complex, and modern system. Khalid was King of Saudi Arabia, Supreme Commander of the Saudi Arabian Armed Forces, President of the Council of Ministers, President of the Consultative Council, and Chairman of the Supreme Committee for Administrative Reform. Assisting him were the Crown Prince, Fahd ibn 'Abd al-'Aziz, First Vice President of the Council of Ministers and chairman of many important decision-making bodies; 'Abd Allah ibn 'Abd al-'Aziz, Second Vice President of the Council of Ministers and Commander of the National Guard; and various ministries, boards, bureaus, committees, and councils.

Reflecting the complexity of government, the Council of Ministers was made up of the Ministers of Defense and Aviation, Public Works and Housing, Interior, Municipal and Rural Affairs, Foreign Affairs, Education,

His Majesty King Khalid ibn 'Abd al-'Aziz.

His Royal Highness Crown Prince Fahd ibn 'Abd al-'Aziz.

His Royal Highness Prince 'Abd Allah ibn 'Abd al-'Aziz.

Saudi Arabia's massive development program is one of the most ambitious ever undertaken by any nation. The ubiquitous earth mover rivals the construction crane as a symbol of industrial expansion that comprises both multi-billion dollar government-sponsored projects and smaller, private manufacturing ventures which help diversify the country's economic base. Among Jiddah industries are a computerized steel rolling mill and an automotive assembly plant, both seen above. Across the peninsula in the Eastern Province, an industrial park at Dammam is site for such factories as one making extruded aluminum products, above left. Facing page: Dammam industries also turn out hoses and fittings for export as well as local sale; plastic and asbestos pipe for water conduction and sewage disposal; structural steel partitions for the building trade.

Finance and National Economy, Petroleum and Mineral Resources, Justice, Communications, Higher Education, Labor and Social Affairs, Planning, Pilgrimage and Waqfs, Agriculture and Water, Information, Health, Commerce, Industry and Electricity, and Telegraphs, Posts, and Telephones, as well as other officials bearing the title of Minister of State.

The Council of Ministers is collectively involved in implementing the second five-year Development Plan, one of the most ambitious programs ever undertaken by a developing country and King Faysal's last major effort on behalf of Saudi Arabia. Basically, the Development Plan calls for expenditure of about $143 billion to provide the kingdom with an enormous industrial infrastructure on which it can build the society its planners envision. But the Plan also aims at providing the kingdom's several million citizens with housing, health, and education. Under a $79-billion allocation for construction, for example, it calls for the building of 2,000 new schools, 175,000 houses — enough to provide better shelter for more than 10 percent of the population — 50 new hospitals, 575 dispensaries, municipal drainage and sewage systems, and new roads for towns and cities.

The Plan also provides for the expenditure of $4 billion on highways, $2 billion on airports, $2.5 billion on seaports, and $10.5 billion for electrical power generation and water desalination, and the construction of complete industrial centers which will include factories, homes, schools, roads, water, electricity, sewage, ports, and transport — each in itself a major undertaking.

The planners saw that some projects are naturally more important than others and, as a result, assigned them higher priorities. One is the immense gas-gathering project (see Chapter 4) which is the key to Saudi Arabia's heavy industrialization program and which, on completion, will make possible almost complete utilization of the gas produced in association with crude oil. This gas will provide both fuel and raw materials for such industrial undertakings as the manufacture of petrochemicals in Saudi Arabia. It will also provide fuel for Aramco's operations, for the desalination of water, and for the generation of electricity in the Eastern Province.

To provide electric power for the growing needs of the kingdom, the government is establishing a number of major power grids — each one covering a sizable segment of the country. The Saudi Consolidated Electric Company in the Eastern Province (SCECO) is the largest of these grids. This integrated network, which the Saudi Government asked Aramco to manage during the first five years (1977-1981) of its operation, merged the independent companies in the Eastern Province with Aramco's grid and tied their facilities together in an integrated system which is expected to provide over 6,000 megawatts of electric power by the mid-1980s. Together with power generated at the government's water desalination plants, this will be fed into a grid of some three thousand miles of transmission lines to provide the electric power needed by Aramco to operate its oil and gas facilities, as well as meeting the needs of the people of the Eastern Province and supplying power to the industries which will be developed in the Jubail industrial complex (see Chapter 4). Similar integrated systems are being established in other areas as well.

A third high-priority project is the improvement of seaports, the inadequacy of which had begun to create serious congestion as early as the 1960s and as a result had hampered the kingdom's preliminary moves toward growth and expansion. In 1966, during Faysal's reign, the government had already begun to modernize and improve its port facilities by building a new port at Yanbu', north of Jiddah, enlarging the port of Dammam, and expanding the port of Jiddah. The government had also improved smaller ports at Qatif, Jubail, and al-Khobar. But with rapidly multiplying volumes of imports (totaling about $22 billion in 1978), even the improved facilities could not offload and move the quantities of materials needed. As a result, incoming ships from the early 1970s to 1976 began to clog all the ports, and the unloading of badly needed cargoes was sometimes delayed for months.

To solve the immediate problem the government initiated or supported such emergency programs as the construction of "barge ports" to bring cargo to shore in barges. As these programs began to take effect, the harbor crisis was overcome, but because forecasts suggest that imports will continue to rise

A high-rise housing complex stands on the outskirts of Dammam.

Ghizlan power plant near Ju'aymah on the Gulf coast will form the hub of SCECO's province-wide transmission system.

Calendar, Clocks

In the seventh century, according to the historian al-Biruni, the Caliph 'Umar ibn al-Khattab, after conquering Persia and driving the Byzantines from Syria, found that administration of the new Islamic empire required extensive correspondence with his far-flung regional governors and generals. That, in turn, involved him in the problem of calendars; in attempting to date the correspondence he learned that the various systems of dating then current were both complicated and linked to other religions and states. As they were therefore for one reason or another both impractical and unacceptable, it was decided to establish a new calendar system based on the advent of Islam.

In establishing the new system 'Umar decided, after consulting with his companions, to use the year of the Hijrah, the Prophet's emigration from Mecca to Medina, as the starting point of the Islamic era, and to start the new calendar from the day of Muhammad's departure from Mecca on July 16, 622. Year One of the Islamic calendar thus corresponds to A.D. 622-623. The Western method of designating Islamic dates is by the abbreviation A.H., for Anno Hegirae or "Year of the Hijrah."

Relying on a number of passages in the Quran (surahs ix: 36–37, and x: 5), 'Umar established the new Islamic calendar, in contrast to most other calendars, on the basis of a strictly lunar year. One lunar month — which is the cycle between two new moons — contains 29 days, 12 hours, 44 minutes, and 2.8 seconds. A lunar year of twelve months, therefore, contains 354 days and 11/30 of a day. This fraction adds up to 11 days in every cycle of 30 years, and these are inserted into the calendar by establishing leap years. Therefore every period of 30 years has 11 leap years of 355 days. The intercalated day is always added to the month of Dhu al-Hijjah, the last month of the year.

The difference between the 354 or 355-day lunar year and the astronomical solar year of 365-1/4 days accounts for the difficulty of converting dates from the Islamic *(Hijri* or "Hijrah") calendar to the Gregorian calendar and vice versa. One method of conversion is to use the following equation on the basis that every 32 Gregorian solar years are approximately equal to 33 Muslim lunar years.

(A.D. = Gregorian year, A.H. = Hijrah year):

$$\text{A.D.} = 622 + (\tfrac{32}{33} \times \text{A.H.}) \text{ or A.H.} = \tfrac{33}{32} \times (\text{A.D.} - 622)$$

It should be remembered that these formulas give only the year in which the corresponding year began. For example, A.H. 1398 began on December 12, 1977, but most of 1398 fell in A.D. 1978.

Some other guides for approximate conversion are: a Gregorian century equals 103 Hijrah years; 100 Hijrah years equal 97 Gregorian years; the year A.H. 1396 corresponded very closely to A.D. 1976.

The twelve months of the Islamic year are:

Muharram
Safar
Rabi' al-Awwal (Rabi' I)
Rabi' al-Thani (Rabi' II)
Jumada al-Ula (Jumada I)
Jumada al-Akhirah (Jumada II)
Rajab
Sha'ban
Ramadan
Shawwal
Dhu al-Qa'dah
Dhu al-Hijjah

In theory the months contain 30 or 29 days alternately, with the odd-numbered months generally containing 30 days and the even-numbered months generally containing 29 days. But the actual length of each month depends on when the new moon is sighted, as the sighting of the new moon marks the beginning of the month and the sighting of the next new moon marks its end.

The lunar year is completely unrelated to the seasons because each year begins 10 or 11 days earlier in the Gregorian year than the previous one. Thus any one of the months of the Islamic year may occur in any season. If your birth date is Rajab 15, you might celebrate the occasion one time in July and fifteen years later in February. Schools in Saudi Arabia, as a result, close for the summer holiday in any three consecutive months that may fall in that season; and Ramadan, the month of fasting (see Chapter 2), may occur in winter, spring, summer, or autumn, making a complete cycle every 33 Gregorian years.

Similarly Muslim festivals, unlike Christmas or the Fourth of July, may occur in any season. But in addition to the difference in timing, there are major differences with regard to festivals. In Western countries, holidays celebrate a variety of religious, historic, social, and military events. But in Saudi Arabia, a country that strictly follows the doctrines of Islam, the main holidays that are recognized and observed are the two religious feasts of *'Id al-Adha* and *'Id al-Fitr.*

'Id al-Adha or "the Festival of the Sacrifice," falls on the tenth day of the twelfth month, Dhu al-Hijjah, and marks the end of the hajj (see Chapter 2). It is celebrated with the sacrifice of a sheep or goat — or sometimes, if the family can afford it, a camel or an ox — which is then given to the poor. Public worship is also performed by the whole

(Continued on page 168)

Calendar, Clocks

community. In most Muslim countries the duration of the festival is three days, during which most people dress in new clothes, exchange presents, visit friends and relatives, and may serve special foods and sweets.

The other feast day, 'Id al-Fitr or "The Festival of the Breaking of the Fast," occurs on the first day of the month of Shawwal and marks the end of Ramadan, the month of fasting. Like 'Id al-Adha, it is celebrated by public worship and by the exchange of gifts and visits, but there is no sacrifice. It is also usually celebrated for three days. As it marks an end to the austerities of Ramadan (see Chapter 2), 'Id al-Fitr is a particularly joyous festival.

Both festivals are primarily religious occasions — designed for expression of communal solidarity as well as individual satisfaction and fulfillment at having carried out two major duties of the faith — and are characterized by the giving of alms to the poor and generous gifts (generally of money) to one's younger relatives.

Although other Muslim countries have introduced a number of additional public holidays, such as the Prophet's Birthday, New Year's Day (the first day of Muharram), and various national Independence Days, Saudi Arabia observes only one general holiday other than the two religious festivals. This is National Day, which commemorates the unification of the country under the name of the Kingdom of Saudi Arabia on September 22, 1932. It follows neither the Hijrah nor the Gregorian calendar, but rather the solar zodiacal calendar, and falls on the first day of the month of Libra, corresponding more or less to September 23 in the Gregorian calendar. That date was picked for the convenience of foreign governments and their diplomats. It is customary for them to send formal congratulatory messages to the Government of Saudi Arabia and for Saudi diplomats abroad to hold receptions on that day.

The adoption of the lunar month also had effects on Saudi Arabia's system of keeping time. As the month begins with the sighting, just after sunset, of the new moon and ends with sighting of the moon of the next month, the Muslim system followed ancient convention in which each day was considered to begin at sunset. For many centuries this system of starting the "day" at sunset, dividing it into twenty-four equal parts — twelve for daylight and twelve for nighttime — worked well.

But in more recent times the element of confusion caused by the fact that in each city and town clocks were set daily to correspond with actual local sunset, and the additional problems caused by the introduction of modern time zones and daylight saving time, caused frequent difficulty and misunderstanding. At one point, a popular gift to newcomers to Saudi Arabia was a watch with two dials, one giving Arabian time, the other whatever time the newcomer himself was using. Eventually the confusion caused by the use of two systems of time became too great, and when the requirements of international telecommunications and such factors as airline schedules began to demand the use of a single system, Saudi Arabia in the 1960s adopted Greenwich Mean Time plus three hours (GMT+3) as the standard time for the entire country.

Dhu al-Hijjah 1399 — NOVEMBER 1979 — Muharram 1400

SUN	MON	TUE	WED	THU	FRI	SAT
			1 / 11	2 / 12	3 / 13	
4 / 14	5 / 15	6 / 16	7 / 17	8 / 18	9 / 19	10 / 20
11 / 21	12 / 22	13 / 23	14 / 24	15 / 25	16 / 26	17 / 27
18 / 28	19 / 29	20 / 1	21 / 2	22 / 3	23 / 4	24 / 5
25 / 6	26 / 7	27 / 8	28 / 9	29 / 10	30 / 11	

Muharram 1400 — DECEMBER 1979 — Safar 1400

SUN	MON	TUE	WED	THU	FRI	SAT
						1 / 12
2 / 13	3 / 14	4 / 15	5 / 16	6 / 17	7 / 18	8 / 19
9 / 20	10 / 21	11 / 22	12 / 23	13 / 24	14 / 25	15 / 26
16 / 27	17 / 28	18 / 29	19 / 30	20 / 1	21 / 2	22 / 3
23/30 — 4/11	24/31 — 5/12	25 / 6	26 / 7	27 / 8	28 / 9	29 / 10

Safar 1400 — JANUARY 1980 — Rabi' I 1400

SUN	MON	TUE	WED	THU	FRI	SAT
		1 / 13	2 / 14	3 / 15	4 / 16	5 / 17
6 / 18	7 / 19	8 / 20	9 / 21	10 / 22	11 / 23	12 / 24
13 / 25	14 / 26	15 / 27	16 / 28	17 / 29	18 / 30	19 / 1
20 / 2	21 / 3	22 / 4	23 / 5	24 / 6	25 / 7	26 / 8
27 / 9	28 / 10	29 / 11	30 / 12	31 / 13		

for some time, the expansion of existing facilities and the development of new ports are still high-priority projects.

THE PILGRIMAGE TODAY: The modernization of Saudi Arabia has also been extended to the kingdom's role as custodian of the Holy Cities of Mecca and Medina. To the House of Sa'ud this role has always been highly important. Immediately upon extending his rule to the Hijaz, 'Abd al-'Aziz took steps toward eliminating the payments extorted from pilgrims by tribes along the caravan routes. Later, when the revenues from petroleum permitted it, he abolished all taxes on pilgrims. He also assigned his son Faysal to improve conditions for the pilgrims who came to Saudi Arabia each year to make the hajj, one of the most significant spiritual events in the lives of Muslims. The pilgrimage has required from the kingdom, the physical as well as historic heartland of Islam, a logistical achievement of impressive proportions. In recent years it has involved the handling of about a million and a half pilgrims, most of whom have to be provided with food, water, shelter, and medical care, and who — in great throngs and on a precise schedule — have to be transported, guided, and instructed during the trip from Jiddah to the holy places and back, generally within three weeks.

For the better part of fourteen centuries Muslims from around the world had been making the holy journey, some on foot, some in caravans, and others, in recent years, by steamer and rail. But starting after World War II — when someone converted a handful of war-surplus bombers into passenger planes and chartered them to pilgrims — more Muslims began to come by air. By the 1960s, when airlines began to build fleets of modern aircraft, Muslims from such distant centers of Islam as Indonesia and the Philippines to the east and Nigeria to the west were flying to Saudi Arabia. By the 1970s most major airlines of Muslim countries were offering such service and some were assigning the biggest jets they owned to carry pilgrims — sometimes at the rate of three hundred flights a day. One of these was Saudia, the national airline of Saudi Arabia. As a result, the numbers of foreign pilgrims increased sharply — from 316,000 in 1967 to 862,520 in 1979, mostly from the neighboring Arab countries and Iran, with smaller numbers coming from the rest of Asia and Africa, and a few thousand from Europe and from North, South, and Central America.

Traditionally, many of the pilgrims' logistical problems were left in the hands of a unique institution: a corps of expert guides called *mutawwifs.* For generations the mutawwifs had arranged transport and accommodations, provided food and water, guided the pilgrims to Mecca and the other holy places, and offered help with regard to the rituals. Today all pilgrims must register with a mutawwif as soon as they arrive. The mutawwif is also responsible for making arrangements for the pilgrims to depart, partly because the visas issued to pilgrims are special visas; they restrict the pilgrims to Jiddah, holy places traditionally included in the pilgrimage and, of course, the *haram,* the sacred "area of the pilgrims," which is strictly forbidden to non-Muslims.

With the swift rise in the numbers of pilgrims during the 1960s and 1970s, however, Saudi Arabia had to do even more. At Jiddah, for example, the government has built huge transit centers and in the haram has constructed a network of roads capable of handling many thousands of vehicles simultaneously. As part of the second Development Plan, the government also began construction of a new international airport at Jiddah with one terminal exclusively reserved for hajj traffic.

The government has also reorganized the tent cities in which the pilgrims live, deployed thousands of police, Boy Scouts, and National Guardsmen to direct traffic and assist the aged and the ill, and taken steps to eliminate or reduce the danger of infectious diseases. In addition it has equipped its pilgrimage staffs with walkie-talkies, closed-circuit television, and helicopters. In all, Saudi Arabia by 1979 was spending over $80 million annually to insure that faithful Muslims everywhere could, at least once in their lifetime, make this holiest of journeys.

Although the kingdom, under 'Abd al-'Aziz and his successors, has emerged as a prosperous nation and an important power in world affairs, its rulers and people have never forgotten the long struggle waged by the House of Sa'ud to adhere to and promote the faith revealed to the Prophet fourteen centuries ago.

A huge and fully serviced tent city at Mina annually accommodates hundreds of thousands of the faithful who come to perform some of the rites of the pilgrimage there.

The many faces of Saudis of different generations at work, play, school, and repose.

OIL AND ARAMCO

Men of ancient civilizations, for example the Sumerians, used natural asphalt to cement blades to handles.

Asphalt, or bitumen, also served as mortar in ancient structures of sun-baked brick.

The Venetian traveler Marco Polo wrote about the "fountains of oil" he had seen at Baku on the Caspian Sea.

Noah, preparing the Ark for the Flood, seems to have been one of the first men to have realized the value of petroleum. He used it to caulk the seams of his primitive vessel "within and without." But even before Noah, prehistoric man undoubtedly had seen, smelled, and tasted this strange blackish-green substance that seeped out of the earth into wells, pools, and streams. For a time ancient man probably had feared it too; strokes of lightning occasionally ignited escaping jets of gas and started fires that in some instances burned for centuries.

Precisely when, and to what degree, ancient man first began to grasp the potential of petroleum are still matters for archaeological investigation; but by 4000 B.C., when the Sumerians were beginning to keep records, he had already started to put it to use. The Sumerians — and later the Assyrians and Babylonians — used natural asphalt to attach blades to handles, treat the sick, and serve as mortar for their buildings.

These civilizations, grouped on the banks of the Euphrates River in what is now Iraq, obtained their asphalt from the "fountains of pitch" in Hit, about a hundred miles west of Baghdad, where large seepages of petroleum existed. But Hit was by no means the only source in ancient times. Other seepages existed along the Dead Sea and near the Yellow River in China.

According to the available evidence, ancient peoples knew more about asphalt than other forms of petroleum. In the Bible there are references to "slime" and "pitch" — that is, bitumen or asphalt, the substance left after the gases and liquids of crude oil evaporate. The basket in which Moses floated in the Nile was waterproofed with asphalt, and the famous wall on which Belshazzar saw the handwriting was mortared with it. Nor was liquid petroleum unknown. There are numerous early references to *neft* (an Old Persian word for petroleum from which the English "naphtha" is derived) and to "burning waters," and in the fifth century B.C. the Greek historian Herodotus described how both bitumen and oil were obtained.

As the centuries rolled on, less benign uses of petroleum were recorded. Byzantine commanders introduced the dreaded Greek Fire, a compound similar to napalm that the Greeks poured on enemy troops beneath city walls or sprayed on enemy fleets through tubes mounted on the prows of ships. It was difficult to extinguish and is credited with being a key weapon in Byzantium's defense when Arab fleets attacked Constantinople in the seventh and eighth centuries.

The Arabs had discovered petroleum too. In the ninth century the scientist al-Razi produced a handbook in which he recorded a description of how to distill neft and about 950 a group of Arab scholars in Basra worked out a theory on the origin of oil. Arabic literature of the period has references to "Eternal Fires," presumably caused by natural gas, seeping from the earth, which had somehow been ignited and burned for many years. One repeated reference was to the oil of Baku, a city on the Caspian Sea that was once part of Persia and is now one of the centers of oil production in the U.S.S.R. The 'Abbasid caliph al-Mu'tamid granted the revenues from naphtha springs at Baku to the people living in the vicinity.

The oil of Baku — where one of the most prolific fields in history was found in the nineteenth century — was undoubtedly known thousands of years earlier, but clear references to it did not appear until the seventh century. In the following centuries, however, Baku attracted considerable attention. The Arab writer al-Mas'udi, who visited Baku about 915, told of a place where "fire... ceases not to burn." Marco Polo, who visited the area about 1271, wrote that he had seen "a fountain from which oil springs in great abundance, insomuch that a hundred shiploads might be taken from it at one time." He also noted that "people come from vast distances to fetch it, for in all the countries round about they have no other oil."

THE NEW WORLD: Similar if less spectacular indications of petroleum were noted in many places in Europe — in Italy, Poland, Germany, and what are now Czechoslovakia and Rumania — and later in the New World. Francisco Pizarro, the Spanish conqueror of Peru, found the Indians there producing asphalt, and Sir Francis Drake used asphalt some fifty years later to coat his ships' hulls during his far-ranging raids on Spanish shipping in the Caribbean. In 1543 Hernando de Soto, on his way to the Mississippi, found asphalt in a Texas creek; and in 1595 in Trinidad Sir Walter Raleigh found asphalt which, he wrote, "melteth not with the sunne as the pitch of Norway." In 1627 a missionary found oil in a spring now called Cuba Lake near Buffalo, New York; it was the first of many such springs that French and British explorers discovered as they pushed into the North American wilderness.

The Indians had collected petroleum from natural springs for centuries and prized it highly for medicinal and other purposes. Physicians followed their example, and petroleum became a familiar item on the shelves of drugstores. It was also used to a small extent for lighting and for lubrication and by the early nineteenth century had been refined experimentally.

During the nineteenth century the development of machines and factories created a large demand for lubricants and lighting oils. Mutton and beef tallow, lard, and castor oil served as lubricants. The demand for lubricants and lamp oil gave rise to a whaling industry so successful that whales were almost exterminated and sperm oil became scarce and expensive.

By the middle of the century scientists in France, Great Britain, Canada, and the United States had begun to develop substitutes. Between 1845 and 1850 a French company began to make illuminating oil from shale, and in 1850 a process to produce oil from coal and oil shale was patented and a geologist named Abraham Gesner demonstrated how to make kerosene from coal. Not long after, in 1855, a Pittsburgh druggist named Samuel Kier, who had been bottling and selling petroleum as a medicine called "Kier Rock Oil," built a distillation system that produced what he called "carbon oil." It was possibly North America's first real oil refinery. Out of these processes came grease for nineteenth-century machinery and the fuel known as kerosene, which provided a fine heating fuel and a clearer, brighter light for living rooms, carriages, and locomotives.

DRAKE'S WELL: By then, of course, it had occurred to more than one alert businessman that oil might be far more useful than anyone had suspected. It had also occurred to them that there might be more oil in the earth than was seeping to the surface and that there must be better methods of obtaining petroleum than skimming it off the surface of the

so-called oil springs. From such conclusions came the experiments that eventually led to the digging of a fifty-foot well in Canada which produced enough oil to justify a small refinery that made lamp oil. This was in 1857, two years before a former railroad conductor, "Colonel" Edwin L. Drake, decided that he could drill for oil the way others drilled for water. Pursuing this idea, Drake hammered an iron pipe thirty-odd feet into the ground and, inside the pipe, drilled a well beside Oil Creek in Pennsylvania, near what is now called Titusville. The well, about seventy feet deep, produced up to thirty-five barrels a day and launched the petroleum industry as it is known today.

At first the search triggered by the Drake well focused on Pennsylvania, which dominated oil production for the next twenty-five years. But throughout the United States men began to take a closer look at any area where streams and wells had ever shown traces of oil. As a result, discoveries were made in Colorado, Wyoming, Ohio, Illinois, California, Texas, and Kansas before the end of the century.

Drake's discovery quickly led to experiments and innovations in refining and transport. In June 1860, a year after the discovery at Titusville, the country's first commercial refinery was opened in Oil Creek Valley in Pennsylvania. In 1861 railroads began to transport oil in vertical wooden tanks mounted on flatcars. Four years later the first successful oil pipeline was built — a two-inch line five miles long — and in 1886 a precursor of the modern oil tanker, the *Glückauf*, was launched. Toward the turn of the century oilmen were even beginning to experiment with offshore drilling. In 1894 they drilled the country's first offshore well at Santa Barbara, California. Drake's well also gave impetus to exploration and development in Burma, Java, Sumatra, Borneo, Venezuela, Rumania, and Russia.

ROCKEFELLER: In those first exuberant years the petroleum industry was turbulent, oilmen wasteful and disorganized. Lacking both knowledge and supporting technology, they first drilled wells haphazardly, worked them inefficiently, and sold kerosene, lubricants, and other rudimentary products in ruinous boom-and-bust cycles of glut and

Sir Walter Raleigh reported huge pools of asphalt on the island of Trinidad.

North American Indians discovered in oil seeps a substance useful as medicine and war paint.

Samuel Kier converted petroleum to lamp oil with a simple distillation system.

Drake's Pennsylvania well gave birth to an industry when it brought oil to the surface by methods earlier used only to drill for water.

shortage, wealth and bankruptcy, until in 1870 John D. Rockefeller, a young Ohio business-man, began to impose a wholly integrated structure on refining and transport through-out the United States. Rockefeller, a grain merchant, started his career in oil with a small 500-barrel-per-day refinery in Cleveland, but by 1872 had bought or annexed nearly eighty refineries in the oil regions and in Pittsburgh, Philadelphia, and New York; and by 1880 his monolithic organization controlled close to 95 percent of all refining in America.

Rockefeller's methods provoked out-raged opposition that plagues the oil industry to this day, and in 1911 the U.S. Supreme Court upheld legislation that dismantled the organization. But it is also true that he and his associates created the disciplined, coordinated structure that standardized the wildly fluctuat-ing cost, distribution, and quality of petroleum products. Their reorganization of the industry contributed enormously to the soaring growth of American industrialism and the national prosperity that industrialism created. It also enabled the United States to hold its own in the strong competition for international pe-troleum markets that developed among Brit-ish, Dutch, Russian, and American companies in the 1880s.

This competition arose as European oil interests began to develop fields in such places as the East Indies, Rumania, and Russia — especially Russia. There oilmen in 1874 had tapped the historic potential of Baku and established Russia as a world leader in oil production. By 1900 Russia was producing some 80 million barrels a year compared to America's 65 million.

SPINDLETOP: In that year, however, a former Austrian naval officer named Anthony F. Lucas drilled a well in a fifteen-foot hillock of land in Texas twenty-five miles from the Gulf of Mexico; a few months later, in one of the most colorful episodes in the history of oil, he brought in Spindletop, the biggest oil field of the period.

For years before the discovery, people in the nearby town of Beaumont had said that you could poke a cane into the hillock and light the gas that escaped. But as most experts (including one of Rockefeller's top geologists) dismissed the possibility of oil, no one but a self-taught geologist named Patillo Higgins

John D. Rockefeller imposed a disciplined structure on a previ-ously disorganized and wasteful oil business.

The infant U.S. oil industry reached maturity with the gigan-tic Spindletop discovery near Beaumont, Texas, in 1901.

The Search For Oil

Until the nineteenth century man rarely searched for oil. He simply noticed it. In some places he detected it seeping into pools or glistening on the surface of streams. Elsewhere he could scarcely miss it — for example, in the "pitch lake" in Trinidad, which is estimated to have held some 200 million barrels of heavy oil and asphalt that could simply be dug by hand.

In the nineteenth century, however, geologists noted that oil seeps often seemed to originate in or near the upward-folding arches known as "anticlines" and specu-lated that these structures might be repeated in layers below the surface of the earth. An anticline is one kind of "structural trap" — a distortion of strata beneath the earth's surface that may hold petroleum. There are several kinds of structural trap, but anticlines are generally the most important in the search for oil because they often contain more petroleum and are easier to detect than other types. In an anticline, or any other kind of trap, petroleum permeates layers of porous rock, rather like water in a sponge. The oil is contained and kept from migrating and dispersing by a layer of impermeable rock called a "cap rock."

The arches in rock strata do not necessarily reveal themselves on the surface, however, and the search for oil must rely on a variety of methods to deduce what lies beneath the surface. The basic tool in this search is a knowledge of the earth itself — how it was formed, what it is made of, and how it was modified through time. The search generally begins with a study of surface features, and the geologist puts to use his knowledge of such disciplines as the study of the origin, composition, and distribution of rock strata (stratigraphy); the physical and chemical properties of rocks (mineralogy); and fossilized animal and plant remains from ancient geological periods (paleontolo-gy). With these he is able to construct maps of the earth's substructure.

At least as important as geology and its various branches is the relatively new science of geophysics (the study of the physics of the earth), which since the 1930s has been increasingly depended upon to supplement and expand the findings of the geologists. Geophysical methods can be used, in effect, to map the underground strata and to determine, usually with considerable accura-cy, the shape and size of any geological structures in these strata. To do these things, geophysics uses three methods: the magnetic survey, the gravity survey, and the seismic survey.

Surveying with the use of the magnetometer is historically the oldest of these three. The magnetometer detects minute variations in the earth's magnetic field and, since sedimentary rocks are practically nonmagnetic while igneous rocks have fairly strong magnetic effects, it can aid in locating and measuring the thickness of sedimentary strata which may possibly be oil-bearing.

The gravity meter, on the other hand, measures minute differences in the earth's gravitational field, and this too is an indication of the nature of the subsurface strata, since variations between the gravity values of sedimentary rocks and the basement rocks underlying them, and between older and more recent rocks, can be interpreted in terms of the shapes and densities of underground structures.

The most widely used of the three geophysical methods and the most productive for studying underground strata is now the seismic survey. Seismology is usually associated with the study of natural earthquakes, but in connection with oil exploration it is the study of man-made vibrations in the earth by means of the seismograph, now one of the most valuable instruments in the search for oil. In seismic surveying an explosive charge is lowered into a drilled "shot-hole" a few feet deep and detonated. The shock wave from the explosion travels downward through the earth, is bounced back to the surface by discontinuities in the subsurface rocks, and is received by highly sensitive microphones called geophones and recorded. The period elapsed between the detonation and the time when the resulting shock wave is picked up by the geophone is measured with an accuracy of up to a thousandth of a second and the resulting figures, when correctly interpreted, give a detailed picture of the depth and nature of the subsurface strata. In some surveys, heavy vibrating metal pads or falling weights are used instead of the explosion to produce the required shock waves.

Information obtained from induced shock waves helps identify underground strata.

Seismic exploration employs two basic techniques — the "reflection" and the "refraction" methods. While both depend on the transmission of shock waves through the earth, there is a fundamental difference between the two techniques. With the reflection method the waves are reflected directly back to the geophone, while with the refraction method they travel laterally along the underground rock layers before angling back to the surface.

Both techniques have the same goal: to provide data from which expert analysts can plot cross-sections of the subsurface strata with considerable accuracy, in some cases all the way down to the basement rock beneath the sedimentary layers and at depths down to 40,000 feet. At one time this data was recorded visually as graphs on long strips of photo-sensitive paper, but since the mid-1960s when digital computer processing replaced the analog computer system the data from the geophones has been recorded on multi-track magnetic tape, translated by a field computer into numerical values, and then sent to a computer center for further processing. This processing involves the preparation by computer of maps, mathematical models, and even visual models presented with three-dimensional effect. Flashed onto a computer terminal or reproduced on film, this data is analyzed and interpreted to help determine the best locations for drilling and even what depth the exploratory well should be drilled to.

Computer-generated record of seismic data shows relative strength of reflected signals.

Techniques such as these are obviously far advanced over the methods used in the early days of the industry, when instinct rather than science was often the guiding force, but even they cannot guarantee the presence of oil. The only sure way to find oil remains essentially the same as it was at Titusville, Pennsylvania, in 1859: drill a well and see if it is there.

Whether their purpose is to find oil or gas or water, wells can be dug by three methods. They can be dug by hand with the old-fashioned pick and shovel; they can be hammered into the earth by percussion; or they can be drilled with what is basically the equivalent of the carpenter's or machinist's drill bit — and all three methods have been used in the search for oil.

The most primitive of these methods is obviously that used in digging a well by hand — with one man at the bottom of a hole chipping away at the earth or rock and sending the debris to the surface in a basket or bucket hung at the end of a rope. Although the history of the next step up the technological ladder, drilling by percussion, can be traced back for well over a thousand years, oil wells were being dug by hand in some parts of the world as late as the early twentieth century.

The drilling of wells by percussion or pounding consists basically of suspending a large sharpened "drilling tool" at the end of a rope and repeatedly raising it and letting it drop into the hole being drilled. The rope is passed over a pulley and attached to a long board or pole which serves as a lever, and for many centuries it was simply the weight of the drilling crew at the end of the lever that raised the tool before letting it drop again. With the advance of mechanization in the nineteenth century, however, the efficiency of this very laborious method of drilling was greatly increased by using steam power rather than man power for the task of raising the drilling tool. This made it possible to employ a very much heavier drilling tool and to

The Search For Oil

use a steel cable instead of a rope, and the new system came to be known as the cable-tool method. These improvements not only greatly speeded up the drilling process but also made it possible to drill much deeper holes than before. It was by an early form of this cable-tool method that Colonel Drake's first well was drilled in 1859.

Early 1800s drilling machine used the "teeter board" method of actuating the tools.

The next step in the improvement of drilling techniques came in the last decade of the nineteenth century with the introduction of rotary drilling. This makes use of a steel drill bit — at first not very different in design from some types of carpenter's bits — which is attached to a long string of steel pipe (the "drilling string") and rotated at the bottom of the hole. One of the chief advantages of rotary drilling, as it is called, is that it enables a hole to be drilled much faster than with cable-tool drilling, and the new method gained additional popularity after it was used to drill the well that discovered the Spindletop field in 1901.

Steam-powered engine and draw works used at Spindletop were the best to be had in their day

Rotary drilling in turn made possible the next advance in drilling methods — the introduction of the cone bit, invented in 1909 by Howard Hughes, Sr. The cone bit, which led to a further significant increase in the speed of drilling, consists of an arrangement of three steel cones fitted with exceptionally hard, durable teeth that rotate as the bit is turned and grind their way through successive layers of rock. Rotary drilling did not supersede cable-tool drilling overnight. In fact, the cable-tool method continued to be used in some places for drilling oil wells

until the 1950s, but the rotary method received a further impetus in the late 1920s with the invention of "self-cleaning" teeth for the cone bit, and after about 1930 rotary drilling became in most cases the method of choice.

No matter what the method used, the cutting tool (whether pick and shovel or high-speed rotary bit) is only one of the essential elements in drilling the well. Another is some means of shoring up the sides of the hole to prevent their caving in. With a hand-dug well this may be accomplished by lining the hole with stone or brick or even wooden boards. In early times the Chinese used hollow bamboo poles to line wells dug by the percussion method, and in the West long semicircular pieces of wood were bound together to form a tube and used as lining. As drilling techniques began to develop in the nineteenth century, iron pipe came to be used to line the well and eventually this was replaced by lengths of steel pipe which could be screwed together end to end and lowered into the hole as it progressed deeper into the earth. At the present time this "casing," as it is called, serves not only to line the well bore and prevent it from caving in but also as a channel through which the broken rock from around the rotating drill bit can be brought to the surface.

Yet another essential element in the drilling process is what is known as "mud" — which actually consists of water to which the drilling engineer adds one or more types of special solids mixed with chemicals to produce the exact consistency and weight that is required. This fluid is pumped down into the hole through the drilling string which turns the bit and it serves two purposes: it lubricates the teeth of the drill bit as they cut into the subterranean rock, and as it flows back to the surface through the space between the drill stem and the casing it carries with it the debris from the bottom of the hole. These pieces of broken rock or "cuttings" serve to show what type of rock the drill is cutting through. The drilling mud has one very important additional purpose: the weight of the column of mud in the hole acts as a plug or stopper and serves to restrain and in most cases to prevent any sudden eruption or "blowout" that might otherwise occur when the drilling tool penetrates an oil-bearing or gas-bearing formation. This explains why blowouts or gushers are far less common today than they were in the days of cable-tool drilling when no mud was used.

The drilling string itself, the long hollow steel shaft which turns the bit, must meet exacting standards. Screwed together section by section on the surface, it must be strong enough to support its own considerable weight suspended from the rig and the additional weight of heavy steel "drill collars" at the bottom of the string that increase the rate of penetration of the bit. At the same time it must also be as flexible, relatively, as a fishing rod, as the upper sections of the string may actually make several revolutions before the bit also begins to turn. The pipe is also subjected to great strain each time the drillers, in order to change bits, hoist it out of the hole, dismantle it, screw the sections back together again, and lower the string back into the hole.

Drilling rigs have also changed considerably since the early days of the industry. The first rigs were no more than simple towers of cross-braced wood whose main purpose was to provide sufficient height so that the cutting tool at the end of the drilling rope or cable could be raised and allowed to drop again. When the well was completed it was usually easier to leave the tower in place than to dismantle it. This gave rise to the popular but mistaken image of an oil field as a forest of rigs or derricks. Today rigs have evolved into a variety of enormous, usually mobile steel structures able to cross deserts and oceans under their own power. The characteristic tower or derrick is no longer needed to provide height for the drop of the cable tool but instead serves as a means of drawing the drill stem from the hole and also as a place in which the drill pipe can be stacked vertically while the bit is being changed. Once the well is completed, the rig is removed, leaving only a few valves on the surface of the earth or, in the case of offshore drilling, a steel platform over the site of the well.

Modern rigs, far more powerful than their forerunners, are also safer and more reliable.

Drilling, of course, varies enormously from country to country and location to location in its difficulty, its cost, and the techniques required. Drilling from a 600-foot 35,000-ton steel platform and tower in the North Sea obviously requires different equipment and methods than drilling from a wheeled rig in the Empty Quarter of Saudi Arabia. Drilling also varies in purpose. Some wells are "wildcats," drilled in an effort to find oil in a new location. Others may be "delineation wells," drilled to find the limits of a known producing location. Still others are "development wells," drilled to bring in additional production from an established field. But today, as always, the crucial well is still the "discovery well." In answering the key question — is there oil there? — the discovery well is the bottom line in the search for oil.

would take Spindletop seriously. Higgins, insisting there was oil there, finally persuaded Lucas and his backers to drill, and on January 10, 1901, at a depth of about 1,150 feet, Lucas brought in the greatest "gusher" ever seen outside Russia: a six-inch plume of oil that came in "like a shot from a heavy cannon," as one witness described it, spouted 150 feet in the air, and set off the most spectacular oil boom in history. Within hours telegraph wires had carried the report across the country, and within days thousands of oilmen, merchants, and speculators were on their way for a share of the excitement and, they hoped, the profits. Some found both as, in the next three months, six other wells came in — one of them topped by a geyser 217 feet high — and the tempo of exploration, as well as the price of land, increased frantically.

Spindletop's gusher — a layman's term coined there to describe North America's first major free-flowing well — quickly became a symbol for the undisciplined oil exploration that characterized the industry before it developed more controlled methods of drilling. The discovery well at Spindletop, for example, disgorged about 800,000 barrels in the nine days required to cap it — and most of that went up in flames eight weeks later. In Mexico in 1910 a well called Potrero del Llano No. 4 spewed some 100,000 barrels a day into the jungle for two months before it could be capped. Another at Dos Bocas caught fire and burned for forty days in a flaming column visible from ships far out in the Gulf of Mexico. Gushers are unquestionably spectacular, but they are also wasteful and dangerous and every effort is now made to prevent their occurrence.

The impact of the Spindletop find was almost as spectacular as the wells themselves. In one stroke American oil production surpassed the rest of the world; according to one estimate six of the wells at Spindletop were producing more oil in one day than the rest of the oil fields in the world combined, and before they gave out the fields there yielded 142 million barrels. Spindletop also gave birth to other oil companies that would soon challenge Rockefeller's nearly impregnable position — companies such as today's Sun, Gulf, and Texaco. Because of the ingenuity of its drillers, Spindletop contributed to the development of the rotary drill and focused

Patillo Higgins had spent eight years in unsuccessful oil ventures before Spindletop made him famous overnight.

Anthony Lucas, Higgins' partner, decided to use a steam-driven rotary rig at Spindletop in what proved to be the first large-scale success of rotary drilling equipment.

A. D. 1848 DISCOVERED IN BORING FOR SALT WATER near

A. D. 1849 Wonderful MEDICAL VIRTUES DISCOVERED.

400

THE Bank of the Allegheny River, IN ALLEGHENY COUNTY, PENNS'A.

about FOUR HUNDRED FEET below

the Earth's surface, is pumped up with the Salt Water, flows into the Cystern, floats on top, when a quantity accumulates, is drawn off into Barrels, is bottled in its natural state without any preparation or admixture. For particulars, get a Circular.

Pittsburgh, Jan. 1st, 1852.

400

S. M. Kier, Proprietor.

A scrapbook page of vintage photographs reconstructs the humble birth of an industry which, despite the cycles of success and failure that marked its adolescent years, grew up to alter the world. 1. Early pump station of the Ohio State Oil Company. 2. Pipeline construction in the pioneering days of oil in Persia. 3. Cement-coated pipeline in Louisiana, 1919. 4. Pseudo bank note issued in 1852 by Samuel Kier to advertise the medicinal virtues of petroleum. 5. Spindletop, the first gusher ever seen by American oilmen, in January 1901. 6. Primitive pumping apparatus in which a weight attached to the pumping level swung like the pendulum of a clock. 7. Pumping well in the Allegheny Mountain fields of Pennsylvania. 8. Traffic jam in a Humble Oil Company field in 1918. 9. "Eternal Fire," the flaming oil seep at Kirkuk in Iraq, known centuries ago and still burning. 10. Pioneer run at Oil Creek, Pennsylvania, 1865. 11. Drilling rig at Chiah Surkh on the border between Persia and Iraq, 1902.

attention on the importance of drilling "mud," a fluid that lubricates the bit and washes cuttings to the surface. Spindletop also showed that oil could be found around salt domes. The Spindletop discovery, furthermore, triggered another dynamic search for oil throughout the United States, a search that in the next ten years would uncover great fields in California, Louisiana, Illinois, Kansas, and Oklahoma.

One of the earliest refineries in the United States was the Monitor Refining Company plant at Oil Creek, Pennsylvania.

THE INTERNAL - COMBUSTION ENGINE: Even more important than Spindletop was the development in the late nineteenth century of the internal-combustion engine and the realization, about 1900, that gasoline could fuel it better than kerosene.

Although a liquid-fuel engine had been developed as early as 1873, and Gottlieb Daimler and Karl Benz experimented with a gasoline engine in 1886, the internal-combustion engine was, until the turn of the century, impractical. For a time, in fact, electric automobiles were far more popular. But oil industry researchers were working hard to find a practical use for gasoline, a volatile by-product from kerosene refining. Although small quantities were used as solvents for paints and varnishes and for special lamps for street lighting, most of it was poured into rivers or burned. One effort to find a use for gasoline led to one of the first advertising campaigns in America. Launched in 1898, it urged housewives to try "cool, convenient, and economic gasoline stoves." The campaign was successful, but its impact was soon eclipsed by the growing awareness that gasoline was precisely the fuel that the internal-combustion engine needed.

Along with the automobile, the 1920s ushered in a new type of small business.

For both automobiles and petroleum these interlocking developments were turning points. Reinforcing each other they created an American automotive industry which after turning out only about 4,000 cars in 1900 produced 187,000 in 1910 — two years after Henry Ford came out with his famous Model T — and a petroleum industry that was thereafter closely geared to the need for gasoline. The leapfrogging demands of the two industries also stimulated such allied industries as steel, glass, and road construction. In addition they transformed petroleum refining into a highly sophisticated science that in the next fifty years improved shipping, revolutionized aviation, transformed agricul-

Gasoline had little market until Henry Ford built a car that everyone could afford.

tural techniques and output, and created new chemical compounds on which numerous other industrial advances — and some entire industries — were based.

REFINING AND GEOLOGY: Before the automotive age, improvements in oil refining came mostly from trial-and-error experiments. Starting with simple distilleries — no more than large iron vats mounted on bricks over a wood fire — the early oilmen had to unlock the secrets of refining one step at a time, on the basis of observation and conjecture. As a result, the first refineries smelled, smoked, and sometimes exploded — as did the kerosene they produced.

Storage, shipping, and distribution methods were equally simple. In some places storage "tanks" were simply holes in the ground lined with planks, kerosene was shipped in oak barrels piled on oxcarts, and gasoline was carried to automobiles in open pails. Even when "gas stations" were introduced they consisted of no more than a metal tank and a garden hose.

The scientific approach, to be sure, was not unknown. As early as 1887 Herman Frasch, a brilliant industrial chemist in Canada, had devised a way of reducing the rank sulfur in oil by stirring metal oxides into raw kerosene during distillation. Frasch also improved several other processes and products. But it was not until the automotive age, with its need for more gasoline, that researchers began to zero in on the basic properties of petroleum, and not until 1912 that they perfected a process called "cracking" — perhaps the most important technological breakthrough in the history of the oil industry.

Cracking, essentially, is the use of intense heat to change the molecular structure of natural crude oil. Discovered accidentally about 1860, cracking was first used to increase the yield of kerosene from a barrel of oil. In 1912, however, as a result of attempts to adapt cracking to the production of gasoline, a process called "pressure cracking" was developed which not only doubled the volume of gasoline obtainable from a barrel of crude oil, but also opened the way to manipulation of petroleum molecules in other ways and to development of the processes on which the whole modern petrochemical industry is built.

From a military standpoint, the development of pressure cracking came none too soon. By then — on the eve of World War I — Western military leaders had begun to convert battleships from coal to oil, introduce gasoline-powered submarines, trade off mules for trucks, and try out the first clumsy tanks and flimsy warplanes. All of this stimulated the demand not only for greater volumes of gasoline, but also for more efficient gasoline.

The problem of efficiency was not satisfactorily solved until the 1920s, when the postwar growth of the automotive industry created additional demands for better gasoline. In trying to provide it, researchers noted that cracked gasoline seemed to "knock" less than "straight-run" or natural gasoline. This led to experiments with an additive called tetraethyl lead which reduced knocking. The process was used for almost fifty years until the passage of antipollution legislation led to its gradual abandonment. As automobile engines with greater compression ratios were introduced, however, refining experts had to delve still more deeply into gasoline's performance characteristics. Out of that research came, in the 1930s, what are called "thermal reforming" processes, which provided greater volumes of higher octane — (that is, better performing) gasolines.

This period — the 1920s and 1930s — was what the oil historian G. A. Purdy calls "the golden years for petroleum engineers." In those days, he wrote, "almost every process could be improved by the application of engineering principles." But researchers made contributions too. Chemists, for example, eliminated the impurities in gasoline that clogged carburetors, left coatings of carbon in engines, and corroded processing equipment. Along the way they also developed new processes and stored up information that would lead to the 1939 breakthrough called "catalytic cracking" — the cracking of petroleum molecules by the use of chemical catalysts rather than by heat and pressure alone.

Oil geology also came into its own in this period. Although theories about anticlines, the arched rock strata in which petroleum is frequently found, had begun to provide guidelines as early as the 1880s, the discovery of oil remained for many years after that more a matter of observation and guesswork than of science. Even as late as 1930, when Columbus M. "Dad" Joiner brought in the giant East Texas field, intuition was still thought by many to work as well as geological study. In 1910, however, geologists C. Willard Hayes and Everette Lee DeGolyer led a British company to Mexico's Potrero del Llano No. 4, and geology began to gain ground. DeGolyer four years later began to determine the shape, location, and structure of underground strata by applying gravity survey information. In the next decade geologists greatly improved their ability to assess underground formations, adapted the seismograph to oil exploration, and, in applying their new techniques, led the industry to other major oil discoveries.

"Dad" Joiner proved he was right about the potential of what came to be America's number-one producing state when he brought in the East Texas field.

Everette DeGolyer pioneered the use of geophysics in prospecting for oil in the U.S., with his greatest success the development of seismic techniques to detect fields associated with salt domes.

MORE DISCOVERIES: These advances were timely. World War I demands for oil had imposed alarming strains on American oil resources and after the war the growth in number of tractors, buses, trucks, and cars — 23 million on the road by 1929 — required ever greater volumes of oil. Partly as a result of the improvement in geology, however, individuals and companies went on to uncover still greater fields in Appalachia, Illinois, Indiana, Louisiana, and California. By the end of the 1920s close to 87 percent of the world's production was coming from North America.

In the meantime, the first major discoveries had been made in what came to be called Mexico's "Golden Lane," and by 1918 Mexico was the second largest producer of oil in the world. In 1914 the first commercial field had been found on the eastern shores of Lake Maracaibo in Venezuela, and subsequent exploration by British, Dutch, and American companies established the Maracaibo Basin as one of the world's greatest oil reservoirs.

The discoveries in the United States, Mexico, and Venezuela, coupled with the drop in production during the post-revolutionary chaos in Russia, gave the Western Hemisphere a lead in oil production that would endure through the 1960s. They also gave the United States and its allies a crucial advantage as, in 1939, war again engulfed the world.

The Tia Juana field under Lake Maracaibo was a major source of oil for the Allied forces in World War II.

WORLD WAR II: Oil played an even more important role in World War II than it had in the First World War. Because Germany lacked sufficient sources of oil it was essential for her to capture the Baku fields of the Soviet Union, and failure to do so was a factor in Germany's defeat. Both Germany and Japan were forced to depend to a significant extent on synthetic oil made from coal which, in terms of both quality and quantity, was inadequate. Germany's aviation fuel, for example, could not compare with the high octane fuel that the American oil industry began to produce after catalytic cracking was developed in 1939. On the Allied side, researchers turned to petroleum to develop a synthetic substitute for rubber after Japan's Far East conquests choked off supplies of the natural product.

The war's unprecedented demands for oil also stimulated construction of pipelines in the United States, increased the size of tankers, and improved exploration techniques. Production also increased; during World War II fully half of U.S. shipments overseas consisted of petroleum products.

In the immediate postwar period, the expansion of American industrial technology, the enormous scale of the physical reconstruction of war-devastated Western Europe and Japan, and the outbreak of hostilities in Korea all continued to stimulate demand. As a result, the United States in 1948 became a net importer of petroleum rather than an exporter. This change, in absolute terms, was slight — on the order of 145,000 barrels a day. But it was a turning point nonetheless. From that day on the United States would be increasingly dependent on foreign oil and eventually on oil from the Middle East — where forty years before another important chapter in the history of oil had begun.

OIL IN THE MIDDLE EAST: In one sense the history of oil in the Middle East is less colorful than its history in the United States. It is far more a story of prolonged and complicated national and corporate negotiations than of the boom-town individualism that characterized so much of American exploration. In the early years some individuals, however, do stand out: Baron Julius von Reuter, who founded the Reuters news agency; Calouste Gulbenkian, who became known to the public as "Mr. Five Percent"; William Knox D'Arcy, a British financier who fathered the first major oil discovery in the Middle East; George B. Reynolds, a tenacious field man-

Baron Julius von Reuter was the earliest of several international financiers to win mineral and oil concessions in Persia.

Calouste Gulbenkian, prime mover in negotiations involving territories of the old Ottoman Empire, was a founder of the Turkish Petroleum Company, forerunner of the Iraq Petroleum Company.

William D'Arcy lost over a million dollars in fruitless oil search in Iraq and Persia before he succeeded.

ager who brought in the first well; and King 'Abd al-'Aziz of Saudi Arabia who in 1923, even before he had unified his kingdom, granted a concession to Major Frank Holmes, a mining engineer from New Zealand who, despite many contrary opinions, insisted that there was oil on the Arabian Peninsula — and was proven spectacularly right.

Baron von Reuter was the first on the scene but his role was relatively small. In 1872 and again in 1889 he obtained from Shah Nasr-ed-Din concessions to search for and exploit minerals and oil in Persia. The company formed by de Reuter drilled three wells but found no oil and in 1899 the concession was canceled.

About the same time the young Armenian Gulbenkian, who had learned something about oil in Russia's Baku fields, submitted a report to the Ministry of Mines of the Ottoman Empire, which until the First World War had actual or theoretical sovereignty over all the Arab lands of the Middle East. This report, calling attention to the historic oil seepages of Mesopotamia, excited Sultan Abdul-Hamid and later led Germany to seek petroleum rights from the Ottoman Empire along the route of the proposed Berlin-to-Baghdad railroad. That move, in turn, lured other competitors into the Middle East, including Royal Dutch Shell and an American admiral representing the New York Chamber of Commerce.

The military coup d'etat and Young Turk revolution of 1900 and the deposition of the sultan in the following year put a temporary stop to all such efforts to obtain concessions in the Ottoman Empire. In 1910, however, a National Bank of Turkey was founded, at the urging of the British and with British capital, and with Gulbenkian as one of the directors. Gulbenkian persuaded the bank to negotiate an agreement by which in 1912 the Turkish Petroleum Company (TPC) was formed, with himself a shareholder. Through TPC Britain and Germany reached an agreement on Turkish oil development that played a considerable part in negotiations after World War I.

Meanwhile William D'Arcy, who had made a fortune in gold in Australia, had begun to investigate the possibility of finding oil in the Middle East. In 1900 D'Arcy sent representatives to Persia to negotiate a concession and scout the terrain. In the following years he obtained the concession, and after his geologists recommended "two unquestionably petroliferous territories" he picked a field manager and dispatched him to search for oil near Chiah Surkh, located in the border area between Persia and Iraq.

Reynolds, the field manager, was a tenacious geologist who spent sixteen months completing the first well, brought in one well that went dry five months later, and endured nearly five years of hardship — including an outbreak of plague — before his and D'Arcy's hopes were fulfilled.

They almost were not. By 1905 D'Arcy was running out of money — he had spent well over a million dollars and had been forced to seek loans. Two years later, as Reynolds began drilling in the Zagros Mountains of the Ahwaz region in western Persia, funds ran out again. D'Arcy tried to hold on but in May 1908 his syndicate decided to withdraw and sent a cable ordering Reynolds to stop work, dismiss his crew, and come home.

MASJID-I-SULAIMAN: At that point Reynolds had been drilling into a ledge in an area called Masjid-i-Sulaiman. As the ledge overlooked a stream where oil had been seeping out for years, Reynolds was certain he was on the verge of success and decided that he would not accept these instructions until he received a letter confirming them. Instead, he kept drilling and on May 26, 1908, at a depth of 1,180 feet, brought in the first commercial well in the Middle East — and uncovered the Masjid-i-Sulaiman field, which by the end of the 1970s had produced well over a billion barrels of oil.

The Masjid-i-Sulaiman field lies in a sedimentary basin rimmed by the mountains of Oman, Iran, Iraq, Turkey, Syria, Lebanon, the Hijaz, and Yemen — a basin that contains the modern oil fields of the Tigris and Euphrates river regions, Saudi Arabia and the other Arab states lying in or on the Arabian Gulf, and the Iranian foothills and coast. No one knew that in 1908, however, and even experienced geologists refused concessions that later turned out to include exceptionally thick porous rocks and reservoir conditions ideal for the recovery of the oil. As a consequence, discoveries that were to alter world patterns of supply and demand were not made for another twenty-five to thirty years.

EARLY DEVELOPMENTS: Development in Persia started almost at once. In April 1909 D'Arcy's Anglo-Persian Oil Company was launched — with the encouragement of Admiral Fisher, First Sea Lord of the British Admiralty, who for many years had been pressing for conversion of the Royal Navy from coal to oil. Five years later, on the eve of the First World War, the British Government gave more concrete support. Under the prodding of Winston Churchill, Parliament voted to acquire a majority interest in the Anglo-Persian Oil Company, which later became the Anglo-Iranian Oil Company and — still later — British Petroleum.

In Persia, meanwhile, Anglo-Persian had laid out and supervised the construction of a 130-mile pipeline to the Arabian Gulf that was completed in 1911. The line ran between Masjid-i-Sulaiman and an uninhabited mud-flat at the head of the Gulf called Abadan; there, in 1913, a refinery with an initial capacity of 2,400 barrels a day was completed. Shortly after, Churchill signed a contract under which Anglo-Persian would supply oil to the Royal Navy. As the Allies needed great quantities of oil in the war it proved to be a wise precaution, although in fact the new discoveries played no more than a secondary role in the eventual Allied victory over the Central Powers.

After the war Middle East oil again came to the fore as the Allies, in negotiating spheres of influence in the territories formerly ruled by the Ottoman Empire, discussed various agreements affecting future discoveries of oil in Mesopotamia. As the discussions were complicated and often involved controversy, some key matters were not finally settled for years. One was the objection of the United States to being excluded from Mesopotamian oil exploration. These objections led to the formation of the Near East Development Corporation, a consortium of five American companies, which spearheaded American participation in Middle East oil development.

In 1928, an agreement was reached under which shareholding in the Iraq Petroleum Company (IPC) was adjusted: Anglo-Persian, Royal Dutch Shell, the Compagnie Française des Pétroles, and the Near East Development Corporation each held a 23.75 percent share — with 5 percent for Gulbenkian, which

The perseverance of George Reynolds was rewarded in May 1908 when he brought in the first commercial oil well in the Middle East.

The Masjid-i-Sulaiman discovery opened up a field that produced over a billion barrels by the end of the 1970s.

OIL FIELDS OF THE MIDDLE EAST

The major oil fields of the Middle East are located in a sedimentary basin lying between the Arabian Shield on the west and the mountains of Iran on the east and contain well over half of the world's total oil accumulations. Saudi Arabia has the largest proved and probable oil reserves in the world and two of the largest oil fields in the world are in the kingdom – the Ghawar field onshore and the Safaniya field offshore. Of the total of forty-seven oil fields that Aramco had discovered by 1980, all but two are located in the northern-most (and largest) of the six areas that remain in the company's concession.

OILFIELDS

ARAMCO CONCESSION AREAS (onshore and offshore)

MAJOR OIL PIPELINES IN SAUDI ARABIA

* Where state of Israel was established in 1948

earned him his nickname. Simultaneously, the companies concerned signed what was called the "Red Line Agreement," whereby each undertook not to seek individual concessions in a large area of the former Ottoman Empire without agreement by the other companies. The area included all of Arabia except Kuwait.

A year before IPC was formed, oil had been found at Baba Gurgur in Iraq, 140 miles north of Baghdad. Within 2,500 yards of Iraq's Eternal Fires — which had burned continuously at least since Nebuchadnezzar's time — oil burst to the surface on the night of October 14, 1927, and like the first Spindletop well in Texas spurted into the air in a gusher 140 feet high. It also took five lives and touched off a crisis that lasted ten days while men in gas masks strove to master it. This well flowed at the rate of 95,000 barrels a day, marked the discovery of the Kirkuk oil field, one of the largest in the Middle East, and confirmed Gulbenkian's predictions made more than a quarter of a century earlier.

One of the largest fields in the Middle East was tapped with the discovery well at Baba Gurgur in Iraq.

THE 1930s AND 1940s: In the 1930s exploration and development in the Middle East proceeded at a steady pace. In Persia Anglo-Persian discovered and began to export oil from the Haft Kel field (1928), the Gach Saran field (1935), and Agha Jari (1944). In Iraq IPC discovered the Ain Zalah field and, through its subsidiary the Basrah Petroleum Company, brought in the Zubair field. In 1930 Standard Oil of California took over a concession originally negotiated by Frank Holmes on Bahrain and on May 31, 1932, found oil — a discovery that stimulated the search for oil in Saudi Arabia and Kuwait. Some two and a half years later the Kuwait Oil Company, formed in 1933 by Anglo-Persian and Gulf Oil Company, received a concession for Kuwait and in April 1938 discovered the giant Burgan field, one of the largest in the world. Exploration and development concessions for oil were granted in Qatar in 1935, in Oman in 1937, and in Abu Dhabi in 1939. And in 1938 oil in commercial quantities was discovered in Saudi Arabia.

In brief, as a team of experts under the leadership of Everette DeGolyer which the U.S. Government sent to the Middle East in 1943 reported, the center of gravity of world oil had begun to shift from the basins of Texas, Mexico, and Venezuela to the Middle East. Crude oil production from the Western

Major Frank Holmes won the first oil concession in what is now Saudi Arabia, but no exploratory work was undertaken and the agreement lapsed.

Hemisphere continued to be a significant part of the world total, but its proportionate share of the total declined steadily after the end of World War II; and while the United States continued to be the world's largest producer until 1974, its share of the total was likewise declining and in fact by 1948 it was already importing more oil than it exported. Certainly by the end of the 1930s it was becoming clear that the Middle East was where the world's biggest reserves were located and that therefore this was where the major share of world oil production would have to come from in future. Eventually it became evident that the Arabian Peninsula — and especially Saudi Arabia — was where the world's largest oil accumulations were located, and the chief role in developing these was played by the company that came to be known as Aramco.

ARAMCO FORERUNNERS: There is no precise beginning to the story of Aramco. In one sense it began on May 29, 1933, when the Saudi Arabian Minister of Finance and a Standard Oil Company of California lawyer signed an agreement in Jiddah giving the company an exclusive right to "explore, prospect, drill for, extract, treat, manufacture, transport, deal with, carry away and export" oil and oil products. In another, it began a few months later when two American geologists landed on the east coast of Saudi Arabia and launched a frustrating five-year search for oil. In still another sense it began on March 3, 1938, the day Dammam Well No. 7 encountered oil in commercial quantities in what is now called the Arab Formation. But the beginning might well be said to be the day in 1930 when King 'Abd al-'Aziz somewhat reluctantly decided to allow foreigners to investigate and evaluate the potential oil and other mineral resources of his country.

The King's first attempt to exploit these mineral resources had been in 1923, before he had fully unified what was to become Saudi Arabia. In that year he granted an oil concession to Major Frank Holmes, an energetic and amiable New Zealander. Holmes, however, represented a London financial syndicate, not an oil company, and the syndicate was unsuccessful in its attempts to persuade any oil company that the chances of discovery of oil in Arabia were enough to risk the necessary capital expenditure. The Holmes concession, covering more than 30,000 square miles in eastern Saudi Arabia, was allowed to lapse through failure to make certain nominal annual payments.

In 1930, as an outgrowth of discussions with his English friend and unofficial adviser, H. St. John B. Philby, King 'Abd al-'Aziz set in motion a series of developments that would eventually bring the two American geologists to the eastern shore of his country. The first of these developments was an invitation to visit Saudi Arabia which 'Abd al-'Aziz sent to Charles R. Crane, a wealthy American businessman who had done philanthropic work in Yemen and who had been co-chairman of the King-Crane Commission, the controversial fact-finding delegation which had been sent to the Middle East in 1919 in order to make recommendations about the future government of the Arab lands that had been part of the Ottoman Empire. Crane accepted the invitation, and during his visit to Saudi Arabia he promised to send the King a mining engineer to examine the country's water, agriculture, and mineral resources. The man Crane selected was Karl Twitchell, a Vermont Yankee who in 1931-32 crossed the peninsula looking for water sources, mineral outcrops, and oil seeps.

In the meantime, Standard Oil Company of California (Socal) had sent two geologists to Bahrain to make recommendations about oil prospects there. One of them was F. A. Davies, later to become chairman of the Board of Directors of Aramco. "From the day we first set foot on Bahrain," wrote Davies some years later, "we had a strong desire to examine the geology of the mainland in Saudi Arabia, not only because of its bearing on what might be expected below the surface of Bahrain, but also because it was thought there might well be oil possibilities in the vastly larger area of the mainland." When, as a result of Davies' recommendations, Socal drilled on Bahrain and discovered oil there in May 1932, it was only natural for Socal's executives to press with considerable vigor to explore Saudi Arabia.

Socal at first attempted to arrange a meeting with the King through Major Holmes (the same Major Holmes who had negotiated an agreement with the King in 1923 and with whom Socal had been associated from the start in Bahrain), but then discovered that the King

had already asked Twitchell to see if he could find an oil company interested in paying for a concession to explore for oil and produce it if found. Socal immediately retained Twitchell to assist in obtaining such a concession.

Socal also attempted to get in touch with the King through Philby. Philby was asked to propose to the King that Socal make a preliminary geological examination of eastern Saudi Arabia, with the idea that a concession would be negotiated if the preliminary investigation appeared to justify it. When Philby indicated that he was prepared to serve as an intermediary and reported that the King was willing to negotiate, Twitchell and Lloyd N. Hamilton, a Socal lawyer specializing in contracts and leases, traveled to Jiddah to negotiate a concession agreement, arriving in February 1933. There Philby joined the team.

Philby served as go-between in the King's early talks with oil-company representatives.

NEGOTIATIONS: The negotiations took three and a half long months. Saudi Arabia's team of negotiators, led by Shaykh 'Abd Allah al-Sulayman, the King's shrewd Minister of Finance, was capable, patient, and tenacious. The Saudi team knew the best terms already won by Persia and Iraq for oil concessions and was determined to obtain no less favorable conditions. There was also competition. The Iraq Petroleum Company (IPC) sent its distinguished negotiator Brigadier Stephen Longrigg to Jiddah at the same time. Although IPC seemed less interested in developing oil in Saudi Arabia than in keeping out other oil companies, it had the full backing and support of the British minister to Saudi Arabia. Even Holmes put in an appearance for a few days, but he was obviously not prepared to meet the minimum demands of the Saudi negotiators.

Hamilton, however, had several factors working in his favor. One was that IPC had at that time more oil available than it knew what to do with. Another was that Hamilton's company had already discovered oil on Bahrain and had demonstrated there that its interests were confined to business and involved no political entanglements or ambitions.

Socal was far from taking on a "sure thing" in moving to obtain a concession in Saudi Arabia. The negotiations were conducted shortly after the United States had gone off the gold standard and President Roosevelt had closed U.S. banks, and at a time

Fred Davies, sent by Socal to explore for oil on Bahrain, was convinced the mainland held promise as well.

Negotiations over the Socal concession were headed on Saudi Arabia's behalf by the influential Minister of Finance, Shaykh 'Abd Allah al-Sulayman.

5   6   7

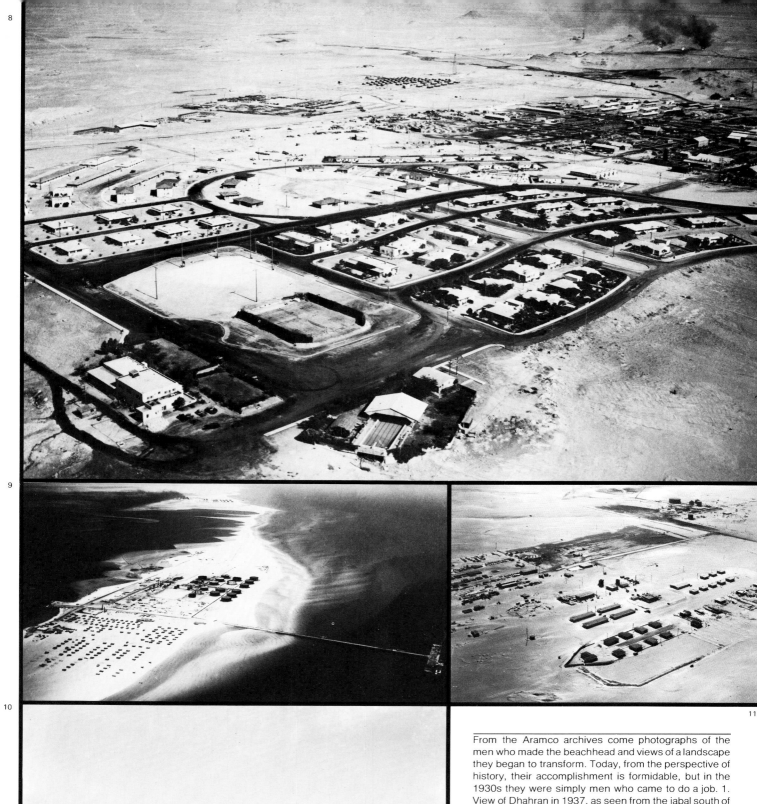

From the Aramco archives come photographs of the men who made the beachhead and views of a landscape they began to transform. Today, from the perspective of history, their accomplishment is formidable, but in the 1930s they were simply men who came to do a job. 1. View of Dhahran in 1937, as seen from the jabal south of Dammam Well No. 1. 2. Jerry Harriss, Fred Davies, Soak Hoover, and Max Steineke camped near Jabal Dam, 1936. 3. Hoover and Harriss at camp on the Abqaiq structure in 1936. 4. Tom Barger-Ernie Berg field party departing in the fall of 1937. 5. Krug Henry and Art Brown shooting the stars at Linah, 1934. 6. Joe Mountain, Dick Kerr, and Russ Gerow with the Fairchild used for aerial reconnaissance. 7. Felix Dreyfuss and Steineke at their Jubail office, 1935. 8. Dhahran in 1946, beginning to look like a town. 9. Ras Tanura tank farm and pier, 1947. 10. Early family housing in Dhahran, late 1937. 11. Abqaiq in 1947.

First man in the vanguard of oil prospectors was Bert Miller.

In the pattern of most early explorers, Krug Henry wore a beard and Arab headgear.

Invaluable to the pioneering effort was a single-engine plane equipped for aerial photography.

The inventive Dick Kerr helped develop special methods for processing photographic film in desert conditions.

when crude oil was selling for less than fifty cents a barrel. The company was in fact taking a calculated business gamble in a period when the economic outlook and business prospects were particularly gloomy.

The concession agreement was signed in Jiddah on May 29, 1933, by Shaykh 'Abd Allah and Hamilton. In the agreement Socal committed itself to loans totaling £50,000 gold (about $250,000 at that time), yearly rentals of £5,000 (about $25,000), and royalties of 4 shillings gold (about $1.00) per ton of oil produced. It also undertook to provide the government with an advance of £50,000 gold once oil was found in commercial quantities. From the government's standpoint, of equal importance were provisions calling for an immediate start of exploration and for drilling to begin as soon as a suitable structure was found (in any case no later than September 1936), and construction of a refinery after oil was discovered.

Socal obtained the exclusive right to prospect for and produce oil in eastern Saudi Arabia and preferential rights (that is, the right to obtain additional areas by matching the terms of other offers) to most of the rest of the kingdom that had any chance of containing oil accumulations. The agreement was to run for a period of sixty years from 1933 and was later extended for an additional six years. It was ratified by the Government of Saudi Arabia by a royal decree issued on July 7, 1933, and became effective on July 14, when it was published in the official gazette.

BEACHHEAD: Less than three months later, on September 23, 1933, the first oil prospectors stepped ashore at Jubail. Like Twitchell, who had driven across Arabia to join them, Robert P. (Bert) Miller and Schuyler B. (Krug) Henry wore beards and were in Arab dress to avoid appearing unnecessarily conspicuous to the townspeople and Bedouins, few of whom had ever seen a Westerner. A house at Hofuf in the oasis of al-Hasa had been obtained for them, and later arrangements were made to rent a small compound at Jubail for use as headquarters.

On the afternoon of their arrival the geologists began to explore the coastal region south of Jubail, including a hill called al-Jubayl al-Barri (the Berri oil field was named after this many years later). On September 28 they

came to Jabal Dhahran, the distinctive feature they had observed from Bahrain. The Dhahran area is today the site of Aramco's headquarters, the University of Petroleum and Minerals, the Dhahran International Airport, and much else that has grown up in the intervening years. It is also a textbook example of a geological dome and it eventually proved to contain oil. They chose to give the name Dammam Dome to the structure underlying Dhahran. It was oil industry practice at the time to name newly discovered structures after a nearby town or village, and Dammam and the little fishing village of al-Khobar were the only settlements in the area. Dammam was chosen because it was larger and because it was felt it would be easier for Americans to pronounce correctly than al-Khobar.

This phase of the job — geological reconnaissance — was done using car odometer, alidade and plane table, geologist's pick and Brunton compass. Heat and sandstorms often confined the geologists to their tents or drove them back to their headquarters. In March 1934 their work was made easier when they acquired a proper tool for the exploration of an area bigger than Texas — an airplane.

To Socal, the use of airplanes was considered so important that permission to use them was sought during the original concession negotiations. By the time Henry and Miller came ashore at Jubail, Socal's chief geologist was already negotiating with a geologist, pilot, and aerial photographer named Richard Kerr to provide aerial reconnaissance, photographs, and support to the geologists on the ground. Socal bought a Fairchild 71 high-winged monoplane, equipped it with extra gas tanks and a big camera, and arranged for special chemicals for developing film in Saudi Arabia's extreme heat, and shipped all these to Egypt on a freighter. From there Kerr and Charley Rocheville, as copilot and mechanic, flew the plane to Saudi Arabia via the Suez Canal, Gaza, and Baghdad, touching down at last on an airstrip made ready for them by the geologists at Jubail.

There were problems, even with the plane. The government at first insisted that it fly high, avoid the interior of the country, and use no radio. Blowing sand grounded it often. The large tires it needed to land on soft sand affected the plane's stability and reduced its

Geology Of Arabia

Photomicrograph shows the pore system of the oil-bearing Arab-D limestone.

Hundreds of millions of years ago vast seas washed up against the mountainous landmass of what is now the western part of Saudi Arabia. This ancient landmass is the Arabian Shield, the first of the peninsula's two distinct geological provinces. Sediments left behind by the primordial seas constitute the second and younger province, the Arabian Shelf.

Far more extensive than the present-day Arabian Gulf, or even the sea known to the peninsula's earliest man, the ancient waters spread north as well as west, intermittently covering the regions now occupied by Iraq, Jordan, Lebanon, and Syria. Through age upon age the sea alternately flooded and abated, exposing bare sediments to erosion and then covering them again. Tiny plants and animals living in the marine waters died and became part of the seabed sediments. Through the long, slow processes of nature the mineral sediments hardened into rock and organic matter was transformed into the petroleum now found so abundantly in the Gulf-Mesopotamia region.

The Arabian Shield is actually part of a greater Afro-Arabian Shield, split today by the Red Sea Rift. Bulging toward the east at its midsection and occupying about one-third of the Arabian Peninsula, the ancient landmass consists of rocks formed from molten magma and from folded, compressed sediments that were fused and altered by the enormous heat and pressure associated with mountain building. In some regions comparatively recent lava flows lie upon the shield. This igneous-metamorphic complex, Precambrian in age, slopes gently eastward beneath the sedimentary strata of the Arabian Shelf, forming the crystalline "basement" that surfaces again in parts of the Iranian mountains.

Laid down some 550 million years ago, the oldest of the Arabian Shelf sediments outcrops on the shield's eastern flank and, along with the progressively younger overlying beds, dips gently and thickens in the direction of the Rub' al-Khali and Arabian Gulf basins. Altogether the sediments are some twenty thousand feet thick in the region below the present-day shoreline of the Gulf. Time has worn away the exposed softer beds at their thinner western edge, leaving those less subject to erosion standing high above the level of the general terrain in the shape of escarpments in which Paleozoic, Mesozoic, and Lower Tertiary beds outcrop. Most notable is the long, curved belt of westward-facing cliffs known as the Tuwayq Escarpment. Resistant limestones cap each scarp, and many of these rock units continue without significant interruption for hundreds of miles across the shelf. In eastern Saudi Arabia many of these are covered by essentially flat-lying Tertiary and younger deposits.

All the known accumulations of hydrocarbons in Saudi Arabia occur in the sedimentary shelf and most of them in rocks of the Late Jurassic. In that period in geologic time, roughly 150 million years ago, a progressive change in sedimentary environment — reflecting the withdrawal of the sea — began in what is now central Iraq and subsequently pushed south into the Arabian Peninsula as desiccation spread. The alternate transgressions and regressions of the generally receding sea set up a fourfold sedimentary cycle in which mainly shallow-water carbonate rocks were overlain by beds formed as seawater evaporated in shallow, enclosed depressions. These particular carbonates are the four members of the Arab Formation. They are of paramount importance (especially the porous and extremely prolific member labeled the Arab-D) for they contain the largest reserves of petroleum in the world.

Millions of years after deposition of the sediments, tectonic forces deformed the strata, and oil accumulated in structural traps where overlying beds of impermeable rock prevent its migration and escape. Dammam, the first oil field discovered in Saudi Arabia, is a domal uplift — probably the result of upward pressure from a deeply buried salt plug. The great majority of known accumulations in the kingdom, however, are in anticlines formed when earth movements forced the sediments to buckle. Major deformation occurred in Cretaceous and Eocene times and resulted in broad, shallow folds, unlike the high mountain ranges uplifted later in Iran. The axis of these gentle flexures in eastern Arabia trends generally north and south, and the longest — which includes Ghawar, the largest oil field in the world — extends for more than two hundred and fifty miles.

RED

SEA

SURFACE GEOLOGICAL FEATURES OF ARABIA

The Arabian Peninsula can be divided into two main geological provinces: the shield and the shelf. The Arabian Shield, shown as "Precambrian basement" on the map, consists of igneous and metamorphic rocks and makes up the western one-third of the peninsula. Bordering the shield on the east is the Arabian Shelf, consisting of sedimentary strata. The shelf slopes gently away into the Rub' al-Khali and Arabian Gulf basins, interrupted by a series of escarpments in which Paleozoic, Mesozoic, and lower Tertiary beds crop out. All known accumulations of oil and gas in Saudi Arabia are in the eastern portion of the shelf.

ARABIAN GULF

ARABIAN SEA

Eolian sand and gravel, mainly quaternary

Volcanic rocks, mainly tertiary and quaternary

Oligocene

Miocene and Pliocene

Paleocene and Eocene

Cretaceous

Jurassic

Triassic

Paleozoic

Precambrian basement

Pilot-photographer Joe Mountain amassed an excellent pictorial record of the oil venture's early days.

Some Saudis called Max Steineke, the indefatigable geologist, "a big man with a big arm and a big voice."

Dammam No. 1 blew oil and gas during a flow test, but the oil accumulation proved to be too small for commercial production.

speed. The pace of the work, nevertheless, quickened and the reach of the exploration effort was extended. When permission was received to use the Fairchild's radio, the pilots were able to coordinate their aerial surveys with geologists working on the ground, and by the end of the first eight months in the field, the reconnaissance teams had seen enough to justify a recommendation to drill the Dammam Dome and to study the general area with geophysical methods.

THE FIRST WELL: By October 1934, after a summer in the cool mountains of Lebanon, most of the original team, plus some new men, were back in Saudi Arabia working for Socal's new subsidiary, California Arabian Standard Oil Company (Casoc), to which it had assigned the concession.

Among the newcomers were two men who, in different ways, typified the pioneers of the reconnaissance period. One was Joe Mountain, a fine pilot and a professional photographer and darkroom technician who produced a fascinating pictorial record of those early days. The other was Max Steineke, whose contribution to the Aramco story would be of inestimable value. Burly, enthusiastic, implacably methodical, Steineke was a field geologist who laid the foundations for the understanding of what lay beneath Saudi Arabia's deceptive sands. Aiding them were Saudi Arabs in a wide variety of jobs (115 were on the payroll by 1935) — the first of thousands who eventually formed the backbone of the company's multinational work force.

In most ways the 1934-35 season was like the first one, but there were differences, too. For one thing, there were more jobs to do — the construction of a pier at al-Khobar, for example, and the construction of bunkhouses. The main difference, though, was that on April 30, 1935, they finally began to drill for oil.

But Dammam Well No. 1 was a disappointment. For one breathtaking day, the men in San Francisco thought they had struck oil on the first go. They received a cable reporting a flow of 6,537 barrels per day from the Bahrain zone, but that figure turned out to be garbled. The estimated flow was about 100 barrels a day. That would have been an oil well in Bakersfield, California, but it was hardly commercial in Saudi Arabia. No. 1 was completed as a gas well, producing from a shallow horizon for domestic cooking and heating and for firing the boilers used to provide power for the drilling of other wells.

Drilling of Dammam No. 2 started in February 1936. By June 20, during a five-day test, it flowed an average of 335 barrels of crude a day. A week later, after acid treatment, it produced at the equivalent of 3,840 barrels a day. San Francisco was jubilant and approved four more wells in the Dammam Dome and a wildcat at Al Alat, some twenty miles northwest of Dhahran. In July plans were made for yet another well, Dammam No. 7. It was scheduled to be a deep test into a zone which had shown gas, but little oil on Bahrain.

They drilled No. 1 deeper, down below 3,200 feet, without striking anything worthwhile. Then No. 2 went bad and started producing more water than oil. No. 3 and No. 4 were both drilled into the Bahrain zone in 1936. The first never produced more than 100 barrels of heavy road oil a day, and the second was a dry hole.

DAMMAM NO. 7: On December 7, 1936, the drillers spudded in Dammam No. 7. It was destined to become the most stubbornly defended route to oil yet encountered. There were accidents, cave-ins, lost circulation, and stuck drilling bits. Everything imaginable seemed to go wrong.

Meanwhile, the geologists were beginning to probe still farther and deeper into Saudi Arabia's geological past. Aiding them was their first paleontologist, Richard A. Bramkamp. It was Bramkamp who confirmed and refined Steineke's intuitive grasp of the peninsula's geology and succeeded Steineke as Aramco's chief geologist.

In the spring of 1937 the first two wives of American employees came to join their husbands in the new houses being constructed not far from the drilling rigs, and in September four more wives and four children arrived. In that same spring Max Steineke crossed the Arabian Peninsula both ways. It was not the first trip (Miller and Hamilton had done it in 1934), but from the standpoint of an understanding of the geology of Saudi Arabia it was of great importance. By the time he returned, after having a comprehensive look at the kingdom's surface geology, Steineke had the data which enabled him to construct a skeleton of the general structure and stratigraphy of the peninsula on which all subsequent geological knowledge was built. It was a tremendous piece of reconnaissance geology.

When he got back to Dhahran, however, Steineke found the camp in gloom. Dammam No. 7, the deep test, was not going at all well. By October 1937, plagued with troubles, it was at a depth of 3,300 feet and still showing, in the terse words of a cable sent to San Francisco, "no oil, no water," and on the last day of the year, while drilling at only 192 feet above the depth at which oil was eventually found, it suffered a gas blowout. Drilling continued, but Casoc's worried officials contacted Steineke to ask for a crucial piece of advice: Shall we go on?

Keep drilling, he advised. As it turned out, Steineke's advice was sound, for on March 3, 1938, Dammam No. 7, now down to 4,727 feet in the Arab Formation, began to flow at a rate of 1,585 barrels of oil a day. By March 22, it was flowing 3,810 barrels a day. That fall, the government was formally told that Dammam was a commercially valuable oil field, and Casoc gladly paid the agreed upon advance of £50,000 gold. Saudi Arabia was in the oil business.

Dammam No. 7 had taken fifteen months to complete. By the time it was finished, the wildcat at Al Alat had been abandoned as a dry hole at 4,530 feet. Dammam No. 2 and No. 4 were eventually deepened to the Arab Formation and became excellent producers. Lucky No. 7 was tough to drill, but it has ever since been a steady and reliable producer, averaging 1,600 barrels a day since 1938 for a cumulative production of over 27 million barrels by 1979.

INTO PRODUCTION: In the story of Aramco the discovery of oil in commercial quantities in Dammam No. 7 was a turning point. Until then the Saudi Arabian venture had been a risky and costly proposition. Now, as a commercially sound operation, it needed large transfusions of money to expand some facilities and to build others. By 1935, in addition, the production of Standard of California in the Middle East and the Netherlands East Indies (now Indonesia) called for additional marketing facilities. At the same time, the marketing facilities that had been developed by The Texas Company (now Texaco) were in need of more accessible production. The two companies therefore combined their interests located between Egypt and the Hawaiian Islands and in this way The Texas Company in 1937 became a half-owner of Casoc and additional funds thus became available for expansion of the operations in Saudi Arabia.

Casoc now had the go-ahead for more housing, for enlargement of the pier at al-Khobar, for pipelines and storage tanks, for a stabilizer plant to remove poisonous hydrogen sulfide gas from the oil before shipment, for a small refinery, and for a marine terminal for tankers. In September 1938 at Dahl Hith, a few miles southeast of Riyadh, Bramkamp and another Aramco pioneer, Tom Barger (who later became the company's chief executive officer), found an outcrop of the same thick anhydrite cap rock that had overlain the producing zone in Dammam No. 7. This confirmed a deduction that Steineke had made and, by showing that conditions favorable for the accumulation and entrapment of oil probably existed not just in the Dammam Dome but over most of eastern Saudi Arabia, it justified a considerable expansion of the exploration program. At the end of 1938 the structure drilling program was extended, with a coordinated study of rock cores brought up to the surface when drilling in deep wells.

Dammam No. 7, the discovery well that put Saudi Arabia into the oil business, is still producing today.

In addition, the men of Casoc had a special sort of deadline to look forward to in the winter and spring of 1939. They had invited King 'Abd al-'Aziz to come to the east coast to take his first look at the oil installations and, on May 1, watch the first tanker being loaded with Saudi Arabian oil.

The King, they knew, was well pleased with Casoc's success — pleased enough to reject some of the offers that in the wake of Dammam No. 7 had come in from Great Britain, Germany, and Japan, then on the verge of World War II. Still, Casoc's owners had decided it would be wise to be ready with matching offers in case they should be necessary. By January 1939 Casoc was again involved in complicated negotiations affecting the two Neutral Zones between Saudi Arabia and its neighbors to the north, Kuwait and Iraq, and parts of Saudi Arabia outside the exclusive area granted in the original concession agreement of 1933. The King's visit was indeed going to be important.

Floyd Ohliger led King 'Abd al-'Aziz on a tour of oil installations during His Majesty's first visit to Aramco.

Air-conditioned trailers long ago replaced the tents of pioneering oil explorers, and many of the exploration tools have been sharpened by technological advances and by the use of computers for sophisticated interpretation. Right, above: Surveyor determines locations for lines to charges to be set off for obtaining seismic data. Right: Exploration camp in the Sand Mountain area of the Rub' al-Khali receives supplies and work crews by air. Facing page: "Strat well" in the Rub' al-Khali is drilled with special tools that cut cores of rock and bring these samples to the surface for stratigraphic study. Below: Thin rock sections are marked for microscopic examination in the paleontology laboratory. Top corner, facing page: Geophysicist computes seismic travel time from a shot point to various stratigraphic reflectors — information that will be used for computer-generated maps.

The visit was a great success. In the spring of 1939 the King and his retinue moved east from Riyadh in a caravan of two thousand people in five hundred cars, and on April 28 they set up a city of white tents near Dhahran. After two days of banquets and formalities, the King inspected the installations, dined aboard the *D. G. Scofield* — the Socal tanker picked to load the first shipment — and, on May 1, 1939, opened the valve that let the first barrel of oil flow into the first tanker at Ras Tanura. During the festivities, the King also made some mild suggestions with respect to the new round of negotiations and personally cleared the way for an amicable resolution of the differences between the negotiating teams. On May 31, 1939, Casoc and the government signed a supplemental agreement extending the northern and southern parts of the concession area westward and also granting the company rights with respect to Saudi Arabian interests in the two Neutral Zones.

The first cargo of Saudi Arabian crude oil was shipped aboard the tanker *D.G. Scofield* in May 1939

WARTIME: Shortly after the King's visit, war engulfed Europe, and life in Dhahran began to change. At that time, of course, Saudi Arabia and the United States were still neutral. On a moonlit night in 1940, nevertheless, the war came unexpectedly to Casoc when four crews of audacious Italian airmen flew from the island of Rhodes in the Mediterranean and bombs fell on Dhahran.

Years later Aramco learned that the raid was an attempt to knock out the Bahrain Petroleum Company (Bapco) refinery on Bahrain, which was a British protected state, and that the attack on Dhahran was a mistake. Approved by Mussolini personally and led by the secretary of the Fascist party, the raid involved four Savoia-Marchetti S-82s which took off from Rhodes, flew all the way to the Gulf, bombed the refinery in Bahrain, and recrossed the Arabian Peninsula to land in Ethiopia. It was a daring and dangerous flight. En route to the target one of the four pilots lost contact with the rest of the squadron, saw the lights of Dhahran, and, thinking it was Bahrain, dropped his bombs.

On the night of October 19, 1940, the Casoc crews and their families did not know it was a mistake. All they knew was that the quiet desert night was suddenly rocked with the thunder of explosions and that the explosions seemed distressingly close. Miraculously, no

Craters from small fifty-pound bombs remained as evidence of a misdirected air raid in the early days of the war.

one was hurt and little was damaged, but it reminded Casoc that there was a war on. Blackout restrictions were imposed, air-raid shelters were excavated, first-aid instructions were given to employees, and shortly afterwards American women and children were evacuated — the first group by tanker to Bombay.

Oil had been struck at 10,115 feet at Abu Hadriya in March 1940 and, soon after the bombing of Dhahran, Abqaiq No. 1 came in. At 9,720 barrels of oil per day, it was a whopper. The war at sea was severely limiting shipping, however, and this and wartime shortages slowly strangled oil development. The two new fields were shut in. The 3,000-barrel-a-day "teapot" refinery at Ras Tanura that had been started up in January 1941 was shut down in June. The tank farm and marine terminal lay idle. The most important activity remaining was the production and shipment by barge of from 12,000 to 15,000 barrels of oil per day from al-Khobar to the Bapco refinery on Bahrain.

The skeleton group that remained in Saudi Arabia found plenty to do. In May 1940 the first school for Aramco's Saudi employees was started in the sitting room of Hijji ibn Jasim's home in al-Khobar. Within two months there was a second school and in six months there was a third. Some of the geologists and engineers became involved in the development of irrigation facilities in the al-Kharj area southeast of Riyadh. At the request of the government a food hauling service to Riyadh was instituted with trucks that became increasingly difficult to keep rolling as the war went on. On one occasion, three Hurricane fighters were hauled out of a salt flat where their RAF pilots had made emergency landings. Most of the fuel, cement, and other material used in the drilling of two wells at Abqaiq and a wildcat at Jauf in 1943 was transported by camel caravan. The Jauf well proved dry, unfortunately, and the movement of materials by camel proved to be neither cheap nor efficient.

To ensure their supplies in a food-short Saudi Arabia, the oilmen began growing their own vegetables and raising poultry, rabbits, cows, and sheep. They introduced incubators and experimented with crossbreeding. At one time, they had a flock of five thousand sheep, and, thanks to an extraordinary Bedouin named Mutlaq, they raised a lot of cattle. On three separate occasions Mutlaq and his son, alone and on foot, rounded up cattle in Yemen and drove them a thousand miles to Dhahran. By breeding them with stock obtained from Bahrain the men in Dhahran built up respectable herds of dairy and meat cattle.

As the war progressed the United States Government became concerned about the rate of oil consumption, and the importance of Saudi Arabia as a source of additional oil became increasingly evident. The U.S. Government gave consideration to plans ranging from the purchase of all or part of Casoc to the construction of a pipeline to the Mediterranean in return for guaranteed access to Saudi crude. None of these proposals were carried out, but late in 1943 scarce steel and other materials were officially allocated for the construction at Ras Tanura of a 50,000-barrel-a-day refinery, to be financed by the American owner companies. Trucks and construction equipment were made available, and high priorities were given to the movement of men and supplies.

The project included not only the large refinery, tank farm, and marine terminal at Ras Tanura but also a submarine pipeline to Bahrain, where the Bapco refinery was to be enlarged. While gearing up for all of this, the California Arabian Standard Oil Company on January 31, 1944, changed its name to the more appropriate Arabian American Oil Company, soon shortened to Aramco.

The quiet of Aramco's restricted operations turned into roaring activity. The tumult and confusion of any large construction project far from its base of supplies were intensified by wartime bottlenecks and shortages. A ship carrying urgently needed supplies was torpedoed and sunk. Men arrived before they could be housed. Men and materials arrived in the wrong order.

Construction of the refinery and related facilities such as tanks and marine installations was put in the hands of a number of American construction companies. In December 1945 these firms alone had some six hundred Americans working in Ras Tanura, and workmen were recruited also from Iraq, India, and Eritrea.

As difficult as it was to obtain drilling equipment, more oil was needed. Drilling therefore resumed at Abqaiq in 1944, and what turned out to be a successful wildcat was

started in Qatif. There were times in 1944 when drilling crews, however, were needed even more desperately elsewhere. For a couple of weeks some of the drillers helped build bunkhouses.

The submarine pipeline to Bahrain went into service in March 1945. Two weeks after the formal terms of Japanese surrender had been signed on September 2 in Tokyo Bay, the first crude still of the new Ras Tanura refinery was fired. With the firing of the second crude still in December Aramco brought to a conclusion, on schedule, an extraordinary wartime project.

POSTWAR EXPANSION: In September 1945 Aramco posted and celebrated its first two-million-barrel month, and by the end of 1945 it had loaded thirty-eight tankers at the new terminal and had produced over 21 million barrels of oil. Nearly three times total production in the previous year, this figure marked the first giant step toward the record achieved in 1976 when Aramco for the first time produced more than three *billion* barrels of oil in a single year.

The American wives who left in 1940 were back again. In October 1945 ten children were enrolled in a one-room, American-curriculum school which had been closed for the duration of the war. At the same time, some 170 Arab young men and boys were enrolled in training classes in what was known as "The Jabal School." It was no Phillips Exeter or Eton, but it was the prep school for a number of Aramco's future Saudi Arab executives. Charley Rocheville, who had accompanied Casoc's Fairchild aircraft to Saudi Arabia, came with another single-engine airplane, a Norseman, to provide support for exploration parties and for pipeline patrols. Aramco had chartered a few C-47s from the U.S. Air Transport Command in 1945, and work was under way to construct a first-class airport on the site of the old Dhahran airstrip.

There was at this time no road across the sands to Abqaiq. One proceeded there across the desert by driving from target to target placed on the highest dunes. It took two hours by fast launch and three hours by regular launch to get to Bahrain. American employees and their families going on leave could catch a flying boat in Bahrain and fly to Cairo via Basra, Lake Habbaniya, and the Dead Sea. Or

The building of a refinery and small tank farm at Ras Tanura was a major undertaking amid wartime restrictions.

Schoolmaster Sam Whipple had ten pioneer offspring in his one-room school in 1945.

Many of the company's earliest Saudi employees took instruction at what came to be called "The Jabal School."

they could take a ship to Abadan in Iran and then make a memorable three-day flight to New York via Egypt, France, Ireland, and Newfoundland. In January 1946 TWA made the first commercial passenger flight out of Dhahran.

King 'Abd al-'Aziz made his second and last visit to Aramco installations in February 1947. This time he and his entourage traveled in a fleet of the kingdom's own aircraft. He spent the better part of a week entertaining and being entertained. He was obviously pleased by what he saw and heard, and he provided visiting foreign journalists with fascinating stories and attractive photographic opportunities.

The year 1948 was an especially important one in the postwar history of the company because in November of that year arrangements were completed for Standard Oil Company (New Jersey) and Socony-Vacuum Oil Company to acquire shares in the ownership of Aramco. The period of phenomenal growth and expansion that followed in the 1950s and later was thus in part a reflection of the cooperation among four of the major oil companies of the world.

Abqaiq — one day to become the largest crude oil processing center in the world — was little more than an outpost in 1946.

Production was up to 500,000 barrels a day by the end of 1949. This was achieved only with an extraordinary expansion of pumping, pipeline, and treating facilities, not to mention warehouses, shops, offices, and housing. Meanwhile the search for new reserves of oil went on. Drilling in the late 1940s was concentrated in the Abqaiq field, but wildcats also discovered oil at 'Ain Dar and at Haradh. Although the geologists recognized that these two places were on one geological structure, it was several years before they could prove that they were not separate fields but all part of the world's largest oil accumulation, the Ghawar field, over a hundred and sixty miles long and twenty miles wide at its greatest width.

Since a pipeline shortcut to the Mediterranean would eliminate the long haul by tanker around the Arabian Peninsula and through the Suez Canal, various plans for such a project had been considered during World War II. In July 1945 Aramco's owner companies incorporated the Trans-Arabian Pipe Line Company, a name easily shortened to Tapline, for the purpose of building such a pipeline, the world's largest privately financed

Tapline, crossing some seven hundred and fifty miles of desert and mountains, cut a much-needed route to the Mediterranean coast.

Exploring The Aramco Concession

A 1934 field party — Tom Koch, Max Steineke, and guide — takes time out for coffee.

The concession agreement signed at the end of May 1933 by the Government of Saudi Arabia and Socal required the company to "commence plans and preparations for geological work" at once and to begin actual field work within four months. The systematic investigation of the sedimentary geology of Saudi Arabia accordingly began in September 1933 with the mapping of the dome in the Dammam area that oilmen on Bahrain had seen and speculated about. S. B. (Krug) Henry and J. W. (Soak) Hoover did the initial work and they were later joined by others, including Max Steineke, who arrived in 1934 and two years later was named the company's chief geologist. As more men and equipment arrived, the pace of geological reconnaissance increased, expanding to nine field parties by 1937 and eventually radiating out across the desert until by 1959 roughly 500,000 square miles of sedimentary outcrop had been surveyed.

Some of the early findings, however, seemed to show little or no correlation between surface features and what lay beneath them, and geologists were perplexed until Steineke identified the problem. Because percolating groundwater had dissolved and washed away a calcium sulfate (anhydrite) member of one of the formations underlying much of the original exploration area, the rocks above it had collapsed in some places and the consequent slumping of surface topography gave a false picture of the subsurface configurations. To get around, or below, this problem Steineke late in 1936 instituted a program of structure drilling — that is, drilling not for oil but for information that would help locate structures containing oil. Careful study of the rock samples taken from these structure holes and their correlation with the results of surface geological work eventually gave a more positive idea of the continuity, depth, and flexure of the strata.

Observation and mapping had shown that the main structural features of eastern Arabia trended north and south. Structure holes, spaced usually half a degree of latitude apart, were therefore drilled in lines running east and west. It was reasoned that in this way the greatest number of structures and the biggest structures (oil-bearing, it was hoped) would be defined most quickly and most economically. In the beginning the holes were shallow, just deep enough to penetrate below where the dissolved anhydrite had been washed away, but as the drills moved westward to central Saudi Arabia and southward to the Rub' al-Khali it became necessary to drill to other deeper horizons (eventually reaching 3,000 feet) to obtain a true structural picture. Today, looking back, it can be said that it was a combination of structure drilling and surface mapping that has identified the structures containing the bulk of the oil found to date in Saudi Arabia.

In 1953 the company moved on to stratigraphic drilling (probing for information on the composition and sequence of rock beds). In the stratigraphic program fewer wells were drilled and they were drilled deeper — to depths of from 5,000 to 10,000 feet — to include the deep-lying and possibly oil-bearing formations. At first spaced mainly around the periphery of the Aramco concession area, they were later spotted at selected locations within the company's operating area. The lithologic information obtained from these holes was basic in making concession-wide correlations of strata, in recognizing changes in rock composition over broad areas, and in pinpointing places where strata either had been removed or were never deposited.

Along with the direct means of obtaining information in all types of exploratory drilling, that is, by examining and testing rock samples brought to the surface, geologists also obtain information indirectly, by running wire-line logs. With testing devices lowered into the hole, this procedure measures and "logs" such data as the electric current within the earth, the earth's magnetic field, or the naturally occurring radioactivity inherent in all sediments. Logs make it possible to infer the presence of particular rocks and to calculate such information as porosity and the nature of reservoir fluids.

To help them reconstruct the history of the earth, geologists — and more especially paleontologists — identify the fossilized remains of tiny animals (often consisting of only a single cell) that yield valuable clues to the environment in which rock beds were deposited, and hence provide a clue to their age. In the early 1960s, Aramco paleontological studies were expanded to include the then new science of palynology, the study of spores and pollen of the earliest known plants. All these investigations served to reinforce the analyses of data obtained by other means, which all together helped determine which areas warranted concentrated oil exploration.

Two additional techniques that the early explorers put to use were employed in a survey that began along the coast in 1939 and twenty years later had covered most of the concession area. One was the gravity meter survey, which measures from point to point the minute variations in gravitational pull caused by differences in either the depths of rocks or their relative densities. The other was the magnetometer survey, which detects variations in the earth's magnetic field. Relatively inexpensive, the gravity-magnetic approach provides limited information that must be supplemented by other geophysical means, and today it is used primarily in attempts to define and refine the deep-seated aspects of certain structural anomalies.

Other geophysical techniques with an even longer history have in recent years come to account for a major share of the company's exploration efforts. Since 1937 Aramco has used seismic exploration, which measures the speed of artificially induced shock waves in the earth and by using these measurements infers the presence of subsurface structures. Programs have alternated between the reflection method, which is more precise, and the refraction method, which provides rapid coverage and can accurately detect any large-scale structural features.

An especially ambitious part of the seismic program got under way in 1958 when Aramco embarked on a refraction survey that eventually resulted in a network blanketing the entire concession area. By integrating this work with results achieved by both drilling and surface reconnaissance, Aramco has been able to outline the structural framework and establish the stratigraphic succession of the entire area in which it operates.

By the time this refraction survey was completed, the largest surface structural features had been drilled. Of necessity the oil search moved on to the smaller, deeper, and more subtle expressions of structure, and to investigate these hard-to-find flexures Aramco turned to high-resolution reflection seismic prospecting. Using conventional energy sources as well as weight-dropping techniques, field parties have surveyed tens of thousands of line miles, recording the data on multichannel computer tapes. This information is then processed by computer to produce subsurface contour maps that help mark the structural highs that are the object of the search — maps which would require innumerable man-hours to produce by conventional means.

Because of the vast size of the area to be covered and because there were so few commanding elevations from which to get a broad view, an airplane equipped with an aerial camera was essential to even the earliest exploration of eastern Saudi Arabia. Beginning with the arrival of Dick Kerr and his Fairchild 71 in March 1934, photogeology has been used extensively, for from the superior vantage point of the cockpit explorers could pinpoint rock exposures for ground investigation, photograph surface structures, and from the overlapping photos piece together bigger and more accurate maps. Between 1949 and 1958 most of the concession area was mapped on a 1:60,000 scale. Using these photos to tie together and reconcile various ground surveys, Aramco then produced a series of geologic and geographic quadrangle maps of the sedimentary rocks of Saudi Arabia in a project which culminated in 1963 with the publication by the United States Geological Survey of English and Arabic editions of a 1:2,000,000 map of the peninsula with supporting publications.

This mapping project represented a cooperation among government, oil company, and private individuals that was unprecedented and it turned the Arabian Peninsula, virtually unknown to the explorers who had arrived thirty years before, into one of the better-mapped areas of the world.

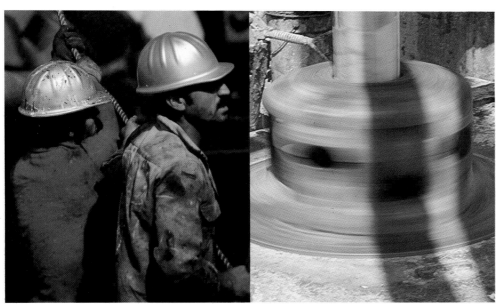

Drilling rigs prospect for oil on land and in the Gulf, their precise locations based on integrated investigations by oil-search teams. Ultimately it is the responsibility of operations personnel to prove the validity of these studies — planning the casing, drill string, mud chemicals, and logging tools — by using the best techniques at their disposal. Engineers who predict reservoir behavior under various programs of production and pressure maintenance then determine future drilling — and always, in the final analysis, the drill bit accomplishes the objective. Aramco Mobile Drilling Platform No. 2, facing page, and the rigs of the desert camp seen above represent the combined exploratory and development effort which may drill as much as one million feet a year.

construction project up to that time. As originally conceived and surveyed, the line would have followed a great circle route from Abqaiq to Haifa in the British mandate of Palestine.

Political tension and later outright war between the Arab states and Israel caused rerouting of the line and delayed the construction program. Though it was first planned to begin construction at both ends at about the same time, the war delayed work on the western end until the autumn of 1949. In January 1948 construction was begun of an Aramco pipeline from Abqaiq to Qaisumah, which would be the actual starting point of Tapline, and work proceeded westward from there, operating from a port and camp built for the purpose at Ras al-Mish'ab, some 160 miles north of Dhahran. Later work began from the western end as well, and the final weld connecting the western and eastern sections was made on September 2, 1950. A few months later, the first tanker was loaded with Saudi Arabian crude at the four-berth western terminus of the pipeline a few miles south of the ancient city of Sidon in Lebanon.

Nearly half of Tapline was constructed above ground, reducing its cost and facilitating the job of inspection crews.

Most of the line crossed desert lands where there were no roads, no water, and no permanent habitations. The terrain included rolling sand dunes, gravel plains, rocky lava belts, and the rugged mountains of Lebanon. Construction of the pipeline through this remote area, a distance of over a thousand miles, required a massive logistical effort. More than 350,000 tons of pipe, equipment, and materials had to be shipped halfway around the world, then trucked long distances overland. At the peak of construction more than sixteen thousand men were employed and over three thousand pieces of automotive and construction equipment were in operation.

A self-propelled Budd car traveled the new railroad link transporting passengers between Riyadh and Dammam.

Towns grew up around the four main pump stations in Saudi Arabia, and the road that parallels the pipeline became an important Middle Eastern transportation artery. The main Tapline pump stations located at Qaisumah, Rafha, Badanah, and Turaif, all in Saudi Arabia, provided an initial capacity of 320,000 barrels daily. In 1957 the capacity was increased to 450,000 barrels daily by installation of auxiliary pumping units midway between the main stations.

Even before Tapline was completed Aramco had become responsible for construc-

tion of another vast project, the 360-mile Saudi Government Railroad between Dammam on the Arabian Gulf and the capital city of Riyadh. Part of this project consisted of building a deep-water port at Dammam. For this a seven-mile causeway and trestle was pushed out into the Gulf, ending in a two-berth wharf. The government has enlarged the port several times during the years and by 1980 it had berthing facilities for forty ships. Aramco did not actually build the railroad and port, which were paid for by deductions from royalties due the government. It contracted the job to a consortium of American engineering firms, but Aramco supervised the project and saw that it was finished almost on schedule. In October 1951 King 'Abd al-'Aziz presided over ceremonies in Riyadh featuring the driving of the traditional golden spike into the final tie, and a new diesel locomotive pulled into the Riyadh station to inaugurate the new service.

CONSOLIDATION: Once the boom period of postwar construction and expansion was ended, Aramco settled down to a relatively quiet period of consolidation and reorganization. The company's manpower — swollen by the temporary forces needed to construct new oil installations as well as new offices, houses, schools, roads, hospitals, and other support facilities — reached a peak of twenty-four thousand in 1952 and then began to decline.

This is not to imply that Aramco lapsed once more into the inactivity of the wartime years. On the contrary, the company's production of crude oil and refined products, once the producing and shipping facilities were in place, climbed steadily, and during each year from 1945 through 1974 the amount of oil produced by Aramco increased at an average rate of about 19 percent. Average daily crude production, which was running at about 500,000 barrels per day (BPD) at the start of 1950, doubled by 1958, doubled again seven years later, doubled once more to 4,000,000 BPD by the end of 1970, and by 1974 it had doubled again. The company's cumulative total production had reached ten billion barrels by 1968; during 1974 it passed twenty billion; and in 1978, forty years after oil was discovered in commercial quantities, the total exceeded thirty billion barrels. Production of refined products also climbed steadily. Refinery runs in 1947 (the first full year of operation after the expansion of the refinery begun during the last years of the war) were slightly over 100,000 BPD and reached a peak of over 500,000 BPD in the early 1970s.

Nor did the company continue to limit its production to crude oil and a basic slate of refined products such as fuel oil, diesel oil, kerosene, and gasolines. Since the early 1960s it has also been increasingly involved in the production, processing, and export of natural gas liquids (NGL), including liquefied petroleum gas (LPG) and natural gasoline.

Aramco had been selling relatively small quantities of LPG in Saudi Arabia for cooking and heating since 1950. This LPG was extracted from refinery process gases. In 1960, however, the company took a step that would eventually bring it into the LPG business in a big way. A plant was constructed in Abqaiq to separate the liquid components of what is called "associated gas," the gas produced along with crude oil. The original idea was to inject these liquids (which were not otherwise economically usable at the time) into the 'Ain Dar field as a means of maintaining the field's reservoir pressure and as a simple conservation measure. Additional studies and cost analysis indicated that while this was a good method of maintaining reservoir pressure, it was economically even more desirable to sell this product than to inject it. After construction of suitable plants this raw LPG was removed at Abqaiq and then sent by pipeline to Ras Tanura for further processing, storage in refrigerated tanks, and sale. In December 1961 the first shipment of LPG was loaded into a specially designed tanker. It amounted to 50,000 barrels, the equivalent of 75 million cubic feet of gas.

Demand for LPG climbed so rapidly that Aramco's facilities, designed initially to process 3,400 barrels of LPG a day, were expanded again and again. Starting in September 1967 the natural gasoline portion (that is, the pentane and heavier hydrocarbon fractions) of the associated gas was removed at new facilities in Abqaiq and shipped to Ras Tanura for blending and sale with LPG. This combination of butane and propane (the constituents of LPG) and natural gasoline is commonly referred to as natural gas liquids (NGL). Production of NGL has risen from 2,900 BPD in 1962 (the first full year of

processing) to over 300,000 BPD in 1979, thus making Aramco the world's largest producer of NGL.

In 1960 most of the tankers leaving Ras Tanura and Sidon with Aramco crude and products were sailing for Europe, which in that year took 42.5 percent of the company's total exports, while Asia and Australia together took the next largest share or 36.7 percent. With one major exception the proportions have remained roughly the same in the succeeding years, with Europe taking between 40 and 50 percent of Aramco's exports, Asia and Australia taking about one third, and the remainder going to other parts of the world. The exception — a significant one — is North America. In 1970 North America was the destination for only 1 percent of the company's export sales. By 1977, however, this figure had risen to 11 percent of the total and by 1979 it was more than 19 percent. This abrupt rise in North American consumption of Saudi Arabian oil reflects the increasing dependence of the United States on foreign oil.

To maintain the enormous flow of oil which has made Aramco the largest producing company in the world has required a constant search for new oil, and the company has always kept up an active exploration and development program. Even during the quiet days of World War II, when production slowed to a trickle and the work force was reduced to a low of 1,825 employees, exploration work continued. Both the very large Abqaiq oil field and the smaller Abu Hadriya field were discovered in 1940, and the Qatif field was found in 1945. The search for new sources of oil continued at an accelerated pace after the war. 'Ain Dar, even bigger than Abqaiq and eventually proved to be part of the mammoth Ghawar field, was discovered in 1948; and Safaniya, the largest offshore oil field in the world, was found in 1951. Other new reserves have been found each year since 1938, and in fact additions to reserves have consistently been greater than the amount of oil produced. The result has been that, in spite of the very large amounts of oil produced, the remaining proved reserves in the Aramco concession area have actually shown a net increase each year.

SHIPPING TERMINALS: As production continued to grow, new and enlarged facilities

Sub-zero temperatures of refrigerated LPG frost loading lines at Ras Tanura.

The first Sea Island berths, built to accommodate the new supertankers, went into service at Ras Tanura in 1966.

Discovery of Safaniya, the world's largest offshore oil field, added tremendously to Saudi Arabia's reserves.

Saudi Arabia is the world's largest exporter of oil and natural gas liquids, and Aramco's marine terminals are among the busiest anywhere. Tankers call at a rate of about ten per day, and their loading necessitates weeks of planning among various company offices to coordinate arrivals and inventories. Right: Berthing master directs a tanker to Ras Tanura piers or Sea Island where the lanky Chiksan arms seen on the facing page will speed loading, often of different products simultaneously. Facing page, below: All eight Sea Island berths are occupied, while another tanker loads at one of the single-point mooring buoys at Ju'aymah, Aramco's deep-water terminal farther north. The concrete trestle at Ju'aymah is designed to carry butane and propane lines to a two-berth loading terminal six miles offshore. Below, this page: Largest crude tanks at Ras Tanura are the 1.25-million-barrel floating-roof tanks such as the one seen under construction at bottom; domed roofs mark refrigerated tanks for LPG.

for storing and shipping oil were required. Since 1950 the three outlets for Aramco's exports have been Bahrain, the Trans-Arabian Pipe Line (Tapline) to the Mediterranean, and tanker-loading terminals at the port of Ras Tanura on the Arabian Gulf, and facilities serving all three have been successively enlarged and improved. The pipeline to Bahrain (the destination for Aramco's first oil shipments back in the 1930s) was "looped" or doubled for part of its distance in 1948 and again in 1952, and auxiliary pumping units were installed along Tapline to increase throughput to the terminal at Sidon in Lebanon.

Since the end of World War II, however, the major outlet for the oil produced by Aramco has been shipment by tanker in the Gulf, and facilities for tanker loading have been repeatedly enlarged and added to in order to keep pace with rising production. The marine terminal at Ras Tanura started with a single pier capable of docking two small tankers. It grew to two piers with a total of ten berths and then to a major oil port able to load giant tankers. To provide berths for the bigger ships Aramco built structures known as Sea Islands. Four Sea Islands have been built and provide berths and loading facilities for eight tankers ranging in size from 60,000 to 500,000 deadweight tons.

As tankers continued to grow in size, and as oil production continued to increase, even the Sea Island facilities were not enough to handle Aramco's export shipments, and other solutions were soon found to be needed. One such solution, a departure from any oil-handling procedure Aramco had previously followed, was implemented in connection with the discovery and bringing into production in 1971 of the offshore Zuluf field.

In 1969 Aramco had built a gas-oil separator plant offshore to separate gas from crude oil produced from the Safaniya field. This plant, however, merely supplemented the principal gas-oil separation facilities for that field, which were on land. Now, for the Zuluf field, Aramco carried out the entire gas-oil separation process offshore. Crude oil from Zuluf wells flowed into a plant mounted on piles over the Gulf surface for removal of the gas, and was then sent on through underwater lines to a 1.8 million-barrel capacity floating storage vessel.

This vessel, actually an oil tanker named the *F. A. Davies* after the former chairman of Aramco's Board of Directors, received the oil and then pumped it to tankers being loaded a mile away. Both tankers were meanwhile free to swing about into the wind while receiving and discharging crude through single-buoy moorings. With the *F. A. Davies* Aramco had two tanker outlets in the Gulf. But with production soaring and both outlets working to capacity, it realized that Saudi Arabia would have to have another, completely new terminal of considerable size.

About fifteen miles up the coast from Aramco's original oil terminal the company therefore began work on a new terminal, Ju'aymah, that would eventually rival the one at Ras Tanura in size and importance. The most conspicuous installations on land at Ju'aymah are a number of enormous crude oil storage tanks, each of them big enough to accommodate a thirty-story building on its side. By the end of 1978 fourteen 1.25 million-barrel tanks had been completed and a year later five 1.5 million-barrel tanks stood ready for filling. Other facilities include a control house for regulating onshore functions, a small-craft harbor for the launches which carry operators to and from their duty stations out in the Gulf, and 56-inch loading lines reaching seven miles out into the water to a platform mounted on piles where meters gauge the crude before it is loaded aboard tankers.

The Ju'aymah terminal went into operation in November 1974 and loaded its first shipment of Saudi Arabian crude aboard the 257,000 deadweight-ton *Esso Indonesia,* tied up at a single-buoy mooring of the same type introduced at Zuluf. By the end of 1977 the terminal had the capacity to load 4.5 million barrels of crude a day into the largest tankers afloat at moorings in a configuration placing each at least a mile from the others. The *F. A. Davies* was taken out of service at the beginning of 1976.

CONSERVATION MEASURES: Oil production from the fields in Aramco's concession areas makes use of the natural pressure of oil and gas within the oil-bearing reservoirs to flow the oil and gas through the well bores to the surface and to move it through flowline gathering systems to plants where the oil and

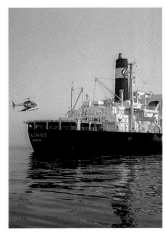
The tanker *F.A. Davies* was specially built to serve as a vessel for offshore storage.

Tanks holding up to one and one-half million barrels each were built to support shipping facilities at Ju'aymah.

Production from Zuluf field called for an offshore GOSP and later a second which, at the time it was built, ranked among the largest of its type anywhere.

gas are separated. As production continues, pressure within the reservoir naturally declines, and unless something is done to maintain the pressure, flowing production could cease before even a small percentage of the oil in the ground had been removed.

In many fields, good oil field practice, which aims at producing in the long run as much oil from the reservoirs as economically possible, requires that this pressure be maintained. This is usually achieved by injecting either gas or water into the oil reservoir. Aramco's injection programs date back to the early 1950s. In 1954 the company's first gas injection plant was completed as part of a pressure maintenance program for the Abqaiq field. Dissolved gas produced with oil was separated from the oil, compressed to a pressure of about 2,500 pounds per square inch, and returned to the oil-bearing formations through injection wells in the higher part of the structure. A second gas injection plant was installed at 'Ain Dar in 1959.

During the development of Abqaiq and Ghawar Aramco decided that the most efficient means of maintaining reservoir pressure in these fields would be through injection of water into the flanks of the producing reservoirs. Water injection can help sustain higher producing rates as well as increasing ultimate oil recovery. Water pumped into subsurface producing reservoirs maintains pressure by moving in behind the oil and gas that are produced. At the same time, water acts to sweep the oil ahead of it toward the centrally located producing wells.

To supplement gas injection at Abqaiq, the injection of water in the northern end of the field was begun in 1956. By the end of the year about 40,000 barrels a day were being injected through three water wells and company engineers were designing additional facilities to bring the daily rate up to 300,000 barrels. Since 1956 the company's water injection programs have expanded considerably (the injection of gas, however, is more effective in some situations and continues in two of Aramco's oil fields or as a temporary conservation measure) and the quantities of water injected increased dramatically during the 1960s and early 1970s, eventually amounting to some 11 million barrels a day. The sources of injection water have been the aquifers of the Wasia and Biyadh formations, which overlie the oil fields of the Eastern Province and in this area are too saline for domestic or agricultural use.

In order to lessen the dependence on aquifer water, plans were made to utilize seawater in its place, and construction began in 1976 of a giant seawater intake and treatment plant on the shore near Qurayyah, east of Abqaiq. This installation, by far the largest of its kind in the world, is designed to supply 4.2 million barrels a day of treated seawater for injection into the central portion of the Ghawar oil field. Seawater taken from the Gulf is treated and pumped through sixty-two miles of dual 56- and 60-inch pipeline into the existing water injection system, replacing the aquifer water previously used.

GROWTH IN THE 1970s: As Aramco moved into the 1970s, it soon found itself faced with a demand for oil which called for expansion that would dwarf the efforts of its earlier years. In some ways the period was reminiscent of the years following World War II when, with both men and materials once again available, Aramco was able to get down to the serious business of defining and developing Saudi Arabia's vast oil resources. In 1947 the company produced less than 250,000 barrels of crude per day, drawing from just three of the four fields it had discovered, yet it stood on the threshold of a period of growth involving projects of unforeseen size and complexity that ultimately made it the number one oil-producing company in the world. Thirty years later, with the oil fields in its concession area — each one major to giant by world standards — numbering over three dozen, Aramco's annual production of crude for the first time exceeded an average of nine million barrels a day; moreover, it had been transformed from a company whose primary interest was oil to one engaged in a variety of other industrial activities.

The postwar development of the 1940s and 1950s, if exciting and challenging to those involved, was steady, predictable, and by and large undramatic, and it went forward with the expectation that huge reserves meant steady, sure growth. Going into the 1970s Aramco was producing less than three million barrels a day, not even one-third of its crude production eight years later. World events altered that situation drastically, however. In quick

Installations at 'Ain Dar compressed gas to be injected back into the reservoir for pressure maintenance.

Seawater treated at the Qurayyah plant replaces a significant amount of non-potable saline aquifer water formerly used for injection into areas of the Ghawar field.

The Ras Tanura refinery, born amid wartime shortages of the 1940s, has grown into one of the world's largest refineries with a throughput capacity of three-quarters of a million barrels of crude and LPG a day. Many of its newest plant areas involve gas handling — as do those across the Arabian Peninsula at Yanbu', site of a fractionation plant under construction for the government gas program, as seen at left. Above: Miles of 26-, 28-, and 30-inch pipe go into the construction of the government's east-west pipeline linking Yanbu' to Eastern Province gas centers. Right: Diver inspects an underwater section that is one small part of Aramco's far-reaching network of crude, gas, and products pipelines. Facing page, far left: Panel signals controllers at the Ju'aymah offshore platform where loading lines from shore are gathered for metering.

succession the Western world enacted strict environmental laws, encountered the energy crisis, and felt the first pangs of a fuel shortage; and other top producing countries imposed production cutbacks just at the moment when demands from Western Europe, Japan, and the United States were skyrocketing. It was time for a sweeping reassessment of the world petroleum picture, and for Aramco the results indicated that it must expand fast.

With an enthusiasm not seen since its pioneer days, Aramco went to work hiring specialists in fields ranging from reservoir engineering to computer programming, making and revising plans, estimating and re-estimating budgets as expansion became the byword of every department. Activity accelerated dramatically as the decade got under way: between 1972 and the end of 1975, for example, Aramco built more than 800 miles of major pipelines, drilled some 1,000 deep wells (four times the number drilled in the previous four years), built 24 gas-oil separator plants, and in increment after increment added more than a billion dollars worth of new turbines, generators, and stabilizing columns to its physical plant. At Ras Tanura the first-anywhere 1.25 million-barrel storage tanks went up, the fourth Sea Island went into operation, and in 1974 alone, the year the new Ju'aymah terminal opened, 4,470 tankers were loaded with the aid of new crude-loading systems, new and bigger loading arms, and record-sized pumps.

Production jumped by roughly 25 percent in 1971, again in 1972, and again in 1973. To keep pace with this growth and the continuing rise in world demand for oil, the company enlarged and strengthened its exploration program and carried on an aggressive search for new oil reserves. Two seismograph crews were operating as the decade began; five years later there were eight, including one using Hovercraft for survey work in shallow marine areas. When the personnel involved in technical support and computer processing and interpreting of data from the field are counted, each of these crews adds up to about five hundred men.

As new manpower began pouring in, the demand for both living and office space soon outstripped what was available. A work force that totaled roughly ten thousand in 1970 was essentially double that by the end of 1975 and

Data-processing systems were expanded to make them faster and more accessible to users.

Storage tanks holding more than a million barrels each and dome-roofed LPG tanks boosted capacity at the Ras Tanura tank farm during the growth period of the 1970s.

Retractable and highly maneuverable Chiksan arms streamline loading procedures at Aramco shipping terminals.

Oil Operations

The oil produced by Aramco is a complex mixture of organic compounds known as hydrocarbons, most of which are normally liquid and some of which are normally gaseous, although they remain dissolved in the liquids as long as they are kept under pressure in the ground. The mixture is different in each field and each producing reservoir — not all crude oil is the same. Some is "light," with a low specific gravity; some is thick and viscous. Some is "sour" or full of sulfur, and some is sulfur-free or "sweet." The different types of crude require different kinds of handling and processing, and Aramco groups them into four standard "grades" known as Arabian Heavy, Arabian Medium, Arabian Light, and Arabian Extra Light. Market demand, refining needs, safety factors, conservation considerations, and availability of manpower and facilities determine how much of any particular grade is produced in any given period. To achieve a proper balance of all these factors calls for a high level of skill in both long-term planning and short-term scheduling.

Aramco operates today in a concession area covering some 85,000 square miles of the Eastern Province and its offshore waters and consisting of six noncontiguous "retained areas." All but two of the forty-seven oil fields that Aramco had discovered by 1979 (and all fifteen of the fields actually being produced) are located in the largest and northernmost of these areas, which lies partly onshore and partly in the waters of the Arabian Gulf. This area, irregular in shape, extends some 250 miles to the north, west, and south of Dhahran, the company's administrative headquarters community located within sight of the Gulf some ten miles from Dammam, the provincial capital. From the northernmost tip of the concession to its furthest southward extension in the Rub' al-Khali is a distance of about 800 miles.

The Aramco concession areas at the beginning of 1980 were estimated to hold some 113 billion barrels of proved crude oil reserves. Probable reserves (those that in all likelihood can be recovered using present-day technology) add another 65 billion barrels for a total of 178 billion barrels of oil. Saudi Arabia thus has the largest proved and probable reserves in the world. The kingdom is also the world's largest exporter of oil and Aramco is responsible for 97 percent of its production. In 1979 the company produced just over 9.2 million barrels per day (BPD) for a total of well over 3 *billion* barrels for the year. This was accomplished with only about 700 producing wells, with the average well flowing over 13,000 BPD. In contrast, the United States requires over 500,000 wells to produce just 8.5 million BPD, with the average U.S. well producing less than 17 BPD.

All Aramco wells flow freely to the surface because of the expansion of the dissolved gas which is trapped under pressure with the crude oil in the reservoir. When the reservoir is produced, the oil flows to the surface together with this dissolved or "associated" gas, while water underlying the oil displaces it. As the oil rises up the well bore, pressure decreases and gas starts to separate out of the oil, much as gas bubbles out of a bottle of carbonated beverage when it is opened.

As oil and the gas associated with it are produced, the pressure in the reservoir naturally declines. To maintain this pressure Aramco injects large quantities of non-potable water at the edges of the reservoir to supplement the influx of water surrounding the oil. A large part of the water used for this purpose is drawn from the Arabian Gulf, while the rest comes from saline underground aquifers. The company injects some 11 million barrels of water daily into selected oil fields and plans further additions to the seawater intake and treatment plant on the coast south of Dhahran at Qurayyah. This is already by far the largest such plant in the world. In two places, both to help maintain pressure and as a temporary conservation measure, Aramco also reinjects limited quantities of compressed gas or gas liquids into the gas cap at the top of the reservoirs.

Some four million barrels of seawater are treated daily at Qurayyah.

Production wells are drilled at carefully planned intervals, so that oil and its associated gas from one field may reach the surface at wellheads spaced over an area of many square miles. A cluster of such wellheads is connected to a central point by a spoke-like "gathering system" of relatively small-diameter pipelines called flowlines. The mixture of oil and gas travels to the central point where the two are physically separated in a series of vessels or traps at a gas-oil separator plant or GOSP. Two or more flowlines are sometimes joined into a single "trunk line" before reaching the GOSP. This is especially true in offshore fields. Aramco has built nearly 2,000 miles of flowlines and trunk lines.

Pipelines stretch across the sands moving oil and gas to and from Abqaiq.

Gas-oil separator plants consist primarily of a series of large steel vessels designed to release the dissolved gas from crude oil in gradual stages at successively lower pressures. This is basically a physical process in which the gas, which is lighter, collects at the top of the vessel, still carrying a very small amount of oil, while gravity causes most of the heavier oil to collect at the bottom. Depending on the initial pressure — which as the oil comes from the well may be as high as 500 pounds per square inch — pressure is reduced in two or three stages to about 50 pounds per square inch. At this pressure the crude still contains some dissolved gas when it leaves the GOSP to be pumped to downstream processing plants. The gas which has been separated out can also be collected at the GOSP.

Gas-oil separator plants numbered fifty-eight by 1980.

Aramco pipes some of the gas to downstream centers for further processing and eventual sale, and some is flared or burned — either for safety reasons or because collecting and processing it has historically not been economically possible or justified in the kingdom. When the Saudi Government's gas program is completed it will provide the major installations needed to collect and process most of

(Continued on page 216)

Oil Operations

the gas from onshore fields and, as part of this program, gas compression facilities are being built at many GOSPs. In addition, desalting facilities — not a part of the gas program — are being built at a number of GOSPs to ensure that the crude oil meets required specifications for salt content. With such additions, many GOSPs are becoming sizable plants in themselves. In 1978 Aramco had a total of fifty-eight gas-oil separator plants, both onshore and offshore.

Aramco's oil operations are divided geographically into two areas. The southern area is administered from Abqaiq, the major processing center for crude oil and natural gas liquids (NGL) located about forty miles southwest of Dhahran. The northern area is administered from Ras Tanura, forty miles north of Dhahran, the site of an oil refinery, liquefied petroleum gas (LPG) plants, and a marine terminal handling both crude oil and oil and gas products. In general, the crude oil and part of the associated gas produced from fields in the southern area are piped from GOSPs in the area to Abqaiq for further processing, while most of that from GOSPs in the northern fields proceeds directly to Ras Tanura. Where compression facilities have been added to a GOSP, "raw" NGL — composed of all the various readily condensable hydrocarbons present in the separated gases and some impurities such as hydrogren sulfide — is also piped downstream to processing plants.

NGL stream reaching Ras Tanura for fractionation becomes LPG and naphtha for export.

The pipelines which carry the oil, gas, or NGL from the GOSPs are large compared with the flowlines of the gathering systems and range in size from six to fifty-six inches. Excluding flowlines but including the lines that run from downstream centers to storage tanks and shipping terminals, Aramco operates some 4,500 miles of hydrocarbon pipelines.

Crude oil leaving all Aramco GOSPs, with the exception of crude from the offshore Safaniya and Zuluf fields in the north, is sour crude. That is, it contains toxic hydrogen sulfide, which in gaseous form is poisonous and when dissolved in water forms a highly corrosive acid. Sour crude can be shipped by pipeline. It can also be used as refinery feedstock, because the hydrogen sulfide can be removed as part of the refinery operation. It is obviously undesirable, however, to transport sour crude on board tankers, and before it can be safely shipped it must be "sweetened." This is done by a process called stabilization, which consists of partial distillation in the course of which the hydrogen sulfide gas is boiled off.

Southern area crude is stabilized at Abqaiq, which handles about 60 percent of all crude produced by Aramco. That portion of the northern area crude that requires stabilization is processed at Abu Hadriya, Ju'aymah, or Ras Tanura. First, however, a final stage of separation brings the crude from the pressure of 50 pounds per square inch at which it leaves most GOSPs down almost to atmospheric pressure. This is accomplished in large spherical vessels called spheroids, operating at 3 to 4 pounds per square inch, which release the remaining dissolved gases.

Well over half of all crude oil produced by the company is gathered and "sweetened" at Abqaiq.

In the the stabilizing process, sour crude containing 350-600 parts per million of poisonous hydrogen sulfide is sweetened to 10 parts per million or less by heating it and passing it downward over a series of trays in the stabilizer column. After cooling, the sweetened crude is pumped to storage tank farms at the Ju'aymah and Ras Tanura marine terminals, to a bulk distribution center at Dhahran belonging to the Saudi Government's General Petroleum and Mineral Organization (Petromin), or to Qaisumah, the starting point of the Trans-Arabian Pipe Line. The Ras Tanura refinery and the Bahrain Petroleum Company refinery on Bahrain Island, which processes some of Aramco's oil, use sour crude as feedstock.

Spheroid gas, gas separated from crude during the stabilization process, and gas piped from the GOSPs can be compressed to a pressure of about 400 pounds per square inch, then cooled and liquefied to recover additional natural gas liquids. Such raw NGL is stabilized by feeding it into "stripper" or deethanizer columns to remove the light gases such as ethane and methane as well as hydrogen sulfide. This is done at Abqaiq and also at a plant at Berri, near the town of Jubail in the northern producing area. Some of these lighter gases are used to fuel power plants and as fuel or feedstock for various local manufacturing plants. The remaining natural gas liquids, now in the form of stabilized NGL, are shipped by pipeline to plants in Ras Tanura for final processing.

Aramco's Ras Tanura refinery — one of the world's largest — consists of a number of plants that break crude oil down into such products as jet fuel, gasoline, kerosene, naphtha, fuel oil, diesel oil, and asphalt. Other plants remove the last traces of sulfur compounds from stabilized

NGL and fractionate it into three main components. The two lightest components, propane and butane, are commonly referred to as liquefied petroleum gas (LPG). In order to maintain them as liquids at low pressure, they must be refrigerated and stored and shipped in specially equipped tanks. The third NGL product is natural gasoline. The refinery processed almost 700,000 BPD of crude oil and natural gas liquids in 1979.

Both crude oil and products are shipped from the marine terminal at Ras Tanura, with its two loading piers and the four offshore sea islands, which provide berths for vessels of up to 500,000 deadweight tons. Located northwest of Ras Tanura, the terminal at Ju'aymah, Aramco's newest export facility, can load the largest crude carriers now in service from moorings in deep water seven miles out in the Gulf. Large storage tanks at both terminals provide loading flexibility. The crude tank farm at Ju'aymah holds 25 million barrels, while the tank farm at Ras Tanura stores over 27 million barrels of crude and products, more than three times the daily oil production of the United States.

Six-mile trestle carries LPG from refrigerated tanks to offshore loading at Ju'aymah.

All of the oil operations, from wellhead to terminal, are links in a long and intricate chain, with each operation dependent on many others. A change in reservoir pressure, the shutdown of a processing unit for maintenance or modification, an emergency of some kind, fluctuating requirements for various grades of crude or different products, even a few days of unusual weather — any one of these can ultimately have an effect on production planning and ship scheduling. These factors and more are constantly balanced by men and computers in a Dhahran nerve center that monitors almost every aspect of Aramco's oil, gas, NGL, and electric power operations. Because oil operations are complex and potentially dangerous, intensive training and safety measures require even more attention than in many other industries.

To support the many specialists who are directly engaged in all these operations there are hundreds of others running water, steam, and cooling plants and still others driving trucks or buses, flying airplanes, or piloting boats. In this oil company there are employees who manage warehouses, operate laboratories, keep accounts, care for the sick, teach classes, run dining halls, and build houses. But all these jobs are ancillary to Aramco's primary task: to find, produce, process, and move oil.

was four times as big by the end of the decade. By that time, furthermore, the company's own work force was augmented by the numbers working for scores of local contractors (many of them partners of giant international engineering and construction firms) who were working on Aramco's own projects as well as on projects that Aramco was supervising and carrying out on behalf of the Government of Saudi Arabia. With about thirty-eight thousand Aramco employees supplemented by another twenty thousand contractor employees, it was as if the entire working population of a good-sized city had gone to work on a single huge project.

To accommodate these masses of people, Aramco found it necessary to build and operate construction-worker camps at eight sites in the Eastern Province, and the overflow was housed in three- and five-story barges anchored offshore. In Aramco's own residential communities of Abqaiq, Dhahran, and Ras Tanura, two-man trailers, prefabricated efficiency apartments, and new family and bachelor houses were added by the hundreds, along with new schoolrooms and new recreation, shopping, and medical facilities. A three-story addition that added over 40 percent more space to Aramco's main administration building in Dhahran in the mid-1970s soon proved inadequate and a new ten-story administrative headquarters had to be built. The camp at 'Udhailiyah, mothballed years before, was reopened and expanded to provide working and living accommodations for some fifteen hundred employees involved in the projected growth in oil development, water injection, and gas facilities in Aramco's southern producing area.

Aramco's payments to contracting firms working for it went up about 800 percent between 1970 and 1973. The company's annual outlay for materials amounted to $65 million in 1970, reached the neighborhood of $450 million in 1974, and climbed to almost $1,800 million in 1978. Of these amounts the purchases through Saudi suppliers of locally manufactured and imported materials rose from $36 million to $737 million in the 1970-1978 period. In 1977, a year of major expansion, Aramco added some $1.7 billion worth of properties, plant, and equipment for its own operations and another $2.0 billion in connection with government programs in

Contractor construction workers live aboard "floating hotels" such as this one anchored offshore at Ju'aymah.

Expansion during the 1970s brought new life — and housing for hundreds of new employees — to 'Udhailiyah in the southern area of operations.

Oil Operations

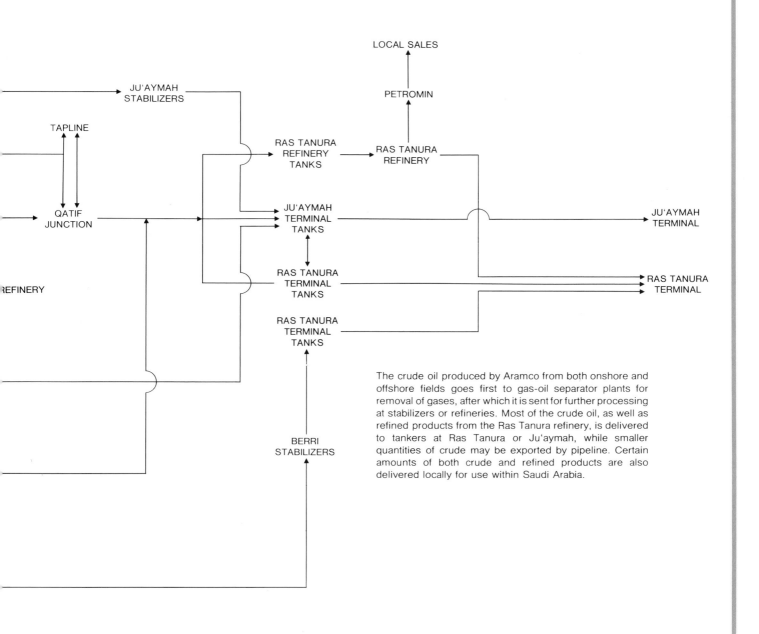

LOCAL SALES

PETROMIN

JU'AYMAH
STABILIZERS

TAPLINE

RAS TANURA
REFINERY
TANKS

RAS TANURA
REFINERY

QATIF
JUNCTION

JU'AYMAH
TERMINAL
TANKS

JU'AYMAH
TERMINAL

REFINERY

RAS TANURA
TERMINAL
TANKS

RAS TANURA
TERMINAL

RAS TANURA
TERMINAL
TANKS

BERRI
STABILIZERS

The crude oil produced by Aramco from both onshore and offshore fields goes first to gas-oil separator plants for removal of gases, after which it is sent for further processing at stabilizers or refineries. Most of the crude oil, as well as refined products from the Ras Tanura refinery, is delivered to tankers at Ras Tanura or Ju'aymah, while smaller quantities of crude may be exported by pipeline. Certain amounts of both crude and refined products are also delivered locally for use within Saudi Arabia.

Three heavy-duty tractors were needed to offload the first of three surge bullets — each seven hundred and fifty tons — when it arrived for the Ju'aymah NGL plant.

His Majesty King Khalid is accompanied by HRH Crown Prince Fahd, HRH Amir 'Abd Allah, and Petroleum and Mineral Resources Minister Shaykh Ahmed Zaki Yamani at the inauguration of the Berri gas plant.

The Berri plant, forerunner in design and principle of the entire gas program, is located not far from the Jubail industrial complex to which it will send sweet, dry gas for fuel.

At the gas treating area of the Shedgum gas plant, largest of the gas-processing centers in the government program, gas supplied by ten GOSPs will be sweetened by removal of carbon dioxide, hydrogen sulfide, and other sulfur compounds.

which the company was involved. And in 1978 the company initiated a Boeing 747 air cargo charter service to help with the volume of cargo being imported — which that year, for the third year in a row, was in the magnitude of one million tons.

"Big lifts" became almost commonplace as mammoth components, many of them the biggest of their kind ever constructed, were brought to Saudi Arabia to form the building blocks of bigger and bigger plants. A 500-ton fractionating column added to natural gas liquids (NGL) facilities at Ras Tanura in 1975 was outdone in 1977 by a depropanizer column lifted into place at the Ju'aymah NGL center that weighed 660 tons, and that in turn was dwarfed by a 750-ton vessel that arrived from Japan aboard an ocean-going barge in 1978. When a gas-oil separator plant for the offshore Zuluf oil field that had gone on stream in 1973 was obsolete just five years later, it was completely rebuilt in a series of twelve "big lifts" with barge-mounted cranes hoisting modules weighing up to 950 tons each.

Working with "the biggest" or "the heaviest" or "the newest" is far from being a new experience for Aramco, however. Because of the extent of its concession area and the unprecedented size of its producing, refining, and shipping operations, Aramco has almost from the start been forced to design, build, or buy the largest and most advanced equipment in the world. Because there was very often nothing else in the world to match its operations, the company has constantly been forced to operate on the cutting edge of advancing technology — that is, to break new ground, try new ideas, and test new methods and equipment.

GOVERNMENT GAS PROGRAM: In the midst of this all-out effort to increase its oil producing and handling capacity and build the necessary supporting facilities, Aramco took on a new role as a working partner in Saudi Arabia's industrialization program, one of the most ambitious any nation has ever undertaken. During the early 1970s the world pricing structure for hydrocarbons as well as growing concern with environmental factors made the conservation and utilization of the high-pressure gas produced in association with Saudi Arabian crude oil economically

feasible for the first time. Accordingly, early in 1975, the Saudi Arab Government asked Aramco to design, develop, and operate on its behalf a nationwide system to gather and process this gas to supply fuel and raw material for the kingdom's multibillion-dollar industrialization program (see Chapter 3) and for export. It was a request that represented "both an honor and a challenge," in the words of the company's chairman, as it expressed government confidence that Aramco could take on the largest industrial project ever undertaken by a single company.

In essence, the gas program was designed to enable Saudi Arabia to utilize for the first time nearly all the gas produced onshore along with crude oil. Upon completion, it will handle some three billion cubic feet of associated gas per day. Desulfurized and treated gas will fuel and feed industrial complexes at the historic site of Jubail, on the Gulf, and across the peninsula at Yanbu', about 220 miles north of Jiddah on the Red Sea. It will also be used to generate several thousand megawatts of power for community and industrial needs, to produce large quantities of fresh water, and to provide NGL for export.

Once the whole program is in operation, gas collected at Aramco gas-oil separator plants will be sent to one of three centers in the Eastern Province. The Berri plant, the first to be completed, was inaugurated in 1977 and stands only a few miles from the Jubail industrial complex it will fuel; the two others, at Shedgum and 'Uthmaniyah, are located at the heart of the kingdom's most prolific oil field. Gas will be first treated at these plants to remove toxic and corrosive sulfur compounds. Further processing produces a sweet, dry residue gas — primarily methane — and a liquid stream — NGL and ethane. The residue gas will be compressed and distributed to fuel water desalination plants, the Eastern Province electrical power network, and planned industrial chemical complexes, while as a by-product of the sweetening process thousands of tons a day of elemental sulfur will be produced, most to be exported. The liquid stream will be pipelined to fractionation centers at Ju'aymah and Yanbu', where it will be split into ethane for industrial plant fuel and feedstock, and propane, butane, and natural gasoline. The propane and butane, termed liquefied petroleum gas or LPG, will be refrigerated and exported from Juʻaymah and Yanbuʻ; the natural gasoline will go out in conventional tankers from Yanbuʻ and Ras Tanura.

Because it crosses some extremely rough terrain, the pipeline that feeds the fractionation center far across the peninsula at Yanbuʻ is a major engineering feat in itself. The longest and most advanced computer-controlled NGL pipeline ever built, the 720-mile high-pressure line will initially deliver 270,000 barrels per day to Yanbuʻ and will parallel a 1.85 million-barrel-per-day crude oil pipeline (not an Aramco project) that a number of American companies are building for the Saudi Arab Government. These two lines thus will link the port of Yanbuʻ to the oil fields and gas facilities of the Eastern Province and give it a new future as an industrial center similar to the one at Jubail, where planned industry ranges from steel mills and aluminum smelters to petrochemical plants. Together the two complexes will form part of an industrial mosaic designed to diversify Saudi Arabia's economic base and provide a lasting foundation for future growth.

ARAMCO AND WORLD ENERGY: Saudi Arabia's present well-being and future growth are heavily dependent on oil. It is the sale of this oil that provides current income for the day-to-day operation of the government as well as the funds that support its huge development plans. It is Saudi Arabia's oil, too — not only the income from its sale but also the mere fact that it exists, and in such quantity — that is the main basis for the major economic and political role that the kingdom now plays on the world stage.

In fact, almost 90 percent of the Saudi Government's income is generated by the three companies that now produce its oil. The American-owned Getty Oil Company holds a concession covering the land area of the kingdom's share of the Neutral Zone lying between it and Kuwait and in 1979 produced 80,900 barrels a day (BPD) of crude oil, and the Japanese-owned Arabian Oil Company has a concession covering the offshore area of the Neutral Zone from which it produced 197,600 BPD. The largest share, however, comes from Aramco, whose 1979 production of 9,251,079 BPD contributed almost 98 per-

cent of the Saudi Government's oil income and over 85 percent of its total income.

By extension, of course, Saudi Arabia depends in turn on the nations of the world that buy its oil. But this is far from being a one-sided relationship. The nations of the world — and especially the industrialized countries of the West and Japan — depend on the oil-producing nations of the so-called Third World (particularly in the Middle East) to supply a significant portion of the petroleum they need to keep their economies going. The relationship is a mutual one, with consumers depending on producers and producers dependent on the consuming countries. Ever since it moved into the forefront of the international petroleum picture the Government of Saudi Arabia has shown its awareness of this interrelationship, and those who control the kingdom's oil policies have taken it as one of their principal guidelines in shaping those policies.

A pipeline originating at Shedgum — built in sections 26, 28, and 30 inches in diameter — will carry NGL across the peninsula to Yanbuʻ.

Stated in the simplest terms, the United States, Western Europe, and Japan are all consuming more energy than they produce, and by far the greatest part of what they consume is in the form of oil and gas. They cannot increase their own production significantly (or even continue it for very long at present levels) because their reserves are not sufficient to allow this — oil production in the United States, for example, began to decline after 1970 and new production from Alaska has only temporarily halted this trend. The growing deficit in the energy balance of the industrialized countries is being made up by oil and gas produced by other areas of the world — primarily Venezuela, Africa, and the Middle East.

In looking at the energy balance of a country or region, oil production and oil consumption are obviously the two main factors to be taken into account. In forecasting what the future position of a country is likely to be, however, and in determining whether any country or region can make a significant long-term contribution to the needs of the energy-short nations, a third factor is equally important: it is necessary to consider what its reserves are — that is, how much oil and gas it has in the ground. Large-scale production over a long period obviously must have large reserves behind it.

The three charts on page 224 show

Towers of the fractionation plant at Yanbuʻ rise in silhouette against the sunset.

Mustering hundreds of "horses" and dozens of wheels, specialized haulage equipment moves tanks, traps, building modules, and gas-plant columns to their destinations at Aramco industrial areas. Transportation epics that begin at the design stage end when trucks as large as the 700-horsepower giant at right and hydraulic 32-wheel trailers, such as those supporting the 500-ton pressure vessel seen at bottom, hook up to haul and help install components that often are the biggest of their kind ever built.

1979 WORLD PRODUCTION

1979 WORLD RESERVES

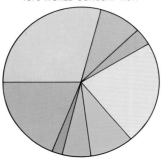

1979 WORLD CONSUMPTION

United States
Venezuela
Other Western Hemisphere
Middle East
Western Europe
Japan
Other Far East
Africa
Communist World

these three factors for the major industrialized areas of the world in 1978. For example, the United States (including Alaska) was consuming 29 percent of the total oil produced in the world, but was producing only 16 percent and had only 5 percent of the total oil reserves. Western Europe, with 4 percent of world reserves, was producing 3 percent of the world's oil but consuming 23 percent. The three elements are even further out of balance for Japan, which has negligible production and no significant reserves but consumed 9 percent of world oil during the year. All three of these areas, in other words, are clearly in a deficit position as far as their energy situation is concerned.

Looking at the supplier regions of the world, the charts show that Venezuela is producing 4 percent of the world's oil (but has less than 3 percent of its reserves), while Africa has 9 percent of reserves and is responsible for 10 percent of world production. The major element in the world oil picture, however, is obviously the Middle East, which in 1978 produced 39 percent of the world's oil and had reserves calculated at 57 percent of total world reserves. In other words, well over half the world's oil reserves are located in the Middle East and it is clear that this is where a major part of the world's supplies will have to come from in the foreseeable future.

In terms of oil and other energy sources, the Middle East actually means, as a practical matter, the countries of the Arabian Gulf, which together are estimated to have over 55 percent of the world's total oil reserves. The most important of these countries is, of course, Saudi Arabia, the largest oil-exporting country in the world and the country with by far the largest reserves. Saudi Arabia's crude oil reserves (of which almost all lie in the Aramco concession area) are calculated at present to amount to about one-fourth of total world reserves, almost one-third of the reserves of the non-Communist world, and about five times the reserves of the United States including Alaska. With 1978 exports of 7,733,000 BPD (of which about 1,228,000 BPD went directly or indirectly to the United States), Saudi Arabia was supplying a large part of the energy needs of the industrialized nations of the world. The completion of the ambitious gas gathering and processing program that Aramco is carrying out for the Saudi Govern-

ment will make a further contribution to the world's total energy supply equivalent to 745,000 BPD of crude oil.

This situation is not an unmixed blessing for the kingdom. In fact, it is a cause for considerable concern on the part of the Saudi Government. Oil is almost the only economic resource that the kingdom has at the present time, but it is a depletable resource. Oil reserves that took millions of years to form may be used up in a few generations — and, unlike a forest or a river or a wheat field, an oil field does not renew itself. Saudi Arabia therefore cannot afford to squander the wealth it now has but must use it to build alternate sources of income for the future, and this is one of the primary objectives of the five-year development plans.

But in using its present wealth to build for the future the kingdom is faced with making a series of sometimes difficult choices between occasionally conflicting alternatives. For example, while it needs very large sums of money to pay for its development projects, it cannot produce its oil at the extremely high rates that world demand sometimes calls for because to do so would unduly accelerate the depletion of its reserves. It could also result in the kingdom's receiving more money income than it can usefully spend or profitably invest — and to the Saudi Government's policymakers it seems obvious that in the long run oil in the ground may be a more desirable form of wealth to hold and to pass on to future generations than vast bank deposits in Western currencies that are steadily shrinking in value.

It is therefore clearly not in the best interests of Saudi Arabia to produce oil at the very high rates that some parties have urged upon it, but on the other hand it realizes the harm that could be done to the consuming countries by a drastic cut in oil output. The planners in the Saudi Government are very much aware that their country coexists with and is interdependent with the industrialized world, and they realize that any move of this nature could lead to a depression or even economic collapse in the West and that this would inevitably have serious results even for Saudi Arabia itself. Faced with this difficult choice between much more production and much less production, Saudi Arabia elected in 1974 to institute relatively moderate controls over its output and imposed a ceiling of 8.5 million BPD on Aramco's crude production. Nevertheless it has demonstrated its readiness to respond to the needs of the consuming nations by administering this ceiling in a fairly flexible manner and by raising it to a higher level when emergency circumstances required it — for example, to help make up the shortage in world supply caused by the very sharp drop in Iranian production at the end of 1978 and during 1979. It has been able to do this because of its very large production capacity and its enormous reserves. These factors have also enabled it to act on its conviction that the oil-producing and oil-consuming nations are dependent on each other by playing a moderating role in the Organization of Petroleum Exporting Countries (OPEC) and opposing the very large price increases that have been proposed by some members of that organization.

NON-OIL ACTIVITIES: On its way to becoming the largest oil-producing company in the world and even before it became involved in large-scale projects such as the Saudi Government's gas program, Aramco was far from limiting its activities to those connected directly with oil operations — the usual mix of exploration, drilling, producing, refining, and shipping. Almost from the day of the first landing at Jubail in 1933 it has been involved in a very wide range of other kinds of activities, sometimes out of necessity and sometimes as a matter of choice.

When Aramco began its operations in Saudi Arabia in 1933 the basic requirements of a modern industrial operation were almost nonexistent there. The company, perforce, had to enter into a wide variety of non-oil-connected activities until such time as the local economy could provide the goods and services needed to support its oil exploration and development operations. In addition there were a large number of other activities that the company undertook either because they were required under its concession agreement or under Saudi laws and regulations or else out of a desire to be a good citizen and in pursuance of a policy of enlightened self-interest — that is, a belief that whatever might help in the development and advancement of the local community in eastern Saudi Arabia would ultimately also be of benefit to Aramco. Many

(perhaps a majority) of the non-oil-related activities that Aramco has engaged in were entered into from a combination of these different reasons and motives.

For example, Aramco's extensive involvement in the construction, staffing, and operation of medical facilities and its sponsorship of preventive medicine and public health programs have been motivated by necessity (the lack, at first, of other adequate medical facilities), enlightened self-interest (based on the realization that a healthy work force would be the most productive work force), and the requirements of Saudi laws.

Facilities and staff of a large, fully accredited hospital, along with ten modern clinics, provide medical care for Aramco employees and their families.

The labor regulations enacted by Saudi Arabia in 1942, four years after Aramco began commercial production of oil, required employers to provide free medical treatment for their workers, and later the obligations of industrial employers were extended to the families of their employees. To discharge these obligations Aramco has built and equipped one major fully accredited 363-bed hospital and ten modern clinics staffed by a total of over sixteen hundred doctors, nurses, technicians, and other employees. In addition to operating its own medical facilities, Aramco has given both financial and technical assistance to encourage the development of private hospitals and clinics in its area of operations.

A new dental clinic in Dhahran, opened in 1978, was part of a comprehensive expansion of Health Center facilities.

Fairly extensive preventive medicine efforts have also been a part of the company's medical programs and many of these, by their very nature, have not been restricted in their application and effect to Aramco employees. The earliest and one of the most important of such efforts began in 1941 and was directed against malaria, which at that time was endemic in the Eastern Province. From 1941 to 1947 Aramco conducted an anti-malaria program at its own expense, from 1948 to 1955 the company and the Saudi Government collaborated in the campaign, and since 1956 the government has conducted the program without Aramco participation. These programs have resulted in the virtually complete eradication of malaria from the Eastern Province.

Almost from the day its geologists first set foot in the kingdom Aramco found itself involved in providing technical assistance in one form or another to the people of the Eastern Province. Most of its early technical assistance was provided on an informal ad hoc basis — often after working hours — by various individuals and organizations within the company. In order to more efficiently organize and channel this activity, which by the end of World War II had become a very sizable informal function, Aramco established an industrial development organization in 1946.

This group (now called the Local Industrial Development Department) sought out local entrepreneurs, giving them the technical, material, and financial assistance required to enable them to provide the goods and services needed by Aramco, its work force, and the developing local communities in the company's area of operations. At the end of the 1970s some four hundred local businessmen were being awarded approximately 900 construction and service contracts with Aramco each year and the annual value of these contract awards was about $2.4 billion. Aramco's encouragement of such contractors has helped bring about the development of a large and experienced construction, transportation, and maintenance capability in the local community.

Helping local farmers establish profitable vegetable farms has been a major goal of Aramco assistance programs.

Agriculture is another field of activity not directly related to its oil operations that the company became involved in very early in its history. Aramco's agricultural assistance efforts grew out of the company's cooperation with the Saudi Arab Government in developing agriculture in the al-Kharj area, some sixty miles southeast of Riyadh. Aramco provided technical and material assistance between 1938 and 1954 to help develop the rich agricultural potential of this area and for several years was responsible for supervision of the al-Kharj project's three farm complexes, which covered some three thousand acres.

Experiments with hydroponic greenhouses led to successful production of certain vegetable crops.

To assist farmers in the oases of al-Hasa and Qatif to realize the agricultural potential of these areas Aramco established an agricultural assistance organization in 1956. This group has concerned itself with helping local farmers to establish vegetable and poultry farms, providing technical information and advice, and developing marketing channels for local produce.

The most recent agricultural project in which the company has been involved is a demonstration farm in the oasis of al-Hasa. Using a 300-acre plot of land provided by the Saudi Government in the heart of the oasis,

Aramco agriculturists set out in 1978 to show local farmers how modern agricultural techniques and labor-saving machinery could turn the desert into profitable farmland. Less than a year and a half after the start of the project the farm was producing sixteen different vegetable crops, often by the use of new techniques improvised on the spot.

ELECTRIC POWER: In the early 1950s Aramco helped to establish a number of private power companies in the local communities within its area of operations — the initial step in what eventually became a very large-scale involvement in the development of electric power in the Eastern Province. When the rapid growth and development of some of the major towns in the late 1950s and early 1960s required considerably larger and more sophisticated facilities, Aramco assisted the power companies in the two largest local communities, Dammam and al-Khobar, to merge and to form the nucleus of a single large company to serve the entire coastal area. Aramco provided the resulting Dhahran Electric Power Company (DEPCO) with significant technical, administrative, and financial help and for many years supplied it with free gas for power generation, thus helping to reduce the cost of power to consumers.

When the industrial growth of the 1970s got under way, it soon became apparent that piecemeal efforts of individual companies would not be sufficient to meet the power needs of the new era. In 1974 the Saudi Arab Government's Central Planning Organization (CPO), the forerunner of its Ministry of Planning, investigated the possibility of consolidating the generating systems of the various power producers in the Eastern Province in order to establish an integrated system, one in which the various government agencies concerned with electric power and water desalination would participate, along with Petromin, Aramco, DEPCO, and over two dozen other private power companies in the region. As the existing Aramco power system was the largest in the area, had been built on the basis of careful economic and technical analysis, and was operating reliably with a relatively small reserve capability, it was decided that expanding and adding to it would be the quickest and most efficient way of creating an integrated Eastern Province network.

The direct result of the CPO's studies was the establishment in August 1976 of the Saudi Consolidated Electric Company (SCECO) by a royal decree which granted the integrated company a renewable thirty-year franchise for the generation, transmission, and distribution of electric power in the Eastern Province. It was planned that Aramco and other power producers transfer their facilities to SCECO in exchange for shares in the new company and the government designated Aramco to manage the company during its first five years.

The immediate aims of SCECO were to support the needs of Aramco's crude oil production program and the gas program upon which the kingdom's heavy industry will depend; to provide the quantities of power required for the Jubail industrial area infrastructure and other industrial users; and to electrify Eastern Province communities that had no electric power and upgrade the systems of those whose supplies were inadequate. About two hundred towns and villages are within the franchise area of SCECO, which at the time of its formation was serving some 100,000 customers.

SAUDI ARAB EMPLOYEES: The concession agreement of 1933 provides that the Aramco enterprise is to employ Saudi Arab nationals as far as practicable, and this requirement has determined both the composition of the Aramco work force and to a large extent the direction in which its employee relations policies have developed.

One very important objective of these policies has been to provide training for the company's Saudi employees in order to reduce the need to bring foreign workers to Saudi Arabia. When the first Aramco pioneers arrived to begin work in eastern Saudi Arabia in 1933, almost none of the people of the region had any acquaintance with modern technology or any experience of working in modern industry. Schools in the area were scarce or nonexistent, literacy (particularly among the Bedouins) was rare, and there was an almost complete absence of the technical and clerical skills needed by an oil company. Training had to begin immediately.

TRAINING AND EDUCATION: At first this training was informal: drillers, craftsmen, and office workers taught their particular specialties on the job. A more intensive effort was required, however, and by 1940 there were twenty-two Saudi employees receiving special training in Dhahran, while another twenty-six had been sent to Bahrain for training. These training activities expanded greatly after the end of World War II and by 1950 over four thousand Saudi employees (about 40 percent of the Saudi work force) were receiving instruction in some 144 different crafts, trades, and skills from a staff of about 250 full-time and part-time teachers.

Aside from the informal training contacts that the Saudi employees had in their work assignments, the education and training of the Aramco work force in the years immediately following World War II took place in traditional American-type schools. By the middle of 1949, however, the need for Aramco to increase production to meet the growing world demand for oil called for both more facilities and accelerated training of the work force. The company therefore embarked on a program of on-the-job training under which one-eighth of the working day was set aside for training by line personnel. This program was extremely successful and in a relatively short time developed a Saudi Arab work force of more than thirteen thousand employees who were capable of doing a very high proportion of the company's work.

After the short-term gains were achieved, however, it became evident that only more formal schooling could provide the theoretical knowledge and special skills that employees would need in order to move up to higher-level technical and management positions. In the mid-1950s, therefore, the majority of Aramco's training activities were centralized in three industrial training centers (one in each of the company's main operating districts) and three industrial training shops. The industrial training shops provided the opportunity to acquire skills such as the ability to read blueprints, wire a house, install and repair plumbing, and handle tools. The industrial training centers concentrated on academic subjects like English, mathematics, geography, accounting, and general science. Class hours were generally flexible: employees could attend classes during the working day or in the evening on their own time.

In 1974 a new industrial training center

SCECO's 230-kilovolt transmission system will ultimately bring electricity to more than two hundred towns and villages of the Eastern Province.

Language study labs form one of the most important areas at the company's industrial training centers.

Hands-on experience enables students to learn such valuable skills as electronics repair at industrial training shops.

Gas Operations

Gas produced with crude oil is collected at gas-oil separator plants and piped to gas plants in the Eastern Province. There, impurities such as hydrogen sulfide are removed and a sweet, dry gas is extracted for use as an industrial fuel or feedstock. From gas processing centers at Shedgum and 'Uthmaniyah the remaining natural gas liquids (NGL) and ethane are piped to plants at Yanbu' and Ju'aymah for fractionation into their separate components. NGL from Berri (which does not collect ethane) goes to Ras Tanura or Ju'aymah for fractionation. In the fractionation plants, ethane is produced in gaseous form for use as a petrochemical feedstock in the industrial complexes at Yanbu' and Jubail. After removal of ethane, the NGL is further fractionated into LPG (propane and butane) and natural gasoline. LPG is exported from Yanbu' and Ju'aymah; in the case of Berri, LPG is exported from Ras Tanura. Natural gasoline is exported from Yanbu' or Ras Tanura.

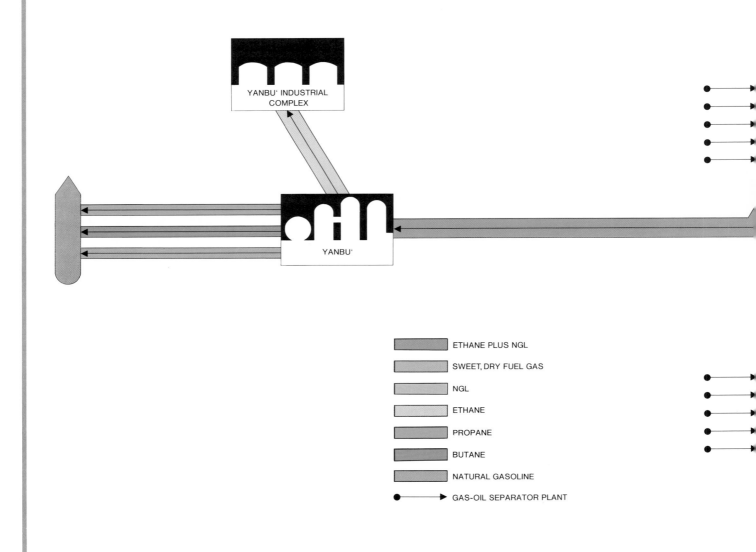

YANBU' INDUSTRIAL COMPLEX

YANBU'

ETHANE PLUS NGL

SWEET, DRY FUEL GAS

NGL

ETHANE

PROPANE

BUTANE

NATURAL GASOLINE

GAS-OIL SEPARATOR PLANT

JUBAIL INDUSTRIAL COMPLEX

BERRI GAS PLANT

SHEDGUM GAS PLANT

'UTHMANIYAH GAS PLANT

JU'AYMAH

RAS TANURA

JUBAIL
BERRI
SHEDGUM
JU'AYMAH
RAS TANURA
YANBU'
'UTHMANIYAH
EAST-WEST NGL/ETHANE PIPELINE

and a new workshop were opened in Dammam and similar facilities were opened in al-Mubarraz in the oasis of al-Hasa. With these additions, and with the enlargement of the Dhahran center in 1977, the combined capacity of the system rose to over five thousand trainees. The facilities of the industrial training workshops, meantime, were enlarged and their curriculum was broadened to include a wide range of subjects from basic industrial principles to advanced training in the maintenance of such things as electronic instruments, industrial control devices, and the like.

In the ten years between 1953 and 1963 the proportion of skilled Saudi workers in Aramco's work force rose from 9 percent to 57 percent. By 1980 there were nearly 9,600 Saudi employees enrolled in the company's industrial training centers and shops, and a further 1,050 were enrolled in one or more of its forty-five on-the-job training and testing programs. Another group of 390 was studying abroad in craft courses, and about 300 more were enrolled in full-time academic courses in educational institutions within the kingdom and abroad. Even more significant as an indication of the success of Aramco's training efforts is the fact that by 1980 over 45 percent of the company's management and supervisory positions were held by Saudi Arab employees.

A broadly based training effort produces skilled workers, operators of sophisticated plants, and supervisory personnel.

SCHOOLS FOR CHILDREN: The company's involvement in education extends to include children of employees. The labor regulations of Saudi Arabia require certain industrial employers to construct schools for the children of their employees. In satisfaction of this requirement, and following discussions with the government, Aramco agreed in 1953 to build elementary schools of sufficient capacity to accommodate a number of students equal to the number of school-age sons of its Arab and Muslim employees resident in Saudi Arabia. "School-age" was defined as meaning between six and fourteen. In 1959 Aramco further agreed to build intermediate schools (grades 7 to 9 inclusive). Under the terms of the agreements between Aramco and the government, all these schools, both elementary and intermediate, are turned over to the Ministry of Education as soon as they are completed and become an integral part of the government school system, with the ministry

Nearly sixty elementary and intermediate schools built by Aramco are integrated into the government system.

taking entire responsibility for operating the school, hiring teachers, and controlling the curriculum. Aramco, however, continues to maintain the schools and pay all the costs of operating them.

In 1960 the Government of Saudi Arabia moved to establish public education for women for the first time, and in the following year Aramco agreed to build elementary and intermediate schools for girls under the same terms and conditions as those of the two earlier agreements covering schools for boys, except that it is the Directorate of Girls' Education in the Eastern Province rather than the Ministry of Education that takes over the operation of the schools when they are completed.

When the company first began to construct schools for the children of its employees its obligation was to build ten elementary schools. By the end of 1979, it had built a total of fifty-eight elementary and intermediate schools and further enlarged four of these by the addition of new wings. These Aramco-built government schools have a total capacity sufficient to accommodate over twenty-five thousand boys and girls.

HOME OWNERSHIP: Another major element of Aramco's efforts to build a competent and stable work force has been its home ownership program, under which the company makes loans to eligible Saudi employees for the construction, renovation, or purchase of homes in local towns and villages. In the early days of the Aramco enterprise most Saudi Arab employees lived as bachelors in company quarters, and at first there was a heavy turnover as men who had until that time lived much as they pleased tried to adapt to the unaccustomed demands of a daily work schedule in a modern industrial operation. As the employee group gradually became more stable, Saudi employees in increasing numbers began to bring their families into the areas of operation. To help these employees develop roots in the area and to head off the possible growth of substandard housing, the company instituted a home ownership program in 1951.

The two key features that form the basis of the program are that the employee acquires free the ownership of a piece of land made available by the government and developed by the company, and that he receives a long-term interest-free loan from the company to help him pay for construction of his house. Aramco subsidizes the acquisition of homes under the program by forgiving 20 percent of the total amount loaned, which includes a 5 percent service charge, and the employee repays the balance through monthly deductions from his pay. An additional feature of the program is that the company forgives the outstanding balance of a loan in the event an employee dies or becomes permanently disabled before he has repaid it.

One important by-product of Aramco's encouragement of employee home ownership has been the strengthening of the local economy by creating a substantial market for all types of building materials and home furnishings. Under the home ownership plan the company has lent over $370 million to its employees and by the end of 1979 over ten thousand individual loans had been made. About 40 percent of the money advanced to employees has gone to local contractor payrolls and given continuing employment to thousands of workers, and some 60 percent has gone for the local purchase of building materials. The program has thus assisted in stimulating the development of diverse independent local industries by assuring outlets for their products and has helped spur the growth and expansion of local communities.

AN INTERNATIONAL WORK FORCE: The work force that has built the Aramco enterprise from its occasionally discouraging early days up to a giant enterprise producing millions of barrels of oil a day has always consisted primarily of Saudi Arabs and Americans, and the company has always tried to meet its obligation under the concession agreement to employ Saudis in preference to other nationalities wherever and whenever possible. While its training and development programs have been very successful in moving Saudi employees up into all levels of company management, however, Aramco has also had to rely on many other nationalities to help build and operate the enterprise, and this has been especially true during periods of rapid growth and expansion like the late 1940s and early 1950s and the 1970s.

In the early years, and up until the last days of World War II, it was mainly men from other Arabian Peninsula and Arabian Gulf countries and from India who formed the major part of this body of "other" employees. In fact, Indians (and later Pakistanis), who had provided much of the trained manpower in the Gulf for many years before the coming of Aramco, have always made up a significant portion of the company's work force.

The period of great expansion that started in 1945 called for a rapid buildup in the company's construction manpower, and a large pool of trained craftsmen was discovered in Eritrea, across the Red Sea from Jiddah. There many hundreds of Italian colonists and former soldiers of Mussolini's defeated armies were marking time as virtual prisoners of war and welcomed the chance to take productive jobs in Dhahran and Ras Tanura. By the end of 1945 Aramco had almost sixteen hundred Italian employees, and although their numbers declined sharply after the period of postwar construction and expansion came to an end in the early 1950s, Italians have continued to form a small part of Aramco's manpower ever since.

A program of subsidized home loans encourages Saudi Arab employees to own their own homes.

The next group to enter the Aramco work force in considerable numbers were the nationals of other Arab countries. Many hundreds of workers from Aden and the Sudan, both craftsmen and clerical and professional personnel, were employed during the late 1940s and early 1950s, and the Sudan has since then continued to be a source of manpower for the company. Late in 1948, following the Arab-Israeli war and the expulsion or flight of many hundreds of thousands of Arabs from their homes in Palestine, King 'Abd al-'Aziz asked Aramco to make a special effort to provide jobs for as many of the refugees as possible, and the next five years saw the addition to the work force of many hundreds of Palestinians, some of whom have remained with the company for twenty-five years and more. Other Arab nationalities that have contributed in smaller numbers to Aramco's manpower have included Egyptians, Jordanians, Lebanese, and Syrians.

With the unprecedented demands for large numbers of additional employees to carry out the expansion of the 1970s Aramco had to look even further afield for trained manpower and found new sources for recruitment in the British Isles and in Asia. By the end of the decade some twenty-five hundred British and Irish employees, both men and

The multinational character of the Aramco work force is
evident throughout the company, whether at the construction site or in the control room, and groups even more varied
can be seen in such areas as refining and plant operations,
producing, or transportation. Aramco employees come from
forty-five countries, but most are Saudi Arabs. By the end of
the 1970s more than 45 percent of the supervisory positions
throughout the company were held by Saudi Arabs, and the
company had further intensified its recruiting efforts, seeking in particular professionals and recent graduates of
universities within the kingdom and abroad.

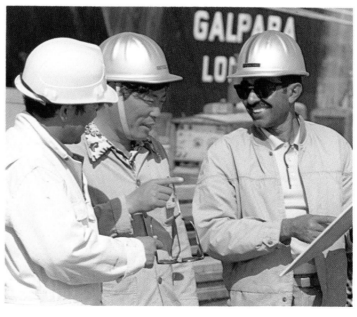

women, were working as Aramco employees, the Philippines had contributed over thirty-eight hundred employees, Sri Lanka was proving to be another source of trained man-power, and the Aramco work force consisted of employees from some forty-five different nationalities. The largest single groups, however, continued to be Saudi Arabs and Americans.

The fact that the company had recruited and trained this large body of skilled employees (both Saudi Arabs and foreigners), many of them with years of experience in the kingdom, was a major factor in the Saudi Government's decision to entrust Aramco with carrying out the kingdom's gas program and with managing the Saudi Consolidated Electric Company during the crucial first five years of its existence.

ORGANIZATION: The management structure of Aramco has evolved and changed through the years to meet the changing needs of the company as it has grown from a small exploration organization to the largest oil-producing company in the world. Shortly after the concession agreement was signed in May 1933 Socal assigned its concession rights to a wholly-owned subsidiary, California Arabian Standard Oil Company (Casoc), with headquarters in San Francisco. The name was retained and the company's offices remained in San Francisco even after The Texas Company acquired a 50 percent interest in Casoc in 1937, but on January 31, 1944, the company was renamed Arabian American Oil Company and from that time on became generally known as Aramco.

Late in 1946, after it became apparent that Saudi Arabia's petroleum reserves were extremely large and would call for great market outlets and enormous capital investments for their full development, negotiations were begun to enable Standard Oil Company (New Jersey) (now Exxon) and Socony-Vacuum Oil Company (now Mobil Oil Corporation) also to become part owners of Aramco. The negotiations were complicated and prolonged by the fact that both these companies were members of the Iraq Petroleum Company group and thus subject to the Red Line Agreement which prevented them from acting individually in a large area of the Middle East. Final arrangements were completed in

With the formation of Aramco Services Company, Aramco-related activities in the U.S. were centered in Houston.

November 1948, and from that time until 1975, when Mobil's share was increased, shareholdings in Aramco were: Standard Oil of California 30 percent, Texaco 30 percent, Exxon 30 percent, and Mobil 10 percent. Saudi Arabian oil as a result gained extensive new marketing outlets, particularly in Europe, and the original two Aramco partners obtained the capital required for construction of the Trans-Arabian Pipe Line from Saudi Arabia to the Mediterranean.

In anticipation of the change in ownership, Aramco moved its offices from San Francisco to New York in 1948. At that time a number of small offices were also maintained in Los Angeles, Tulsa, Chicago, and Washington, D.C., to carry out various recruiting, purchasing, shipping, and other functions in support of the operations in Saudi Arabia. The New York and Washington offices have remained in operation, and in fact during the middle and late 1950s Aramco had almost a thousand employees working in New York, but in 1952 the company's corporate headquarters were moved to Dhahran, which became the residence of the chairman of the Board of Directors, the president, and most of the principal officers of the company. In 1959 two representatives of the Government of Saudi Arabia — Shaykh Hafiz Wahba, a former Ambassador of Saudi Arabia in London, and Shaykh Abdullah H. Tariki, the Director General of Petroleum and Mineral Affairs — were appointed to Aramco's Board of Directors.

In 1974 almost all the operations of the New York office were transferred to Houston, where they became the responsibility of a subsidiary company, wholly owned by Aramco, named Aramco Services Company (ASC). This company, which within five years grew to have over a thousand employees, performs engineering, purchasing, and shipping services and carries out various financial, recruiting, and other functions for Aramco, including the important one of coordinating the oil purchasing requirements and shipping schedules of Aramco's offtaker companies so that production of crude oil and refined products can be planned to meet export demand.

In the years following the end of World War II many of the countries which were the principal purchasers of the oil produced by

Aramco had neither dollars nor other convertible currencies to pay for their imports, and Aramco and its owner companies therefore worked out new arrangements to sell oil for nondollar currencies and use these currencies to buy supplies and services. To carry out these arrangements Aramco in November 1948 formed another subsidiary company, Aramco Overseas Purchasing Company, later called Aramco Overseas Company (AOC). Located at first in Rome, AOC's headquarters were moved in 1954 to The Hague in Holland, and the company maintains other offices in Beirut, Tokyo, Dhahran, and Sydney. Its approximately eight hundred employees perform services in engineering, purchasing, and other fields for Aramco and its affiliated companies.

RELATIONS WITH THE GOVERNMENT: Article 36 of the oil concession granted to Socal on May 29, 1933, stated that "it is distinctly understood that the Company or anyone connected with it shall have no right to interfere with the administrative, political or religious affairs within Saudi Arabia." The fact that Aramco has always adhered strictly to this requirement is undoubtedly one reason why its relations with the Government of Saudi Arabia have generally been good. Another is that Aramco has always been ready to listen to the government's point of view and to make changes in its arrangements with the government when these seemed reasonable and necessary. Brigadier Stephen Longrigg, who was the Iraq Petroleum Company's negotiator in competing with Socal for the Saudi Arab concession in 1933 and later became managing director of IPC, noted admiringly many years later that Aramco's policies had "earned gratifying and no doubt sincere tributes from King ibn Sa'ud and his ministers."

This is not to say that there have never been differences between the company and the government or that the course of relations between them has always gone smoothly. There have been differences between the two — and sometimes major ones — but these have always been resolved through negotiation and agreement rather than through confrontation and crisis as has sometimes been the case with concessionaires in other countries. As Saudi Arabia's Minister of Petroleum and Mineral Resources, Shaykh Ahmed Zaki Yamani, once put it, "In a closed room we sit down and

quarrel, but finally we reach an agreement." As a result, the concession agreement of May 1933 has been repeatedly modified and amended over the years, though it remains the basic charter of the relationship between Aramco and the Government of Saudi Arabia.

Some of the changes that have taken place have been concerned only with the arrangements between Aramco and its host government, while others have reflected the influence of trends at work all over the Middle East or in the international oil industry as a whole. The agreements between the two parties have dealt with the size and duration of the Aramco concession and with a variety of other matters. The great majority of the later agreements, however, have dealt with financial arrangements and have been entered into in response to the government's desire to gain a greater return from and greater control over the oil and gas resources from which it derives about 90 percent of its income.

The headquarters of Aramco Overseas Company is located in The Hague in Holland.

The first modification to the original concession agreement was signed on May 31, 1939 — some seven months after Aramco had formally notified the government that it had discovered oil in commercial quantities. It dealt with various additional payments to the government and a number of other matters and also extended Aramco's concession area to the northwest and southwest as well as over Saudi Arabia's undivided half interest, "of a maritime or of a territorial nature," in the two Neutral Zones — one shared with Iraq and the other shared with Kuwait. With the signing of this agreement the area of Aramco's concession rights, comprising an Exclusive Area and a Preferential Area, reached its maximum historic size, about 673,000 square miles.

The next major agreement between the parties, in October 1948, defined the offshore portion of Aramco's concession area, stipulated that the government would receive an additional five cents per barrel in royalty on each barrel produced from the offshore area, and guaranteed that royalties paid on offshore oil would amount to at least $2 million a year.

The concession agreement of 1933 specified that "from time to time" the company would relinquish parts of its concession area which it decided not to explore further or make other use of — a concept unknown in the early oil concessions — but for many years the government did not wish the company to

Shaykh Ahmed Zaki Yamani, Saudi Arabia's Minister of Petroleum and Mineral Resources.

RED

SEA

THE ARAMCO CONCESSION AREA

The concession area granted to Socal by the Saudi Arab Government in 1933 consisted of an exclusive area covering all of eastern Saudi Arabia as far as the westerly edge of the Dahna and a further area of preferential rights extending west of that as far as "the contact between the sedimentary and igneous formations." In 1939 the concession was extended to include additional areas in the far northwest and southwest of the kingdom as well as Saudi Arabia's interests in the two Neutral Zones to the northeast. Since then the concession area has been reduced by successive relinquishments until at the end of the 1970s it consisted of six separate pieces covering a total of about 85,000 square miles.

GULF OF OMAN

ARABIAN GULF

PREFERENTIAL AREA

ARABIAN SEA

———— 1933 Exclusive and Preferential Areas

———— 1939 Additional Areas

Relinquishments

| 1947 | 1948 | 1949 | 1952 | 1955 | 1960 | 1963 | 1968 | 1973 |

Present Concession Areas 1-6

make any such relinquishments. The supplemental agreement of 1939, in fact, specifically provided that for the next ten years Aramco would be under no obligation to relinquish any part of its Exclusive Area. Under the 1948 agreement Aramco relinquished all its concession rights in the Neutral Zone between Saudi Arabia and Kuwait and all of its Preferential Area west of longitude 46° E and undertook to relinquish an additional 33,000 square miles on six specified dates from 1949 to 1970. This was superseded by an agreement concluded in March 1963 under which Aramco relinquished all the rest of its Exclusive Area except for approximately 125,000 square miles in five separate blocks or "retained areas" and undertook to make six further relinquishments at five-year intervals.

In March 1963, Shaykh Ahmed Zaki Yamani, Minister of Petroleum and Mineral Resources, and Robert I. Brougham, senior vice president and Aramco's chief negotiator, signed a number of major agreements between the government and the company.

What was probably the most important change in the concession relationship took place in December 1950 with the signing of the so-called 50-50 agreement. Under this agreement, which followed by some months a precedent set earlier in Venezuela and was the first of its kind in the Middle East, Aramco submitted to an income tax (the concession agreement of 1933 had exempted it from all taxes) and undertook to pay the government 50 percent of its gross income less operating expenses. An additional tax of 5 percent on export sales of crude oil and refined products was imposed by a royal decree issued in December 1970.

By this agreement the Saudi Government's income from Aramco's operations came to be linked primarily not to the number of barrels of oil produced and sold, as before, but rather to how much profit the company made. After 1950, therefore, the government showed increasing interest in the prices charged for oil, the cost of running the business, and the accounting methods used in determining these things, since all of them affected the size of the kingdom's revenues. Many of the subsequent modifications of the Aramco concession dealt with matters such as these. At the same time, as the government was increasingly successful in developing a group of technically trained oil experts in its Ministry of Petroleum, it also became more and more interested in and involved with the actual operations of the company — such things as exploration programs, drilling practices, pressure maintenance, and so forth.

The theory of "participation," first publicly put forward by Petroleum Minister Yamani in June 1968, was the logical culmination of these trends. Under participation the government would have not only a specified share of the income of the company but also a share in the ownership of its assets and in the top-level direction of its operations. On December 20, 1972, after long negotiations, participation became a reality when the major oil concessionaire companies operating in the Arabian Gulf signed a so-called "general agreement" with their host governments. As a signatory of this agreement, the Government of Saudi Arabia acquired, as of the beginning of 1973, a 25 percent interest in Aramco's crude oil concession rights, the crude oil it produced, and its crude production facilities.

Discussions continued during 1973 and led to agreement increasing the Government of Saudi Arabia's participation interest to 60 percent as of the beginning of 1974. Negotiations leading toward a 100 percent Saudi Government interest resulted in final payments being made in 1980, although by mid-1981 final agreements had not yet been signed.

In many respects the new agreements only confirm and reinforce important trends in an amicable and continually evolving relationship between Saudi Arabia as a sovereign state exercising its rights over its oil resources and the American shareholders as partners in the Aramco enterprise. The new agreements will not shift the focus of policymaking and decision: the crucial aspects of Aramco's oil operations — production, conservation, and so on — were already the prerogative of the Saudi Arab Government long before it had a share in ownership. Apart from other advantages, Saudi Arabia will benefit under the agreements by keeping the oil companies' accumulated expertise in exploration, production and refining, and worldwide marketing, and from the stability that firm, long-term purchase agreements bring. The American companies involved — and through them the United States as an oil-importing country — will also benefit from the new arrangements. Their access to large quantities of Saudi Arabian oil will be guaranteed and they will retain their close working relationship with the only member nation of the Organization of Petroleum Exporting Countries (OPEC) capable of producing the increasingly large quantities of oil that the U.S. will be importing in the 1980s and beyond unless it is able to reverse the trends of the past thirty years. They will retain their ties as well with the nation that has consistently stood, within OPEC, for moderation in price and stability of supply of the crude that the energy-hungry world relies on.

The new agreements will simply open another chapter in which Aramco will continue to play a vital role in a period of economic and social transformation that is probably without precedent in the long history of the Middle East.

GROWTH AND TRANSFORMATION: The changes occurring today throughout the Middle East are especially remarkable in the Arabian Peninsula, where developments are so often in dramatic contrast to even the recent past. In Saudi Arabia the transformation is happening at such a rate and on such a scale that it is difficult to take in and grasp as a whole. The changes taking place in the Eastern Province, the area along the Arabian Gulf coast in which Aramco operates, represent in microcosm what is happening throughout the kingdom.

Air conditioning is perhaps one of the most visible and pervasive symbols of the changes that have already occurred, since the coming of the oil industry, in the life of the Eastern Province. Thousands, tens of thousands of "window units," many manufactured in Saudi Arabia, protrude through the concrete block walls of new apartment towers, throb in serried ranks in prefabricated wood and metal construction camps, and drip lukewarm condensation on the necks of shoppers thronging the packed sidewalks of booming al-Khobar and Dammam. August is the month of peak loads on the Eastern Province electricity grid, the month which closes each summer with a practical test of how well electric company planners have forecast the constantly multiplying demand for more lights, more household appliances, and more air conditioning. It is a month when temperatures in the towns along the Arabian Gulf's western shore frequently top 110 degrees and the relative humidity hovers near 100 percent. But air conditioning and oil money are doing for stretches of the Eastern Province of Saudi Arabia what air conditioning and oil money

have done for the Texas Gulf Coast around Houston, transforming a muggy coastal scrubland into a sprawling, modern urban conglomerate where today it is possible to work and live not only comfortably, but also pleasurably.

The air conditioners are in widespread use only from mid-April through October. Most of the Eastern Province is technically a desert — it receives an average of less than three inches of rain a year and virtually all of that precipitation comes from November through April, six gentle months when the sands can be brushed with green and the name desert barely seems to apply, when days are pleasantly warm and sunny and evenings cool, sometimes even chilly.

The market area, or suq, of al-Khobar in 1946 consisted of a few shop stalls along an unsurfaced street.

AS IT USED TO BE: Although the winter rains along this coast provided better grazing for the sheep, goats, and wide-ranging camels of the Bedouins than some other parts of the peninsula, it was not rainfall that gave the region its modest prosperity and sustained man since earliest times. Rather, ground water from distant mountains, welling up clear and plentiful from artesian springs or 'ayns in two major oases, nurtured broad date gardens, while the turquoise, shoal-filled waters of the Gulf provided fish and pearls and carried the commerce of distant shores.

According to local legend, a Gulf pirate once occupied the fort that years ago stood offshore from Dammam.

Hardy Bedouins, farmers painstakingly tending groves of palms and the silver webs of irrigation channels, fishermen, divers, sailors, townsmen, merchants and traders supplying the simple needs of these and of others in the far hinterland — these were the people of the Eastern Province, surviving, occasionally thriving, in a harsh and demanding land. They lived, as one writer said, "lives of unselfconscious, pervasive religiosity, the name of God constantly on their lips; His intercessions sought; His interventions praised."

Their pleasures, when work was done, were the pleasures of the family and the home, playing with their children, talking with friends and neighbors over endless cups of coffee. Children imitated their parents and at an early age began to share their work. Women, secluded and protected from men outside their family by custom, were honored in their role as mothers. Polygamy, a practice now fading, was then widespread. Men in this land felt affection and loyalty to family and to

At one time, Jubail sent out as many as two hundred pearling boats, but the trade declined in the early 1930s.

Climate

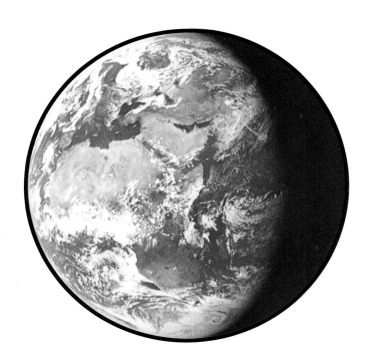

Like most of the rest of the peninsula, the Eastern Province region is an area of environmental extremes. The best known features of the climate are the intense summer heat and frequent strong winds. However, the Eastern Province has experienced freezing temperatures, torrential rains, thunderstorms, and extended sandstorms which add to the contrasting extremes of this desert climate.

The year can be divided into seasons in this region. The length of the summer is greater than in more temperate zones and can be considered as lasting from May until September, with the hottest months being from June through August. There is normally no rain during this period, and evaporation rates are high. Relative humidity values are low in inland areas during the summer season though coastal humidities remain quite high.

Beginning in late May and June, an extensive low-pressure area develops over the Asian continent as a result of the early summer heating of this large landmass. The counterclockwise wind circulation around this low is a permanent feature over and adjacent to the continent of Asia during the entire summer. The eastern coast of Arabia lies on the southwest edge of this low-pressure zone and winds blow predominantly from a north-northwest direction. Increased winds during June and occasionally early July are known as *shamals,* the Arabic word for northerly wind. Sustained winds for two- to three-day periods at speeds of 25-30 miles an hour create blowing dust and limited visibility. Shamals with gusts of 60 miles an hour lift sand-sized particles three feet or more above the desert surface and dust hundreds of feet. By mid-July there is no longer an appreciable pressure difference between Asia and Arabia, and the still predominantly northwest winds are weaker than in the early summer. August is normally the calmest month, though the hottest.

The autumn months of October and November are a transitional period in which temperatures fall and relative humidity begins to rise. The Asian low-pressure area weakens, and by November the first winter storms begin to affect the area. These move eastward across the Mediterranean and the Middle East. As the centers of these storms approach the Arabian Gulf, the leading boundary of the front frequently creates southeast or south winds. These are then usually followed by northwesterly winds as the front passes. Wind speeds and directions associated with these storms thus show wide variations in frequency of occurrence. Severe tropical cyclones from the Arabian Sea weaken as they approach southeast Arabia.

The winter months of December through February are characterized by stormy periods with strong winds, some rain, thunderstorms, and blowing dust interrupted by periods of relatively mild weather. February is usually the windiest month. Freezing temperatures, though rare, have been recorded in December and January in the Eastern Province.

The winter storms diminish in frequency and intensity during the spring months of March and April, though strong thunderstorms may occur locally during this period. Temperatures again begin to rise with the approach of summer, and the humidity decreases.

The climate over the Arabian Gulf is essentially the same as that of the Eastern Province since this extremely shallow marginal sea is virtually surrounded by land. The only connection with the open ocean is through the narrow Strait of Hormuz, so that the Arabian Gulf can be considered as a restricted arm of the Indian Ocean. Offshore sea surface temperatures vary from 60°F in winter to 90°F in summer, while coastal bays and lagoons have an even wider temperature fluctuation range, attaining temperatures of 104°F. Salinities are high in the Gulf due to excessive evaporation from the extreme temperatures and strong winds, as well as salt addition from numerous piercement salt domes and brackish undersea springs.

tribe; their respect was for devoutness, age, learning, good manners, generosity, and strong, fair leadership. Hospitality extended to strangers and even, under an elaborate code, to enemies.

Al-Hasa, about forty miles inland from the nearest point on the coast, is the larger of the two principal oases in the Eastern Province. In fact, with some 30,000 acres under cultivation, it is one of the largest anywhere. Some three million palm trees are estimated to grow there, watered by more than fifty natural springs and several hundred dug wells. Each of the two largest of the natural springs gushes from the ground at the rate of some 20,000 gallons per minute. Aside from dates, and the various fruits and vegetables cultivated in the shade of the palms, the people of the oasis once exported their sturdy breed of tall white donkeys and wove a fine beige wool cloth used in making the billowing cloak locally known as the *bisht*.

Although few details are known about the earliest history of al-Hasa, archaeologists have determined that men were living there as long as seven thousand years ago. Surface remains indicate that the oasis supported a substantial population in the Middle Ages. The House of Sa'ud first ruled al-Hasa in the eighteenth century, but the area later came under first Egyptian and then Ottoman Turkish administration. The Ottomans built a fort at Hofuf, the largest of al-Hasa's dozens of villages and towns, with a mud brick wall that at its strongest points was thirty feet high and six feet thick.

In 1913 'Abd al-'Aziz, the founder of modern Saudi Arabia, scaled the walls with a force of six hundred men and recaptured the town from the Turks. Garrisons in the other large towns of the area surrendered shortly after. The Saudis kept the name al-Hasa Province, a Turkish usage, for the whole coastal region and retained Hofuf as its capital. It remained so until 1956, when the administrative center was moved to the growing port city of Dammam and the region was given its present name, the Eastern Province.

Just north of Dammam and some eighty miles from Hofuf is Qatif, the second of the two major oases. Smaller than al-Hasa, but also comprising many villages and dozens of natural springs, the Qatif oasis is three miles across at its widest point. Its date gardens, though

interspersed with *sabkhahs* or salt flats, stretch some fourteen miles along the shore of Tarut Bay. In the bay, across the shallows from the large town of Qatif which gives the oasis its name, is the island of Tarut, once accessible only by boat at high tide and by wading at low tide, but now joined to the mainland by a causeway.

On the desert coast of Arabia plentiful water and safe anchorage have made Qatif and Tarut trading centers since at least the third millennium B.C. They probably served — as nearby Bahrain Island did — not only as a source of pearls and dates, but also as a link between the ancient civilizations of Mesopotamia and the Indus Valley. Persian Zoroastrians, Jews, and Nestorian Christians all lived and worshipped in Qatif and on Tarut before the coming of Islam. The Turks and perhaps the Portuguese had garrisons or outposts in the area and either built forts or added to ones they found already existing. It was on Tarut, in 1915, that the British Government, which had established protectorates elsewhere in the Gulf to help safeguard its sea lanes to India, signed a treaty recognizing the authority of 'Abd al-'Aziz Al Sa'ud as the independent "Ruler of Najd, El Hassa, Qatif and Jubail, and the towns and ports belonging to them," that is to say, most of central and eastern Arabia.

Jubail, about forty miles further up the coast from Qatif, with only two small springs, was not a large or, as far as anyone knows, an ancient oasis. Its importance was as a port of entry for goods destined for Riyadh (lying as it did at the beginning of one of the principal trails across the Dahna sands) and to Buraydah and 'Unayzah and other towns of northern Najd, and it had an advantage over Qatif and al-'Uqayr in its deeper waters which allowed larger vessels to unload cargoes there. The pearling fleet once based there and at Tarut never recovered from the world depression of the early 1930s and later competition from Japanese cultured pearls. It was at Jubail, in 1933, that two American geologists came ashore after crossing by dhow from Bahrain to begin the search for Arabian oil.

Down the coast some sixty miles south of Dammam is the port of al-'Uqayr, once counted as about a day's journey by camel from al-Hasa and the most favored port of entry to Riyadh and the interior by way of

Coffeepot-making is a traditional craft in al-Hasa oasis.

Date gardens and farms of Qatif oasis stretch for miles along Tarut Bay.

Remains of a fortress on Tarut Island — here seen in an aerial photo of the late 1940s — have been found to rest atop evidence of centuries-old civilizations.

The ruins of an old fort, now demolished, were a landmark in the harbor of old Dammam.

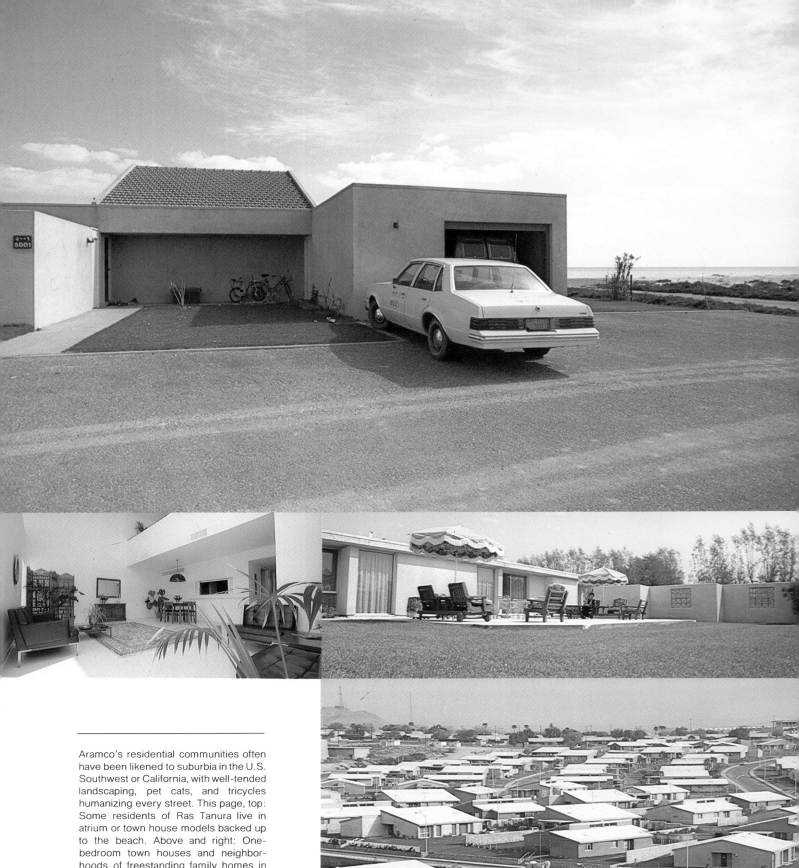

Aramco's residential communities often have been likened to suburbia in the U.S. Southwest or California, with well-tended landscaping, pet cats, and tricycles humanizing every street. This page, top: Some residents of Ras Tanura live in atrium or town house models backed up to the beach. Above and right: One-bedroom town houses and neighborhoods of freestanding family homes in Dhahran. Opposite page: Supermarket and barbershop in the Abqaiq Mall. Classroom in Dhahran School. "Twin towers" of the newest section of administrative headquarters in Dhahran.

Arrival of oilmen at Jubail between 1933 and 1935, when this photo was taken, gave a temporary boost to the coastal village which some four decades later was selected as the site of a vast industrial complex.

Dependent for their very survival on desert wells, Bedouins lived a life unchanged for centuries.

In the spring of 1935 when drilling began on Dammam Dome, the basic accommodations of the first Dhahran camp were the only buildings in sight.

Hofuf. Since the development of ports further up the coast with deeper water and more modern facilities, and with the completion of roads and a railroad from Dammam, the importance of al-'Uqayr has declined and its harbor today is little used.

And that, as recently as forty years ago, was the Eastern Province: "El Hassa, Qatif and Jubail, and the towns and ports belonging to them." The latter phrase included, of course, a number of smaller fishing villages and scattered oasis farming hamlets. There were also the lonely wells and distant encampments more familiar than the towns to the Bedouin tribes as they roamed the land in search of grazing.

Except for its people, eastern Arabia had few riches, although compared with much of the world at that time the people of the region were well enough off. But before the discovery of oil brought new jobs for the young and increased income for government social services, this was not an easy place to live. Schools and hospitals had yet to be built. Smallpox, cholera, and malaria were endemic. There were no paved roads and few cars to use them if there had been. There were few radios, no telephones, no electricity except from the odd generator, and of course no air conditioning.

From the air today much of the coastal Eastern Province appears to be laced with the sinews of the twentieth century: four-lane highways, a railroad, an endless maze of pipelines of all sizes carrying oil, gas, and natural gas liquids, water pipes, irrigation canals, chain-link fences, telephone lines, and electric transmission cables. Along the sweeping crescents of shore where desert and gulf merge, the physical manifestations of change loom up in concrete and steel. The empty land is filling fast. Today even the meanings of names have changed across this landscape. Places known in the collective memory of generations of Bedouins or seafarers as hills, plains, wells, capes, and islands are printed on maps and become oil and gas fields, pumping stations, industrial plant sites, and new communities.

LIFE IN ARAMCO: Aramco's exploration teams have covered the ground from the Iraqi border in the north to the far reaches of the

Rub' al-Khali, some eight hundred miles to the south. By the end of 1979 the company had discovered, on land and offshore, forty-seven oil fields and three gas fields. The main producing, treating, and shipping activities, however, and the multitude of diverse and technologically complex installations and facilities required to support them, are concentrated in a smaller area of the province. This is roughly a semicircle, with a radius of about 180 miles, centered on Aramco's headquarters community of Dhahran and sweeping from Marjan and Safaniya offshore in the north to Khurais and Haradh in the south.

Dhahran, principally an administrative center, is the oldest and largest of the four oil communities and has grown up over the Dammam field, where the company first discovered oil in commercial quantities in 1938. Ras Tanura, on a narrow headland about forty miles north of Dhahran and not far from the Qatif oasis, is the site of a major refinery and a marine terminal. Abqaiq, built over the oil field of the same name some forty miles southwest of Dhahran, is a producing and processing center. The newest and smallest of the communities is 'Udhailiyah, located atop the central portion of the giant Ghawar field, where large-scale gas projects are under way, about seventy miles south of Abqaiq and twenty miles from the oasis of al-Hasa.

In the beginning Dhahran was a rustic camp, an all-male outpost which provided mainly Arab and American oilmen with the bare essentials: workshops and offices in which to do the job they were there to do, and basic board and bed. Today Dhahran and the three smaller communities are much like modern towns anywhere — with a few noticeable differences. Americans often say the communities remind them of quiet suburbs in the U.S. Southwest: trim one- and two-story houses surrounded by well-watered lawns set off with hedges, trees, and flowers, and curving streets with cars parked by the curbs, the kind of small town where many people bicycle or walk to work and most still go home for lunch. Each community has tennis courts, a swimming pool, bowling alley, baseball diamond, and golf course. Each also has a mail center, barbershop, laundry, snack bar, library — its shelves crammed with the latest books and magazines — and a supermarket stocked with familiar brands.

Some American families living here feel so much at home that several hundred of their sons and daughters have returned to become second-generation employees of the company, and already there are even a few third-generation American workers with Aramco.

The biggest difference from a small U.S. town, of course, is the international character of these oil communities. A newcomer finds that living in the apartment or house next door, or working in the office across the hall, there may be a Saudi Arab or an American — or a Canadian, an Englishman or Scot, an Indian or Pakistani, a Lebanese, a Palestinian, or perhaps a Dutchman. Aramco is the Eastern Province's largest employer. In 1979, for example, some thirty-eight thousand persons were on its rolls. By far the largest number, almost twenty-two thousand, were Saudi Arabs, and over thirty-four hundred were from the United States, but in all they represented some forty-five different countries.

Most Saudi Arab employees live in the long-established towns closest to the various oil operations centers, most in their own homes built with company loans. Their children, both boys and girls, attend schools run by the Saudi Arab Government, many of which were built and are maintained by Aramco. For the children of employees living in the four oil communities, the company operates schools following the American system, in which non-Arab students study Arabic as a second language.

Sometimes, amid this diversity of people, different cultures flow together. For example, Saudi Arabs and foreigners learn to enjoy each other's cooking and exchange friendly greetings in each other's language. Sometimes the cultures meet unchanged in mutual respect, as when non-Muslims refrain from eating or smoking in public during the fast of Ramadan or conservative Saudi Arabs accept the fact that Western women go unveiled.

When they are not at work, employees and their families in the four communities keep busy in a seemingly endless variety of pursuits. In Dhahran there exist more than fifty clubs and associations dedicated to sports, hobbies, crafts, and professional interests of all kinds. Similar groups, equally active, exist in the other communities, with interests ranging from stamp collecting to sailing, rugby, and karate, and from amateur theatricals, choral singing, and square dancing to ceramics, weaving, natural history, and gardening. Through the years various forms of group endeavor — annual art and garden shows, scouting jamborees, community choruses, "county" fairs with booths, games, and a parade — have become something close to local institutions.

Interwoven with such familiar activities, which would be common enough in most European or American towns, there are special, sometimes unique, opportunities which come from living in the Eastern Province. Some employees keep and ride their own Arabian horses, others learn about and collect Oriental carpets. Scuba divers sail by dhow to remote islands to fish or photograph in the teeming waters of the Gulf. Others indulge their penchants for geological and historical field trips; they watch birds, collect shells, and learn to identify desert plants. A few even take up such unusual and esoteric interests as falconry. Teenagers enjoy racing across dune country on motorcycles, and families with four-wheel-drive off-road vehicles camp in the desert, sometimes driving long distances by compass along the fringes of the Rub' al-Khali sands.

Students find their recreation opportunities almost unlimited.

Because they are interested in seeing more of Saudi Arabia outside the Eastern Province, some foreign employees take advantage of short holiday periods to drive to the capital city of Riyadh, or on to Jiddah, the major port city of the Red Sea coast, to the majestic ruins of Madain Salih in the northwest, or to the cool green mountains of 'Asir in the southwest. For longer vacations, with paved highways all the way, it is not at all unusual or difficult these days to drive outside the kingdom north to Jordan and Syria or on to Europe. Only an adventurous few, however, yet drive in the other direction to the two remote areas of the peninsula which have perhaps seen the least change in recent years, the picturesque and colorful mountain strongholds of Oman and Yemen.

Closer at hand, Western newcomers in the oil communities of the Eastern Province often wonder if they have missed out completely on the age of the romantic and exotic East they read about in their schoolbooks. Old-timers in Aramco tell them stories about donkey-drawn wells where now there are diesel pumps, of

Camping enthusiasts with off-road vehicles delight in the rugged beauty of the desert.

Since the company's earliest days, its workers have managed time for recreation, and as the communities grew, so did organized programs. The proximity of the Gulf guaranteed that boating, fishing, and swimming would become favorite sports, and today one or more swimming pools are available in each community. Golf, tennis, and racquetball are played throughout the year, and such seasonal sports as basketball and softball are joined by soccer and rugby, games which reflect the international composition of the work force. The equestrian arts attract both adults and young people, and an annual horse show draws competitors from all over the kingdom to Dhahran. For the less athletically inclined, there are clubs embracing interests from stamp collecting to scouting; each community has an active women's group and each has a well-stocked library; a company-wide employees' association sponsors programs with imported entertainers. Most however, succumb to the lure of the outdoors — where the sun shines nearly every day of the year.

arrow-shaped reed fish traps on tidal flats where now there is landfill, of camel markets where now there are parking lots. True, there are still potters in al-Hasa who make wood-fired clay water jugs, there are basket makers in Qatif yet who braid straw into circular floor mats, and there are Bedouin women still weaving homespun wool into colorful strips of sturdy textile.

Today it is not uncommon to see the beast once called the "ship of the desert" defer to a faster mode of travel.

THE EASTERN PROVINCE TODAY:

Change comes in little ways as well as big. It comes quickly and is all-pervasive. Nowadays Bedouins carry barrels of water to their sheep in pickup trucks, and when they move their black tents they load them — along with transistor radios and cylinders of bottled cooking gas — onto gaily decorated trucks. Townsmen, when they sit together in the evening, watch color television on any one of a number of channels and offer their guests soft drinks and canned juices as often as tiny cups of cardamom-flavored coffee. Children in villages ride tricycles and young men's sports clubs organize long-distance bicycle races. Middle-class families go for a weekend drive in their air-conditioned cars and stop for ice-cream cones or pastries. Increasingly, in the larger towns and cities, some women attend mixed social functions or go to restaurants with their husbands.

What were once simple village markets have become showcases for manufactured goods from all over the world.

The art of bargaining is still practiced in covered *suqs* which have the smell of spices and musty carpets and the glitter of tin, brass, copper, and gold. But among the goods for sale are tape cassettes of the latest hits from Cairo and London, battery-powered toys from Hong Kong, watches and lighters and pens from Tokyo, Geneva, and Paris. In the fish market the fish — in tempting variety — are fresh from the Gulf, and stacked in the next aisle of stalls are baskets of dates and bags of rice. But there are also carrots, cucumbers, and cabbages grown on local farms, apples shipped from Lebanon and Washington State, oranges from Morocco and from Jordan, mangoes from India, and bananas from Honduras.

Hofuf and Qatif have spilled beyond their walls and nearby date gardens are yielding to houses and streets as did the orange groves of Los Angeles. Inexorably, Dhahran and its two coastal neighbors, al-Khobar and Dammam, are growing together. By day, clearly,

stretches of desert still separate the three towns, but at night countless clusters of lights already join them.

Dhahran itself has spread out with new housing, both permanent for families and temporary for construction workers. Next to it, like an acropolis crowning a low limestone *jabal,* is the magnificent campus of the University of Petroleum and Minerals. Below the university, toward the Gulf, is Dhahran International Airport, then the town of Thuqbah. Al-Khobar, laid out in orderly city blocks along a new waterfront boulevard, is a bustling shopping center with traffic jams, flashing neon lights, and glass and chrome-fronted stores selling most of the consumer products of the industrialized world. It now has a number of office towers, several first-class hotels, and any number of good places to eat out, including that most ubiquitous of institutions, the Chinese restaurant. In the expanding residential neighborhoods pastel stuccoed houses and apartments, schools, mosques, and corner grocery stores flank newly tree-lined streets which have scarcely been paved before they are dug up again to lay new pipe and cable.

The twin roads along the coast are a succession of housing compounds, wholesale showrooms, construction storeyards, and light industrial areas. On the outskirts of Dammam, the provincial capital, are a fertilizer plant, a growing industrial estate with several dozen factories producing items as varied as plastic pipes, aluminum buildings, paints, paper bags, and air conditioners, and the railroad yards and warehouses supporting the busy commercial harbor. Most government ministries have established branches here; a daily newspaper is published; a large new soccer stadium draws capacity crowds; and King Faisal University, the kingdom's youngest, plans a new campus in the city.

Probably in only a few of the world's great capitals at a few moments in history since the days of Babylon and Rome have men from so many far-flung nations come to live and work at one place and time as they have to this once-remote, relatively small port city in eastern Saudi Arabia at the beginning of the final quarter of the twentieth century. They stroll and shop each evening, shoulder to shoulder, in the streets of Dammam's commercial center between the principal mosque and the public gardens: Americans, Koreans in stenciled T-shirts, Filipinos in visored caps and sports slacks, bearded Afghans and clean-shaven Pakistanis in long, full shirts over loose-legged pants, tall Eritreans, turbaned Sudanese, Indians, Mediterraneans — Syrians, Turks, Greeks, Italians — Frenchmen in fashion-cut blue jeans, Germans in shorts and sandals, lanky mustachioed Englishmen. It is an international work force, skilled laborers and craftsmen, technicians, teachers, engineers, drawn here by the jobs created by the changes under way in the Eastern Province.

There are more changes to come. Planning is under way for a network of new highways and a causeway across the Gulf to Bahrain, and design work has been started for a major new international airport and a railroad along the coast. In a few years Jubail will be a major city, totally planned, built almost from scratch. Its industrial complex — various petrochemical plants, a refinery, and steel and aluminum mills are being planned for it — will be fed and fueled by products from gas which, coming out of the ground along with the oil, will be separated, gathered, and processed in an immense government-sponsored program. New desalination plants to be built near Jubail will soon gush forth as much fresh water each day as all of the age-old springs of al-Hasa and Qatif combined. The electricity they generate, added to the planned capacity of the Eastern Province's existing consolidated power network, will be more than enough, even when all the other jobs are being done, to keep many many air conditioners humming.

For the most part the people of al-Hasa, of Dhahran, al-Khobar, and Dammam, of Qatif, Tarut, and Jubail, like their fellow countrymen throughout the kingdom, realize that the oil and gas resources which are bringing all these changes will not last forever. They understand the need to exchange these depletable sources of wealth for others which are enduring — technology, industry, education — so that their grandchildren will not experience the hardships their grandparents knew. They also realize that wealth is not only bringing material changes, but also, in countless ways, is changing the time-tested patterns of their lives.

Not many years ago the people of the Eastern Province lived by a kind of natural rhythm determined by the changing seasons: the Bedouins clustered near the wells when summer was at its zenith and moved on with the first flicker of lightning on the night horizon in the fall; seamen followed the monsoon winds into the Indian Ocean, pearlers and fishermen each had their time; in the oases farmers gathered their dates in the heat of late summer and early autumn and planted other crops beneath the palms to harvest before the burning winds of June.

Today families plan holiday trips according to the vacation periods at their children's schools, while Saudi university students in America and Europe return to the kingdom to join their colleagues at institutions here in seeking summer jobs. Merchants schedule business trips with a close eye on trade fair calendars around the world. Imported fruits and vegetables know no season, and if in the coastal towns August is still very hot and very humid, today it no longer really matters.

The pace of life is different now. People are concerned that traditional values will change too. The wealth they had was their faith, a code of conduct, a generosity of spirit, a foundation man could build on. Now education, travel, television, contact with foreigners — all have made Saudi Arabia a full partner in the modern world. Through technology its people hope to strengthen their future in it, but not at the cost of destroying the foundation, of losing what they had: the closeness of the family with its loyalties and responsibilities, their respect for custom and pride in the richness of their language, the sustaining strength of their religion.

People in the Eastern Province and the kingdom as a whole believe that tradition and modernity can live honorably side by side; that women will be able to take a more active part in society and in the development of their country within the context of Islam without neglecting their roles as wives and mothers; that boys and girls can go to school and learn how to flourish in the larger world and still cherish their past and esteem their elders. They believe also that man can take the time, even in the rush of twentieth-century commerce and industry, to close a shop or stop work at the amplified call of the muezzin to prayer or, pulling a truck to the side of the road at sunset, kneel in the vastness of the desert and offer thanks to God for what He has given.

Even in the remote reaches of the silent desert, men hear in their hearts the call to prayer ... and they answer.

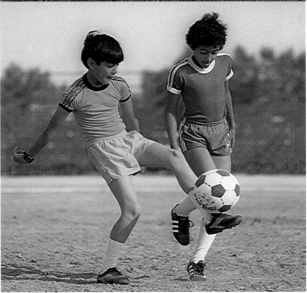

Aramco employees and their family members come from many different countries. All these nationalities contribute to the unique character of the Aramco community — not so much melting pot as multi-cultured mosaic. With employment need-and-supply cycles always changing, the mixture is constantly in flux; nationality groups that were rare in past decades become major ingredients, and the faces, the costumes, and the menus change. Saudi Arab employees live for the most part in nearby towns, in homes built with loans from Aramco. The children of those who choose to live in company communities depart by early-morning bus for government schools, but they can be seen after hours back on the Aramco sports field.

Books For Further Reading

This selection of books for further reading about the subjects covered in this volume does not pretend to be more than an introduction to the vast number of works that have been published on the Middle East and the Islamic world. The books listed are all in English, and they have been chosen for their intrinsic worth, readability, and availability. Many have been published in paperback editions. Although most of the authors are specialists, the books are — with few exceptions — general works written for the nonspecialist. Many offer annotated bibliographies enabling the reader to pursue particular subjects in as much detail as desired.

Following common present-day practice, no attempt is made to list publishers. It is not uncommon now for books to have separate publishers for hardbound and paperback editions in America and in Britain. It is impractical to list all and unfair to list only one.

Brief descriptions of certain books are provided, especially where titles do not clearly indicate the material covered (e.g., *The Loom of History*). On the other hand, descriptions are not normally provided books as explicitly titled as *The Middle East: A Physical, Social, and Regional Geography.* All books included are recommended, though they are not, of course, of equal merit. The selection is unabashedly weighted in favor of books on the Arabs and the Arabian Peninsula.

A good source of well-illustrated general articles on a wide variety of subjects connected with the Middle East is the magazine *Aramco World,* published six times a year.* Special issues of particular interest have dealt with the pilgrimage (November-December 1974), Arab women (March-April 1971), food of the Middle East (November-December 1975), the sights and scenery of Saudi Arabia (January-February 1975), and American economic ties with Saudi Arabia and other Arab countries of the Arabian Gulf (January-February 1977).

---

* The magazine is available from: Public Relations, Aramco, Dhahran, Saudi Arabia; or Aramco World Magazine, 55 Laan van Meerdervoort, The Hague, Netherlands; or Aramco Services Company, 1100 Milam, Houston, Texas 77002, U.S.A.

THE MIDDLE EAST AND THE ISLAMIC WORLD: SURVEYS AND COMPILATIONS

Beaumont, Peter; Blake, Gerald H.; and Wagstaff, J. Malcolm. *The Middle East: A Geographical Study.* London and New York, 1976.

Berger, Morroe. *The Arab World Today.* Garden City, N.Y., 1962.

Coon, Carleton S. *Caravan: The Story of the Middle East.* Revised edition. Huntington, N.Y., 1976.

Fisher, W. B. *The Middle East: A Physical, Social, and Regional Geography.* 6th edition. London and New York, 1971.

Hayes, John R., editor. *The Genius of Arab Civilization, Source of Renaissance.* New York, 1975.

Lewis, Bernard, editor. *The World of Islam: Faith, People, Culture.* London, 1976.

Lutfiyya, Abdulla M., and Churchill, Charles W., editors. *Readings in Arab Middle Eastern Societies and Cultures.* The Hague and Paris, 1970.

Malone, Joseph J. *The Arab Lands of Western Asia.* Englewood Cliffs, N. J., 1973.

Mansfield, Peter. *The Arabs.* London, 1976. Published in New York as *The Arab World: A Comprehensive History.*

Rogers, Michael. *The Spread of Islam,* in the series The Making of the Past. Oxford and New York, 1976.

Schacht, Joseph, and Bosworth, C. E., editors. *The Legacy of Islam.* 2nd edition. Oxford, 1974. The first edition (1931) was edited by Thomas Arnold and Alfred Guillaume.

The Legacy of Islam and the handsome books edited by Hayes, Lewis, and Rogers contain excellent essays by specialists on many aspects of Middle Eastern and Islamic civilization. Berger writes as a sociologist, Coon as an anthropologist, Malone as a political scientist, and Mansfield as a journalist.

THE MIDDLE EAST AND THE ISLAMIC WORLD: HISTORY

Antonius, George. *The Arab Awakening: The Story of the Arab National Movement.* London, 1938; New York, 1965.

Atiyah, Edward. *The Arabs.* London etc., 1955; New York, 1968.

Brockelmann, Carl. *History of the Islamic Peoples.* Translated by Joel Carmichael and Moshe Perlmann. New York, 1960.

Dunlop, D.M. *Arab Civilization to A.D. 1500.* London and Beirut, 1971.

Fisher, Sydney Nettleton. *The Middle East: A History.* New York, 1959.

Hitti, Philip K. *The Arabs, A Short History.* Princeton, 1949.

———. *History of the Arabs.* 10th edition. London and New York etc., 1970.

Hodgson, Marshall G. S. *The Venture of Islam: Conscience and History in a World Civilization.* 3 vols. Chicago and London, 1974.

Holt, P. M.; Lambton, Ann K. S.; and Lewis, Bernard. *The Cambridge History of Islam.* 4 vols. Cambridge, 1977.

Hourani, Albert. *Arabic Thought in the Liberal Age, 1798-1939.* London etc., 1962.

Kirk, George E. *The Middle East in the War,* in the series Survey of International Affairs. London etc., 1953.

———. *The Middle East 1945-1950,* in the series Survey of International Affairs. London etc., 1954.

———. *A Short History of the Middle East, from the Rise of Islam to Modern Times.* 6th edition. New York, 1960.

Lenczowski, George. *The Middle East in World Affairs.* 2nd edition. Ithaca and London, 1956.

Lewis, Bernard. *The Arabs in History.* 4th edition. London etc., 1966.

——, editor and translator. *Islam: from the Prophet Muhammad to the Capture of Constantinople,* in the series The Documentary History of Western Civilization. 2 vols. New York and London, 1974.

Monroe, Elizabeth. *Britain's Moment in the Middle East, 1914-1956.* London, 1963.

Nutting, Anthony. *The Arabs.* New York, 1964.

Runciman, Steven. *A History of the Crusades.* 3 vols. Cambridge, 1951-54.

Toynbee, Arnold J. *The Islamic World Since the Peace Settlement,* in the series Survey of International Affairs. London, 1927.

Watt, W. Montgomery. *The Majesty That Was Islam.* London, 1976.

The works of Brockelmann, Hourani, and Hodgson are scholarly and thorough. Antonius writes of the political renaissance of the Arabs in this and the last century. Watt tells of Islamic history to A.D. 1100, and Hitti brings his history of the Arabs down to the establishment of the Ottoman Empire in Egypt in 1517. The books by Toynbee and Kirk are particularly valuable for their treatment of the Palestine problem.

THE RELIGION OF ISLAM

Ali, Abdullah Yusuf. *The Holy Qur-an: Text, Translation and Commentary.* 2 vols. Lahore, 1934; New York, 1946; and other editions.

Amin, Mohamed. *Pilgrimage to Mecca.* London, 1978.

Amin, S. M. *The Holy Journey to Mecca.* Naples, 1976.

Arberry, Arthur J. *The Koran Interpreted.* 2 vols. London and New York, 1955.

'Azzam, 'Abd-al-Rahman. *The Eternal Message of Muhammad.* Translated by Caesar A. Farah. New York, 1964.

Donaldson, Dwight M. *The Shi'ite Religion: A History of Islam in Persia and Irak.* London, 1933.

Esin, Emel, and Doganbey, Haluk. *Mecca the Blessed, Madinah the Radiant.* London, 1963.

Gibb, H. A. R. *Mohammedanism: An Historical Survey.* 2nd edition. London etc., 1961.

Guellouz, Ezzedine, and Frikha, Abdelaziz. *Mecca: The Muslim Pilgrimage.* New York and London, 1979.

Hamidullah, Muhammad. *Introduction to Islam.* 2nd edition. Paris, 1959.

Morgan, Kenneth W., editor. *Islam — the Straight Path: Islam Interpreted by Muslims.* New York, 1958.

Nasr, Seyyed Hossein. *Ideals and Realities of Islam.* London, 1966.

Pickthall, Marmaduke. *The Meaning of the Glorious Qur'ân: Text and Explanatory Translation.* 2 vols. Hyderabad, 1938, and other editions.

Smith, Wilfred Cantwell. *Islam in Modern History.* Princeton, 1957.

Von Grunebaum, G. E. *Muhammadan Festivals.* New York, 1951.

Watt, W. Montgomery. *Muhammad at Mecca.* Oxford, 1953.

——. *Muhammad at Medina.* Oxford, 1956.

There are many translations of the Quran. Each has its strong points. Those by Arberry and Pickthall are particularly good. Abdullah Ali's translation is especially useful for its explanatory notes. The newcomer to the subject is well advised, however, to start his study of Islam with a general introduction, such as is provided by 'Azzam or Gibb or Hamidullah. Von Grunebaum's book is a pleasant introduction to the Muslim at prayer and on pilgrimage. Esin and Doganbey are Turkish Muslims who describe the Holy Cities by word and picture.

ARCHAEOLOGY AND
THE ANCIENT NEAR EAST

Bibby, Geoffrey. *Looking for Dilmun.* New York, 1969.

Breasted, James Henry. *A History of Egypt from the Earliest Times to the Persian Conquest.* 2nd edition. New York and London, 1909 etc.

Burney, Charles. *The Ancient Near East.* Ithaca and Oxford, 1977. The title of the British edition is *From Village to Empire.*

Childe, V. Gordon. *New Light on the Most Ancient East.* "Rewritten" edition. London, 1952.

Harding, G. Lankester. *The Antiquities of Jordan.* Revised edition. London, 1967.

Johnson, Paul. *Civilizations of the Holy Land.* London, 1979.

Saudi Arabia, Ministry of Education, Department of Antiquities and Museums. *An Introduction to Saudi Arabian Antiquities.* Riyadh, 1975.

Simpson, William K., et al., editors. *Ancient Egypt: Discovering Its Splendors.* Washington, 1978.

Winnett, F. V., and Reed, W. L. *Ancient Records from North Arabia.* Toronto and Buffalo, N.Y., 1970.

Childe and Harding are the authors of standard works in their fields of archaeology. The book on Saudi Arabian archaeology is unusually well illustrated. Bibby describes recent archaeological discoveries on the western side of the Arabian Gulf.

LITERATURE AND
VISUAL ARTS

Arnold, Thomas W. *Painting in Islam: A Study of the Place of Pictorial Art in Muslim Culture.* Oxford, 1928; New York, 1965.

Blunt, Wilfrid. *Splendours of Islam.* London and New York, 1976.

Burckhardt, Titus. *Art of Islam: Language and Meaning.* London, 1976.

Dimand, M. S. *A Handbook of Muhammadan Art.* 3rd edition. New York, 1958.

Du Ry, Carel J. *Art of Islam.* Translated by Alexis Brown. New York, 1970.

Eiland, Murray L. *Oriental Rugs: A Comprehensive Guide.* Revised edition. Boston, 1976.

Ettinghausen, Richard. *Arab Painting,* in the series Treasures of Asia. New York, 1977.

Formenton, Fabio. *Oriental Rugs and Carpets.* London, New York etc., 1972.

Gibb, H. A. R. *Arabic Literature: An Introduction.* 2nd edition. Oxford, 1974.

Hawley, Walter A. *Oriental Rugs, Antique and Modern.* New York, 1913, 1970.

Haywood, John A. *Modern Arabic Literature, 1800-1970: An Introduction, with Extracts in Translation.* London, 1971.

Kritzeck, James. *Anthology of Islamic Literature, from the Rise of Islam to Modern Times.* New York etc., 1964.

Lichtenstadter, Ilse. *Introduction to Classical Arabic Literature.* Boston, 1974.

Lings, Martin. *The Quranic Art of Calligraphy and Illumination.* London, 1976; Boulder, Colorado, 1978.

Nicholson, Reynold A. *A Literary History of the Arabs.* 2nd edition. Cambridge, 1969.

Rice, David Talbot. *Islamic Art.* London, 1975.

Ross, Heather Colyer. *Bedouin Jewellery in Saudi Arabia.* London, 1978.

Safadi, Yasin Hamid. *Islamic Calligraphy.* London, 1978.

Scerrato, Umberto. *Islam,* in the series Monuments of Civilization. New York, 1976.

Schroeder, Eric. *Muhammad's People: A Tale by Anthology.* Portland, Maine, 1955.

Gibb, Lichtenstadter, and Nicholson offer introductions to the literature of the Arabs, and Kritzeck, Haywood, and Schroeder have compiled anthologies of that literature in translation. Bernard Lewis's two volumes entitled *Islam* and listed above under histories are a fascinating compilation of translations from Arabic, Persian, and Turkish literature up to the fifteenth century. Blunt, Burckhardt, Dimand, Du Ry, and Rice survey the visual arts, with Blunt and Scerrato accenting architecture.

CLASSICS

Arabian Nights. Many editions, but the most famous translations are by Richard F. Burton and Edward William Lane.

Burckhardt, John Lewis. *Notes on the Bedouins and Wahábys.* 2 vols. London, 1831; New York and London, 1967.

———. *Travels in Arabia.* 2 vols. London, 1829; Beirut, 1972.

Burton, Richard F. *Personal Narrative of a Pilgrimage to Al-Madinah and Meccah.* 2 vols. London, 1893; New York, 1964.

Doughty, Charles M. *Travels in Arabia Deserta.* 3rd edition. London and New York, 1921. This and later editions have an introduction by T. E. Lawrence.

Hurgronje, C. Snouck. *Mekka in the Latter Part of the 19th Century.* Translated by J. H. Monahan. Leiden and London, 1931.

Lane, Edward William. *An Account of the Manners and Customs of the Modern Egyptians.* London, 1836, and many later editions.

Lawrence, T. E. *Seven Pillars of Wisdom: A Triumph.* London and Garden City, N.Y., 1935.

Palgrave, William Gifford. *Narrative of a Year's Journey through Central and Eastern Arabia (1862-63).* 2 vols. London, 1865, 1969.

Pelly, Lewis. *Report on a Journey to the Wahabee Capital of Riyadh in Central Arabia.* Bombay, 1866; Cambridge and New York, 1978.

———

As the entries above indicate, a number of publishers have recently been bringing out new editions of some of the best-known older books on Arabia and the Middle East – in some cases a hundred years and more after they were first published. The books by Burton, Doughty, and Lawrence listed here are classics of the English language, quite apart from their merits as authorities on matters Arabian. None of these works are easy reading, but any effort by the reader will be well rewarded. In some bibliographies works by Hurgronje will be found listed under *S* for Snouck Hurgronje.

THE ARABIAN PENINSULA AND THE GULF

Abdullah, Muhammad Morsy. *The United Arab Emirates: A Modern History.* London and New York, 1978.

Anthony, John Duke. *Arab States of the Lower Gulf: People, Politics, Petroleum.* Washington, 1975.

Azzi, Robert. *An Arabian Portfolio.* Manchester, N.H., 1977.

———. *Saudi Arabian Portfolio.* Manchester, N.H., 1978.

Belgrave, Charles. *Personal Column.* London, 1960.

Beling, Willard A., editor. *King Faisal and the Modernisation of Saudi Arabia.* Boulder, Colorado, and London, 1980.

Bidwell, Robin. *Travellers in Arabia.* London, 1976.

Brent, Peter. *Far Arabia: Explorers of the Myth.* London, 1977.

De Gaury, Gerald. *Faisal, King of Saudi Arabia.* London, 1966.

Dickson, H. R. P. *Kuwait and Her Neighbours.* London, 1956.

Freeth, Zahra, and Winstone, H.V.F. *Explorers of Arabia: From the Renaissance to the End of the Victorian Era.* London etc., 1978.

Hawley, Donald. *The Trucial States.* London, 1970.

Hill, Ann and Daryl. *The Sultanate of Oman: A Heritage.* London and New York, 1977.

Hopwood, Derek, editor. *The Arabian Peninsula: Society and Politics.* London, 1972.

Ingrams, Harold. *Arabia and the Isles.* 3rd edition. London, 1972.

———. *The Yemen: Imams, Rulers & Revolutions.* London, 1963.

Kelly, J. B. *Britain and the Persian Gulf, 1795-1880.* Oxford, 1968.

Kiernan, R. H. *The Unveiling of Arabia: The Story of Arabian Travel and Discovery.* London etc., 1937; New York, 1975.

Long, David E. *The Persian Gulf: An Introduction to its Peoples, Politics and Economics.* Revised edition. Boulder, Colorado, 1978.

———. *Saudi Arabia.* Beverly Hills, Calif., 1976.

Marlowe, John. *The Persian Gulf in the Twentieth Century.* London, 1962.

Monroe, Elizabeth. *Philby of Arabia.* London, 1973.

Pesce, Angelo. *Colours of the Arab Fatherland.* Riyadh, 1972.

———. *Jiddah: Portrait of an Arabian City.* London, 1974.

Peterson, J. E. *Oman in the Twentieth Century: Political Foundations of an Emerging State.* London and New York, 1978.

Philby, H. St J. B. *Arabia of the Wahhabis.* London, 1928.

———. *Arabian Jubilee.* London, 1952.

———. *Arabian Oil Ventures.* Washington, 1964.

——— *The Empty Quarter: Being a Description of the Great South Desert of Arabia Known as Rub' al-Khali.* London, 1933.

———. *A Pilgrim in Arabia.* London, 1946.

———. *Sa'udi Arabia.* London, 1955.

Rihani, Ameen. *Ibn Sa'oud of Arabia: His People and His Land.* London, 1928; Salisbury, N.C., 1977.

Sheean, Vincent. *Faisal: The King and His Kingdom.* Tavistock, England, 1975.

Stacey International. *The Kingdom of Saudi Arabia.* Revised edition. London, 1979.

Stookey, Robert W. *Yemen: The Politics of the Yemen Arab Republic.* Boulder, Colorado, 1978.

Troeller, Gary. *The Birth of Saudi Arabia: Britain and the Rise of the House of Sa'ud.* London, 1976.

Twitchell, K. S. *Saudi Arabia.* 3rd edition. Princeton, 1958.

Wilson, Arnold T. *The Persian Gulf: An Historical Sketch from the Earliest Times to the Beginning of the Twentieth Century.* Oxford, 1928; London, 1954.

Winder, R. Bayly. *Saudi Arabia in the Nineteenth Century.* New York etc., 1965.

Beling's book is a compilation of papers on a wide range of topics connected with Saudi Arabia. Belgrave's autobiographical work is about Bahrain and the author's years there as an advisor to the ruler, while Kelly and Winder collect detail for the historian. Ingram's *Arabia and the Isles* is about the area known as Hadhramaut. Bidwell, Brent, Freeth, and Kiernan write of the development of knowledge of Arabia by European explorers. Azzi's two books consist for the most part of beautiful color photographs of Arabia and its people. Pesce's books are also color photographic reports in the main, but the volume on Jiddah has much descriptive and historical text as well.

Philby's historical works are sound, and his records of exploration are valuable compendiums of information. *Arabian Oil Ventures* contains Philby's story of the negotiation of the Aramco concession and of Major Frank Holmes's earlier concession covering much the same area. Rihani's book is a first-hand account of the Saudi State in the 1920s by an American of Arab descent who was with King 'Abd al-'Aziz at the conference of al-'Uqayr in 1922.

SYRIA, LEBANON, AND IRAQ

Haley, P. Edward, and Snider, Lewis W., editors. *Lebanon in Crisis: Participants and Issues,* in the series Contemporary Issues in the Middle East. Syracuse, N.Y., 1979.

Harris, George L. *Jordan: Its People, Its Society, Its Culture,* in the series Survey of World Cultures. New Haven, 1958.

Hitti, Philip K. *History of Syria, Including Lebanon and Palestine.* 2nd edition. London and New York, 1957.

Hourani, A. H. *Syria and Lebanon: A Political Essay.* London etc., 1946.

Khadduri, Majid. *Independent Iraq, 1932-1958: A Study in Iraqi Politics.* 2nd edition. London etc., 1960.

———. *Republican 'Iraq: A Study in 'Iraqi Politics since the Revolution of 1958.* London etc., 1969.

Lloyd, Seton. *Twin Rivers: A Brief History of Iraq from the Earliest Times to the Present Day.* 3rd edition. London etc., 1961.

Longrigg, Stephen Hemsley. *Four Centuries of Modern Iraq.* Oxford, 1925; Beirut, 1968.

———. *'Iraq, 1900-1950: A Political, Social, and Economic History.* London etc., 1953.

———. *Syria and Lebanon under French Mandate.* London etc., 1958.

Penrose, Edith and E. F. *Iraq: International Relations and National Development,* in the series Nations of the Modern World. London and Boulder, Colorado, 1978.

Salibi, Kamal S. *The Modern History of Lebanon.* London, 1965; Westport, Conn., 1976.

Seale, Patrick. *The Struggle for Syria: A Study of Postwar Arab Politics, 1945-1958.* London etc., 1965.

Thesiger, Wilfred. *The Marsh Arabs.* London, 1964.

Thesiger's book is about the inhabitants of the marshes of southern Iraq.

PALESTINE/ISRAEL

Barbour, Nevill. *Nisi Dominus: A Survey of the Palestine Controversy.* London etc., 1946. Published in New York in 1947 as *Palestine: Star or Crescent?*

Ellis, Harry B. *The Dilemma of Israel.* Washington, 1970.

Hirst, David. *The Gun and the Olive Branch: The Roots of Violence in the Middle East.* New York and London, 1977.

Hurewitz, J. C. *The Struggle for Palestine.* New York, 1950.

Peretz, Don. *Israel and the Palestine Arabs.* Washington, 1958.

Quandt, William B. *Decade of Decisions: American Policy toward the Arab-Israeli Conflict, 1967-1976.* Berkeley and Los Angeles, 1977.

Rodinson, Maxime. *Israel and the Arabs.* Translated by Michael Perl. New York, 1968.

Safran, Nadav. *Israel: The Embattled Ally.* Cambridge, Mass., and London, 1978.

Sayegh, Fayez A. *The Arab-Israeli Conflict.* New York, 1956.

Taylor, Alan R., and Tetlie, Richard N., editors. *Palestine: A Search for Truth: Approaches to the Arab-Israeli Conflict.* Washington, 1970.

Virtually all books about the Middle East in this century discuss the partition of Palestine and the creation of the State of Israel. There are, in addition, a growing number of books about individual aspects of these events, few avoiding the tendentious. However, those recommended here are good introductions to the most pressing current problem of the Middle East.

IRAN AND TURKEY

Lenczowski, George. *Russia and the West in Iran, 1918-1948: A Study in Big Power Rivalry.* Ithaca and London, 1949.

Lewis, Bernard. *The Emergence of Modern Turkey.* 2nd edition. London etc., 1968.

Muller, Herbert J. *The Loom of History.* London and New York, 1966.

Wilber, Donald N. *Iran, Past and Present.* 8th edition, Princeton, 1976.

Wittek, Paul. *The Rise of the Ottoman Empire.* London, 1958.

Muller's book is considered a minor classic on civilization in Asia Minor from Troy to Ataturk.

EGYPT, NORTH AFRICA, AND SPAIN

Burckhardt, Titus. *Moorish Culture in Spain.* Translated by Alisa Jaffa. London, 1972.

Knapp, Wilfrid, editor. *North West Africa: A Political and Economic Survey.* 3rd edition. Oxford, 1977. The first two editions (1959 and 1962) were edited by Nevill Barbour.

Sordo, Enrique, and Swaan, Wim. *Moorish Spain: Cordoba, Seville, Granada.* New York, 1963.

Vatikiotis, P. J. *The Modern History of Egypt.* London, 1969.

Waterbury, John. *Egypt: Burdens of the Past, Options for the Future.* Bloomington, Ind., and London, 1978.

MIDDLE EAST OIL

Anthony, John Duke, editor. *The Middle East: Oil, Politics, and Development.* Washington, 1975.

Barger, Thomas C. *Energy Policies of the World: Arab States of the Persian Gulf.* Newark, Delaware, 1975.

Hartshorn, J. E. *Objectives of the Petroleum Exporting Countries.* Nicosia, 1978.

——— *Oil Companies and Governments: An Account of the International Oil Industry in Its Political Environment.* 2nd edition. London, 1967.

Longrigg, Stephen Hemsley. *Oil in the Middle East: Its Discovery and Development.* 3rd edition. London etc., 1968.

Mikdashi, Zuhayr. *The Community of Oil Exporting Countries: A Study in Governmental Co-operation.* London, 1972.

Stegner, Wallace. *Discovery!* Beirut, 1971.

Stocking, George W. *Middle East Oil: A Study in Political and Economic Controversy.* Nashville, Tenn., 1970.

Tughendhat, Christopher. *Oil: The Biggest Business.* London, 1968.

Turner, Louis. *Oil Companies in the International System.* London, 1978.

Vicker, Ray. *The Kingdom of Oil: The Middle East, Its People and Its Power.* New York, 1974.

Longrigg, Stocking, and Tughendhat present surveys, each with its own strength. Longrigg provides the most detail, and Tughendhat is easiest to read and the widest ranging. Stegner tells the story of Aramco's pioneering days. Vicker describes the Middle East oil industry and its setting as it was in the early 1970s.

BEDOUINS, OASIS DWELLERS, AND SAILORS

Dickson, H. R. P. *The Arab of the Desert: A Glimpse into Badawin Life in Kuwait and Sau'di Arabia.* London, 1949.

Hawkins, Clifford W. *The Dhow: An Illustrated History of the Dhow and Its World,* in the series Nautical Historical Record. Lymington, Hants., 1977.

Thesiger, Wilfred. *Arabian Sands.* London etc., 1959.

Vidal, F. S. *The Oasis of al-Hasa.* Dhahran, 1955.

Villiers, Alan. *Sons of Sinbad.* New York, 1940.

Weir, Shelagh, editor. *The Bedouin: Aspects of the Material Culture of the Bedouin of Jordan.* London, 1976.

Thesiger's work is already considered a classic. It describes the Bedouins of the sands of southern Arabia with great perception. Dickson is rich in material on the people of eastern Arabia. Vidal's study is the most complete work in English on an area with which Aramco has had close ties. Villiers gives a popular account of the life of the Arab sailor, while Hawkins describes and illustrates the ships he sails.

NATURAL HISTORY

Baron, Stanley. *The Desert Locust.* London, 1972.

Basson, Philip W.; Burchard, John E.; Hardy, John T.; and Price, Andrew R. G. *Biotopes of the Western Arabian Gulf: Marine Life and Environments of Saudi Arabia.* Dhahran, 1977.

Benson, S. Vere. *Birds of Lebanon and the Jordan Area.* London and New York, 1970.

Bodenheimer, F. S. *Animal and Man in Bible Lands.* Leiden, 1960.

Brown, William Robinson. *The Horse of the Desert.* New York, 1947.

Cloudsley-Thompson, J. L., and Chadwick, M. J. *Life in Deserts.* London, 1964.

Dickson, Violet. *The Wild Flowers of Kuwait and Bahrain.* London, 1955.

Harrison, David L. *The Mammals of Arabia.* 3 vols. London, 1964-72.

Migahid, Ahmad Mohammad. *Flora of Saudi Arabia.* 2 vols. 2nd edition. Riyadh, 1978.

Mountfort, Guy. *Portrait of a Desert.* London, 1965.

Nelson, Bryan. *Azraq: Desert Oasis.* London, 1973.

Schmidt-Nielsen, Knut. *Desert Animals.* Oxford, 1964.

Täckholm, Vivi. *Student's Flora of Egypt.* 2nd edition. Cairo, 1974.

Vincett, Betty A. Lipscombe. *Wild Flowers of Central Saudi Arabia.* Milan, 1977.

The book on marine life in the Arabian Gulf by Basson and others is a well-illustrated and already standard work that will appeal to the general reader as well as the professional. The many illustrations in Migahid's flora will aid the non-specialist seeking names of Saudi Arabian plants, while Täckholm's *Student's Flora* includes many plants of the Arabian Peninsula as well as of Egypt and its keys are clear enough to be used by the motivated amateur. With these and the standard field guides to the birds of Europe, Asia, and Africa (many of which migrate through the Middle East), the natural history buff is off to a good start.

Index

S

T